THE SCIENTIFIC WORLD-PERSPECTIVE AND OTHER ESSAYS
1931–1963

SYNTHESE LIBRARY

MONOGRAPHS ON EPISTEMOLOGY,

LOGIC, METHODOLOGY, PHILOSOPHY OF SCIENCE,

SOCIOLOGY OF SCIENCE AND OF KNOWLEDGE,

AND ON THE MATHEMATICAL METHODS OF

SOCIAL AND BEHAVIORAL SCIENCES

VOLUME 108

KAZIMIERZ AJDUKIEWICZ

THE SCIENTIFIC WORLD-PERSPECTIVE AND OTHER ESSAYS 1931-1963

Edited and with an Introduction by

JERZY GIEDYMIN

D. REIDEL PUBLISHING COMPANY

DORDRECHT-HOLLAND / BOSTON - U.S.A.

Library of Congress Cataloging in Publication Data

Ajdukiewicz, Kazimierz.
    The scientific world-perspective and other essays, 1931–1963.

    (Synthese library; v. 108)
    'Bibliography of Ajdukiewicz's works': p.
    Includes indexes.
    Translation of essays selected from the author's Jezyk i poznanie,
with two articles added.
    1. Knowledge, Theory of—Addresses, essays, lectures. 2. Logic,
Symbolic and mathematical—Addresses, essays, lectures. 3. Languages—
Philosophy—Addresses, essays, lectures. I. Giedymin, Jerzy. II. Title.
B4691.A42E5   1977   199'.438   77–21887
ISBN 90–277–0527–5

Selection based on the Polish book
JĘZYK I POZNANIE
published by PWN – Copyright by Państwowe
Wydawnictwo Naukowe, Warszawa 1960 (vol. 1) and
Warszawa 1965 (vol. 2)

Published by D. Reidel Publishing Company,
P. O. Box 17, Dordrecht, Holland

Sold and distributed in the U.S.A., Canada, and Mexico
by D. Reidel Publishing Company, Inc.
Lincoln Building, 160 Old Derby Street, Hingham,
Mass. 02043, U.S.A.

To Mrs. Maria Ajdukiewicz

TABLE OF CONTENTS

Editor's Preface   ix
Ajdukiewicz's Life and Personality   xiii
Acknowledgements   xvii
Editor's Introduction: xix
    Radical Conventionalism, Its Background and Evolution: Poincaré, LeRoy, Ajdukiewicz

1. On the Meaning of Expressions (1931)   1
2. Language and Meaning (1934)   35
3. The World-Picture and the Conceptual Apparatus (1934)   67
4. On the Applicability of Pure Logic to Philosophical Problems (1934)   90
5. On the Problem of Universals (1935)   95
6. The Scientific World-Perspective (1935)   111
7. Syntactic Connexion (1936)   118
8. A Semantical Version of the Problem of Transcendental Idealism (1937)   140
9. Interrogative Sentences (1934/1938)   155
10. Logic and Experience (1947)   165
11. Epistemology and Semiotics (1948)   182
12. Change and Contradiction (1948)   192
13. On the Notion of Existence (1949)   209
14. Conditional Statement and Material Implication (1956)   222
15. The Problem of the Rationality of Non-Deductive Types of Inference (1958)   239
16. The Problem of the Foundation of Analytic Sentences (1958)   254
17. Syntactical Connections between Constituents of Declarative Sentences (1960)   269
18. Axiomatic Systems from the Methodological Point of View (1960)   282
19. The Problem of Foundation (1963) [posthumous]   295
20. The Problem of Empiricism and the Concept of Meaning (1964) [posthumous]   306
21. Intensional Expressions (1967) [posthumous]   320
22. Proposition as the Connotation of a Sentence (1967) [posthumous]   348
Bibliography of Ajdukiewicz's Works   363
Index of Names   371
Index of Subjects   373

KAZIMIERZ AJDUKIEWICZ 1890–1963

Though with considerable delay, most of the writings of Polish logicians of the inter-war period are now available in English. This is not yet true of Polish philosophy. In the present volume English-speaking readers will find, for the first time, a sizeable collection of the articles of one of the most original and distinguished of Poland's philosophers of the present century, Kazimierz Ajdukiewicz (1890–1963).

To be sure, Ajdukiewicz was a philosopher-logician from the beginning of his career. His first work of some importance, a monograph entitled *From the Methodology of the Deductive Sciences* (1921 post-dated; two abstracts published in 1919/20) exhibited two features which were to become characteristic of the style of his later philosophy: On the one hand the monograph was the result of Ajdukiewicz's deep interest in the systems of modern logic, the foundations of mathematics, in the properties of deductive systems and their relevance to philosophy; on the other hand the monograph was an attempt at developing an 'understanding methodology' (in the sense of German 'Verstehende Methodologie') of deductive sciences, i.e. a pragmatic study of axiomatic systems which would supplement purely formal investigations of those systems. The former made him a close ally of logical empiricists; the latter was rooted in the hermeneutic tradition of the second half of the 19th century (Dilthey) which spilled over into the 20th century (Spranger) and which was not cherished at all by logical empiricists. Moreover Ajdukiewicz's early preoccupation with the foundations of mathematics and logic brought him into close contact with the ideas of Poincaré and other French thinkers, notably Couturat and LeRoy; a thorough appreciation of Kant's epistemology and philosophy of mathematics as well as of some ideas of Bolzano and Husserl (e.g. the classification of 'semantical categories') were also responsible for the fact that Ajdukiewicz's philosophy defied the stereotype of logical empiricism.

From the Methodology of Deductive Sciences proved to be, at least in some respects, a pioneering work and to have an influence on the development of logic in Poland. For example, it contained (in the first of the monograph's three parts entitled 'The Logical Concept of Proof: A Methodological Essay') formal (syntactical) definitions of such meta-logical concepts as 'proof', 'theorem' 'consequence', 'logical theorem', 'logical consequence' and so initiated in Poland the structural method of defining these concepts. Ajdukiewicz clearly distinguished the concept of 'logical entailment' from 'material entailment (implication)' at a time when this was not yet common-place. Tarski's early formulation of the deduction-theorem (1921) was inspired by a discussion contained in the monograph (Cf. A. Tarski: 'On Some Funda-mental Concepts of Meta-Mathematics', *Logic, Semantics, Meta-Mathematics*, Oxford, 1969, p. 32). Moreover in his analysis of the concept of mathematical existence (in the third part entitled 'On the Notion of Existence in Deductive Sciences') Ajdukiewicz used the concepts of satisfaction, truth and domain of a theory though the difference between the logical semantics and the logical syntax was not quite clear to him (or anyone else) at the time. Finally, in connection with his discussion of the consistency proofs by interpretation and of the existence of absolute consistency proofs (the second of the three essays, entitled 'On Proofs of Consistency of Axioms') Ajdukiewicz refutes the then common claim that any proof of the consistency of the axioms of logic would be circular (Cf. A. Tarski: 'The Concept of Truth in Formalized Languages', *Logic, Semantics, Meta-Mathematics*, p. 237).

Among Ajdukiewicz's contributions to the logical syntax perhaps the best known is his analysis and definition of 'syntactically connected expressions'. This analysis includes a notation for the categories of expressions and an algorithm for testing whether an expression compounded of simple expres-sions of a language will belong to a definite 'semantical category' i.e. will be syntactically connected. The algorithm shows, for example, that the formula which expresses Russell's paradox is not syntactically connected. Since the idea of 'semantical categories' (which originated with Husserl and was introduced into foundational studies by S. Leśniewski) is related to the classification of 'parts of speech' in colloquial language, Ajdukiewicz's analysis of 'syntactical connection' is of relevance to the logic of natural and not only of formal languages. This is why 'syntactical connection' and Ajdukiewicz's 'categorial grammar' are used and discussed in the writings on the syntax and semantics of natural languages in contemporary philosophical logic (Cf. P. T. Geach: 'A Program for Syntax' and D. Lewis: 'General Seman-tics' *Synthese* 22 (1970), Nos. 1/2.) Apart from the fundamental article 'Syn-tactic Connexion', the present volume contains several until now not easily accessible articles in which Ajdukiewicz applied the 'categorial analysis' either to some traditional philosophical problems (e.g. the problem of universals) or to linguistics (in 'Syntactical Connections between Constituents of Declarative Sentences') or to the philosophy of language (in 'Intensional Expressions', and 'Proposition as the Connotation of a Sentence').

The logic of questions and answers was another area, now being extensively investigated, to which Ajdukiewicz made pioneering contributions (Cf. D. Harrah: *Communication – A Logical Model*, M.I.T., 1963). His earliest writings on the logic of questions date back to 1923 and 1926. 'Interrogative Sentences' included in the present collection first appeared in 1934.

Ajdukiewicz's main contributions to philosophy were in the area of epistemology, philosophy of language, philosophy of science, of mathematics and of logic. It is hoped that this volume will amply show the originality of his ideas and their relevance to the problems debated in contemporary philosophy. One of those ideas introduced between 1930 and 1934 was an essentially pragmatic conception of language, based on three types of 'meaning (acceptance) rules', coupled with a notion of intersubjective, 'ideal' meaning. Language was conceived as a rule-determined structure and the meaning of the expressions of a language was seen to be due to their ability to occupy definite positions within the language matrix. An epistemological doctrine, labelled by Ajdukiewicz, radical conventionalism, was a consequence of this view of language and meaning. The main problems which Ajdukiewicz's epistemology was designed to answer were, firstly, the relation between the data of experience and our world-picture; secondly, the nature of the growth of our scientific knowledge. With the philosophy of Henri Poincaré, Ajdukiewicz shared the view that experience does not uniquely determine our scientific world-picture, the latter being codetermined by the choice of a conceptual apparatus. Contrary to Poincaré, however, and with a reference to Edouard LeRoy, Ajdukiewicz claimed that there exist conceptual apparatuses which are not intertranslatable and that the growth of scientific knowledge occurs, at least sometimes, through the replacement of one such conceptual apparatus by another. As one of the fundamental tasks of epistemology Ajdukiewicz saw the study of the evolutionary tendencies in our conceptual frameworks. In his critical revision of the doctrine of radical conventionalism after 1935 Ajdukiewicz extended his original conception of language to structures based exclusively on deductive meaning rules or on these and empirical meaning rules. In such languages, which have no axiomatic rules, analytic sentences do not exist. The extended conception of language in turn gave rise to the view that the task of methodology should consist in constructing and evaluating a plurality of conceptual structures in which present and future science could be practised.

Readers familiar with philosophy of science will no doubt see from this account how much of the so-called 'new empiricism' of today was anticipated by Ajdukiewicz in the early thirties and the early fifties.

Articles included in this selection have been ordered chronologically according to dates of their publication. Readers interested primarily in radical conventionalism, rather than in the development of Ajdukiewicz's theory of meaning, may be advised not to read first the article 'On the Meaning of Expressions', but to start from 'Language and Meaning' or even from 'The World-Picture and the Conceptual Apparatus' (which contains a brief abstract of the main results of 'Language and Meaning'). The last three articles in the present selection were published from manuscripts posthumously. All three were read by Ajdukiewicz as papers before his death but were not intended in the present form for publication. In fact, just before his death, Ajdukiewicz began rewriting 'The Problem of Empiricism and the Conception of Meaning' and the extant fragment of this new version is included here together with the text of the original paper.

The Polish texts of all but the last two of the articles in this selection may be found in *Język i Poznanie (Language and Knowledge)*, vol. I (1960), vol. II (1965).

Logical notation used throughout this volume is not uniform. Different systems of logical symbols used by Ajdukiewicz in his articles have been retained here in their original form.

In making this selection I have relied on the valuable advice of Professor Klemens Szaniawski from Warsaw University. I should like to thank my colleagues, Professors Klemens Szaniawski, Marian Przełęcki, and Dr Peter Williams, as well as Mr David Pearce for reading and commenting on my introductory essay 'Radical Conventionalism, Its Background and Evolution'. It goes without saying that none of them should be held responsible for any of its inadequacies.

Without the help and understanding of Miss Freda Williams, who typed the manuscripts, conducted the correspondence, kept the timetable and patiently reminded me of innumerable things which escaped my attention or memory, this selection would never have been completed.

Logic and Scientific Method Division,   JERZY GIEDYMIN
School of Mathematical and Physical Sciences,
University of Sussex,
1977

AJDUKIEWICZ'S LIFE AND PERSONALITY

Kazimierz Ajdukiewicz* was born in 1890, the son of a civil servant. Tarnopol, the place of his birth, had been since the partitions of Poland in the 1770's part of Galicia, a province of the Austrian Empire. Ajdukiewicz completed his secondary education in Lwów and enrolled there at the University to read philosophy, mathematics and physics. In 1912 he was awarded a Ph.D. degree in Philosophy on the basis of a thesis on Kant's philosophy of space. Among his university teachers in Lwów were, in philosophy, Kazimierz Twardowski – himself a disciple of Franz Brentano – in logic, Jan Lukasiewicz and, in mathematics, Waclaw Sierpiński. In 1913 Ajdukiewicz went to Göttingen University where at the time David Hilbert was lecturing on the foundations of mathematics and Edmund Husserl on philosophy. A year later, however, he was conscripted into the Austrian army and served on the Italian front. Towards the end of World War I he joined the newly-formed Polish army, from which he was demobilized in 1920 with the rank of an artillery captain, to return to university life. He was habilitated docent in Warsaw University in 1920 having submitted a habilitation dissertation entitled *Z metodologii nauk dedukcyjnych (From the Methodology of Deductive Sciences)*, Lwów, 1921. At that time he married Maria Twardowska, Kazimierz Twardowski's daughter; they subsequently had a son and a daughter. Until the outbreak of World War II he was, at first, docent and then professor of philosophy in the universities of Lwów and Warsaw (in Warsaw from 1926 to 1928). During World War II he continued to live with his family in Lwów. Forced under German occupation to earn his living as a clerk, he found time nevertheless to teach in clandestine Polish schools. After the war ended he accepted the Chair of the Methodology and Theory of Science (afterwards re-named the Chair of Logic) in the Faculty of Mathematical and Physical Sciences of the University of Poznań. In the years 1948–52 he was Rector of Poznań University. He left Poznań for Warsaw in 1955. As professor of Logic in the University of Warsaw and head of the Division of Logic in the Institute of Philosophy of the Polish Academy of Science, he continued until retirement in 1961, retaining, however, the latter post after retirement. Ajdukiewicz died in his sleep quite unexpectedly one night in 1963 of heart failure.

* Phonetic transcription [aidu:ˈKevitʃ].

By any standard Ajdukiewicz's academic career in Poland, interrupted only by World War II, was a brilliant one. He achieved all possible academic distinctions and for more than thirty years he exercised a great influence on the development of philosophy and logic in Poland. He was a member of the Polish Academy of Science from its creation after World War I. In the inter-war period he was, together with Leśniewski, Lukasiewicz, Kotarbiński and Tarski, among the most active members of the Polish (Lwów-Warsaw) School of Logic. (On this subject interested readers may consult Z. Jordan: *The Development of Mathematical Logic and Logical Positivism in Poland between the Two Wars*, OUP, London, 1945.)

After World War II, with Leśniewski no longer alive, Lukasiewicz and Tarski abroad and Poland's leading logicians engaged in the pursuit of logic as a purely mathematical discipline, it was left to Ajdukiewicz, Kotarbiński and to their pre-war and post-war disciples (now junior colleagues) to continue the tradition of the logical approach to philosophy, in particular to the philosophy or methodology of science. Among those of Ajdukiewicz's former students who are well-known outside Poland, one should mention Henryk Mehlberg (*'Positivisme et science'*, Studia Philosophica; *The Reach of Science*, 1958 and many articles on the philosophy of mathematics and of science), now in the U.S; Roman Suszko (apart from articles on mathematical logic, 'Formal Logic and the Evolution of Knowledge' in *Problems in the Philosophy of Science* in A. Musgrave and I. Lakatos (eds.), Amsterdam, 1968); Marian Przełęcki (*The Logic of Empirical Theories*, London, 1969, numerous articles on the semantics of empirical theories); Klemens Szaniawski (present Editor of *Studia Logica*, contributions to the foundations of probability, statistics and decision theory); and Jerzy Pelc (editor of *Semiotic Studies* and author of many contributions to semiotics), the last three at present professors of Logic in the Faculty of Philosophy of the University of Warsaw. Of two favourite assistants Ajdukiewicz had in Poznań, Zbigniew Czerwiński and Andrzej Malewski, the former (author of many articles on the foundations of probability, statistics and inductive logic published in *Studia Logica*) now has a Chair of Econometrics in the Poznań School of Economics and the latter, having made very interesting contributions to the philosophy of the social sciences (e.g. 'Generality of Levels of Theories Concerning Human Behaviour' in H. L. Zetterberg and G. Lorenz (eds.), *A Symposium on Theoretical Sociology*, N.Y., 1964) died prematurely in tragic circumstances.

Between 1955 and his death in 1963, Ajdukiewicz was responsible for organizing regular seminars in Warsaw and conferences in several other places. The majority of those professionally interested in logical methodology in Polish universities, some mathematical logicians, e.g. Suszko, Loś, Grzegorczyk, and invited scientists (physicists, biologists, social scientists, linguists) participated in those gatherings.

Ajdukiewicz was an excellent teacher by nature; nevertheless, he used to prepare his weekly lectures for undergraduates as carefully as public lectures or presidential addresses. The problem of how to improve teaching methods, and especially how to make logic as an academic subject attractive to students not majoring in logic, was a great concern to him throughout his life, during which he wrote seven textbooks on logic and methodology of science. He was a man of action as much as a philosopher. Teaching and research were for him important social activities which had social consequences and were, therefore, associated with social responsibility. As a professor he was an academic in the grand manner; during his years as Rector of Poznań University he was usually referred to as Kazimierz the Magnificent. But it was part of his nature to see to it that any job he undertook was done properly. One can conjecture that he would have been successful in any career he might have chosen. Reminiscing on his years as a commanding officer during World War I he would sometimes say to his friends and colleagues that perhaps he should have chosen the career of a general rather than of an academic (K. Szaniawski: 'Język i poznanie', Kultura, November 1973). Though he defended in his writings the ideal of 'pure science' against narrow-minded practicality, thinking to solve intellectual and practical problems and teaching were for him an important part of a life worth living.

Another feature of his personality, which many of his former students and colleagues emphasize, was his ability, or at least his efforts, to understand other people's interests and points of view, however difficult this might have been on occasions. Though schooled primarily in mathematics and physics, he had an exceptionally good understanding of the peculiarities of the humanities. And though his foremost interest was in logic, the foundations of mathematics and of science, he was by no means narrow-minded in supporting other people's research. For instance, back in the 1920s he encouraged one of his first assistants to do research on the philosophy of Duns Scotus ('The Concept of Intention in Duns Scotus' Philosophy') and of Aristotle (Cf. Stefan Świeżawski: Wspomnienie o profesorze Ajdukiewiczu' Tygodnik Powszechny, No. 1265, 1973).

In private life Ajdukiewicz had many interests, ranging from music (Beethoven, Wagner) and literature to game shooting. He was a nature-lover and the Tatra Mountains were particularly close to his heart. He was a great conversationalist.

The qualities of Ajdukiewicz which most impressed me personally back in the 1950s – when I belonged to the circle of his disciples and subsequently junior colleagues — were his dignity, independence of mind, and the rare ability to display apparently worn-out problems in a new light. On re-reading Ajdukiewicz's works recently, I have been struck by the extent to which his philosophy between 1920 and 1963 revolved around a few main themes seen through and illuminated by changing perspectives.

JERZY GIEDYMIN

ACKNOWLEDGEMENTS

My deep gratitude is due to those who translated articles numbered 2, 3, 6, 7, 21 and 22 for their kind permission to reprint those articles with suitable terminological adaptations. I extend my thanks to the original editors and publishers of all articles included in the present volume for their kind permission to translate those articles into English and to reprint them here. Specific acknowledgements may be found on the first page of each article.

JERZY GIEDYMIN

RADICAL CONVENTIONALISM, ITS BACKGROUND AND EVOLUTION: POINCARÉ, LEROY, AJDUKIEWICZ

I. THE EVOLUTION OF AJDUKIEWICZ'S PHILOSOPHY

The dominant theme of Ajdukiewicz's philosophy throughout his life was the problem of the dependence of our knowledge and of our conception of knowledge on language. Two related questions, on two different levels, were involved: one was the question whether our scientific world-view may be uniquely determined by experience or whether it is rather co-determined by the 'choice' of a language; the other is the question whether the solutions of the fundamental epistemological problems — in particular our conception of knowledge — are independent of the choice of a conception of language. Epistemology, philosophy of science, of mathematics and of language were the areas in which Ajdukiewicz's philosophical interests were concentrated and to which he made the most important contributions.

The philosophy which emerged from his preoccupation with two main epistemological problems mentioned, underwent within over forty years of his more mature intellectual life an interesting, though perhaps not unusual evolution.

In the *first period*, roughly before 1936, it was dominated by the doctrine which Ajdukiewicz himself labelled *Radical Conventionalism*. Radical conventionalism resulted from an original pragmatic conception of language combined with a concept of intersubjective meaning which Ajdukiewicz developed between 1929 and 1934 ('On the Meaning of Expressions', 'Language and Meaning'). The doctrine affirmed: (1) the existence of languages or conceptual frameworks which are not intertranslatable, (2) the necessity of articulating any knowledge in one of those languages, (3) the possibility of choosing one of the languages or of changing from one to another, hence of the existence of a decisional or conventional element in all knowledge, (4) the discontinuous nature of changes in science throughout its history. It is not difficult to see in radical conventionalism a continuation of the post-Kantian conventionalist tradition and also an anticipation (by some thirty years) of many of the current doctrines in contemporary philosophy of science.

Radical conventionalism, conceived and developed at the time when Logical Positivism in Central Europe reached its climax, was presented to the

J. Giedymin (ed.), Kazimierz Ajdukiewicz: The Scientific World-Perspective and Other Essays, 1931–1963, XIX–LIII. *All Rights Reserved.*

philosophical world outside Poland in a series of articles in *Erkenntnis* in 1934/5 ('Language and Meaning', 'The World-Picture and the Conceptual Apparatus', 'The Scientific World-Perspective'). Like the philosophy of the Vienna Circle and the Berlin Circle, it was inspired by various developments in mathematics and in science which occurred during the nineteenth century and in the first two decades of the present century, viz. the discovery of non-Euclidean geometries, the crisis in the foundations of mathematics (set-theoretic paradoxes) and various methods of resolving the crisis, the development of mathematical logic (in particular of meta-logic), the transition from classical to relativistic and quantum physics, etc. However, unlike the logical positivists of the Vienna Circle, Ajdukiewicz was never under the influence of phenomenalism (of either Berkeley's, Hume's or of Mach's type); nor did he dismiss as absolutely meaningless all the problems and theses of traditional metaphysics. So, for example, in his critique of the reistic analysis of the problem and doctrine of universals he argued in 1935 ('On the Problem of Universals') that it is illegitimate to 'translate' a metaphysical thesis formulated in one language (in this case of Aristotle) into another language (e.g. conforming to Kotarbiński's reistic criteria) and to criticize the 'translation' as if it were the original thesis; it is illegitimate to do so because the languages of different philosophical systems are not mutually translatable.

On the whole, the doctrine of radical conventionalism had a much wider — hence, more liberal — philosophical background than its contemporary, logical positivism. Ajdukiewicz himself saw radical conventionalism as a critical, revised (radicalized) continuation of the philosophy of the New Critique of Science *(la nouvelle critique de la science)* in France, in particular of Henri Poincaré and Edouard LeRoy. He emphasized strongly the Kantian features of his doctrine, as well as the indebtedness of his philosophy of language to some ideas of Bolzano and Husserl. Finally, he appreciated and endorsed the 'hermeneutic' idea of understanding (Dilthey, Spranger) as the method — or at least as one of the methods — of the humanities, including epistemology and the history of philosophy. The latter view was never abandoned by Ajdukiewicz.

The retreat from radical conventionalism was first acknowledged at a public discussion in 1936 and, again, many years later, in a polemical article.[1]

However, it seems that its fundamental ideas never ceased to fascinate Ajdukiewicz. A critical re-thinking of those ideas was certainly responsible for some of the most original articles produced during the *second period* of his life. In particular, it was responsible for his clarification and defence — against his own arguments put forward during the radical conventionalism period — of the thesis of Radical Empiricism, according to which all knowledge consists of empirically revisable sentences ('Logic and Experience'); towards the end of his life, it developed into the outlines of a new research programme in epistemology and in the philosophy of language ('The Problem of Empiricism and the Concept of Meaning').

So far as epistemology is concerned, Ajdukiewicz's philosophy during the second period of his philosophical life seemed to waver between Moderate Conventionalism (henceforth MC) and serious entertainment of Radical Empiricism (henceforth RE), to progress finally towards a Pluralist Epistemology, i.e. the view that the duty of an epistemologist is not to take and defend one of the positions in the Radical Apriorism-Radical Empiricism spectrum (See his *Problems and Theories of Philosophy*) but rather to elaborate and thereby understand many possible conceptions of language and knowledge which could be used either to account for past and existing science or to anticipate further developments within its epistemological and linguistic framework.

So far as language and its philosophy are concerned, during the post-radical conventionalism period Ajdukiewicz made more extensive use of the ideas developed within logical syntax and logical semantics, though the pragmatic aspects of language continued to be at the centre of his interests ('Axiomatic Systems from the Methodological Point of View', *Pragmatic Logic*). As an indication of Ajdukiewicz's gradual withdrawal from radical conventionalism one may perhaps mention the fact that in 1937 ('A Semantical Version of the Problem of Transcendental Idealism') and again in 1948 ('Epistemology and Semiotics') he gave semantical paraphrases of the doctrines of subjective and logical idealism and a critique of those doctrines based on his 'translation', though he was careful to admit that he could not be certain of the adequacy of the translation and that the authors of those doctrines would in all probability not regard his translations as adequate. In the rest of this introductory essay we shall have the opportunity to comment on those aspects of Ajdukiewicz's conception of language which were fundamental to radical conventionalism and on those which he was able to retain in the post-radical conventionalism period.

From the point of view of what is currently fashionable in contemporary philosophy of science radical conventionalism may seem more congenial than Ajdukiewicz's more mature philosophy of the later period. At any rate it should be interesting to know how radical conventionalism originated, why it seemed at first so attractive to its author and what reasons or arguments persuaded him later to modify his philosophy. Moreover, because of the importance of conventionalist philosophy both for the development of science and of the philosophy of science, it is instructive to see how radical conventionalism compares with the philosophy of French conventionalism (commodism) and what was implied by either. In the rest of the present essay I shall outline first those philosophical views of Henri Poincaré and of Edouard LeRoy which were relevant to radical conventionalism, then discuss in more detail radical conventionalism and finally the transition to the post-radical conventionalism of Ajdukiewicz.

II. THE CONVENTIONALISM OF HENRI POINCARÉ

By choosing the name of radical conventionalism for his earlier philosophy and by making explicit references to Poincaré's philosophy and to his polemic with LeRoy, Ajdukiewicz left no room for doubt that the views on mathematics, science and language of those two French philosophers were in some respects similar to his own.

Poincaré's whole philosophy was rather complex. He was a Kantian in his views on the epistemological status of arithmetic, claiming that some of the axioms of arithmetic, in particular the principle of mathematical induction, were synthetic a priori truths. On the other hand, he rejected Kantianism in the philosophy of space, geometry and physics, replacing it by a combination of Genetic Empiricism (concepts and statements in geometry and physics originated from experience) and Conventionalism. In the foundations of set-theory his position was anti-Cantorian, constructivist, pre-intuitionist. In the philosophy of physics his conventionalism left room for empirical elements and so was within the bounds of the empiricist tradition. It was also coloured by many neo-Kantian and evolutionary ideas, like most philosophical doctrines of the time.

It is mainly Poincaré's philosophy of geometry and, to some extent, of physics that is of relevance here.

Against the Kantian view of geometry Poincaré used the following counter-claims and arguments:

(i) Geometrical space, the object of geometry, is not identical with representational space (in its triple form of visual, tactile and motor space); the former is a theoretical construct and has properties different from the latter (*Science and Hypothesis*, henceforth SH, 1902, p. 56).

(ii) Both concepts of space are of empirical origin: a motionless being could not have acquired a concept of space (SH, 59); were there no solids in nature, there would be no geometry (SH, 61); representational space is the result of the effects external objects exert on our senses and of the way our senses are built, both these factors being contingent, not necessary (SH, 56).

(iii) We do not represent to ourselves external objects in geometrical space, rather we reason about objects as if they were situated in geometrical space (SH, 57); geometry is only the summary of the laws of succession of images, not a framework imposed on individual images (SH, 64); this is why it is possible to change geometry: the same images may be arranged according to different laws (SH, 64).

(iv) Beings with minds and senses like ours but without our experiences might receive from a suitably chosen external world impressions which would lead them to construct a geometry different from Euclid's. If, on the other hand, we were transported to that different world, we should have no difficulty in referring phenomena to our Euclidean space, which we owe to the experiences of our world (SH, 51).

(v) Euclidean (or any other) space is not an a priori form of our sensibility without which no spatial experiences are possible; the axioms of Euclid are not synthetic a priori truths, necessary and universal; in fact, they are not truths at all: the distinction between truth and falsity does not apply to them (SH, 50).

Poincaré also argued against 'geometric empiricism' by which he could have meant either the philosophy of geometry associated with Newton's philosophy of space some aspects of which may be found in B. Russell's *An Essay On the Foundations of Geometry*, 1897 and in some polemical articles written by Russell in that period) or the philosophy of space and geometry associated with relevant discoveries made by Gauss and Riemann (*Über die Hypothesen welche der Geometrie zu Grunde liegen*, 1854). Some of Poincaré's arguments and claims against geometric empiricism are as follows: (a) geometric objects, points, straight lines, circles etc. are 'ideal objects' not given in experience, though experience plays an essential role in the origin of corresponding concepts (SH, 70); (b) if geometry were empirical, it would be hypothetical, subject to revisions; it would not be an exact science (SH, 49–50); (c) it has been suggested (e.g. by Lobatchevsky) that astronomical observations of stellar parallax may decide between alternative geometries ("If Lobatchevsky's geometry is true, the parallax of a very distant star is finite. If Riemann's is true, it will be negative ...", SH, 72). However, "What we call a straight line in astronomy is simply a path of a ray of light. If, therefore, we were to discover negative parallaxes ... we should have a choice between two conclusions: we could give up Euclidean geometry or modify the laws of optics and suppose that light is not propagated in straight lines" (SH, 72–3). (d) 'distance', 'straight line' etc. are not definable independently of the axioms of a specific geometry ('Des fondements de la géometrie', *Revue de Métaphysique et de Morale*, **VII** (1899), 279); (e) the fundamental hypotheses underlying each of the alternative geometries are not 'experimental facts' although in our choice of one of those geometries we are guided by the observation of certain physical phenomena (e.g. movements of solid bodies, properties of light propagation) ('Sur les hypotheses fondamentales de la géometrie', *Bull. de la Soc. Math. de France* (1887), p. 215); (f) "Experiments only teach us the relations of bodies to one another. They do not and cannot teach us the relations of bodies and space, nor the mutual relations of the different parts of space ... experiments have reference not to space but to bodies" (SH, 79, 84).

Poincaré concluded from his criticism of the Kantian philosphy of geometry and of 'geometric empiricism' the following doctrines:

(1) The axioms of Euclid's geometry, though they originate from empirical generalizations, form an implicit definition of the primitive terms of the system (e.g. 'point', 'lies between', 'is equidistant'); they are *terminological conventions* neither true nor false but more or less convenient (commodes) (SH, 50); the same applies to the status of the axioms of other geometries[2].

(2) Alternative systems of metric geometry are different metric systems or metric languages which are *translatable* one into another on the basis of a suitable dictionary (SH, 42–3).

(3) Mathematical space to which we refer physical phenomena in our physical theories is a mathematical continuum (an idealization of the 'physical continuum' of our sensations) in itself amorphous; it can be metrized only if specific conventions are laid down concerning 'congruence' or 'distance'; this can be done in different ways yielding either Euclidean or non-Euclidean geometry – hence the conventionality of metrics and of metric geometries (SH, chap. II; *The Value of Science*, chap. III, p. 37).

(4) From the group-theoretic point of view one can say that geometries (metric and non-metric) are studies of invariants under various groups of transformations[3]. With respect to metric geometries it was pointed out by S. Lie that the congruence of two figures means that they are able to be transformed the one into the other by a certain point transformation in space; moreover, the properties in virtue of which congruence is an equality depend on the fact that displacements of figures are given by a group of transformations[4].

(5) What is a priori is the general concept of group; however, it is not an a priori form of sensibility but rather of understanding (in Kant's sense); within the general concept of group we can choose one particular group of transformations which will determine our geometry.

Poincaré used exactly analogous arguments against the Kantian and the empiricist views of the laws of mechanics and concluded that their status as well as that of 'absolute time', 'absolute space', was conventional (SH, Part

III, chap. 6, 'La mesure du temps', *Revue de M. et de M.*, 1898). Moreover, he extended the group-theoretic viewpoint to physics: The principle of relativity, according to which the laws of physical phenomena are the same for a fixed observer as for an observer who has a uniform motion of translation relative to him (so that we have not nor can we possibly have any means of discovering whether or not we are carried along in such a motion), is equivalent to the principle that all laws of physics should be invariant under Lorentz transformations; in effect, physics is a study of invariants of the Lorentz group (which leaves invariant the form $x^2 + y^2 + z^2 - c^2 t^2$). The preference for the Lorentz group over the Galilean transformations, under which the laws of classical dynamics remain invariant, is not a matter of truth or falsity or of experimental findings but rather of simplicity: Maxwell's equations are not invariant under the latter but are invariant under the former. The choice of the Lorentz transformations, however, has a profound effect on the conceptual system of physics; for example, simultaneity becomes relative.

Apart from the discovery of non-Euclidean geometries, it seems that there were two other important sources of conventionalism in the philosophy of physics of Poincaré (and Duhem): one was an essentially *neo-Kantian conception of (empirical) meaning* (shared, however, both by pragmatists and by many nineteenth- and twentieth-century empiricists); the other was their reading of the history of science coupled with other arguments to the effect that there have been and always will be both *observationally equivalent and experimentally indistinguishable theories* in science.

The mentioned conception of (empirical) meaning may be stated, for example, in the following way: If two sets of sentences, S_1 and S_2, are observationally equivalent (i.e. have indentical observational consequence classes), then they have the same scientific meaning or content; or − in a stronger form − the problem of choosing between two theories T_1 and T_2 is empirical if and only if T_1 and T_2 are neither observationally equivalent nor experimentally indistinguishable (given available observation and measurement techniques).[5]

The relativity of motion, and the associated principles of relativity, starting with the kinematic or visual principle of relativity, known already to ancient Greeks, and including the more recent ones (e.g. the one mentioned before, the Poincaré principle) were referred to in support of the claim of the existence of observationally equivalent theories. But any, apparently rival theories, pretending to account for the *nature* of matter, light, etc. were regarded by both these authors as possibly observationally equivalent. Now, *observationally equivalent* − and even experimentally indistinguishable −

theories according to Poincaré differ one from another in their theoretical part only linguistically, they are different *façons de parler*, they are alternative *languages,* more or less convenient, more or less inspiring or misleading (since they contain fictions and metaphors); again, as in the case of geometries, the question of truth or of falsity does not arise. The only way *a language* in a sense reflects reality is through its structure; in the transition from an old theory to a new one metaphors may change while the empirical laws as well as the relations expressed by differential equations of the theory's abstract part may remain true (SH, 161). In this sense the growth of science *is* cumulative rather than disruptive despite the ephemeral nature of theories (SH, 160–5). Physical reality – the world – is knowable only up to the observational equivalence of alternative theories and up to the isomorphism of their theoretical postulates. This is essentially the Kantian sceptical doctrine concerning the limits of knowledge, expressed in a new form.[6] The term 'instrumentalism', sometimes applied to this view of scientific theories (e.g. by Karl Popper[7]), may be misleading since it overemphasized the pragmatist element explicitly renounced in Poincaré's polemic with LeRoy and in his praise of the ideal of 'pure science' (*The Value of Science*, 1905, last chapter).

Poincaré did not classify either the axioms of geometries or the conventional principles of science (empirical laws elevated to the status of conventions) as analytic, presumably because traditionally analytic sentences were regarded as analytic truths whereas Poincaré denied any truth-value to both implicit definitions and to principles. However, Poincaré's philosophy had a tremendous impact on the later development of the idea of analyticity: firstly, when the concept of analyticity was suitably extended to cover all terminological conventions (Ajdukiewicz sentences dictated by axiomatic meaning rules; Carnap's meaning-postulates), analytic sentences came to be seen as determinants of language; secondly, Poincaré's genetic empiricism combined with conventionalism and his insistence that statements in science have been changing their status (perhaps the most famous case in point being the principle of relativity which – Poincaré claimed – had been an empirical generalization elevated to the status of a convention and then was threatened in this status by the outcome of Kaufmann's experiment[8]) made it necessary to relativize analyticity to language understood in a more precise and rigid way (Ajdukiewicz, Carnap) or else to question our ability to distinguish between the analytic and non-analytic sentences (Quine, White and others[9]) if 'language' is used in the usual loose and amorphous sense; finally, Poincaré was one of the first, if not the first, to suggest that conventional and non-conventional components occur in one and the same sentence and might be split artificially (VS, Part III, chap. 10, p. 124).

Ajdukiewicz's interest in Poincaré's philosophy antedated at least by fifteen years his articles on radical conventionalism published in the nineteen-thirties. In several papers read at the meetings of the Philosophical Society in Lwów in 1919 and 1920, as well as in his habilitation dissertation entitled *Z metodologii nauk dedukcyjnych* (Lwów, 1921; English translation, as 'From the Methodology of Deductive Sciences', henceforth MDS, in *Studia Logica* **XIX**, 1966) Ajdukiewicz discussed various problems in the foundation of mathematics and logic and tried to clarify various foundational concepts (e.g. the concept of proof, entailment, mathematical domain, satisfaction, truth, existence, etc.) In the last of the three essays of which that dissertation consists, viz. in the essay entitled 'On the Notion of Existence in the Deductive Sciences', he criticized Poincaré's claim, expressed in *Science and Method* (1909) and in three articles in *Revue de Métaphysique et de Morale* (**XIII**, **XVI**), that "existence in deductive theories amounts to consistency" (in mathematics 'exists' means 'is free from contradiction'). Against Poincaré Ajdukiewicz argued that though consistency is a necessary condition for mathematical existence it is not a sufficient condition; 'exists' in mathematics means 'is an element of a proper (intended) domain of the specific mathematical theory'. Ajdukiewicz's critique seems interesting for at least two reasons: firstly, his explication of 'exists' with respect to mathematical theories is, in a sense, more constructivist and relies more heavily on an idea of mathematical intuition than Poincaré's purely formal requirement of consistency. Secondly, by insisting that absolute existential claims in mathematics make no sense, only relative ones do ("... in the deductive sciences we do not speak of existence in absolute sense but only relatively to a given system", "We may speak only of existence in a system as we speak of inclusion in a domain", "... there exist Euclidean straight lines and *non*-Euclidean straight lines; however, both cannot co-exist", "... the role of an existential postulate ... consists in enumerating those objects ... which may be substituted for the variables in the axioms", p. 45) he not only anticipated the thesis of 'ontological relativity', at least with respect to mathematics, but also left a clue as to how a critical analysis of Poincaré's views in the foundations of mathematics and science may have inspired his 'linguistic relativism' or 'conceptual perspectivism' essential to radical conventionalism.

First of all, Ajdukiewicz obviously accepted Poincaré's general conventionalist thesis according to which there are conventional elements in our knowledge and there are problems not solvable without such conventions. However, he radicalized this claim, as we shall see later. He also agreed with Poincaré that the conventional elements in our knowledge are not isolated conventions but rather close-knit conceptual systems of languages, which play a fundamental inferential role apart from being able to describe relations between the phenomena and, possibly, directly unobservable structures. It seems that Ajdukiewicz was influenced by Poincaré's preoccupation with the changes in science and mathematics, though he did not accept Poincaré's view of the fundamentally cumulative, non-disruptive nature of such changes. This is because Ajdukiewicz rejected both Poincaré's conception of meaning (of theories) and of language. Poincaré's discussion of alternative metric geometries as intertranslatable languages and his imaginary accounts of the communication between the inhabitants of non-Euclidean worlds must have been heuristically important. But the idea of the relativity of mathematical existence (in hyperbolic geometry rectangles do not exist, for example, and one cannot speak about rectangles in the language of that geometry), coupled later with an entirely different concept of language and of meaning (the origins of which may be found in Ajdukiewicz's 1921 dissertation MDS), presumably persuaded Ajdukiewicz to disagree with Poincaré's and to agree with LeRoy's view on the role of the change in linguistic conventions and on the question of the existence of languages which are not mutually translatable. An outline of the dispute over this last problem will be given presently in the section dealing with LeRoy's conventionalism.

III. LEROY'S NOMINALISM AND THE CONTROVERSY OVER THE EXISTENCE OF A 'UNIVERSAL INVARIANT'

Edouard LeRoy[10], mathematician and philosopher, combined the most extreme elements of conventionalism of the New Critique of Science with Bergsonian Evolutionism and Life-philosophy in order to argue for a spiritualist 'philosophy of freedom', for the superiority of intuition and religious experiences over science. It is his extreme form of conventionalism as well as some of his views on language that are of relevance here.

In 'Science et philosophie' (*Revue de M. et de M.* **VII**, 1899; henceforth SP) and in 'Un positivisme nouveau' (henceforth PN; *Revue de M. et de M.* **IX**, 1901) LeRoy presented a very extreme version of a conventionalist philosophy of mathematics and of science as the result of 'the new critique of science' referring indiscriminately to the works of M. Boutroux, Poincaré, Duhem, G. Milhaud, J. Wilbois as well as his own.[11] Poincaré felt it necessary to reject — in a polemical article — LeRoy's 'Nominalism' and to clarify by contrast his own position ('Sur la valeur objective des théories physiques', *Revue de M. et de M.*, 1902, *The Value of Science*, 1905, Part III 'The Objective Value of Science'; the September issue of *Revue de M. et de M.*, 1900 is likewise relevant). Pierre Duhem claimed priority over the other authors mentioned by LeRoy (though he carefully disassociated himself from their extra-scientific conclusions) and suggested that Poincaré's reply was intended as much for him as for LeRoy.[12]

The philosophy of science reported with approval by LeRoy as the result of the new critique of science consists of (1) the critique of 'facts', (2) the critique of 'laws' and (3) the critique of 'theories'.

1. *The Critique of 'Facts'*

The traditional empiricist and Comtian positivist philosophy of science, perpetuated by numerous text-books on the subject, contrasted 'positive science' consisting of facts, with theories and hypotheses. Facts were claimed to be objective, theory-independent and simply discovered, stated and collected by impartial observers. However, Claude Bernard already pointed out that this is a naïve view of science since abstract concepts and theories play an important role in the study of even the simplest facts (SP, 513); constant preoccupation of philosophers and scientists with rigour and objectivity too often results in the failure to see the role of the *free activity of the mind* in the determination of experimental truth (SP, part II, 514). Hence the need for a *new theory of scientific truth*. A visit to a scientific laboratory would show that scientists themselves have the impression of *constituting* facts, of *creating* from some amorphous material the particular objects of observation (SP, II, 515; PN, 145).

Reality is not accessible directly to the observer but only through the mediation of conceptual forms or schemes which are contingent on our past experiences as individuals and as a race, on our aims and prejudices as men of action, on everything life has imprinted on our minds. There are no isolated objects in nature, everything is diffused in everything. The process of separation or of objectification of nature, necessary and convenient for our thinking expresses ultimately nothing but the weakness of our bodies, exigencies of our actions or the variety of our points of view (SP, II, 516). Our practically oriented senses are filters which leave only a residue of reality in our experience. There are no absolute facts, intrinsically definable as such. Any result of isolation, classification or approximation is relative to a viewpoint chosen in advance. In conclusion, far from being received passively by our mind, *facts are* in a way *created* by it (SP, II, 517).

There is a difference, however, between common-sense facts and scientific facts; the latter are *theoretical interpretations* and differ from the former in the degree of conventionality, artificiality and relativity. The sentence 'All men are mortal' may serve as an example of the former; 'Phosphorus melts at 44 °C', 'The earth rotates' are examples of the latter. A 'bare' or 'pure' fact does not become a scientific fact unless it is placed within a system of concepts (PN, 145). Admittedly, there is a mysterious residue of objectivity in facts, but science is not concerned with facts from the point of view of objectivity but rather as artefacts, as 'atoms' in conventional schemes representing various points of view on nature (SP, II, 518).

2. *The Critique of 'Laws'*

According to the naïve traditional view, laws exist objectively, imprinted on facts; all that is necessary is to discover them among many irrelevant details.

In fact, laws are constant *relations*, or − to use a mathematical metaphor − they are *invariants* under universal tranformation; they represent the element of stability in our changing experiences. Logically, they are abstract formulae, or schemes of classification, which summarize in a convenient way individual occurrences; they are also *mnemonic instruments, shorthands*. Furthermore, laws are second-order facts − more simplified, abstract and so more convenient; they replace first-order facts thus removing us further from the immediate contact with nature. All laws, far from being simply abstracted from things, are constructions of our mind, symbols of our ability to vary infinitely viewpoints from which the constancy of the world may be seen; once laws have been formulated, the situation is reversed: facts now are nothing but intersections of laws (SP, II, 520). Are laws objective? − They are above all the results of our discursive operations which they express more than nature (SP, II, 523). Laws as we know them are *contingent on* general forms (concepts) of common sense such as *space, time, motion* whose sense we understand relative to practical needs of discursive thinking and of action, individual or social; they also depend on other conditions such as the *concepts of Euclidean geometry* which modern research has shown to have originated from the peculiarities or our experiences and from the habits of our life. Moreover, in so far as laws are quantitative they express the *conventions* on which measurements are based. Methodologically speaking, laws are *neither verifiable nor falsifiable*; they have often been saved from falsification by inventing new entities or by pleading that the conditions have not been exactly satisfied for the occurrence of predicted phenomena, or finally by pleading the limited sensitivity of our observational and measuring instruments. The physicist wants to have regularities, this is why he finds them with the help of ingenious violence to which he subjects nature (SP, II, 523, PN, 143). *Laws are implicit definitions of terms* (PN, 143).

Are then scientific laws nothing but pure games or caprice of our mind? Such a claim would be untenable; they are, at least, *expressions of organized life* and of an *intentional attitude of our mind* (SP, II, 525).

3. *The Critique of 'Theories'*

Theories are *schematic and symbolic representations of* laws, *implicit definitions*; they are unverifiable and not subject to empirical control; they are rules of grammar; rival theories are like different dialects (SP, II, 528).

From any theory by small variations one may construct infinitely many *observationally equivalent* or *experimentally indistinguishable theories* (SP, II, 529).

Rival theories are "innumerable solutions of the same indeterminate problem" (Milhaud), they are distinct but *intertranslatable languages*; (SP, II, 529, PN, 142) each has its advantages and scientists ought to be able to choose them according to their personal preferences; it is essential to have rival theories because each of them emphasizes something that others disregard (SP, II, 530). Theories, like laws, are neither verifiable nor falsifiable; once established, they become convenient languages (SP, II, 531).

There is no true theory in the limit, only the preferred one (SP, II, 532).

The aim of rational science is to construct a schema of the universe which would permit discursive thought to reproduce at will, without appeal to experience, all the developments of nature. Scientists strive to construct a table (diagram) with double entries in which symbols and phenomena correspond one to another, a dictionary of Real-Rational, like words of two languages coordinated for translation. The external world is conventionally represented, like a symphony by the score or celestial order by the differential equations (SP, II, 544). The fundamental scientific ideas are those of *correspondence* and *representation*; two objects represent one another if any change in one is associated with a change in the other and, consequently, it is sufficient to act on one of them to induce an action on the other; two objects so related are logically substitutable, since knowledge of one suffices – by translation – to obtain knowledge of the other (SP, II, 545).

In conclusion, the results of the new critique of science undermined the traditional belief in the necessity and objectivity of science. Facts, laws and theories are all conventional, relative, contingent. Those results have shown that scientific conclusions are not necessary unless one adopts a certain attitude; they explain the rigour of science by showing that the latter results from a decree of our mind, from conventions; freedom of our mind is the source of knowledge; in effect science in not shown to be purely arbitrary – except from a logical point of view – for science grows out of life, i.e. our practical and spiritual activities (PN, 148). This is why *it is not possible to understand science as a purely intellectual enterprise*, for as such it is either merely a vast symbolism without any significance, or based on a vicious circle. One has to appeal to the *primacy of action*, either *practical or spiritual*.

The new critique of science has destroyed the old, naïve and narrow positivism of Comtian kind, which mistook common sense, crude facts for immediate intuitions, and saw in industry, in production the only worthwhile activity. By its opponents the new critique was accused of *scepticism*. However, it has given birth to *New Positivism*, which is not sceptical: it is positivism in the sense that its highest ideal is also *action*, though not primarily practical action in the narrow sense but rather 'profound action', i.e. the spiritual life (PN, 147, 151); the new positivism realizes that there are *diverse orders of knowledge* (the rational attitude is a legitimate but not the only and not the most valuable attitude one may take); even the most contrary views may contain correct elements; one must not reject outright a method merely because one has not been used to it; one can study things profitably from many different biases, there are many different ways of arriving at the truth. The superstition that there is one unique procedure, inevitable and perfect, usually results from lack of criticism (SP, II, 377).

In his polemic with LeRoy Poincaré argued that (a) as a philosophy of action LeRoy's extreme conventionalism or nominalism was self-defeating; (b) scientific facts are merely common-sense facts translated into a specialized, technical language of science, and, therefore, not 'created' by scientists in any clear sense; (c) there is a 'universal, objective invariant' under changes of the conventions implicit in laws and theories, so that all conventional, theoretical languages are intertranslatable. ('Sur la valeur objective des théories physiques', *Revue de M. et de M.*, 1902; *The Value of Science*, Part III, The Objective Value of Science; henceforth VS):

In connection with the first of these three points Poincaré simply argued that if it is true as LeRoy following Bergson claimed that science and its language have been geared primarily to practical actions, distorting reality in order to provide us with simplified recipes for actions, then it cannot be true that science consists exclusively of conventions. For conventions are arbitrary, free creations of our mind whereas 'practical recipes' cannot be such. "There is no escape from this dilemma; either science does not enable us to foresee and then it is useless as rule of action; or else it enables us to foresee in a fashion more or less imperfect, and then it is not without value as means of knowledge" (VS, 115).

With regard to the second point, Poincaré's position was that the distinction between 'bare' or 'rough' (pure, common sense) facts and 'scientific' facts made by LeRoy (and Duhem) was not illegitimate. He objected, however, to LeRoy's (and Duhem's) view that 'rough' or 'common-sense' facts are outside science and of no relevance to it and that 'scientific' facts, the only facts relevant to science were 'created by scientists' in a conventional way, dependent merely on their choice of one of many possible theories (which are themselves nothing but conventions). In Poincaré's own view it is the 'rough' or 'crude' fact that imposes the scientific fact upon the scientist (VS, 116). The following are examples of statements of fact: (1) It grows dark (a report of a layman's impression of an eclipse of the sun), (2) The eclipse happened at nine o'clock, (3) The eclipse happened at the time deducible from the tables constructed according to Newton's laws. Of these the first is supposed to represent a 'bare' or 'crude' fact, while the remaining ones are interpretations. To verify the first one, all we need is to specify the language in which it is formulated and to appeal to our senses, whereas in other cases ('scientific facts' or 'interpretations') we have also to specify certain additional *conventions*; but — so Poincaré argued — these conventions are merely rules of languages though more esoteric because used only by scientists and those who know science. In certain cases also some empirical laws are presupposed in the scientist's language which affirm, for example, that alternative methods of measuring (or detecting the presence of) certain effects will produce the same results: "To measure a current I may use a very great number of types of galvanometers or besides an electrodynamometer ..."; should the underlying law (of the equivalence of results) turn out to be false "it would be necessary to change the scientific language to free it from a grave ambiguity". Poincaré concluded: "The scientific fact is only the crude fact translated into a convenient language" (VS, 119, 120).

The last of the quoted claims was contested by Duhem on the ground that 'translation' in this case would be 'indeterminate' (to use a Quinean expression) and that the assumed laws which assure the equivalence of observational results form a theory, i.e. are conventional:

"It is therefore clear that the language in which a physicist expresses the results of his experiments is not a technical language similar to that employed in the diverse arts and trades. It resembles a technical language in that the initiated can translate it into facts, but differs in that a given sentence of a technical language expresses a specific operation performed on very specific objects whereas a sentence in the physicist's language may be translated into facts in an infinity of different ways" (*The Aim and Structure of Physical Theory*, p. 149). "... The role of the scientist is not limited to creating a clear and precise language in which to express concrete facts; rather, it is the case that the creation of this language presupposes the creation of a physical theory ..." (op. cit., p. 151).

The distinction between 'facts' and 'interpretations' ('scientific facts') made by all three French philosophers was later to become the subject of Ajdukiewicz's criticism and the outcome of that criticism one of the bases of his radical conventionalism ('The World-Picture and the Conceptual Apparatus', this volume p. 67).

Finally, in his polemic with LeRoy, Poincaré credited him with formulating the problem of the *existence of 'the universal invariant'* under changes of language, i.e. the problem of the *existence of languages* which are *not inter-translatable* (VS, 126—7). "Since the enunciation of our laws may vary with the conventions that we adopt, since these conventions may modify even the natural relations of these laws, is there in the manifold of these laws something independent of these conventions and which may, so to speak, play the role of *universal invariant*? ..." (VS, 127). In replying to this question Poincaré referred to fictitious non-Euclidean beings "educated in a world different from ours" and argued that their non-Euclidean language could always be translated into ours on the basis of a dictionary or — if they came to live with us in our world — both sides would end up understanding each other just "... as the American Indians ended by understanding the language of their conquerors after the arrival of the Spanish" (VS, 127). There were some conditions necessary for such understanding or translation, viz. some common 'humanity' (e.g. similar sense organs), common principles of logic (there would be no translation, for example, "... if those beings rejected our logic and did not admit, for instance, the principle of contradiction", VS, 128). Now, what is the nature of this invariant making all human-like languages intertranslatable?

"... The invariant laws are the relations between crude facts, while the relations between the 'scientific facts' remain always dependent on certain conventions" (VS, 128).

As was pointed out in our account of LeRoy's philosophy, though he saw conventional (logically and empirically arbitrary) elements not only in laws and theories but also in scientific facts and was thus forced by the logic of his own thoroughgoing conventionalism to formulate the problem of trans-latability between alternative conventional languages, he explicitly admitted the intertranslatability (even 'exact translatability') of all theoretical languages without clarifying what the 'universal invariant' under such translation would be; he did this possibly under the pressure of the authority of Poincaré's earlier writings on the subject. It was Duhem who questioned this universal translatability thesis having pointed out that a scientific fact (and 'interpreta-tion') can be mapped onto infinitely many 'common sense facts' whose equivalence is always based on a suitable law, and a law was for Duhem part of a theory, i.e. of a conventional language. Thus by removing all 'bare' or 'pure' facts from science and by insisting that all scientific facts are theory-dependent (for their meaning and acceptance) both Duhem and LeRoy opted for a more subjectivist and relativist view of science which deprived the latter of its superiority — in terms of objectivity and rationality — over religious beliefs and other 'spiritual experiences'[13]. Poincaré — whose views are often misrepresented as thoroughly conventionalist[14] — remained faithful to the tradition of scientific objectivity admitting that one may adopt a strictly nominalistic attitude with respect to all theories, laws and facts but insisting at the same time that such a nominalist attitude is alien to science as we know it (VS, 122–4). Conventions do play an important part in science; but once some conventions have been laid down, the problems scientists are interested in are of empirical nature and are solved on the basis of experimental procedures (VS, 120, 122). Moreover, there is no sharp and unbridgable frontier between science and common-sense which we decide in everyday life (VS, 122).

The controversy over the translatability of languages between Poincaré and LeRoy (involving also indirectly Duhem) must have had some influence on Ajdukiewicz's radical conventionalism. He himself refers to it (in 'The World-Picture and the Conceptual Apparatus', 1934) only in connection with the disagreement between Poincaré and LeRoy concerning so-called 'bare' or 'pure' facts, apparently siding with LeRoy's claim that scientists 'create (scientific) facts' in fact arguing against all three French authors' distinction between 'bare (pure) facts' (observational reports) and 'interpretations', and their implicit belief that one might be free to change more artificial scientific conventions but not those traditionally embedded in everyday language.

It is plausible to suggest that LeRoy's challenge to Poincaré's thesis of the translatability of all human languages and his Bergsonian and Pragmatist conception of language as "part of life", as expressing various "attitudes, ways of life, points of view" and associated with "action", did exert some influence on radical conventionalism. If so, then one must also emphasize the counterbalancing influence of the mathematical logician's conception of language as uniquely given by its vocabulary and rules. While Poincaré and LeRoy discussed translatability (or otherwise) of languages in terms of firstly, 'shared humanity' of speakers (e.g. having sense-organs like ours), secondly, the properties of the worlds in which they lived (Euclidean, non-Euclidean worlds), and thirdly, of the existence of 'bare' or 'pure' facts, Ajdukiewicz based his thesis of the existence of not-intertranslatable languages on more rigorous conceptions of language, meaning and translation. Finally, notwithstanding the latter thesis, science according to Ajdukiewicz's radical conventionalism is far *less* arbitrary and subjective than LeRoy would have had it.

IV. THE AJDUKIEWICZ LANGUAGES AND
RADICAL CONVENTIONALISM

According to Ajdukiewicz's own statement (in 'Language and Meaning', henceforth LM, and 'The World-Picture and the Conceptual Apparatus', henceforth WPCA), the epistemological theses of radical conventionalism are consequences of the definition of 'meaning' associated with the conception of language which he developed in 'On the Meaning of Expressions' (henceforth ME) and in LM. Different conceptions of meaning give rise to different views concerning the cognitive role of language. Some of them imply that the cognitive role of language reduces simply to its role as a means of communication and since all sufficiently rich languages are mutually translatable, the choice of one of them does not affect our knowledge in any essential way, though it may make a difference in other respects. Such, as we have seen, was the view of Poincaré. But there is another view, according to which the cognitive function of language is of crucial importance and transcends that of a means of communication being comparable to the role Immanuel Kant attributed to the a priori forms of sensibility and of understanding (WPCA, p. 86), except that there are, so it is claimed, *many different, mutually not translatable languages* which may provide completely *different world-perspectives* when combined with suitable experiential data. Such different linguistic world-perspectives might perhaps be compared to the radically different world-pictures envisaged briefly and dismissed by Poincaré (in his polemic with LeRoy) when he mentioned beings with sense organs different from ours (more sensitive to some, less sensitive to other stimuli) and using a logic different from ours (VS, III, Chap. X, 128). This other view, according to which languages play a much more dramatic role in cognition led Ajdukiewicz to the doctrine of radical conventionalism.

Language as actually spoken by men is for Ajdukiewicz — as it was for LeRoy — part of our biological and social life, adaptive behaviour, goal-directed and rule-governed activity. Apart from the rules of phonetics and syntax, the language of a community of speakers might be seen as governed by the *rules* which would express the speakers' *dispositions* to definite *motivational relationships* whereby experiences of certain types *motivate the acceptance* of definite sentences of the language (this is a pragmatic conception of inference). However, an empirical study of language — wherein to discover if a speaker associates with sentence S the meaning assigned to it by the meaning rules of L one places him in a situation appropriate to S and elicits his assent to or dissent from S (LM, p. 40) — would soon reveal that in a natural language there are no fixed and universal motivational relationships, in other words, that a natural language should rather be seen as a family of languages each of them with fixed and binding rules, each of them corresponding perhaps to a different way or form of life (languages of different social strata, professions, etc.). However, there is more to language than the psychological processes. The logical aspect (judgements in the logical sense), relevant to knowledge in the objective sense, rests in the intersubjective meaning which expressions have relative to a language-structure and not relative to individual speakers. If this is granted, then a transition is made to a more abstract study of language in which the latter is an idealization ('idealized type'), intended to reflect the inherent, though latent structure of a part of a natural language (LM, 63); (ME, 26). In an abstract study of this type, language is reconstructed in terms of its vocabulary, the rules of syntax and the *meaning-specification,* or the *meaning-*(acceptance) *rules.* The latter determine the *structure* or *matrix of the language* and the *meaning* of expressions is then conceived as an abstract property they have in virtue of the *positions* they may take *in the matrix* (LM, p. 62). Three kinds of meaning-rules may be distinguished as basic: (1) *axiomatic meaning-rules* specify sentences which are to be accepted unconditionally: the rejection of any sentence dictated by an axiomatic meaning-rule amounts to the violation of the meaning-specification characteristic for the language; (2) *deductive meaning-rules* specify ordered pairs of sentences (or ordered pairs whose first element is a sentence-class and the second element is a sentence) such that if one accepts the first of them one is thereby committed to accepting the second on pain of violating the meaning-specification of the language; (3) *empirical meaning-rules* assign to definite experiential data sentences (simple empirical meaning-rules) or to definite experiental data and sentences, other sentences (compound empirical meaning-rules) such that in the presence of those data (possibly conjoined with the acceptance of some sentences) one is forced to accept the coordinated sentence if one is to avoid violation of meaning. Axiomatic and deductive meaning-rules are *discursive* rules, they are sufficient for purely discursive languages, e.g. of pure mathematics (LM, p. 47, 'Scientific World-Perspective', WPCA, p. 68). Each meaning-rule has a *scope*: the scope of an axiomatic meaning-rule is a set of sentences (the axioms or principles of the language); the scope of a deductive meaning-rule is a set of ordered pairs of sentences (or of sentence-class/sentence); the scope of an empirical meaning-rule is a set of ordered pairs of experiential data and sentences (or experiential data-*cum*-sentences-sentence). The scopes of the meaning-rules of the same type may be summed. The sum of the scopes of all meaning-rules of the same type is their *total scope.* Two expressions of a language have *the same meaning* (are synonymous or intertranslatable) if their interchange leaves the total scopes of the meaning-rules unaltered, i.e. if they are *isotopes* in the total scopes of the meaning-rules. This statement may be made more precise in terms of the matrix of the language (LM, p. 62). The meaning-specification of a language is the correlation between its expressions and their positions within the scopes of the meaning-rules (and, consequently, within the matrix). Thus for a change of the meaning-specification of a language a change in the total scope of at least one of the types of meaning-rules is necessary. Two expressions of a language are said to be *directly (immediately) meaning-related* if they both occur in the same element of the scope of a meaning-rule; they are *indirectly (mediately) meaning-related* if they are linked by a finite chain of expressions which are directly meaning-related among themselves. A language in which any two expressions are directly or indirectly meaning-related is called *connected*; a *disconnected* language is an assemblage of connected languages. A language *L* is said to be *open with respect* to another language *L'* if *L'* contains all the expressions of *L* with the same meanings they have in *L* and also some expressions which do not exist in *L* and such that at least one of them is directly meaning-related to an expression in *L*. A language is *open* if there exists another language with respect to which it is open. A language which is not open is *closed* (LM, p. 50). The distinctions just introduced are crucial for Ajdukiewicz's analysis of *meaning-change* ('variance') and thus of *language-change*, as well as for his analysis of the relations between different languages. In effect, they are crucial for the theses of radical conventionalism.

Not every change in the scope of individual meaning-rules results in the change of the total scope of the meaning-rules: different individual scopes may yield identical scope-sums; hence there are changes in the individual scopes which leave the meaning-specification of the language (and thus the meanings of its expressions) unaltered (LM, p. 49). When the meaning-specification of a language does change, this can occur either through the introduction of new expressions or without such enrichment of the vocabulary. The latter change occurs, for example, when a sentence which originally was an empirical hypothesis is elevated to the status of a 'principle' (convention) in Poincaré's sense. According to Poincaré, we may remember, the postulates of Euclid's geometry, the laws of Newtonian mechanics, conservation laws, the principle of relativity all changed their status in this way at one time or another. However, from Poincaré's point of view all these changes occurred within one and the same language, or at least did not involve any change in the meaning of the sentences in question. By contrast on Ajdukiewicz's conception of language and meaning a radical change in meaning occurs whenever the status of a sentence is altered in this way; for the rejection of an empirical hypothesis does not violate any meaning-rule whereas the rejection of a sentence dictated by an axiomatic meaning-rule, e.g. a 'principle' or terminological convention, does. According to Ajdukiewicz's view of language it is logically impossible to reject a sentence dictated by an axiomatic meaning-rule, i.e. a sentence analytic in the given language, if one understands it in conformity with the meaning-specification of the language. For a proper use of a sentence dictated by an axiomatic meaning-rule requires that it should be accepted (SWP, p. 111).

As regards the introduction of new expressions into a language's vocabulary, an open language behaves under such a change differently from a closed one: one can introduce into an open language L a new expression E which is not synonymous with any expression already in L and such that E is directly meaning-related to some expression L, without thereby altering the meaning of the old expressions of L. A closed language, on the other hand, becomes disconnected if it is enriched with a new expression synonymous with some of those already in the language (LM, p. 51).

If two languages L and L' are both closed and connected and if some expression of L has a translation in L' then the two languages L and L' are *intertranslatable*. An open language can close to two closed and connected languages which are mutually translatable but cannot close to two closed and connected languages which are not intertranslatable. If the totality of the expressions of a closed and connected language together with their meanings (i.e. positions in the total scopes of the meaning-rules) is called a *conceptual apparatus* and the totality of accepted sentences of such a language a *world-picture*, then the *theses of Radical Conventionalism* may be formulated as follows:

Of all the judgements (meanings of sentences – JG) which we accept and which accordingly constitute our entire world-picture, *none* is unambiguously determined by experiential data; every one of them depends on the conceptual apparatus we choose to use in representing experiential data. We can choose, however, one or another conceptual apparatus which will affect our whole world-picture (WPCA, p. 67; for a more precise statement see same article, chapter 3, 'Radical Conventionalism, p. 72).

Apart from the above doctrine of radical conventionalism, Ajdukiewicz also subscribed to a weaker thesis of radical conventionalism, formulated in his polemic with Poincaré and other French conventionalists, and independent of the concept of closed and connected languages which is essential for the formulation of the 'stronger' theses of radical conventionalism. The weaker thesis of radical conventionalism is as follows:

There is no essential difference between so-called observational reports ('bare' or 'pure' facts) and interpretations so far as their epistemological status is concerned; the former are governed by the meaning-rules of the ordinary language, whereas the latter are governed in addition by explicitly introduced conventions whose purpose is to make the expressions of the ordinary language more precise (WPCA, p. 78; 'W sprawie artykulu prof. A Schaffa o moich pogladach filozoficznych', Jezyk i Poznanie, I, p. 181).

If we call *universal* a language in which all judgements (meanings) can be expressed, then science in its actual development does not show a tendency towards universality; a universal language would be disconnected, a loose assemblage of conceptual apparatuses. Science tends towards a connected world-view (WPCA, p. 79).

A conceptual apparatus together with a set of experiential data is called *a world-perspective* (corresponding to those data) SWP, p. 112). The set of sentences dictated by the meaning-rules of a conceptual apparatus (together with well-confirmed hypotheses framed in the concepts of the language) form *a world picture* (WCPA, p. 81). Two different world-pictures (associated with conceptual apparatuses which are not mutually translatable) are neither logically nor experimentally comparable. One could extend a conceptual apparatus L by introducing a *concept of truth*, perhaps with the help of the following meaning-rule: Only that person speaks the language L who having accepted a sentence S of L is on that basis prepared to accept the sentence 'S is true in L'. So introduced, the concept of truth would apply to the sentences of L only. Using one conceptual apparatus one cannot predicate 'truth' or 'falsity' of any sentence belonging to the world-picture associated with a different conceptual apparatus, not translatable with one's own (SWP, p. 117).

If different world-pictures cannot be compared either logically (through inferences or with respect to their truth or falsity) or experimentally, are they equally good or can they not be compared in any way whatever? — They can be compared and evaluated in the process of *'humanistic understanding'* (SWP), p. 117) or from an *'evolutionary'* point of view. The former is in effect a study of the motives which guide scientists in bringing about changes in science. The latter is concerned with the question: Which of the conceptual apparatuses is closer to the (*quasi-*) goal discernible from the evolutionary tendencies in actual science? (SWP, p. 117).

Let us label as *Ajdukiewicz languages* the (idealized) languages given by the vocabulary, the syntax and the three types of meaning-rules, as described before.[15] The Ajdukiewicz languages have several interesting properties, among them the following ones: (1) they are axiomatic systems; (2) for any of the language speakers they are axiomatic systems not only in the formal but also in the pragmatic sense; (3) assuming Ajdukiewicz's definition of meaning, they are interpreted axiomatic systems in a sense of 'interpreted' different from the usual semantical-extensional one; (4) they are theories in a literal and quite precise sense.

The Ajdukiewicz languages are *axiomatic systems* since the meaning-rules of each such language define a relation of consequence on the class of its sentences. This is obvious in the case of languages which are based only on discursive (axiomatic and deductive) meaning-rules. The empirical meaning-rules, however, can be reduced to axiomatic ones, as has been shown by Ajdukiewicz (in *'Empiryczny fundament poznania'*, 1936; *'W sprawie arty-kulu prof. A. Schaffa o moich pogladach filozoficznych'*, *Język i poznanie*, II, p. 163).

Since the axioms of an Ajdukiewicz language have to be accepted by any speaker of the language together with all their consequences, an Ajdukiewicz language is for any of its speakers *an axiomatic system in the pragmatic* and not only in the formal *sense*.

In his 1921 dissertation MDS Ajdukiewicz distinguished between the formal (syntactical), semantical and methodological (pragmatic) properties and studies of axiomatic systems, though at the time he did not use the terms 'semantics' or 'pragmatics'. In a couple of articles published in the post-radical conventionalism period ('Axiomatic Systems from the Methodological Point of View', included in the present volume, also *'Metodologia i metanauka'*, *Zycie Nauki*, 1948, translated as *'Methodology and Metascience'* in *25 Years of Logical Methodology in Poland*, M. Przełęcki, R. Wójcicki (eds.), Reidel, 1976), Ajdukiewicz discussed the differences between the meta-logical (formal and semantical) and the methodological aspects of axiomatic systems in mathematics and in science. From the methodological point of view one is interested in the pragmatic relations between the axiomatic systems and men who use them, e.g. in the question whether or not their axioms and derived theorems are asserted (accepted) by those who use them and how such acceptance is justified. Ajdukiewicz proposed to distinguish three types of axiomatic system from the methodological or pragmatic viewpoint: An axiomatic system is *assertive-deductive* (for X) if both its axioms and derived theorems are accepted (by X) and the acceptance of derived theorems is motivated by the acceptance of the axioms. An axiom system is *assertive-reductive* (for X) in case the acceptance of the axioms is motivated by the acceptance of some of the derived theorems (so-called hypothetico-deductive systems in science are of this type). Finally an axiomatic system is *neutral* (*non*-assertive (for X)) if neither its axioms nor its derived theorems are asserted (by X) but merely 'assumed' or 'entertained'. Though this distinction was made by Ajdukiewicz not for semantical but for methodological purposes and no reference was made by him in that context to his earlier conception of language and 'meaning' (understood in an inter-subjective sense), it is tempting to characterize the Ajdukiewicz languages in the light of this classification of axiomatic systems, and assuming Ajdukiewicz's definition of 'meaning'. On the assumption mentioned, the Ajdukiewicz languages are, of course, assertive-deductive axiomatic systems for any speaker of those languages (if one disregards semantic requirements, avoided in LM). However, since not all sentences of an Ajdukiewicz language are dictated by axiomatic meaning-rules — hypotheses, for example, are not — within a language of this type there may be embedded either an empirical theory or an abstract theory which is assertive-reductive or else neutral; this would allow one to treat not only empirical hypotheses, but also some mathematical axioms, e.g., the axiom of infinity, the axiom of choice, etc. as 'hypotheses' rather than as sentences dictated by the axiomatic meaning-rules, i.e. as analytic.[16]

Assuming Ajdukiewicz's definition of 'meaning', and disregarding for the time being certain inadequacies in it to be discussed later, an Ajdukiewicz language is an *interpreted system*, since every expression of such a language has meaning, i.e. position in the total scope of the meaning-rules which govern the acceptance of sentence. This is a sense of 'interpretation' different from the usual semantical-extensional one, as a mapping of the expressions of the language onto an abstract or empirical domain (structure). For although every expression of an Ajdukiewicz language has meaning, not every one has a referent (denotation). Moreover, two co-extensive expressions, i.e. which have identical denotations in a domain, may have different meanings. Indeed, one of Ajdukiewicz's objectives was to do justice to these differences between 'meaning' and 'denotation' (LM, p. 39, also his reference to Mill's distinction between 'denotation' and 'connotation' there). As can be gathered from our previous comments, an axiomatic system may be interpreted in either an abstract domain, e.g. of numbers, or in an empirical domain, and yet remain uninterpreted in the present sense; this happens, of course, if it is a neutral axiomatic system with respect to whose axioms and derived theorems one takes no assertive attitude. Such a system, on its own, would *not* be an Ajdukiewicz language (in the present sense; see, however, section 5 for the Ajdukiewicz languages without axiomatic meaning-rules), since its axioms are not dictated by axiomatic meaning-rules, though it could be embedded in one to give its expressions meaning in Ajdukiewicz's sense. 'Meaning' in Ajdukiewicz's sense was understood in a non-psychological sense of 'objectified meaning', relativized only to a language. The latter in its logical aspect is a relatively autonomous entity. The actual linguistic performance of the language-users somehow participates in it, since the language-users are committed to the acceptance of those sentences of the language which its meaning-rules dictate. Linguistic expressions on this conception acquire meaning in a way analogous to the process in which 'life-expressions' acquire 'objective sense' (*Sinn*) within a cultural structure, according to the philosophy of the 'Objective Mind'. Meaning (interpretation) in this sense may be given directly to the most abstract expressions whether mathematical, scientific, theological or metaphysical in general. For what is essential to 'meaning' so understood is not — as in the case of indirect interpretation through so-called 'bridge-principles' — the relation of an expression to observables, but its position (valence) in a language-structure.[17] The methodological question of the justification of such commitments is distinct from the semantical one. Needless to say, the existence of referents is not guaranteed by having a meaning in this sense nor — as we shall see — is identity of referents of synomymous expressions. Finally and trivially — in virtue of previous properties — an Ajdukiewicz language is a *theory* in the clear and precise sense of a deductively systematized set of asserted sentences. Let us repeat, a user of an Ajdukiewicz language is committed to accept some of its sentences — those dictated by the meaning-rules — in order to understand its expressions in a way appropriate to the given language ("There is no understanding without some belief" as a contemporary hermeneuticist wrote). By contrast, Poincaré's view was that an abstract *theory* in theoretical physics is merely a *façon de parler*, — a language of symbols and metaphors which *does not commit* one to any assertion, apart from the empirical laws invariant under change of theoretical language and possibly its invariant structure. Similarly, for Carnap, realism and idealism were two observationally equivalent metaphysical theories and thus two different *façons de parler* without any commitments. In at least one of the senses of 'instrumentalism' a scientific theory from the instrumentalist viewpoint is a system of unasserted (though possibly semantically interpreted) sentences, i.e. is a neutral (non-assertive) axiomatic system in Ajdukiewicz's terminology.[18] Such a view expresses either the instrumentalist's scepticism with respect to the specific scientific theory (or to any scientific theory) or else his commitment to an apparently incompatible metaphysical or religious doctrine and to the ideal of consistency of one's assertions. It is worth noting, first of all, that Poincaré's view of physical theories was not instrumentalist in this sense (whereas Bellarmino's and Osiander's, for example, were); secondly, that a sceptic-instrumentalist (in the sense just explicated) may use an Ajdukiewicz language to embed in it a neutral, unasserted scientific theory. Ajdukiewicz himself never held an instrumentalist view of scientific theories in any of the senses mentioned, except possibly the last one with respect to mathematics at the time when he wrote his 'Axiomatic Systems from the Methodological Point of View'.

The stronger thesis of radical conventionalism implies that there are at least two different mutually intertranslatable conceptual apparatuses, i.e., closed and connected languages. Three concepts are important for the understanding and assessment of the truth of this claim: 'Meaning' (since 'translation' is defined in terms of 'sameness of meaning'), 'closed language', 'connected language'. The first two turn out to be associated with certain difficulties which will be discussed in the final section of this essay. Ajdukiewicz's general conception of language as based on vocabulary, syntax and the meaning-rules (the Ajdukiewicz languages as we have called them here) was largely unaffected by these difficulties and continued to be used by him for various purposes in the later period of his life.

V. BEYOND RADICAL CONVENTIONALISM

Radical conventionalism grew out Ajdukiewicz's conviction that to solve epistemological problems in a satisfactory, clear and precise fashion one needs a *more rigorous conception of language and meaning* than those used in traditional epistemological discussions. For *knowledge* consists, in traditional terminology, of judgements and concepts and the latter are simply *meanings* which sentences and other expressions have relative not to individual knowing subjects but *relative to a language* (or a family of languages) (LM, p. 35). The same applies to scientific laws and theories. Newton's laws of gravitation, for example, is the meaning a particular sentence has in a specific language and which is shared by all its *translations*. The controversy between the apriorists and the empiricists as to whether there are a priori elements (judgements) in our knowledge and if so whether they are all analytic or not, concerns articulated knowledge and this presupposes a language, i.e. a system of expressions endowed with meaning (LM, p. 39). One cannot hope to resolve the controversy without having a clearer notion of language and meaning. The same applies to a more specific controversy between the apriorists, radical empiricists and conventionalists (moderate empiricists) concerning the status of Euclid's axioms or of the laws of Newtonian mechanics. The controversy presupposes a concept of analyticity (as well as other related concepts) and, clearly, Kant's definitions were unsatisfactory, especially in the light of Poincaré's insight into the changes of the status of the components of mathematical and scientific theories (from empirical generalizations to conventional principles). This insight is wasted if one does not see those changes as indicative both of the changes in language and of the relativity of status. Finally, the dispute between Poincaré and LeRoy concerning the existence of the 'universal invariant' under translation from one language into another and the question whether all languages are intertranslatable, is hopelessly undecidable as long as it is conducted in obscure and vague terms (e.g. 'shared humanity', 'universal invariant', and unanalyzed concept of 'translation'). However stimulating these controversies are, one should approach them in a more rigorous fashion if one takes them seriously.

In order to realize this research programme Ajdukiewicz set out in the early nineteen-thirties to construct a concept of language and of meaning at once more precise than the traditional ones and yet embodying some, at least, of the traditional insights. Language itself was to be seen as both rooted in psychological phenomena susceptible of empirical research (judging process, attitudes, assertive behaviour) and as transcending them into the sphere of intersubjective structures given by rules, viz. meaning-rules constituted by and abstracted from human activities. Meaning was conceived as an abstract, intersubjective property expressions have in virtue of their positions or role (inferential valence) in the language-structure. Language was thus both a humanistic or cultural structure knowable through participation in it (under-standing, acceptance, assertion)[19] and a formal structure (an axiomatic system) which could be studied with the help of formal methods.

Having adopted this view of language in the first period of his philosophical development, Ajdukiewicz was in a position to argue that there were many linguistic structures or conceptual apparatuses and that one's world-perspective depended not only on experiential data but also on the choice of one such conceptual apparatus. Moreover, he was able to give a definition of analyticity in L (the set of sentences dictated by the axiomatic rules of L and their consequences by virtue of deductive rules) and to argue both that the alleged synthetic a priori sentences were analytic in his sense and that the presence of the a priori analytic sentences in our knowledge is unavoidable since it is simply due to the fact that knowledge has to be articulated in a language. In this way, *the clarification of the concepts of language and of meaning had important epistemological consequences*: the first was that one's world-view was co-determined by experiential data *and* the choice of a language; the second was that the solutions of various traditional epistemological problems were determined by the essential properties of language and were given once the relevant properties of language were exhibited in a satisfactory theory of language. The latter seemed also to give an extra bonus: semantical concepts such as 'denotation' ('reference'), 'truth', 'falsity', etc. which had been known to generate paradoxes, were dispensable. 'Meaning' was neither identified with nor defined in terms of 'denotation'. Individual sentences and world-pictures were not characterized as true or false but rather as dictated by meaning-rules, i.e. as derivable immediately or mediately by meaning-rules. If the term 'true' were to be introduced at all, it would be governed by a meaning-rule which restricted its application to the sentences of one's language already dictated by the meaning-rules of the language (Cf. Ajdukiewicz's preface to *Język i Poznanie, 1960*).

Ajdukiewicz's articles on language, meaning and radical conventionalism appeared at the time when in Vienna logic as the method of philosophy was identified with logical syntax. However, their publication roughly coincided with the emergence of logical semantics: Alfred Tarski's memoir *Pojecie prawdy w jezykach nauk dedukcyjnych* (*Towarzystwo Naukowe Warszawskie*, Warszawa) appeared in 1933 and soon, in 1936, was made more accessible in German translation as 'Der Wahrheitsbegriff in formalisierten Sprachen' (*Studia Philosophica* I). Pragmatics, mainly empirical pragmatics and as a research programme rather than as an accomplished technique, was to be enshrined a bit later as a part of the Logical Empiricist Theory of Language (Ch. Morris – 'Theory of Signs', *Int. Enc. of Unified Science* I (1938), 2.

The impact of logical semantics on Ajdukiewicz's philosophy was three-fold: Firstly, he at once joined in the programme of developing epistemology based on logical semantics, since semantical concepts were now shown to be free from the paradoxes, provided the use of those concepts was suitably restricted; secondly, he began to doubt whether a satisfactory definition of 'meaning' could be given without the use of semantical concepts (in the narrower sense). Thirdly, he came to the conclusion that the classical conception of truth (explicated by Tarski) was essential for realist epistemology. As regards the first and third points, one should mention his article 'A Semantical Version of the Problem of Transcendental Idealism' (hereafter SVPTI), 1937, in which Ajdukiewicz used both some results of semantics (e.g. 'The class of theorems of an incomplete theory is not identical with the class of true sentences in the language of the theory') and his own conception of language (meaning-rules as defining the relation of consequence on the set of sentences of a language) to paraphrase the thesis of transcendental idealism and to subject it to criticism. In the same article he observed that, if dissatisfied with the application of the law of the excluded middle to sentences with vague terms one were to replace 'true sentence' with 'provable theorem' (or 'sentence derivable in virtue of meaning-rules'), then one would be committed to epistemological idealism (a similar claim may be found in *Problems and Theories of Philosophy*, translated by H. Skolimowski and A. Quinton, Cambridge U.P., 1973, p. 21).[20]

Meanwhile it was pointed out by Tarski (as reported by Ajdukiewicz in 'The Problem of Empiricism and the Concept of Meaning') that, at least for a language L based exclusively on axiomatic and deductive meaning-rules one can construct two expressions A and B such that the meaning-rules of L are invariant under the interchange of A and B and yet A and B have *non*-identical denotations. This shows that, if one demands (as one usually does) that two synonymous expressions should have identical denotations, then *the invariance of the meaning-rules under the interchange of expressions – though necessary – is not sufficient for those expressions of a language based on axiomatic and deductive meaning rules to be synonymous*. Let us remark, first of all, that the objection does not apply to languages without axiomatic meaning-rules. However, if one accepts Tarski's criticism – as Ajdukiewicz did – then 'synonymity' and 'meaning' are no longer explicitly defined in terms of the language matrix and the equivalence class of positions within the matrix. They are defined only *partially* by the implication: If two expressions of L are synonymous, then the meaning-rules of L are invariant under interchange of those two expressions. This implication, unaffected by the objection, was enough for Ajdukiewicz to be able to continue claiming that the presence in our knowledge of analytic (a priori) sentences is unavoidable since it is due to our use of language. The same implication also suffices as a criterion of meaning-change (variance), since it provides a criterion of the difference in meaning. Thus many problems of meaning-change discussed in contemporary philosophy of science under the heading of 'incommensurability' can still be handled within the framework of Ajdukiewicz languages. Finally, the objection could have been met by making the relevant adequacy condition part of the definition of 'synonymity': Two expressions of L are synonymous if and only if the meaning-rules of L are invariant under the interchange of those expressions and if the denotations of the expressions in question are identical. In later years one of the alternative definitions of 'meaning' which Ajdukiewicz considered, and which he thought would be neutral with respect to different epistemological positions, was in terms of 'co-denotation', i.e. in terms of the denotation of a compound expression and of the syntactical positions (within the expression) of its constituents. The latter concepts he developed in his very influential 1935 article 'Syntactic Connexion', and used in many later articles, including the posthumously published 'Proposition as the Connotation of a Sentence' and 'Intensional Expressions'.[21]

Apart from the mentioned objection to Ajdukiewicz's definition of 'synonymity', some criticisms were also made of his concept of a closed language, i.e. of a language which cannot be further enriched without becoming disconnected. Critics argued that closed languages did not exist that – a fortiori – closed not-intertranslatable languages did not exist either. Since Ajdukiewicz's definition of 'meaning' was given for closed and connected languages, this criticism may seem to be directed against the definition of 'meaning' also. Now, the assumptions of connectedness and closedness were made by Ajdukiewicz with full awareness of their idealized nature (LM, p. 64; WPCA, p. 87). A disconnected language is not *one* language but a *family* of connected languages. Similarly, an open language is an 'unfinished' language, a language which is in the process of growth or, at least, of potential growth; in other words, such a language is only part of a 'complete language'. It is, therefore, impossible to construct a matrix either for a disconnected or for an open language. In the former case it would have to be a set of matrices; in the latter, the matrix would not be complete and could be extended further in many different ways by introducing different meaning-rules for new expressions; consequently one could never know if the condition of the invariance of the total scope of rules of one type or another was satisfied or not. In other words, the claim that closed languages did not exist could not be a serious objection to the idealized assumption of closedness whose sole function was to make sense of the concept of the language matrix (used in turn to define synonymity and meaning); all idealizations would be affected by similar objections. On the other hand, if substantiated, the claim would constitute a valid objection to one of the theses of radical conventionalism, viz. the thesis that there are at least two different conceptual apparatuses (i.e. connected, closed and mutually non-translatable languages). For though one may be permitted to make use of simplified assumptions in one's definitions and theories, one must not draw existential conclusions from such assumptions.[22]

These and similar criticisms naturally undermined Ajdukiewicz's confidence in radical conventionalism in its stronger version (the weaker was unaffected); they also made his views on language and meaning more flexible which in turn – not surprisingly – led him to embrace a position not unlike his original conventionalism except that it was now *conventionalism at the meta-level*. Radical conventionalism implied the existence of different mutually non-translatable object-languages, from which one at a time could be chosen to articulate our experiences and discursive thoughts. It originated from an analysis in which Ajdukiewicz believed to have captured, as it were, the nature of language in its cognitive function as it is known to us from everyday experience in practical life, in existing science and mathematics. At least three types of meaning-rule (axiomatic, deductive and empirical) are characteristic of any existing empirical language and two (axiomatic and deductive) of any known discursive language. But just as the concept of Euclidean space and geometry, though they originated from our everyday experiences (with rigid bodies), were supplemented by 'non-Euclidean spaces' and *non*-Euclidean geometries, the standard concept of an empirical Ajdukiewicz language may be supplemented by the idea of a language based on deductive and empirical meaning-rules exclusively ('Logic and Experience', 1947, p. 68.)[23] In such a non-standard empirical Ajdukiewicz language there are no analytic sentences since there are no axiomatic meaning-rules necessary to generate analyticity. The role of logic would be performed either by the deductive meaning-rules alone or also by formulae which would be used together with empirical premises in inferences and which — in view of the Duhem-thesis — would be affected by the outcome of the experimental testing of the conclusions. An Ajdukiewicz language without axiomatic meaning-rules is in effect a Quinean language for no sentence is accepted in it 'come what may', i.e. unconditionally; there is no way of distinguishing in it analytic from other sentences because all have the same status epistemologically, all are revisable on the basis of observation. However, one must not conclude that, having rejected his earlier views on language, analyticity, etc., in 1948 Ajdukiewicz embraced a position identical with Quine's ('Truth by convention', 1936; 'Two dogmas of empiricism', 1953).[24] This would not be correct. The point of introducing the concept of a language without axiomatic meaning-rules was rather to argue that the epistemological thesis of radical empiricism (according to which all science — including mathematics and logic — consists of empirically revisable sentences) and the thesis of moderate empiricism (which claims that, apart from empirical components of science, there are also a priori analytic ones), need not be mutually incompatible. They are not, if either they refer to different types of language or express programmes for constructing science in a certain way, rather than describe existing science. One cannot escape the feeling that this new view concerning the relationship between the two epistemological doctrines originated from the analysis of the same examples (given by Poincaré) of sentences changing status (from empirical generalizations to conventional principles). On the previous occasion Ajdukiewicz saw this change as indicating meaning and language variance, and therefore demanded that status be relativized to a language. *Now* he concluded that epistemologists only appeared to contradict one another when they attributed a different status to 'the same sentence'. In fact, they were talking at cross purposes, since either they had in mind different existing languages (e.g. different historical stages in the development of a scientific theory) or else were proposing or demanding that different types of language should be used in articulating science. When radical conventionalism seemed to have been undermined at the object-language level (since it was questioned whether there existed different, not-inter-translatable object-languages), it was in a sense being resurrected at the meta-level of different conceptions of language and different epistemological programmes (choice of types of language). However, if one transforms an Ajdukiewicz language based on all three types of meaning-rules into one with only deductive and empirical meaning-rules, two such object-languages are mutually non-translatable at least in their discursive parts.

This was not a transient feature of Ajdukiewicz's philosphy peculiar to his 1947 'Logic and Experience'. In the posthumously published paper 'The Problem of Empiricism and the Concept of Meaning', which he had read in 1962 at a conference (organized in Warsaw to celebrate his 70th birthday), Ajdukiewicz distinguished the epistemological from the methodological version of the problem of empiricism. Whereas the former is concerned with *questio facti*, the latter is concerned with the question whether it is *possible* to construct science without a priori elements and, if it is, how to do it? Accordingly, methodology was on this programme to study various *possible ways of doing science*, rather like geometry which studies possible spaces.[25]

This was the *coda* of Ajdukiewicz's life-long work, the first movement of which, radical conventionalism, had been conceived back in the early thirties. Methodological Pluralism, which does not preclude one from having a preferred epistemological, methodological or ideological position, has always been part of the conventionalist tradition. It seems a particularly suitable conclusion to the work of a philosopher who all his life was more tolerant towards and more ready to learn from different traditions than most of his contemporaries.

August 1976   JERZY GIEDYMIN

NOTES

[1] Cf. Ajdukiewicz's preface to the first volume of *Język i Poznanie* (Language and Knowledge), 1960, as well as his article *'W sprawie artykulu prof. A. Schaffa o moich pogladach filozoficznych'* (A Reply to Prof. A. Schaff's Article Concerning my Philosophical Views), *Język i Poznanie*, Vol. II, 1965, p. 176.

[2] As we know, both Dedekind and Peano believed that the axioms of arithmetic *do* implicitly define arithmetical primitives. Dedekind seems to have identified the set of natural numbers with what is common to all simply infinite sets, Cf. Hao Wang: 'The Axiomatization of Arithmetic', *Journal of Symbolic Logic* **22** (1957), 152. Poincaré's argument against regarding the axioms of the Dedekind-Peano system as an implicit

definition of arithmetical primitives was as follows: for an axiom system to serve as an implicit definition of its primitives it must be proved to be consistent (and categorical); non-Euclidean geometries have been proved consistent relative to Euclid's geometry and the latter relative to arithmetic; however, a proof of the consistency of the axioms of arithmetic could be only given by recursion, i.e. it would make use of the axiom of induction and would thus involve a *petitio principii.* This may be avoided only by regarding the axiom of induction as a synthetic a priori truth (*Science and Method*, pp. 151–160). It seems therefore that according to Poincaré one can prove the consistency of arithmetic only by an appeal to our mathematical intuition (if we believe in such proofs). However, if the proofs of the consistency of geometries ultimately depend on an intuitive proof of the consistency of arithmetic, one wonders why they should have a different epistemological status, i.e., why they may be regarded as terminological conventions whereas the axioms of arithmetic cannot. In any case, it is questionable whether Poincaré was right in claiming that any consistency proof of arithmetic is bound to involve a *petitio principii.* In view of Gödel's result on consistency proofs, which appeared long after Poincaré's death in 1912, he was right if by *petitio principii* is meant the use in a proof of premisses 'not previously justified'. He need not have been right if by *petitio principii* is meant a circular proof, i.e. one in which the conclusion occurs explicitly or implicitly among the premisses used. If in a proof of the consistency of arithmetic we were to use the axiom of induction the proof would not thereby be circular: the conclusion is a meta-theorem which is neither identical with nor does it imply the axiom of induction. For an analysis of the *petitio principii* along these lines, cf. Ajdukiewicz 'Logic and Experience', this volume, p. 169; also Ajdukiewicz's argument against the charge of the circularity of all consistency proofs of logic *Z metodologii nauk dedukcyjnych;* 'Axiomatic Systems from the Methodological Point of View'.

[3] In his 1872 *Erlangen Programm* F. Klein defined geometry as the study of the properties of figures which remain invariant under a particular group of transformations. This influenced H. Minkowski's space-time geometry.

[4] For each of the metric geometries there is an infinite set of different congruence classes. Cf. R. Bonola: *Non-Euclidean Geometry,* Dover Publications, 1955, pp. 153–4; A. Grünbaum: *Philosophical Problems of Space and Time,* 1963 chap. I; and *Geometry and Chronometry in Philosophical Perspective,* 1968, chaps. I and II.

[5] Two non-empirical theories may be regarded as observationally equivalent. The idea of experimentally indistinguishable laws played a more important role in Pierre Duhem's philosophy of physics. Cf. his *The Aim and Structure of Physical Theory,* Dover Publications, Part II, chap. 5, 'Physical Law'.

[6] The present fomulation of this doctrine is mine but it is very close to Poincaré's own. It seems to imply both the 'inscrutability of reference' (of the theoretical terms of a theory) and the 'indeterminacy of translation' of the theoretical language of a theory.

[7] 'Three Views Concerning Human Knowledge', *Conjectures and Refutations.* For a different account of 'instrumentalism' see my 'Instrumentalism and its Critique: A Re-Appraisal', *Boston Studies in the Philosophy of Science* (forthcoming). Pierre Duhem suggested that Poincaré's account of the epistemological nature of physical theories was inspired by his study of Maxwell's theory. In 'The Value of Physical Theory' (*Revue générale des sciences pure et appliquées* **XIX** (1908); reprinted as appendix in *The Aim and Structure of Physical Theory,* Princeton University Press, 1974) Duhem wrote: "... Is there a physics which has less claim to *knowledge* and which is more clearly and purely utilitarian than that English physics in which theories merely play the role of *models* without any connection with reality? Is it not that physics which first of all enticed Henri Poincaré when he was studying Maxwell's work and so inspired the famous pages in which physical theories were considered solely as convenient instruments for experimental research? ..." (p. 319).

[8] *The Value of Science*, chap. VIII, 'The Present Crisis in Physics', in particular, 98–100, 103.

[9] For an earlier criticism of the analytic-synthetic distinction, see B. Russell's *An Essay on the Foundation of Geometry*, 1897. On p. 57 of that book Russell wrote: "... It will be my aim to prove ... that the distinction of synthetic and analytic judgements is untenable ..."; "... The doctrine of synthetic and analytic judgements ... has been ... completely rejected by most modern logicians ..."; the logicians in question were Bradley and Bosanquet. "... Thus no judgement *per se*, is either analytic or synthetic, for the severance of a judgement from its context robs it of its vitality, and makes it not truly a judgement at all. But in its proper context it is neither purely synthetic nor purely analytic; for while it is the further determination of a given whole, and thus in so far analytic, it also involves the emergence of *new* relations within the whole, and is so far synthetic" (p. 59).

[10] Edouard Louis J. LeRoy (1870–1954), a student of both Poincaré and Bergson, succeeded Henri Bergson, both in Collège de France and in l'Académie Française.

[11] G. Milhaud, 'La science rationelle', *Revue de M. et de M.*, May, 1896; J. Wilbois, 'La méthode des sciences physiques', ibid. September, 1899; E. LeRoy, 'La science positive et les philosophies de la liberté', *Bibliothèque du Congrès internationale de Philosophie*, vol. I.

[12] In *The Aim and Structure of Physical Theory* (*La Théorie physique*, 1906) part II, chap. IV 'Experiment in Physics', in a footnote on p. 144, Duhem refers to his article 'Quelques reflexions au sujet de la physique expérimentale', *Revue de Questions Scientifiques*, 2nd series, III, (1894). Cf. also op. cit., p. 150, footnote 7.

[13] No mention has been made here of Duhem's doctrine of 'natural classification' which has a more realist flavour.

[14] A very accurate short account of Poincaré's philosophy of science may be found in Peter Alexander's note on Poincaré in 'The Philosophy of Science, 1850–1910' in D. J. O'Conner (ed.), *A Critical History of Western Philosophy*.

[15] These must, of course, not be confused with so-called 'Ajdukiewicz categorial grammars' which originated from his 'Syntactic Connexion'; see the present volume, p. 118 also P. T. Geach, 'A Program for Syntax', *Synthese* 22 (1970), Nos. 1/2 and D. Lewis, 'General Semantics', ibid, p. 20.

[16] Every sentence dictated by an axiomatic meaning-rule of an Ajdukiewicz language is an axiom in the formal sense, but *not* vice versa. An axiom of a 'neutral' (non-assertive) axiom-system, though it is of course an axiom in the formal sense, is not dictated by an axiomatic meaning-rule in Ajdukiewicz's sense, since such a rule would require its unconditional acceptance (assertion) by any speaker of the given language. However, a neutral axiomatic system may be an Ajdukiewicz language based on deductive and empirical or only on deductive meaning-rules.

[17] Subject to qualifications – to be discussed in Section 5 of this essay – this point might perhaps be of some interest to those philosophers of science who – like, for example, R. Tuomela – use logical methods in discussing the semantics of empirical theories and insist on direct interpretation of theoretical terms. Cf. R. Tuomela, *Theoretical Concepts*, Wien-New York 1973, p. 118.

[18] I distinguished this sense of 'instrumentalism' in my 'Instrumentalism and Its Critique: A Re-Appraisal', *Boston Studies in the Philosophy of Science* (forthcoming).

[19] Cf. Ajdukiewicz references to E. Spranger and his *Lebensformen*, e.g. 'Kierunki prady filosofii wspolczesnej', 1937, *Język i Poznanie* I, p. 202; 'The Problem of Foundation'. See also his reference to G. Simmel in WPCA, p. 85.

[20] Cf. also E. W. Beth's discussion of SVPTJ in chap. 22 'Realistic Tendencies in the Philosophy of Mathematics', pp. 619–621, in *The Foundations of Mathematics*, Amsterdam 1959.

[21] Ajdukiewicz also considered the pragmatic view of Ajdukiewicz languages on which 'meaning' would no longer be 'ideal' and intersubjective (Cf. 'The Problem of Empiricism

and the Concept of Meaning', p. 319). All these concepts, unlike the earliest one, had no epistemological consequences.

[22] In my note 'Logical Comparability and Conceptual Disparity between Newtonian and Relativisitic Mechanics', *B.J.P.S.* **24** (1973), 263–276, I argued that there are languages which, though not closed in an absolute sense, are closed with respect to a set of sentences. For example, the language of relativistic mechanics may be seen as closed with respect to the theoretical sub-language of Newtonian mechanics. A similar line of thought, in a much more elaborate formal framework, was pursued by P. Williams in his 'On the Logical Relations between Expressions of Different Languages', *B.J.P.S.* **24** (1973), 357–367.

[23] Since in 1935 Ajdukiewicz managed to reduce empirical meaning-rules to axiomatic ones (as regards the unconditional acceptance of sentences dictated by them), the innovation under discussion here may be seen as the outcome of the process of varying the essential properties of Ajdukiewicz languages which Ajdukiewicz had begun over a decade before.

[24] A suggestion to that effect seems to have been made by H. Skolimowski and A. Quinton in their Preface to *Problems and Theories in Philosophy*, p. XVII. I criticized that suggestion in my review of their translation in *B.J.P.S.* **25** (1974), No. 3. However, it may be that their suggestion was tantamount to the statement – which I have made in the text – of the Quinean nature of Ajdukiewicz language without axiomatic meaning-rules.

[25] In 'The Problem of Foundation', which came only one year before 'The Problem of Empiricism and the Concept of Meaning', Ajdukiewicz expressed his support for empirical methodology whose aim is to study science as it actually is and has been. In the latter of the two articles he seemed to be more sceptical about the feasibility of such empirical research.

1. ON THE MEANING OF EXPRESSIONS*

(1931)

I. ON VARIOUS USES OF THE TERM 'MEANING'

1. *'Meaning' in the Sense of 'Purpose' and 'Importance'*

The words 'means' and 'meaning' are used in discussion of the role of
the elements of language and are also used in entirely different contexts, not
concerned with language or its elements. Such is the case, for example, with
the sentence: 'Life ceased to have any meaning'. In this, so to say, extralinguistic context the word 'meaning' could be replaced by 'purpose' without
altering the sense of the sentence. In other similar contexts 'meaning' is
synonymous with 'importance' or 'value'.

2. *Meaning as a Property of Signs*

There are contexts in which the words 'means' or 'meaning' are used in an
extralinguistic sense different from the previous ones. We say, for example:
'He trumped my club, this means he has no clubs'. On other occasions we
say: 'The barometer falls, this means it will rain', and also 'The enemy's
bombardment intensifies: this means, they will attack'. In all these examples
'this means' could be replaced by 'therefore' without altering the meaning of
the sentences. Instead of saying 'The barometer falls; this means that it will
rain', we may say synonymously 'The barometer falls, therefore it will rain'.

It is perhaps a similar sense in which we speak of the meaning of signals.
A signal is an artificially produced phenomenon whose perception — initially
in conjunction with a remembered convention and afterwards on its own —
induces a person familiar with the convention to infer the occurrence of
another phenomenon or to make a decision. The relevant convention consists
in the undertaking given by other persons that they will produce the
phenomenon intended to be a signal only if the signalized phenomenon
(which may also be a command) has occurred. In the case when the apprehen-

* Translated by Jerzy Giedymin. First published in *Księga Pamiątkowa Polskiego
Towarzystwa Filozoficznego we Lwowie*, 12,2.1904—12,1.1929, Lwów 1931, 31—77.
Translation based on the text reprinted in *Język i Poznanie*, Warszawa 1960, PWN. I,
102—136. Reprinted here by kind permission of PWN.

sion of a signal has resulted in a decision, one may say, in conformity with established usage, that the apprehension of the signal (on its own or together with the awareness of the convention) has motivated a decision; in saying this one has in mind not only the fact that the signal and the decision are causally related but also that the relevant decision was made with the awareness of its dependence on the perceived signal. Psychologically this situation seems analogous to the one in which the apprehension of a signal has given rise to the inference concluding the occurrence of another fact. We assert the inferred fact also with the awareness of its dependence on the perceived signal. This is why it seems to me quite proper also to use the terms 'motivation' and 'motivate' in those cases when the apprehension of a signal results in a belief and not necessarily a decision. This extension of the application of these terms follows Marty [1] and Husserl [2] . However, we shall extend the application of these terms more than Husserl, since in the case of any inference we shall say that the beliefs expressed by the premisses motivate the belief expressed in the conclusion; in still further cases, to be mentioned later, we shall speak of the motivation of beliefs.

In all cases in which the word 'means' linking two sentences may be replaced by 'therefore' we shall say that the state of affairs asserted in the first sentence is a sign of the state of affairs asserted in the second.[3] So, for example, the appearance of a red traffic light is a sign that the road is not free, the falling of the barometer is a sign of the coming rain, etc.

Uttered sentences, considered as physical phenomena, are also signs (though not necessarily signals). A sentence is an occurrence which is a sign of the fact that the speaker thinks thus. This kind of 'meaning' characteristic of signs, takes us close to the kind of meaning characteristic of language and its elements.

3. 'Meaning' as 'Semantical Function'

Sometimes by meaning one understands any semantical function of the expressions of a language, i.e. every property of linguistic expressions as such, apart from their external form. In the case of *terms*, 'meaning' will then apply both to their property of denoting and to their property of connoting; in the case of *verbs* it will apply to their property of forming sentences when conjoined with terms, etc.

In place of 'meaning' we propose to use the term 'semantic function' to refer to any property of expressions as such, apart from their external appearance. Sometimes, however, 'meaning' is used in such a way that the term 'the meaning of this expression' does not refer to each semantic function of the expression separately but to all of them jointly. 'Meaning' is used in this way when we say 'I shall distinguish in the meaning of a term its property of denoting'.

4. *'Meaning' in the Narrower Sense*

It is customary in scientific terminology to apply the term 'meaning' to one particular semantic function. Let us consider, for example, the terms 'The woman who shared the Nobel prize in physics in 1903 with Pierre Curie and A. H. Becquerel' and 'The woman awarded the Nobel prize in chemistry in 1911'. The two terms denote the same person, viz. Maria Sklodowska-Curie; they differ however from one another in that, speaking metaphorically, each concerns a different aspect of that person. This is why one would say that the first of the two terms, though it denotes the same as the second, 'means' something else. In this context we have used 'means' in a technical sense which is narrower than 'meaning' identified with 'semantic function'. The term 'meaning' in this narrower, technical use is interchangeable with 'sense'.

Our present inquiry will be concerned with meaning in this restricted sense. In order to focus the reader's attention better on the subject of our inquiry it may help to give one more example of the use of the term 'meaning' in the relevant sense. We say, for instance, that the term 'triangular' denotes the same as the term 'trilateral' but that they have different meanings. The meaning of a term in this context is something which decides how, or in what aspect, an object must present itself to us for the term to apply to it and which, conversely, is uniquely determined by that aspect. In the case of terms the meaning is not determined by their denotations, i.e. by what they denote. All terms have some meaning, but not only terms. So, for example, we believe the sentence 'five is greater then three' to have a meaning different from the meaning of the sentence 'three is less than five'. We shall not decide one way or another the question whether every linguistic expression has a meaning in the relevant sense. It seems doubtful that any meaning may be assigned to exclamations like 'ouch' or interrogative expressions like 'who'; in other words, it seems doubtful that meaning can be assigned to expressions which are not (in *suppositione simplici*) components of sentences in the logical sense (i.e. true or false). In any case when speaking of expressions we shall have in mind only those which are components of sentences in the logical sense. We shall be concerned therefore with meaning in the cognitive (intellectual) sense, not in any other, e.g. emotive sense.

Before we take up our subject we want to emphasize that it is not of interest to us merely as an item in the scientific dictionary. We are concerned not so much with the critical discussion of other authors' definitions of meaning and the exposition of our own. Our concern is quite different and can be explained at this point only in general terms. We believe that language plays a very important role in the cognitive process. Different theories of meaning imply different views concerning the cognitive role of language. According to some, that role is a minor one. Cognition could exist without language; language is only a means to record and communicate our cognitions to others. According to others the role of language is essential; linguistic expressions present objects to us, just as do the data of our sense perceptions and memories and there are objects which cannot be presented at all except by linguistic expression. One's view about the nature of the meaning of expressions is related more or less closely to one's position with respect to the cognitive role of language. By investigating the concept of meaning we hope to shed some light on this role.

II. THE RELATIVIZATION OF THE MEANING OF EXPRESSIONS TO A LANGUAGE

1. *The Ambiguity of Expressions in Quotation Marks*

Before we proceed with our analysis it is useful to observe the following. In the sentences which we used in order to indicate the relevant sense of the word 'means', there were expressions consisting of quotation marks and an expression inside those marks. Such expressions may be used as (1) singular names of those individual inscriptions which occur within quotation marks, (2) universal names which denote all inscriptions of the same type as the one inside the quotes, (3) singular names of the individual string of sounds with the help of which the expression inscribed inside the quotes is being uttered, (4) universal names of all strings of sounds equivalent to the one with the help of which the expression inscribed inside the quotes is being uttered. Apart from these four there is a fifth way of using those expressions. Let us consider the following inscription: ' "also" stands for "therefore" '. Some people will regard this inscription as true, namely those who take the expression ' "also" ' as the name of the words in written German which have the same shape as (are homomorphous with) 'also'. Those, however, who take the expression ' "also" ' as the name of those words in written English which have the same shape as 'also' will not agree that "also" stands for "therefore". These examples show that quotations may be understood in a way different from the four distinguished above. For sometimes a quotation is used as a name of all expressions homomorphous with the inscription within quotes, provided that those expressions are used as expressions of a given language. This was our understanding of quotations in the examples of the uses of the word 'means', e.g. in the sentence ' "triangular" does not mean the same as "trilateral" '. It is obvious that in this context the quotation-expression "triangular" was used as a name of words homomorphous with "triangular" provided that those words are employed as words of the English language.

In general quotations are understood in the way just mentioned. This has, however, a serious drawback. So understood, quotations are ambiguous since similar words occur in different languages whereas quotation marks themselves do not indicate whether what we are concerned with are words of the relevant form as employed in one or another language. For example, the sentence ' "*rana*" is a noun' is ambiguous, since I have not indicated at all whether what is intended are inscriptions of the type '*rana*' as expressions of Latin or of Polish.[4] Usually when expressions in quotes are used as names of inscribed or uttered expressions of a certain type, provided they are employed as expressions of a given language, one assumes implicitly that the language in question is the one containing the sentence with the quotation. There are other contexts, however; the sentence: ' "also" stands for "therefore" ' is an example. In this context the inscription "also" may be taken as the name of homomorphous expressions in German though the whole sentence is in English.

In semantic investigations the ambiguity of quotations understood as names of expression-types in a specific language may be the source of many difficulties. To avoid this ambiguity we will never use quotations in this sense. Whenever a quotation is used it will be understood either as a universal name of all inscriptions homomorphous with the one inside the quotes or as a universal name for all sounds homomorphous with the one we use to read the relevant inscription. Context will make clear in each case whether inscriptions or sounds are concerned.

Having given up the use of quotations in the sense just discussed, we shall have to indicate explicitly in our semantical sentences the relevant language. Consequently, we shall not say, e.g. ' "*rana*" means the same as "torn part of the body of a man or animal" ', nor ' "triangular" is not synonymous with "trilateral" '. Instead we shall relativize explicitly such sentences to a language. We shall say explicitly: ' "*rana*" in Polish means the same as "torn part of a human or animal body" ', or, 'in English, "triangular" and "trilateral" are not synonymous', etc.

2. *Three Meanings of the Expression 'to Speak Polish'*

The phrase 'to speak Polish' is used in at least three senses (the same applies to phrases 'to read in Polish', 'to write in Polish', etc.). Firstly, we may be concerned only and exclusively with the phonetic side of utterances. 'To speak Polish' would then mean to make utterances which consist of speech sounds provided for by the lexicon of Polish and in conformity with Polish syntax. In this purely phonetic sense one may say of a parrot or of a gramophone that they 'speak Polish'. To avoid misunderstandings we decide that from now on in order to state of someone or something that they are merely making utterances consisting of sounds from the lexicon of Polish and in accordance with Polish syntax, we shall not say that they speak Polish but that they *are using speech-sounds which belong to the phonology of Polish*. When making utterances one may use sounds which belong both to Polish phonology and to the phonology of some other language. Whoever utters *'rana'* uses speech-sounds which belong to Polish (phonology) but at the same time uses speech-sounds which belong to Latin (phonology).

Surely we would not say of the Romans that when they were using the string of sounds (or inscription) *'rana'* they were speaking Polish, though in fact those speech-sounds also belong to Polish phonology. Apparently in this case we understand the phrase 'to speak Polish' in a different way than before. Speaking Polish in this sense consists not only in producing speech-sounds which belong to Polish phonology but also in experiencing, simultaneously and in connection with those speech-sounds, mental acts in a manner assigned, whether uniquely or ambiguously, by the rules of Polish to those speech-sounds. The views concerning the nature of those acts which accompany utterances vary with different theories. According to the view held by many linguists those acts which accompany utterances consist in the formation of mental images whose object and content are either uniquely or ambiguously assigned to given utterances by the language. Those parallel acts are closely related to the meaning possessed by utterances as elements of a language.

In order to state of someone that while making an utterance which phonetically belongs to a language he also acts in a way prescribed by that language, we shall say that he has *used a string of speech-sounds belonging to the phonology of the language as an expression of that same language*.

To be able to speak Polish is not only to know how to use speech-sounds which belong to that language but also to have the disposition to use those speech-sounds as expressions of Polish. Whenever we use certain speech-sounds as expressions of a language, we actualize such a disposition. It is not uncommon for a person to speak several languages. It also happens that the same speech-sounds may belong to different languages. People who know both Latin and Polish have two different dispositions to engage in those acts, mentioned before, which accompany the utterance of *'rana'*. When they utter it as an expression of Polish they realize some of their dispositions different from those which they have when uttering '*rana*' as an expression of Latin. This suggests that we should distinguish one further sense of the phrase 'to speak Polish'.

There are utterances which belong to the phonologies of two different languages and which, moreover, are such that the associated act sufficient for the use of the given utterance as an expression of one language is the same as the accompanying act sufficient for the use of the utterance as an expression of the other language. A case in point is the inscription '*brat spał*' when pronounced '*braat spow*'.[5] Whenever I make this utterance (which belongs to the phonology of Polish) as an expression of the Polish language I also make an utterance (which belongs to the phonology of Ukrainian) as an expression of Ukrainian. However, in a certain sense of 'speaking Polish' we are inclined to say that when one is speaking Polish one is never at the same time speaking Ukrainian. Of many Poles living in Western Poland it is true that when making the utterance '*brat spał*' (belonging to Polish phonology) as an expression of Polish they did not speak Ukrainian though they were using a Ukrainian utterance as an expression of Ukrainian.

In saying this we understand the phrase 'to speak Polish' (or 'to speak Ukrainian') neither in the sense of 'to make speech-sounds which belong to Polish phonology (Ukrainian phonology)', nor in the sense of 'to use speech-sounds belonging to Polish phonology as expressions of Polish'. For then we understand the phrase 'to speak Polish' in such a way that to speak Polish at a certain time it is necessary not only to make at the time speech-sounds which belong to Polish phonology and to use them as expressions of Polish, but also to do so while having a set of dispositions to respond to Polish speech-sounds which all and only those people have who can speak Polish. In this last sense one speaks Polish only if one has, so to say, tuned one's responses to the speech-sounds, in a way appropriate to the Polish language. We shall rest satisfied with this metaphor in the conviction that with its help and with the help of our examples the reader has some idea as to the third sense of 'speaking Polish'. We shall henceforth use the phrase 'to speak Polish' in this third sense. To speak Polish in this sense is then to make speech-sounds in accordance with the rules of Polish and to be 'tuned' to Polish, i.e. to have dispositions to respond to Polish speech-sounds in ways appropriate to Polish.

III. THE ASSOCIATIONIST THEORY OF MEANING

1. *Linguistic Associationism*

As we mentioned before, there is a view according to which the answer to the question whether or not an utterance made by a person has been used in conformity with the given language depends on the kind of thoughts the person in question has when making the utterance (or listening to it) and which are due to his dispositions to associate ideas. The view in question is known under the name of linguistic associationism. For on this view, apart from the phonetic or graphic properties of linguistic entities, the most important aspect of language resides in dispositions to associate representations of those entities with other ideas. So, for example, on this theory knowledge of a language consists in having dispositions to associate representations of sounds and expressions of the language with other thoughts in ways appropriate to the particular language. To speak a language (in the third of the senses we have distinguished) amounts, on this theory, to using the sounds which belong to the phonology of the language and to actualizing exactly those associative dispositions appropriate to the particular language. The theory under discussion is the most popular one among linguists. Characteristic of this theory is a rather superficial view of the cognitive role of language: on this view language merely suggests, helps to record thoughts and makes it possible to communicate them; thinking and speaking are parallel and related only through association, i.e. one recalls to mind the other. The associationist theory also comprises a definition of the meaning of expressions which we shall presently subject to closer analysis.

2. *The Original Associationist Definition of Meaning and Its Critique*

Associationists usually define the meaning of an expression as an idea associated with the representation of the expression. As an example may serve the definition given by Professor Szober in his *Outline of General Linguistics* (Warszawa 1924): "The factual meaning of a word is the image of an extralinguistic object associated, on the basis of inner experience, with the representation of the word". Such a definition is subject to several objections. Doctor Niedzwiecka-Ossowska in her critical essay entitled 'Professor Szober's Semantics' (*Przeglad Filozoficzny* 28 (1925), 258–272) points out that in accordance with this definition the meaning of the term 'teacher' would be, for example, the idea of a blackboard if the word 'teacher' should suggest to someone the idea of a blackboard. In his 'Reply' to this criticism (ibid., pp. 272–276) Professor Szober rejects this objection in the following way: "The idea of a blackboard cannot be part of the meaning of the word 'teacher' because the association which is the basis of the factual meaning of the word is established by linguistic usage, hence it is invariable, whereas the association in the example is accidental ...". In his reply Professor Szober mentions associations determined by linguistic usage by which he presumably means those dispositions to association whose possession and actualization are the necessary conditions for the user of the expressions of a language to speak just that language.

3. *The First Modification of the Original Definition and Its Critique*

In our critique of the associationist theory of meaning we shall engage in a dispute with ourselves. In the dispute we shall formulate definitions of meaning, which satisfy the apparent intentions of the proponents of the theory, and then subject those definitions to criticism; the latter will, in turn, suggest further modifications of the definitions.

The objection quoted in the previous paragraph suggests the following improved definition:

> The meaning of expression E in the language L is the thought (idea) associated with the use of E and whose presence, when E is being used, is necessary and sufficient[6] for the speaker to have used E at the time in conformity with the language L.

The objection that the meaning of the word 'teacher' would be the idea of a blackboard if the latter were associated with the perception or idea of the word 'teacher', no longer applies to the present definition, for the meaning of the word 'teacher' in English is to be only such a thought which is necessarily associated with the use of the word for the speaker to use the word in a way appropriate to English; the idea of a blackboard is not such a thought.

The following further objections may, however, be raised against the present definition: every thought is a mental phenomenon and as such occurs only once in someone's consciousness. Similarly, expressions are certain physical particulars, located in a definite place and time. Therefore, if John utters 'dog' at a certain time and Peter utters 'dog' at another time, it is impossible that a thought which was present in John's mind at the time of his utterance of 'dog' should accompany another utterance of 'dog' at a different time in Peter's mind. Furthermore, if John utters 'dog' and Peter listens to this utterance, then certainly no thought which in John's mind accompanies this utterance also accompanies in Peter's mind the hearing of that utterance.

In view of what has just been said the definition of meaning under discussion implies that whenever John utters E and Peter listens, if John uses E in conformity with the language L, Peter certainly does not do so. For, when uttering E, were John to use it in conformity with L, a thought M which is the meaning of E in L would have to be present in John's mind, i.e. the occurrence of that thought – as the meaning of E – is necessary for John to use E in conformity with L. Since, furthermore, no thought of Peter is a thought in John's mind, no thought which accompanies the use of E by Peter is identical with M. Therefore, the use of E is not accompanied in Peter's mind by the thought whose presence is necessary to use E in confomity with English usage, hence Peter did not use E as an expression of English, hence he did not use it in conformity with L.

Orthodox associationists would presumably reply to this criticism in the following way: by saying that the meaning of E is a thought M they do not intend to identify the meaning of E with a particular thought, occurring *hic et nunc*, but rather with a thought-type which may comprise numerous individual thoughts.

4. *The Second Modification of the Original Definition*

Indeed, the source of the objections just discussed is in the ambiguity of expressions such as 'thought M' and 'expression E'. For instance, the expression 'the thought that $2 \times 2 = 4$' may be understood either as a universal term denoting numerous thoughts with given content, or as a singular term denoting only one object which is not a specific thought but rather a *universal*, a type of thought. Similarly, 'the expression "$2 \times 2 = 4$"' may either be understood as a universal term denoting all inscriptions homomorphous with the arithmetical equality within (double) quotes or as the term denoting only one object which is not identical with any specific inscription but is a universal, viz. the type of expressions comprising all those homomorphous with the one within (double) quotes.[7] To avoid these ambiguities, let us decide to use the expression 'thought M' as a universal term which denotes several particular thoughts and the expression 'the type which comprises thoughts M' or briefly 'thought-type M' in the other sense.

The same ambiguity also affects various statements concerning associations of ideas. Statements concerning the associations of two thoughts are sometimes used to make claims about two specific thoughts, on other occasions to make claims about types of thoughts. The following terminology will be used to avoid misunderstandings: 'Thought-type M is immediately associated with thought-type N in the mind of person X' means by definition: 'X has a disposition such that having experienced a thought of type M, immediately afterwards X will experience a thought of type N (irrespective of external conditions) and vice versa.' On the other hand, we shall say: 'A specific thought A of type M is associated in the mind of X with a thought B of type N' by definition means: 'Thought-type M is immediately associated in X's mind with thought-type N, thought A is of type M, thought B of type N and X has experienced A either immediately before B or immediately after B'.

Having removed by these terminological conventions the misunderstandings

from which the objections against the last version of the associationist definition of meaning arose, we shall give another one, which is closer to associationist intentions. The new definition is as follows:

> Thought-type M is the linguistic meaning of expression-type E in
> L if and only if: (1) expressions of type E belong to L, (2) the
> necessary and sufficient condition for a person X who makes use
> of an expression A of type E, to use it as an expression of L is
> that the use of A qua use of an expression of type E[8] should be
> associated in the mind of X with a thought B as a thought of type
> M.[9]

5. *The Critique of the Last Definition*

Among the consequences of the definition of linguistic meaning given in the
previous section the following may be found. For every expression-type E
there exists a thought-type M such that an expression of type E is used by
a speaker as an expression of L if and only if the use of that expression is
accompanied through association in the mind of the speaker by the thought
A of type M. This type is in fact the linguistic meaning of the expression-
type E in L. Now if we had good reasons for denying this consequence we
would have to reject the definition itself. This consequence may be
formulated more simply as follows: For an expression of sound-type E (e.g.
'dentelles') belonging to the phonology of a given language (e.g. French)
to be used by a person as an expression of that language, it is necessary and
sufficient that the use of the expression be accompanied in the mind of the
person in question by a definite thought (in our example, some thought
concerning lace, e.g. the representation of lace).

This consequence seems, indeed, false. For let us imagine, a person, who
knows absolutely no French, often admiring magnificent laces displayed in a
shop-window together with an eye-catching notice bearing the inscription
'dentelles'. In the mind of that person a process will develop whose result will
be that whenever in some other place she sees *'dentelles'* inscribed, she will
experience a representation of laces. Should this happen, would she be using
that expression as an expression of French? We are inclined to deny this
emphatically. The fact that the use of the inscription by the person was
accompanied through association by a certain thought is not only insufficient
for the inscription to have been used as an expression of a given language, it
was also insufficient for it to have been used as a linguistic expression at all.
In this way we reveal our view (or at least its negative side) concerning the
nature of that additional act which is necessary to transform the mere use of

a string of word-sounds belonging to the phonology of a language into the use of an expression of that language. We firmly believe the following: the mere fact that a word-sound, which in a language functions as the name of an object, recalls to a person's mind the idea of that object is not yet sufficient for that person to have used the word-sound as an expression of that language. We believe that between the use of the word-sound and the idea involved there must be a much closer link than simply an association. To conclude, for a word-sound belonging to the phonology of a language to be used as an expression of that language it is not sufficient that its use be accompanied through association by a thought of a certain type.

Nor is the association necessary for that purpose. Let us consider our usual behaviour when reading with comprehension an abstract text. When we read with understanding the sentence 'if a is smaller than b, then b is greater than a', do we in fact find in our mind after the use of that expression (perhaps separated by a vanishingly small lapse of time) a thought whose presence alone would be responsible for our using those sounds as an expression of English? Associationists usually operate with examples of one-word names denoting concrete objects. They claim, for example, that unless the inscription (or utterance) 'house' through association produces in the user's mind the representation of a house, that inscription (or string of sounds) is not being used in accordance with English. This one-sided selection of examples facilitates consensus on the generalization that for any word-sound to be used as an expression of a language it is necessary that the use of that word-sound should produce through association a thought of a suitable kind. However, this generalization is false even when restricted to monosyllabic names of concrete objects. For when we read, for example, the word 'house', using it as an expression of English under normal conditions, i.e. when we are not concerned with testing the associationist thesis, we do not experience at all any idea linked with its sounds through association which alone would be responsible for the fact that we have used the word as an expression of English.

For word-sounds to be used as an expression of English (or of some other language) it is not at all necessary that they should be accompanied through association by a thought of a suitable kind. The behaviour of a person reading under normal conditions a comprehensible text in English does not differ — with respect to the feature relevant here — from the behaviour of someone reading the text of a strictly formalized deductive theory.

In support of our claim we have to resort to introspection. Let us consider what is going on in our consciousness when we are reading or hearing 'Charlemagne lived in the 9th century' as an expression of English. Undoubtedly the reading of that inscription produces through association various thoughts.

In the minds of some readers it may produce the image of Charlemagne's crown; others will imagine a majestic figure in mediaeval attire; I myself recall the words *'Pepin le Petit'* and visualize the map of France, etc. But we are unable to indicate a thought associated with the use of that inscription (or string of sounds), i.e. preceding or following it, which would be of such a nature that the presence of just such a thought is necessary for that inscription to be used as an expression of English.

Perhaps, nevertheless, someone will find such a thought and will say: For the inscription 'Charlemagne lived in the 9th century' to be used by anyone as an expression of English, it is necessary that its reading should produce through association in his mind a thought of the type that Charlemagne lived in the 9th century. Now we agree that for anyone to use 'Charlemagne lived in the 9th century' as an expression of English it is necessary that he should somehow think that Charlemagne lived in the 9th century. What we deny is that for this end it is necessary for a thought of Charlemagne living in the 9th century, as such, to accompany through association the use of that inscription as an inscription of that type. For if we say that a given *hic et nunc* thought A is present through association with another given *hic et nunc* thought B, then thoughts A and B are distinct if only because they occur not quite simultaneously. On the other hand, we do claim that to use the inscription (or sounds) 'Charlemagne lived in the 9th century' as an expression of English it is necessary to think in some way of Charlemagne living in the 9th century; but not to think this 'apart' from having the representation of a suitable sentence, rather in such a way that the thought which constitutes the use of that inscription as an expression of English should itself be a thought of Charlemagne living in the 9th century.

A thought may be characterized from various points of view. Just as a given physical object may be classified both as a fair-haired man and a student, a given thought may fall under various types of thoughts. Let us consider the thought which is identical with the use of 'Charlemagne lived in the 9th century' as an expression of English. On the one hand it may be characterized as the experience of a certain sense-content; on the other hand, it may be characterized as the thought of Charlemagne living in the 9th century. Not every experience of sense-content which a person with normal sight has when looking at the inscription 'Charlemagne lived in the 9th century' is at the same time the thought of Charlemagne living in the 9th century. This sense-content may be experienced by someone who does not understand English and does not think of Charlemagne living in the 9th century. Conversely, a German reading with comprehension in his own language the inscription *'Karl der Grosse lebte im 9.Jahrhundert'* thereby thinks of Charlemagne living in the 9th century without experiencing the sense-content mentioned before.

In order to use 'Charlemagne lived in the 9th century' as an expression of English it is necessary that the thought corresponding to that sentence and consisting in the experiencing of perceptual data should be such that it could be described as the thought that Charlemagne lived in the 9th century. It is, however, not necessary that the sense-perception resulting from a normal reading of that sentence should be accompanied by such a thought through association, the way our representation of the words 'Our father' is associated with our representation of the words 'thou art in heaven'.

Thoughts which could be (ambiguously) described as the experiencing of sense-content specific to the inscription 'Charlemagne lived in the 9th century', may be of various kinds. A person who does not know English and investigates this inscription as a physical object, concerned merely with the kind of types used by printers, will have a thought different from that of another person who understands English; the latter has that sense perception when reading the sentence with his attention directed in the normal way towards 'the sense' of the sentence.

We have thus outlined our view as to how a psychological description should be given of the process of using verbal-sounds as expressions of a language. This view, we believe, has clearly been influenced by Husserl's discussion of the so-called 'act of meaning' in the 2nd volume of *Logische Untersuchungen,* part I, chapter *'Ausdruck und Bedeutung'.* According to Husserl the 'act of meaning', i.e. the use of written signs (or verbal sounds) as an expression of a language consists in the fact that in our consciousness there appears a sense-content due to which one might have a visual representation of that inscription (or verbal sound) provided a suitable intention directed upon that inscription (or sound) were also present. However, when we use the inscription as an expression of a language the sense-content is joined by a different intention, not necessarily representational, and directed in general upon something else than the inscription (or string of word-sounds). This intention, together with the sense-content, forms a homogeneous experience (unitary total act); however, neither the awareness of the sense-content nor the intention itself is a complete and self-contained act of consciousness. Each forms a complementary component of the act of consciousness. The meaning of an expression (as an expression-type) of a language for Husserl would be that type of intention which must be attached to the sense-content in order that the inscription (or string of word-sounds) is used as an expression of that specific language.

We have been trying to show that a certain consequence of the associationist definition of meaning is not correct, for it is not the case that in order to use written signs (or verbal sounds) as an expression of a language it is sufficient or necessary that the use of those written signs (or verbal sounds) should be accompanied through association by a thought of the type assigned by the language to the type of those written signs (or sounds). We have made this claim on the basis of introspection which seems to support the view that whatever thought may be associated with the use of the written signs, it is not sufficient for the use of an expression of a language; for it is also necessary that the act of using those signs itself be a thought of a certain type, such that its characteristic feature is not what kind of thoughts accompany thoughts of the given type. On the other hand, we do believe that to use written signs as expressions of a language it is sufficient that that use be a thought of a certain type which does not depend on the kind of associated thoughts. The presence of associated thoughts is thus not a necessary condition either.

We realize that serious criticisms can be made of our 'psychological arithmetic', criticisms which focus on the difficulty of knowing whether in a given situation one is dealing with one thought having two properties or with two thoughts experienced simultaneously or almost so. It seems to us, however, that in order to describe (or perhaps rather 'to paint') what is going on in someone's mind at an instant of time it is not sufficient to say: *X* experiences this and *X* experiences that; it is necessary, in addition, to be able to indicate the relation which holds between those experiences. So, for example, in order to give an account of what occurs in the consciousness of a person reading and understanding the English sentence 'Charlemagne lived in the 9th century', it is not sufficient to say that the person in question has a visual representation peculiar to those written signs and, in addition, experiences the thought that Charlemagne lived in the 9th century. For one can experience these two thoughts very differently, depending – among other things – on how they are related. If we let a German, who does not understand English, read the sentence 'Charlemagne lived in the 9th century' and simultaneously utter the sentence '*Karl der Grosse lebte im 9.Jahrhundert*', then he will have the sensory experience peculiar to perceiving the sentence 'Charlemagne lived in the 9th century', and by understanding the uttered sentence '*Karl der Grosse lebte im 9.Jahrhundert*' he will also think about Charlemagne living in the 9th century. However, these two experiences will be only loosely related in his consciousness. On the other hand, anyone who reads with understanding the English sentence 'Charlemagne lived in the 9th century' has the sensory experience and also things that Charlemagne lived in the 9th century. But there is obviously a difference between the experiences of these two persons. The difference concerns the way the sensory experience and the thought about Charlemagne are related to each other in the consciousness of either person. To emphasize this relation we said before that there is one thought which is simultaneously a visual representation and the thought that Charlemagne lived in the 9th century; we realize, however, that we would be in a difficult position if challenged by a critic to produce criteria for telling when one has to do with one and when with two thoughts.

Nevertheless one must not expect the language used for a psychological description to satisfy the same criteria as the language used for a physical description.

In our criticism of associationism we used the sentence 'thought A of type M accompanies by association thought B of type N in the mind of X' to mean that whenever A accompanies by association B, then A and B are distinct and only connected by a casual, temporal relation. The sentence 'thought-type M is associated in the mind of X with thought-type N' was also taken to mean that the association consists in the disposition to have thoughts of type M followed by thoughts of type N or vice versa.

It may be objected that our arguments are based on too narrow a concept of association and that, consequently, our criticism applies only to this restricted form of associationism. For we sometimes say that thought-type A is associated with thought-type B, though it is not even generally the case that after a particular thought of type A another particular thought of type B follows; we say this whenever, in the past, our thoughts of type A happened to be thoughts of type B and henceforth habitually thoughts of type A are thoughts of type B.

For instance, suppose until now John happened to see only rectangles whose horizontal side was longer than the perpendicular side. Owing to this circumstance, it may happen that from now on when John visualizes a rectangle he has, in most cases, a representation of it lying horizontally rather than standing upright. Here we have two types of representations: firstly, type A which includes all representations of rectangles, secondly type B embracing only representations of rectangles in a horizontal position. Owing to the fact that coincidentally John's thoughts of type A happened to be also of type B, so henceforth without any special circumstances, and by habit, his thoughts of type A are, in most cases, also thoughts of type B. Using the term 'association' in the extended sense we would be prepared to say that in John's mind the representation of a rectangle became associated with the representation of a rectangle in a horizontal position.

Whoever saw men always, or in most cases bearded and with a moustache will afterwards probably visualize them also bearded and with a moustache. But surely it will not be the case that whenever there is firstly a representation of the type of a man-representation it will be followed by another one of the type of representation of a bearded man with a moustache. One cannot, therefore, apply to this case the concept of association in the narrower sense, but one can apply the concept of association in the wider, extended sense. From an associationist who accepts our previous analysis of the use of written signs as expressions of a language and who uses the concept of association in the extended sense, we might expect to be given the following definition of meaning:

A thought-type M constitutes the meaning of expressions of type E in a language L if and only if: (1) expressions of type E belong to the phonology of L, (2) any person X is using an expression A of type E as an expression of L if and only if (a) the type of sense-experiences specific to expressions of type E is associated (in the extended sense) in the mind of X with the thought-type M, (b) the sense-experience specific to the expression A is also a thought of type M.

The following is a consequence of this definition: For a person X to use certain written signs as expressions of language L it is necessary that by force of habit the sense-experience specific to expressions of type E should usually be in X's mind a thought of type M which is the meaning of expression-type E. This is implied by condition 2a of the definition and is its only remaining element of associationism. However, it appears that this consequence is false. For it seems to us that even when we come across certain written signs of a language for the first time, we can nevertheless use them as expressions of a language; for this to happen it is sufficient that the thought consisting in the sense-experience specific to those written signs be also the thought of the type assigned by the language to signs of that type. But it is implausible to assume that a person who encounters certain signs for the first time has already formed a habit to use those signs in a certain way. The same objection may also be applied, *mutatis mutandis*, to the previously criticized associationist definition of meaning.

We believe that the last definition of meaning has no false consequences provided condition 2a is deleted from it. So modified, however, its uninformativeness renders it unsatisfactory. All that we can learn from it is that the meaning of a type of expressions E in L is a thought-type M restricted only by the condition that one uses written signs of type E as an expression of L if and only if their use constitutes a thought of type M. There are as many types of thoughts as there are properties which thoughts may have. But one may distinguish types of thoughts from the point of view of their clarity or from the point of view from which psychologists usually classify them into representations, judgments, etc. or from the point of view of the person who experiences them and so forth. Now the last definition which we have been discussing shares with the previous ones the defect that it fails to specify the point of view from which the types of thoughts are to be distinguished that are the meanings of the various types of expressions. Some authors claim that those types are distinguished from the point of view of the contents of thoughts, others that they are distinguished from the point of view of the quality and matter, or the matter alone, of thought-acts. However, the content, quality and matter of mental acts are usually characterized in metaphorical terms which help to reach some understanding but are insufficient for clearly formulated definitions. Hence there are no clear criteria which would enable one to decide in particular cases whether or not two expressions have the same meaning. This is why we shall not be content with the last modification of the definition of meaning but shall rather search for another, more informative one, providing moreover a criterion which – at least in languages with precise meanings – would enable one to decide of two expressions whether or not they have the same meaning. The basic idea of such a definition has been suggested to us by a certain passage in Mill's discussion of his concept of connotation. We shall, therefore, first consider Mill's theory of connotation.

IV. MILL'S THEORY OF CONNOTATION

1. *One of Mill's Definitions of Connotation*

According to Mill some terms, apart from having denotations, also connote, i.e. have meanings. So, for example, "The word 'man' ... denotes Peter, James, John, and an indefinite number of other individuals, of whom, taken as a class, it is the name. But it is applied to them because they possess, and to signify that they possess, certain attributes. These seem to be corporeity, animal life, rationality and a certain external form which for distinction we call human ...". "... The name, therefore, is said to signify the subjects *directly*, the attributes *indirectly*: it *denotes* the subjects, and implies, or involves or indicates or as we shall say henceforth *connotes*, the attributes. It is a connotative name". "... Whenever the names given to objects convey any information, that is, whenever they have properly any meaning, the meaning resides not in what they *denote* but in what they *connote* ...".[10]

2. *An Analysis of Mill's Definition*

According to the quoted passage: attributes $C_1, C_2, \dots C_n$ constitute the connotation of term N if and only if we apply N to particular objects because those objects have attributes $C_1, \dots C_n$ and in order to indicate that those objects possess these properties. Several expressions in this definition require clarification.

For example, what may one mean by saying that a term is applied to a particular object? One of the possible answers to this question is as follows: I am applying term N of language L to object X if I believe in the truth of a singular sentence of L whose subject is a singular term as the name of X in L and whose predicate is N. For example, I apply the English term 'man' to Socrates if I believe in the truth of the English sentence 'Socrates is a man'. Again, one applies the German term '*Mensch*' to Socrates if one believes in the German sentence '*Socrates ist ein Mensch*'. The expression 'X believes in the truth of the sentence S as a sentence of language L' will be very important in the rest of our investigation. Whenever we make such a claim we are attributing to X a certain thought which ought to be characterized in three respects. Firstly, it is a conviction or belief. Secondly, it is a thought which consists in experiencing the sense content specific to that particular sentence. Thirdly, it is a thought consisting in the use of the sentence as an expression of language L. Without prejudging whether there are any inarticulate convictions, we think that at least the majority of our distinct convictions consist in such 'beliefs in sentences'. The belief in a sentence S as a sentence of language L is an experience familiar to everybody and it occurs whenever we say or hear something with conviction. In the previous section concerned with our criticism of associationism we were anxious to dispel the erroneous claim according to which the use of written signs (or uttered sounds) as expressions of a language consists of two distinct thoughts: the presentation of those signs (sounds) and the thought which allegedly imparts to those signs a sense, i.e. makes them expressions of the language. In our view, the use of e.g. the signs 'Poland is a republic' as an expression of Polish, consists of one thought only which, on the one hand, may be characterized as the experiencing of a sense content specific to those signs and, on the other hand, as the belief that Poland is a republic. Now it is such uses of signs as expressions of a language which constitute convictions that we call 'beliefs in the truth of sentences'.

Another expression in need of clarification in the context 'we apply N to objects because those objects possess properties $C_1, \dots C_n$' is the word 'because'. What is involved here is undoubtedly not the claim that the application, e.g. of the term 'man' to Socrates is caused by the objective fact of his having a body, being rational, etc. Presumably we are concerned here with a relation between the belief that Socrates has a body, is rational, etc. and the application of the term 'man' to him, i.e. the belief in the truth of the sentence 'Socrates is a man'. This relation may be characterized by saying: we believe in the (truth of the) sentence 'Socrates is a man' on the basis of accepting that Socrates has a body, is rational, etc. What is relevant here is that between the belief in Socrates having a body, being rational, etc. and the belief in the sentence 'Socrates is a man' there is a relation of the same type as between the belief in the premisses and in the conclusion of an inference. We will refer to such a relation as motivation.

We have to clarify one last point in the definition under discussion. It is the *pluralis impersonalis* and the *praesens intemporale* of the verb 'apply'. The application of terms to objects is an activity conducted by someone at some time. If it is said 'The term N connotes properties $C_1, \ldots C_n$ if and only if we apply N to objects because ... etc.', then it should be specified who is meant by 'we'. For a term N to connote properties $C_1, \ldots C_n$ is it enough that one single man should on one occasion apply N to object P because he believed that P had properties $C_1, \ldots C_n$? Or is it rather necessary that a whole group of people (and if so, which group?) should apply it to objects P (to all of them or some?) always motivated by their belief that P has properties $C_1, \ldots C_n$? I suppose that this ambiguity will be removed by relativizing connotation to a language, which anyway seems quite natural. Taking this into account, one would say for example: The term 'man' in English connotes the properties of having a body, being rational, etc. if and only if anybody speaking English is prepared to accept a singular sentence of English of the type 'A is a man' on the basis of knowing that the object denoted by the subject term of the sentence has the property of 'corporeity', being rational, etc. If this interpretation is accepted then one would assume that to speak a language it is necessary to have dispositions towards particular motivational relations, viz. dispositions to accept certain sentences, which belong to the phonology of the language, on the basis of other experiences, e.g. on the basis of certain other beliefs.

The motivational relation assumed in the above example of the definition of 'man' in English, is understood in a very wide sense. Accordingly, any belief in Socrates having a body, being rational, etc., no matter what form this belief takes, would predispose an English-speaking person to accept on this basis the sentence 'Socrates is a man'. However, the belief that Socrates has a body, is rational, etc. may occur in various forms. For the belief in (the truth of) the sentence 'Socrates has a body, is rational, etc.' as well as in the sentence 'Xanthippe's husband has a body, is rational, etc.', or the sentence 'Sophroniskos's son has a body, is rational, etc.' and in the sentences which are translations into German of those sentences, and many more besides, are all beliefs in Socrates having a body, being rational, etc. Hence a new ambiguity: for the connotation relation to hold is it necessary that *every* belief in Socrates having a body, being rational, etc. should be able to motivate the belief in the truth of 'Socrates is a man' or is it sufficient that *some* such belief can motivate the acceptance of that sentence?

If we insist on 'every', implausible consequences would follow. Let us, therefore, agree provisionally on 'some' and let us focus our attention on the remainder of the definition of connotation. We read in it that: A term N is applied to objects in order to indicate that they possess properties $C_1, \ldots C_n$. Since we are not concerned with historical accuracy, we shall interpret this phrase somewhat arbitrarily. If by the sentence 'A is N' we want to indicate that A has the properties $C_1, \ldots C_n$ this is apparently because we believe that by saying 'A is N' we shall inform anyone in command of the language that A has properties $C_1, \ldots C_n$. One may, therefore, suppose that, according to Mill, if the term N connotes in English properties $C_1, \ldots C_n$, then anyone speaking English is able to infer that A has properties $C_1, \ldots C_n$ on the basis of his belief in 'A is N'.

After these interpretative proposals the definition of connotation for English will assume the following form: A term N connotes in English properties $C_1, \ldots C_n$ if and only if every English-speaking person is prepared, on the basis of his belief that an object A has properties $C_1, \ldots C_n$, to accept as an immediate conclusion any singular sentence of English whose subject is a name of A, whose predicate in N and whose joining copula is the word 'is'; and vice versa, on the basis of his acceptance of such a singular sentence he is prepared to believe that A has properties $C_1, \ldots C_n$.

3. *Critical Analysis of the Definition*

We have reconstructed the above definition because in our view it points to the right direction in which one should go in order to make explicit and precise the concept of 'meaning'. The meaning of a term is indeed in our view determined by the information concerning an object which is sufficient for the term to be applied to that object. A definition of meaning which would identify it with connotation is, however, not satisfactory for a number of reasons.

First of all, if meaning were to be identified with connotation then − since only terms have connotations − one would have to conclude that no other expressions except terms have meanings. Moreover, some terms have no connotations and, therefore, these also would have no meaning.

The third and most important reason will become clear presently. The connotation of a term N is uniquely determined by properties such that if we know an object P to possess those properties, then this information is sufficient to conclude immediately that P is N. Now the information that P

has properties C may take various forms. Let us take as an example the property of being a quadrilateral which can be inscribed within a circle. Anyone who accepts the sentence 'A has the property of being a quadrilateral which can be inscribed within a circle' has thereby the information with respect to that property that A has it. However, anyone who without believing in the previous sentence accepts the sentence 'A is a quadrilateral in which the sums of opposite angles are equal' also believes with respect to the property of being a quadrilateral inscribable in a circle that the object A possesses that property. This is because the terms 'the property of being a quadrilateral which can be inscribed within a circle' and 'the property of being a quadrilateral in which the sums of opposite angles are equal' have the same denotation. For the same state of affairs which consists in having the first of these properties is also a fact which consists in having the second property. Having the first of these properties is nothing more than having the second of the properties. The two terms differ with respect to their connotation but not with respect to what they denote.

Now assume that a person X is able to accept the sentence Z_1: 'A is a rectangle' on the basis of his belief in the sentence Z_2: 'A has the property of being a parallelogram and A has the property of being a quadrilateral inscribable within a circle' but is unable to accept Z_1 on the basis of accepting the sentence Z_3: 'A has the property of being a parallelogram and A has the property of being a quadrilateral in which the sums of opposite angles are equal'. Assume also that another person Y is able to accept Z_1 on the basis of Z_3 but not on the basis of accepting Z_2.

On these assumptions the connotation of the term 'rectangle' is the same for X as for Y. Knowledge concerning the same properties (viz. the property of being a parallelogram and the property of being a quadrilateral inscribable within a circle) and consisting in the information that object A has these properties, is sufficient for either of them to accept the sentence 'A is a rectangle'. For the acceptance of either Z_2 or Z_3 amounts to a belief concerning the same properties, viz. that object A has them.

This is why we are not inclined to identify the meaning of a term with its connotation. For in accordance with our own conception of 'meaning of a term', we would have to say that in our example the meaning of the term 'rectangle' for X is different from the meaning of the same term for Y, since X will accept the sentence 'A is a rectangle' as soon as X learns that 'A has the property of being a parallelogram and the property of being a quadrilateral inscribable within a circle' while Y will not be able to do so. If one identifies the meaning of terms with their connotations, then one is searching for meanings in an objective sphere, in the properties of objects denoted by those terms whereas associationists and others conceive of meanings as something belonging to the psychological world. In our own attempt at characterizing the meaning of terms we shall not go outside the language itself. We shall now present our own definition of meaning.

V. AN ATTEMPT AT DEFINING 'MEANING'

1. *In Ethnic i.e. Natural Languages Terms Do Not Have Connotations*

Should anyone claim that a term N has a connotation in the language L, e.g. connotation c, then in accordance with the definition of 'connotation' they would be committed to the following consequence: For any person to speak L it is necessary that they should be prepared to apply N to objects which are known to have the property c.

This consequence amounts to the view that to speak a language it is necessary to be prepared to accept sentences on the basis of certain experiences as motives. This is either correct or not depending on how one understands 'language L'. So far as the ordinary usage of phrases like 'the English language' is concerned, the consequence in question seems to be incorrect. In order to say that a person does not speak English it does not seem sufficient to ascertain that that person is not prepared to apply a term to objects though he knows that the objects possess certain specified properties. However, in semantical investigations the phrase 'to speak a language' is usually used to refer to something much more determinate than what is ordinarily meant by speaking English, for example. For English is spoken by the inhabitants of London as well as by the inhabitants of New York and their speech is different not only because they use expressions which differ phonetically and graphically but also because often the same speech sounds as expressions have different denotations and connotations. Consequently, not only connotation but also phonetics, syntax, denotation and meaning cannot be relativized to English just as they cannot be relativized to the Indo-European language. The term 'the English language' does not refer, loosely speaking, to any determinate semantic system but rather is a general term denoting a number of such systems.

2. *Motivational Relations Are Only to Some Extent Characteristic of Ethnic Languages*

We have just stated that if connotations of terms were to be relativized to English (or any other ethnic language) then one would have to conclude that no term in a language has a connotation. We have reached this conclusion by denying that the disposition to certain specified motivational relations (viz.

to apply a term to objects on the basis of knowing that they have certain specific properties) should be necessary to say of someone that they speak English. Undoubtedly the majority of English speaking people have indeed dispositions to motivate the belief in some sentences by their beliefs in others. An English speaking person is in general prepared to accept the sentence 'Fire!' on the basis of having a visual representation, viz. the representation of fire, which will then motivate the acceptance; similarly, to accept the sentence 'Motor-cars have replaced horse-drawn carriages', on the basis of having accepted the sentence 'Automobiles have replaced horse-drawn carriages'; or, finally, to accept the sentence 'Sometimes a rainfall is accompanied by the fall of barometers' on the basis of having accepted 'Sometimes the fall of the barometer is accompanied by rain'. The same dispositions to motivational relations will not be found, for example, among people who speak only German. For what is involved is the belief in (the truth of) a *sentence*, i.e. a linguistic entity and not something else. In other words, we are not claiming, of course, that a person who speaks only German is unable to believe that there is fire when he sees one but simply that such a person is unable to believe in (the truth of) the English sentence 'Fire' on the basis of seeing fire. No one is able to accept the sentence 'Fire!' unless they speak a language to whose phonology this string of sounds belongs. Similarly, a person speaking only German is unable to accept the sentence 'Some birds are predators' on the basis of accepting the sentence 'Some predators are birds', though they can accept that some birds are predators on the basis of believing that some predators are birds. (The sentence 'I believe that some birds are predators' is taken here as synonymous with the sentence 'I believe in (accept) the English sentence "Some birds are predators" or in some other sentence which is its translation').

We believe that learning a language consists, among other things, in forming dispositions to accept some sentences on the basis of certain motives. A baby gradually acquires the ability to use the language of adults but at first speaks its own language. Expressions of that language often sound like terms of the adults' language though they function in the baby's language as sentences. They are not used by the baby in a parrot-like fashion but in a meaningful way. The difference (between a baby and a parrot in this respect) consists, firstly, in that certain sense-perceptions motivate the acceptance of some sentences. For example, seeing certain faces motivates the baby not only to utter 'mama!' but also to believe in the sentence whose translation into the adults' language might perhaps be 'mother is here' or 'mother is here now'. Babies learn to use their language by acquiring dispositions to accept sentences on the basis of experiences motivating them. Those experiences consist in having visual representations. A similar process occurs in an adult person when they are taught a foreign language with the help of the direct (Berlitz) method. In this case during the first lessons the teacher asserts certain sentences while pointing at or demonstrating objects and students acquire dispositions to accept certain sentences in response to seeing certain objects, etc.

This earliest stage in the learning process is then followed by a more advanced stage when students acquire the ability to accept some sentences on the basis of others which serve as motives. So, for example, during a lesson of arithmetic students acquire the ability to accept sentences of the type 'the square of a number a has such and such a property' on the basis of accepting sentences of the type '$a.a$ has this property'. This motivational relation is formed in the student by the definition of 'the square of a' which he has learned from the teacher.

3. Disposition to Certain Motivations is an Important Part of the Disposition to Use a Language

None of the mentioned motivational relations, however, appears to be such that the mere fact that a person does not have a disposition to any of these relations should suffice to say of him that he does not speak English. Suppose, for example, that an individual is unable to accept the sentence 'Fire!', in spite of seeing a house on fire, simply because he is as yet unfamiliar with this expression; we shall not say on this account that he does not belong to the community of English-speaking persons. Suppose, however, that in spite of seeing a chair he cannot accept the sentence 'Here is a chair' either, or – in spite of seeing a table – is unable to believe in the sentence 'Here is a table' and, in general, in spite of seeing perceivable objects he is not in a position to believe in any sentence which, under such circumstances, is normally accepted by English-speaking people. Then we should certainly say that he does not speak English. A comparison with the well-known paradox of the bald man suggests itself. By removing one hair from the head of a man who is not bald one does not make him bald; a lot of hair has to be removed to make him bald. Similarly, in the case of motivational relations. Suppose there are two men, one of whom, say X, can speak English and the other, Y, who differs from X language-wise only in that he is unable to accept a sentence in the presence of a motivation which normally induces X to accept the same sentence when he is set on speaking English; we shall not say of Y on this account alone that he cannot speak English. It is only if on many occasions Y were found to be unable to respond in a way, in which X normally does when attuned to speaking English, that we should feel entitled to say that Y does not speak English.

Now from the point just made, viz. that having a disposition to every relevant motivational relation is not necessary (or sufficient) for a person to speak English, one must not conclude that some motivational relations are unimportant for speaking English. Such inference would be just as invalid as the argument that since no single hair is necessary to prevent one from becoming bald, therefore keeping your hair is unimportant for not becoming bald.

The ordinary idea of a bald man is a typical example of an unclear and vague concept. Our comparison suggests that the ordinary concept of the English language is similarly unclear. Unclear concepts are not suitable as a basis for scientific analysis which are expected to be precise. The blurredness of the denotation of an unclear concept would result in the blurredness of other concepts constructed with its help. This is why in our endeavour to define the meaning of expressions of a language we are not going to use the term 'language' with its usual vagueness and lack of clarity; we shall rather remove that vagueness contributing thereby to the precision of the term 'meaning' which is to be defined. In doing so, however, we will try to ensure that the extension of our term 'language' is not too different from the extension of 'language' in ordinary sense. In this way our concept of meaning, though precise, will still be applicable to languages in the ordinary sense; however, in such applications it will cease to be precise and will become as vague and imprecise as the ordinary concept of language.

4. *Our Remaining Investigations Will Be Confined to Languages with Fixed Motivational Relations*[11]

We now abandon 'language' in the ordinary sense and declare that henceforth we shall use this term in such a way that for every language L there is given a vocabulary, rules of syntax and those motivational relations in which we are now interested. By saying that for every language L the relevant motivational relations are fixed, we mean that in every language to every sentence of a certain form Z at least one type of experience (mental act)[12] is assigned such that one will not be regarded as a speaker of that language unless one is prepared to accept a sentence of that form in the presence of an experience of the given type. Hence, for every language L, in this sense, there exists a characteristic relation R which assigns to every sentence-type at least one type of experience (mental act) in such a way that X is a speaker of L at time t if and only if the following conditions are satisfied: (a) X utters at t a sentence of type K belonging to L, (b) X is prepared at the same time to accept any sentence Z of type K on the basis of (motivated by) an experience P if and only if the relation R holds between P and K. In short, we assume here that to be a speaker of L it is necessary to utter sentences belonging to L and at the same time to be prepared to accept sentences of L of a suitable form on the basis of motives in such a way that to each sentence-type of L a suitable motive is assigned. If, therefore, English were to be a language of this type with fixed vocabulary, syntax and motivational relations, then in order to speak English it would be necessary (1) to utter a sentence belonging to English, (2) to be prepared to accept, e.g. the sentence 'Fire!' when seeing a building on fire, (3) to be prepared to accept 'Fire'! on the basis of the acceptance of an equivalent sentence, e.g. 'It is burning!', (4) to be prepared to accept the same sentence on the basis of accepting any sentence of the form 'If C has occurred, then it is burning and C has occurred', etc., (5) to be prepared similarly to accept other sentences of English on the basis of suitable motives; the sentences and suitable motives being clearly correlated among themselves.

5. *Language Rules*

In deductive systems, in particular in certain formalized axiomatic systems, e.g. the propositional calculus based on the rules of substitution and detachment (but without definitions), the vocabulary and syntax are completely determined by the definition of so-called well-formed formulae. Similarly, the conditions under which a sentential formula may be accepted (asserted) are completely determined. This is effected by the rules of the system. In a system based on substitution and detachment (for the sake of simplicity we consider only systems without definitions) the following directive is observed: A well-formed formula of type A may be asserted if either (1) two sentences have been asserted, one of which is a conditional whose consequent is equiform with A and the other is equiform with the antecedent of the conditional, or (2) a sentence has been accepted from which A results by substitution. In short: one may assert a well-formed sentential formula of type A either if A is obtainable from already asserted sentences by detachment or if A results from an asserted sentence (s) by substitution. By such a rule the motivational relations, in which we have been interested, are completely determined. Every sentence A is correlated with either (1) the acceptance of two sentences from which A results by detachment, or (2) the acceptance of a sentence from which A results through substitution, as the only admissible motive for accepting A.

If, in general, for a unique characterization of a language we regard as necessary not only its vocabulary and syntax but also the motivational relations, then the language of the propositional calculus, used as our example, would be characterized not by the definition of well-formed formulae alone but jointly by that definition and the rules of the system. From this point of view one would speak not only of the vocabulary and laws of syntax of a language but also of language rules.

Now for every language with fixed motivational relations, i.e. for every language whose command would require dispositions to accept its sentences on the basis of suitable motives (assigned to each sentence-type), one might – theoretically – formulate a rule which would assign suitable acceptance-motives to each sentence-type. Just as there is a rule (or rules) in a deductive system, one might speak of the rules of a language.[13] A single rule of a deductive system determines which sentences it is necessary and sufficient to assert in order that another sentence (which is not one of the axioms) may, on their basis, also be asserted as a thesis of the system. If more than one rule is given, e.g. separate rules of substitution and of detachment, then each rule determines sentences which it is sufficient to assert in order to assert another sentence as a thesis.

One single language rule would determine what experiences (mental acts) are necessary and sufficient in order that one may accept (assert) a sentence of the language. In order to speak a language (with fixed motivational relations) it is necessary that one should be prepared to accept its sentences on the basis of those experiences (mental acts) assigned by the language rule as necessary and sufficient for the acceptance of those sentences. Particular language rules determine what relation is sufficient between a sentence and some experiences (mental acts) so that if one has those experiences (mental acts) one may accept the sentence. For example, according to the rule of substitution: It is sufficient for a sentence Z to result from another G by substitution in order that one may accept Z having previously accepted G. A necessary condition to speak a language L based exactly on rules D is to be prepared to accept sentences of L on the basis of experiences (mental acts) which are related to corresponding sentences by any of the rules of L, and only on the basis of such experiences (mental acts). Only that person speaks the language of the propositional calculus, for example, who is prepared to accept any well-formed propositional formula Z of the calculus on the basis of the acceptance of sentences from which Z is obtained by detachment or by substitution and only on this basis. It seems superfluous to add that in stating our conditions for speaking a language we do not at all require that the speaker should be conscious of the rules which, and which alone, he should follow. It is enough, if in fact he is prepared to follow all and only the rules of the language in question.

Having clarified the term 'language rule' we shall introduce another phrase, borrowed from the methodology of deductive systems, viz. 'a sentence Z is derivable immediately (directly) from P according to the rules of L'. We have said that any language rule of L specifies a relation between a sentence Z of L and an experience which jointly with having the relevant experience (mental act) is sufficient for a speaker of L to accept Z. Let us introduce the term 'the relation on which the particular language rule is based' or 'the relation specified by the (particular) language rule' to refer to that relation. Now we shall say that a sentence Z is derivable immediately from an experience (mental act) P in accordance with the language rules of L if and only if a relation specified by any of the language rules of L holds between Z and P. So, for instance, in the propositional calculus based on the rules of detachment and substitution, a sentence Z is derivable immediately, in virtue of those rules, from the acceptance of sentences A if and only if Z results by substitution or detachment from any sentence in A.

6. *Verbal and Intuitive Derivation (Inference)*

Being prepared to act in accordance with language rules is what we call the disposition to use the language. This disposition is uniquely determined only in artificial languages, e.g. in the language of mathematical logic. In natural languages it is not precisely determined as we have argued extensively before. The disposition in question for natural languages (e.g. English) is not fixed, i.e. a small change in the way we accept sentences on the basis of suitable motives is insufficient to constitute change of the speaker's language but a considerable change in his acceptance habits will constitute such a language-shift. In order, however, to support our arguments with examples, let us make the fictitious assumption that the disposition to speak English is fixed, in other words, that the language rule for English is given.

Our previous examples of beliefs in sentences motivated by other mental acts of people speaking natural languages have shown that in our view the disposition to speak a natural, ordinary language permits not only beliefs in particular sentences to act as the basis for the acceptance of others. Other mental acts may also be a basis for the acceptance of sentences, e.g. having a perceptual presentation with a certain content. The sensation of certain sounds may be the motive for the acceptance of the sentence 'It's thundering'. Motives (for the acceptance of sentences) which themselves consist in the acceptance of sentences will be referred to as verbal; otherwise as non-verbal. We take *verbal derivation* (inference) to mean the process of accepting a sentence on the basis of accepting other sentences; otherwise we shall speak of *intuitive derivation*.

7. *Synonymity as Inferential Substitutivity*

We have arrived at our definition of meaning guided by the following basic idea: two terms in a language have the same meaning provided that when we are presented with a certain aspect of an object we are prepared to apply to the object either of the two terms. An object may be given either through an intuitive presentation (perceptual or 'reproductive') or else through verbal description. So, for example, 'lift' and 'elevator' mean the same in English since every intuitive presentation which may induce us, when we are set on speaking English, to accept a sentence involving 'lift', may also induce us to accept a sentence obtained from the previous one when 'lift' is replaced in it by 'elevator'; furthermore, every sentence from which we are prepared — when set on speaking English — to infer immediately a sentence involving 'lift' is at the same time a sentence from which we are able under these circumstances to infer immediately another sentence obtained from the previous one when 'lift' is replaced in it by 'elevator'. In a generalized form the same idea may be expressed as follows: Two expressions are synonymous if they are mutual substitutes with respect to immediate inference. We shall presently try to formulate this intuitive idea more precisely exhibiting at the same time certain necessary restrictions.

As a first approximation we proposed the following definition: An expression A in a language L is synonymous with another expression B if and only if: (1) all and only those experiences (mental acts) P from which, in virtue of the language rules of L, a sentence Z involving A is immediately inferable are also experiences from which, in virtue of the language rules of L, another sentence is immediately inferable which differs from Z only in that some of the occurrences of A have been replaced by B, (2) each and only such a sentence which, in virtue of the language rules of L, is immediately inferable from a sentence Z involving A is also immediately inferable (in virtue of the language rules of L) from Z by replacing some occurrences of A with B.

8. *An Objection to the Above Definition of Synonymity*

However, the provisional definition given above is not satisfactory: it disregards a certain point as a consequence of which no two expressions are ever synonymous in this sense. As examples of two synonyms we have used 'lift', and 'elevator'. They would not be synonymous given our definition. For the sentence 'Every lift is subject to inertia' is immediately inferable in virtue of the rules of syllogism (applied to English) from the sentence 'every lift is a body and every body is subject to inertia'. Nevertheless, from this conjunctive sentence it is not possible to infer immediately (in virtue of the language rules of English) the sentence 'Every elevator is subject to inertia'. The terms 'lift' and 'elevator' are, therefore, not mutual substitutes with respect to immediate inference in the sense defined previously.

To avoid this difficulty let us introduce the following expression: 'from the experience (mental act) P the sentence Z is inferable in a manner essential for A'. Examples will clarify its meaning. In virtue of the language rules of English from the acceptance of the sentence 'Some Englishmen are sailors' the sentence 'Some sailors are Englishmen' is immediately inferable in a way essential for 'Englishmen'. This is because if in both sentences (i.e. the one whose acceptance may motivate and the one whose acceptance may be motivated) the expression 'Englishmen' is replaced by any other syntactically suitable expression, the result would be sentences whose acceptances again may motivate one another in English. This would not be the case if in both sentences 'are' is replaced by any other syntactically suitable expression, e.g. 'like'.

In general: a sentence Z in L involving the expression A is immediately inferable from an experience P in virtue of the language rules of L in a manner essential for A if and only if: I. from P the sentence Z is immediately inferable in virtue of the rules of L, and II. either (1.a) P consists in the acceptance of sentence(s) S, (1.b) either Z or S contains A, (1.c) there is in L an expression B such that the sentences S and Z are transformed on replacement of all occurrences of A and B, into S_B, Z_B respectively such that from the acceptance of S_B the sentence Z_B is not immediately inferable in virtue of the rules of L, or (2.a) P does not consist in the acceptance of a sentence and (2.b) Z contains A, and (2.c) there is in L an expression B whose substitution for all occurrences of A transforms Z into a sentence Z_B which is not immediately inferable from P in virtue of the rules of L.

9. *A Definition of 'Synonymity' and of 'Meaning'*

The defect discovered in our provisional definition of the synonymity of two expressions in a language may be removed if the phrase 'is inferable' is replaced in it by the phrase 'is inferable in a manner essential for A'. When modified in this way the definition reads as follows:

An expression A in a language L is synonymous with another expression B if and only if (1) Each and only such an experience (mental act) of type P from which in virtue of the rules of L a sentence Z of L containing an expression A is immediately inferable in a manner essential for A is also an experience from which in virtue of the rules of L another sentence Z' obtained from Z by replacing some occurrences of A by B, is immediately inferable in a manner essential for B, moreover (2) all and only those sentences which are immediately inferable from the acceptance of Z (containing Z) in virtue of the rules of L and in a way essential for A, are also immediately inferable in virtue of the rules of L and in a manner essential for B from the acceptance of a sentence Z' obtainable from Z by replacing some occurrences of A by B.

The fact that from the acceptance of the sentence 'every lift is a body and every body is subject to inertia' one may immediately infer by the rules of English the sentence 'every lift is subject to inertia', whereas one cannot infer 'every elevator is subject to inertia', does not prevent us from regarding 'lift' and 'elevator' as synonymous since the sentence 'every lift is subject to inertia' is not inferable from those other sentences in a manner essential for 'lift'.

This is the definition we decide to propose. We cannot think of any objection similar to the one which we have avoided by introducing 'inferability essential for ...'. It may be, however, that such an objection may be found.

In order to obtain a definition of meaning from the definition of synonymity, one would have to use the well-known schema of definition by abstraction. This schema may be used only under the condition that synonymity has been defined as a reflexive, symmetric and transitive relation. Now the synonymity relation *is* guaranteed all these three properties by our definition. There are, therefore, no formal difficulties in defining 'meaning' on the basis of our definition of synonymity. Such a definition by abstraction would define the meaning of an expression W in L more or less as that property of W which is common to all and only those expressions synonymous with W in L.[14]

10. *Verbal and Intuitive Meaning*

Most definitions of meaning which one finds in the literature are concerned with just one kind of meaning, viz. what might be called verbal meaning. For our part we shall distinguish expressions which have intuitive meaning from expressions which have purely verbal meaning. Expressions such as 'red', 'green', etc. have in English an intuitive meaning. For there are experiences, not consisting in the acceptance of a sentence (in this case perceptual presentations) from which sentences containing those expressions are immediately inferable by the rules of English in a manner essential for those expressions. For example, on the basis of a perception of a fresh leaf and in virtue of the rules of English we are able to accept the sentence 'this is green'. On the other hand, expressions occurring in sentences which are not inferable from intuitive presentations but are only immediately inferable from other sentences in virtue of the language rules, have only verbal meaning and are devoid of intuitive meaning. For example, the term 'atom' has a purely verbal meaning. A sentence may be justified directly by experience only if it contains at least one expression with intuitive meaning.

11. *Of So-Called Intention of the Act of Meaning*

Towards the end of the section concerned with the associationist theory of meaning we considered but did not evaluate the following claim: For every type of expression (written signs or utterances) W in L there is a thought-type M such that a particular expression of type W is used by a person as an expression of L only if that use is at the same time a thought of type M. We pointed out that this claim is imprecise, since it is not explained from what point of view those types of thought are to be distinguished. Some authors try to clarify this point as follows: For the word 'table' to be used as an expression of English it is necessary and sufficient that its use be a thought of a table and not of something else, moreover of a table as such and such a thing (e.g. concerned with its appearance or function). This, however, raises a question as to what it means to think of a table as such and such a thing. In order to reply to this question it would not be plausible to suggest that one should introspect on one's experiences when using the word 'table' when attuned to speaking English. Intro- or retrospection of one's experience of using 'table' when set on speaking English (under normal conditions and not when we decide to find out, as if experimentally, what the thought is like) does not reveal to me anything which might be identified with what the phrase 'thinking of a table as such and such' refers to. (In artificial conditions of an experiment in which I attempt to discover the content of my thoughts when I use 'table' there will be in my consciousness a lot which is not present in it under normal conditions; for example, some vague intuitions, some intruding words from which a synonymous expression might germinate, etc.).

In our view the following may be said on this matter: One uses the word 'table' as an expression of English if one is prepared to accept certain sentences of English in which 'table' occurs and if one is prepared to accept them on the basis of some motives rather than others. If when using 'table' I am prepared to accept sentences like 'A table is a piece of furniture', 'One takes meals at a table', etc. and if, besides, I am prepared to accept the sentence 'This is a table' on the basis of certain intuitive presentations, then I am using 'table' as an expression of English. The question whether this preparedness is exclusively in the sphere of dispositions or whether some of its components are actualized in consciousness, is difficult to answer. In our view those who say that the word 'table' is used as an expression of

English if one has a thought of certain objects as being such and such merely state the following: one is then thinking in such a way that one is prepared to respond to certain intuitive presentations by accepting the sentence 'this is a table', furthermore one is prepared to accept other sentences containing 'table' given those and not other motives. In our view 'the intentional (object-directed) nature of acts' and 'the matter of acts' reduces to just such dispositions.

NOTES

[1] A. Marty, *Untersuchungen zur Grundlegung der allgemeinen Grammatik und Sprachphilosophie*, Halle 1908, vol. I, p. 281.

[2] E. Husserl, *Logische Untersuchungen*, 3rd edition, Halle 1922, vol. II, part 1, pp. 25ff.

[3] Cf. 'S. Ossowski Analiza pojęcia znaku', *Przegląd Filozoficzny* 29 (1926), p. 29ff.

[4] [Translator's note: *'rana'* in Polish means 'a wound'.]

[5] [Translator's note: The Polish sentence *'brat spał'* means 'the brother slept (or: was asleep)'. The pronunciation of *'spal'* given in the text is one of two existing in contemporary Polish. Apparently the pronunciation of the whole sentence then coincides with the pronunciation of the corresponding Ukrainian sentence.]

[6] If we remove the word 'necessary' from the definition, then the objection to be made presently against it will no longer be valid. However, the objection in Section 5 will still apply, for it is directed against the view that the association of a thought with the use of an expression is sufficient for that expression to be used as an expression of the given language.

[7] The difficulties and contradictions which some authors see in the conception of universals are due to the fact that they treat the names of universals as expressions of the same semantical category as the names of individuals. I believe that these difficulties do not appear in a language in which the names of universals form a separate semantical category. The ordinary language is of this type.

[8] By the use of an expression A is meant here not the purely physical process of utterance but an act of consciousness. The latter is usually characterized as an act of perceiving or remembering the expression or in other ways. In any case, the use of A as understood here is a mental act which makes it possible to apply the term 'association' (in the relevant sense) to it.

[9] To simplify things we ignore the fact that there are expressions which are ambiguous in the particular language.

[10] J. S. Mill, *A System of Logic Ratiocinative and Inductive*, Longmans Green & Co., New York, 1911, New impression, pp. 19, 20, 21.

[11] [A short eleven-line paragraph summarizing the preceding chapter has been omitted here in the translation – Translator.]

[12] [Translator's note: 'experience' is used in this context roughly in the sense of German *'Erlebnis'* (*erleben*) and not exclusively as sense-experience.]

[13] In most deductive systems there is more than one rule. So far as we know, only Professor Leśniewski's system is based on one single rule.

[14] Throughout our analysis we have been ignoring languages with expressions which have more than one meaning. Nor have we considered synonymity of expressions taken from two distinct languages. We believe, however, that both these problems might be solved within the framework of our proposed conception of meaning.

2. LANGUAGE AND MEANING*

(1934)

1. *Purpose of the Investigation*

Our intention in the present article is to clarify certain semasiological concepts which (in our opinion) have great significance for the methodology of the sciences and also for epistemology. There will be proposed, among other things, a definition of the meaning of an expression. The conception of 'meaning' considered is not a conception of subjective meaning, which subsists in certain psychic acts constituting for an individual his understanding of an expression. Rather, we take 'meaning of an expression' to be something intersubjective which attaches to an expression of a language in relation to the language and *not* in relation to a person. That such a conception of intersubjective meaning should have great importance for methodology and epistemology is plausible for this reason: the theorems of the sciences are nothing other than the meanings of certain sentences, meanings which attach to these sentences in the languages in question; and knowledge (in distinction to knowing), at least in its most mature form, consists in those same meanings of sentences and eventually of other expressions.

Despite the great importance for epistemology of this conception of meaning, in my opinion it has hitherto not been defined precisely. One has contented oneself, for the most part, with attempting to call up a sort of intuitive view of what is to be understood by 'meaning'. The procedure we will follow in securing a definition of 'meaning' is in part analytic, in part synthetic and arbitrary. That is to say, in defining 'meaning' we do as much justice as possible to the generally accepted signification of the term. Only a certain degree of justice can be attained, of course. The usual conception of 'meaning' is not sharply delimited. We want a definition which specifies our concept exactly and strictly. For this reason, in attempting to delimit the concept sharply, we will take the liberty of arbitrarily drawing precise boundaries within the blurred outlines of the usual conception. The boundaries could be drawn this way or that, and each way could be justified in respect

* Translated from the German by John Wilkinson. First published in *Erkenntnis* **IV** (1934), 100–138. *Język i Poznanie*, I, 145–174. Reprinted here by kind permission of the publishers of *Erkenntnis* and the University of Chicago Press. Copyright © 1951 by University of Chicago Press.

to the customary fuzzy conception. But these several ways are not of equal value respecting usefulness, i.e. respecting the results which can be obtained with their help.

The definition of 'meaning' we adopt has far-reaching consequences. As a matter of fact, it leads to an epistemological standpoint which we call 'radical conventionalism'. To such consequences of the present study we devote a separate article (*The World-Picture and the Conceptual Apparatus*) in the next issue of *Erkenntnis*.[1] However, we wish in this article to prepare the way to those theoretical epistemological consequences. We turn our attention first, therefore, to certain distinctions among knowledge processes, especially among judgment processes.

2. *The Judgment and Its Kinds*

We distinguish between judgments in the psychological sense and judgments in the logical sense. Judgments in the psychological sense are certain psychic phenomena concerning whose characteristics much argument has occurred in the past. We will keep clear of this debate. It is our wish simply to direct the reader's attention to certain kinds of *judgment-processes*. In so doing, we shall avoid strict definitions and be content with informal suggestions.

There are judgment-processes (hereafter we designate judgments which are psychic phenomena as 'judgment-processes', to distinguish them from logical judgments which we designate simply 'judgments') that can be adequately expressed in the sentences of a language, and judgment-processes that cannot be so expressed. The former we call 'articulate judgment-processes'; the latter, 'inarticulate judgment-processes'.

Let us illustrate these matters by an example involving an inarticulate judgment-process. The porter comes into the room with my mail while I am at my desk writing these words. I become aware of this without interrupting my work, and as I become aware of it various events — among them certain judgment-processes — occur in me. Suppose I wish to express these judgment-processes in speech. Clearly, by no matter what words I choose for this purpose do I express adequately those processes which have gone on in me. The judgment-processes have a pretty nebulous form; those which actually receive verbal expression have comparatively sharper outlines. Let us try to express the judgment-processes verbally. 'The porter is coming into the room.' 'Eugene is coming into the room.' 'Eugene is opening the door.' 'There's Eugene.' 'There he is.' etc. Each of these sentences adequately expresses a different judgment-process because all the judgment-processes adequately expressed thereby are differentiated respecting their content.

But what I thought as I became aware of the porter entering the room is as well expressed by one of these sentences as by another, and consequently is perfectly exactly expressed by none of them. (The situation is similar to that which arises when we try to draw a line between red and orange in the spectrum of sunlight. Lines can be drawn in various places, and one line is as good as another; but since all the lines are different, one of them is as bad as another.)

In the daily affairs of life, we have to do with just such judgment-processes as these. Catching sight of an approaching auto as I cross the street, I make a judgment; but no statement of language corresponds exactly to this judgment. A similar thing happens when we recall some finished piece of business, or when we have the first thought in the solution of a scientific problem. Indeed, everyone knows what it costs to get that first utterly inexpressible notion clear enough for utterance.

I am not interested here in wrangling over the question: Do the psychic processes I have called 'inarticulate judgment-processes' deserve the name 'judgment-process'? My purpose has been simply to point out their existence. This is important to us, because I want to emphasize that in the course of the present study we shall consider only articulate judging.

Articulate judging takes place mostly (if not always) in reference to voiced or unvoiced speaking, viz. reading, writing, listening, etc. That is to say, articulate judging is a composite psychic process in which usually there can be discerned a more or less fragmentary intuitive representation of a word-image. This intuitive representation is then mixed with certain others (without analysis of the distinguishable components) into the unity of the articulate judging. We consider it fallacious to characterize matters in such a way that in the cases above judging is linked to the sentence-representation simply on the basis of association. The representation enters fully into the judgment-process and, indeed, forms its essential part. This has been convincingly demonstrated by Husserl.[2]

An articulate judgment-process whose essential part is the intuitive representation of a sentence we shall call 'verbal judging'. (Here we leave open the question whether there are in general articulate but non-verbal judgings.) Scientific judgment-processes in mature form are always of the verbal sort.

Among the non-intuitive components of a verbal judgment-process we distinguish the conviction – or assertion-moment. This assertion-moment can be positive or negative, according as the judgment-process involves acceptance or rejection; and it can have various degrees of strength, according to the intensity of acceptance or rejection. When there is no assertion-moment, we are involved with Meinong's *Annahmen*. We call a verbal judgment-process

whose assertion-moment is positive a 'positive conviction'; one whose assertion-moment is negative, a 'negative conviction'.

The further course of this study will show frequent use of the expressions
'X accepts the sentence Z' and 'X rejects the sentence Z'. The first of these is
taken to be equivalent to 'X expresses by the sentence Z a positive conviction'.
In this interpretation, X need neither pronounce nor write the sentence Z;
he may simply hear it or read it; and in general he may even not perceive Z
sensibly, but merely form a mental representation of it. In every case,
however, X is to experience a verbal judgment-process with a positive assertion-moment; and the intuitive component of this judgment-process is to
consist in a representation of the sentence Z. Contrariwise, by 'X rejects the
sentence Z' we mean 'X experiences negative conviction of such a sort that
if its negative assertion-moment were replaced by the positive counterpart
thereof, then he is ready to express by the sentence Z the resulting positive
conviction'. A negative conviction which contains the rejection of a sentence
and a positive conviction which consists in the acceptance of that same
sentence are called 'opposing convictions'.

To the foregoing definitions we add the following remark. By saying that
X accepts the sentence 'It is snowing', we do not in general intend to claim
that X is actually expressing that very judgment which the English customarily
state by 'It is snowing'. Rather, we leave it undecided whether X is using this
sentence as the English language prescribes or perhaps as some other language
might. If, therefore, one says 'X accepts the sentence 'It is snowing''', it
should not be inferred that X believes it is snowing. The remark means only
that X expresses some positive conviction by the sentence 'it is snowing';
and while the conviction may be of the sort associated with 'it is snowing' in
English, it may perhaps be of another kind.

Brentano has made us familiar with sentences of the form 'X accepts Y',
having us understand thereby that Y is an object whose existence X believes
in. Our previous explanation of such expressions makes clear that we use
them in a completely different sense. We emphasize this difference strongly.

So much for the judgment as a psychic process.

Now let us turn to the logical aspect of the judgment. We take the logical
aspect of a judgment to be the meaning which attaches to a sentence of a
language. If we have to do with an articulate judgment-process that is
expressible by a sentence Z of a language S, we shall also refer to the meaning
of Z in S as 'the content of the judgment-process'. (We shall not try to decide
here whether something like content can be coordinated with inarticulate
judgings.) The logical aspect of a judgment-process can involve affirmation
or negation; but it cannot involve acceptance or rejection, because assertion-

moments are part of the psychology of the judgment-process and not part of its content.

3. *Specification of Meaning as a Necessary Characteristic of Language*

A language is not unequivocally characterized solely by its vocabulary and the rules of its syntax; it is also characterized by the way meaning is coordinated with its words and expressions. If someone used the sounds of the English language but associated with them meanings other than the customary ones, we would not equate his language to English; instead, we would consider it as some language or other of his own invention. Thus the specification or the coordination between the sounds of a language (or its written characters) and their meanings is part of the unique characterization of that language. We shall call this coordination the 'specification of meaning' of the language.

For such specification of meaning it is not sufficient to fix the correspondence between the words (or expressions) of the language and the objects which, presumably, they denote. The reason for this is two-fold. First, not all expressions designate objects, but only those of a nominal character, i.e. names; nevertheless all words and expressions of a language have meaning. Second, two expressions can designate the same object and yet have distinct meanings (e.g. the expressions 'the highest mountain in Europe' and 'the highest mountain in Switzerland' designate the same object and yet have distinct meanings).

Traditional logic was not concerned with the meaning of all expressions but only with the meaning of names. It equated the meaning of a name with the content of the concept connected with that name. The example we have just given should clarify the difference between the meaning of a name and the object denoted by the name. Our example could also serve, in traditional logic, to fix the difference between the content and the scope of a (nominal) concept. The notions of the conceptual content of a name and the meaning of a name are rather frequently identified, although of course they are distinct.

4. *Rules of Meaning*

To attempt a definition of 'meaning of an expression' at this point would lead us too far afield.[3] What we have said so far on that score has only the limited aim of removing the grossest misunderstandings.

We intend to propose in this section a thesis which is fundamental to the further course of our study. A provisional and quite inexact statement of this thesis is as follows: the meaning possessed by the expressions of a language determines to some extent the rules of its use. Before formulating this thesis precisely, we wish to discuss its origin and import.

The meaning one attaches to an expression depends on the type of ideas in whose assertion he uses – or ought to use – the expression in question. By the meaning of an expression, therefore, a coordination is established between the expression and a type of idea. Obviously, those who use the same expression in the same sense need not attach to this expression absolutely the same idea (in the sense of a unique real psychic process). This is naturally impossible for different persons, and even for the same person using the same expression at different times. What is necessary is that those who want to use the same expression constantly in the same meaning should always conjoin with this expression ideas belonging to a type of idea which is unambiguously determined by the meaning of the expression.

We shall not attempt here to decide how these types (which are coordinated with expressions by way of their meaning) are formed. Rather, we shall investigate a procedure for revealing misunderstandings. That is to say, we shall consider a procedure which is effective for revealing whether someone attaches to an expression (e.g. a sentence) a meaning *other than* ours.

Let us begin by illustrating the procedure. Suppose an exposed sensitive nerve in someone's tooth is touched, and he winces and cries out. In this case, very likely, we can dispense with asking whether the victim has felt any pain. But suppose the question *is* put, and our guinea pig responds by rejecting the sentence 'it hurts'. How are we to assess his behaviour? First, we might suppose that the person lied; that therefore he did not actually reject the sentence 'it hurts', but only apparently rejected it. Second, it is possible that the person did not lie; that therefore he actually rejected the sentence in question and felt no pain. Lastly, it is possible that the person did not lie and so actually did reject the sentence 'it hurts' and nevertheless that he really felt pain, but attached to the sentence a meaning other than ours. Now let us exclude the possibility that anyone feels pain and simultaneously rejects the sentence 'it hurts', if he attaches to this sentence the same meaning we do. Thus, if someone feels pain and rejects the sentence 'it hurts', we can conclude that he attaches to this sentence a meaning other than ours.

The illustration suggests a procedure for discovering misunderstandings. The schema of this procedure can be formulated as follows: wishing to decide whether someone used a certain sentence with the same meaning we do, we first seek out for this sentence a certain particularly characteristic class of experiences which to us are sufficient for a decisive acceptance of the given sentence; if then, despite the occurrence of an experience in this class, we establish that the person in question rejects the original sentence, we can conclude that he attaches to this sentence a meaning different from ours.

We remark again that the chosen class of experiences should be a markedly characteristic one. Note that its distinctive character cannot consist solely in the fact that we are entirely satisfied to accept the sentence in any of the experiences of the class. Something more is needed. Any experience of the chosen class must satisfy us *immediately*, i.e. the transition from that experience to an acceptance of the given sentence should not occur in several steps. (To illustrate. Suppose we accept certain premisses – this, too, can be considered an experience – as sufficient for some remote conclusion. Someone else, though he accepts these same premisses, rejects the sentence by which we express the conclusion. This is not conclusive proof that between that individual and us there is a misunderstanding regarding the sentences of the premisses or the sentence of the conclusion, for another interpretation of the situation is possible.) What class of experiences we select as characteristic of the given sentence depends in each separate case on our linguistic intuition.

The procedure sketched above would lead to unquestionable results were it not that in practice one cannot determine with complete certainty whether the other person actually does have experience of the kind in question, and whether he really rejects the given sentence or only apparently rejects it. Nevertheless, the basic proposition of the procedure (i.e. anyone who rejects the sentence Z despite his perception of experience of type D attaches to Z a meaning other than ours) is apodictically certain whenever an experience of the proper type is coordinated with the given sentence. It seems superfluous to add that our procedure permits us to detect misunderstanding, but not to secure agreement; i.e. the procedure indicates a necessary but not sufficient condition for deciding whether someone else attaches the same meaning as ours to a sentence.

Consider still another example of such disclosure of misunderstandings. Suppose someone accepts a sentence of the form 'if A, then B'; and suppose, further, that he simultaneously accepts the premiss 'A' but rejects the conclusion 'B'. If he actually does this (and is not merely pretending), we can explain his behaviour by assuming he has already forgotten both of his positive convictions when he rejects 'B'. If he is conscious of both of them while rejecting 'B', we can certainly conclude that he used at least one of the three sentences (i.e. 'if A, then B'; 'A'; and 'B') in a sense different from ours. We rule out entirely the possibility that anyone could use the English language with its established meanings and simultaneously accept both 'if A, then B' and 'A', and reject 'B'.

Let us give closer attention to the theses of the two illustrations presented above. The first thesis affirms the impossibility of entertaining simultaneously a feeling of pain and a negative conviction expressed by the rejection of 'it hurts', when this sentence is rightly understood in accordance with the rules of the English language. The thesis thus excludes the conjunction of an experience of a certain kind (feeling pain) with the appearance in consciousness of another experience (a negative conviction of a certain kind). For the second thesis, designate by 'H' the type of idea coordinated with 'if A, then B', by its English meaning; by 'V' the type of idea coordinated with the antecedent 'A' by its English meaning; and by 'N' the type of idea coordinated with the consequent 'B' by its English meaning. This thesis then can be formulated as follows: the occurrence of two positive convictions of types H and V respectively excludes the simultaneous experience in consciousness of a negative conviction which opposes an idea of type N.

So conceived, these theses — fundamental to our procedure for detecting misunderstandings — appear to be concerned simply with psychological-empirical truths. But we hold that this is not the case, because the two theses (in their preceding formulation) are analytic and do not derive from experience. There is no danger that experience could ever overturn them, just as it cannot, e.g. the sentence 'water heated to 100 °C boils under normal pressure.' A general sentence of the form 'every A is a B' requires empirical verification and can be overthrown by experience just in case one can establish that there is an x which is an A without being a B or without having any property from which the B-ness may be deduced. If the question whether x is A cannot be decided without first ascertaining (in the above sense) that x is B, then we shall say that B is for the concept A constitutive. Thus the sentence 'all cocks crow' is subject to empirical verification and can be refuted by experience. On the other hand, 'every cock is a bird' is not subject to experience; it is impossible to establish for any x that it is a cock as long as there is doubt whether x is a bird. Similarly, 'water heated to 100 °C boils under normal pressure' is not an empirical statement and is immune to the test of experience; indeed, the property 'boils under normal pressure' is constitutive for the concept of water heated to 100 °C.

Is this not exactly the case with our two theses, as we formulated them just above? Consider the assertion 'no one who rightly understands the sentence 'if A, then B' can reject the consequent 'B' if he accepts the conditional 'if A, then B' and the antecedent 'A''. In what way can it be settled definitely whether someone understands 'if A, then B' in its correct English significance as long as it is not clear whether this individual intends to reject the consequent 'B' while accepting the conditional sentence and its antecedent 'A'? Or how is it possible to decide whether a person attaches to 'it hurts' the proper English meaning as long as it is possible for that person to reject the sentence and simultaneously feel pain? We believe this to be impossible. Thus we hold that the theses previously formulated do specify for their sentences the constitutive properties of the concept of use according to meaning.

A conclusive proof of our last claim cannot be given here because our study has not yet reached the stage where concepts are precise and theorems can be proved. For the present we shall simply maintain the claim (confident that the reader will go along with us in it) and not give additional discussion to the matter.

Our discussion of the procedure for detecting misunderstanding has brought out a connection between the meaning one attaches to the expressions of a language and the way one uses these expressions. The connection can be formulated as follows: only that person connects with expressions of the English language (in particular, the sentence 'it hurts') the meanings coordinated with them, who is prepared to accept this sentence upon undergoing such and such a characteristic type of experience (a feeling of pain). Our second example contributes the following: only that person connects with expressions of the English language the meanings coordinated with them in that language who is prepared to accept the sentence 'B' as soon as he has accepted sentences of the form 'if A, then B' and 'A'.

Thus it appears possible to set up for any language (in which expressions have unambiguously determined meaning) rules whose formulations accord with the following scheme:

> Only that person connects with the words and expressions of a language S the meanings coordinated with them by that language who in situations of type L is prepared to accept a sentence of the sort Z.

(This scheme, of course, admits the possibility that Z may be a function of L or of a component of L, as was the case in our second example.) Here we take the sentence 'X is prepared in situation L to accept sentence Z' to have the same meaning as 'If X in situation L answers the decision-question which framed sentence Z as a problem, then X will accept sentence Z'. Now answering the decision-question which frames Z as a problem can consist only in accepting or rejecting sentence Z. Instead of 'X answers the decision-question which frames Z as a problem', therefore, one can say 'X accepts sentence Z or else X rejects sentence Z'. Our concept of being prepared thus comes down to: 'X is prepared in situation L to accept sentence Z' has the same meaning as 'if X is in situation L and either accepts sentence Z or else rejects it, then X will accept sentence Z'. This explanation completely eliminates the mythical notion of a psychic disposition from our conception of 'being prepared'.

As we said, it is possible to set up rules of this form for a language. Such rules we call 'rules of meaning', or, concisely, 'meaning-rules'. With certain sentences these meaning-rules coordinate the particularly characteristic classes of data described above in such wise that to perceive a class of data and to reject its coordinate sentence can occur only in violation of the meaning of that sentence.

Meaning-rules cannot be formulated precisely for each language. (Later a reason for this will be suggested.) But such a formulation can be carried out easily and completely for the artificial language of symbolic logic. The usual sentential calculus based on primitive symbols '$\supset$' and '$\sim$' has two so-called 'rules of inference': the rule of detachment, which permits from '$A \supset B$' and 'A' the inference of 'B'; and the rule of substitution. Definitions (if regarded as rules governing the replacement of certain expressions by certain others) constitute still other rules of inference. All these rules of inference can be transformed with ease into rules of meaning. For example, a rule specifying the meaning of the sign '$\supset$' can be extracted from the rule of detachment as follows: only that person connects with the signs of the language of sentential calculus the meanings coordinated with them by that language who is prepared to accept sentence 'B' if he accepts sentences of the form '$A \supset B$' and 'A'. Again, from the definition of the sign '$\vee$' (according to which, '$A \vee B$' can be substituted for '$\sim A \supset B$') the following rule of meaning can be formed: only that person connects with the signs of the language of sentential calculus the meanings coordinated with them by that language who is prepared to accept each sentence S_2 which results from sentence S_1 by replacing an expression of the form '$\sim A \supset B$' with '$A \vee B$', provided he accepts the original sentence S_1. In ways similar to those for this artificial language, analogous meaning-rules can be set up for natural languages. But the undertaking would encounter great difficulties, and could not be carried through completely.

The rules of meaning of a language, requiring of each user of the language to accept certain sentences of this language in certain situations, are thus determined by the meaning of the words and the expressions of the language. Whoever violates these rules of meaning shows thereby that he does not attach to the word-sounds of the given language the meaning coordinated with them in this language; and therefore that he is not using this language, but some other one which employs the same sounds. One observes the rules of meaning just as he observes the rules of phonetics or the rules of syntax. Without, perhaps, knowing the meaning-rules explicitly, he sees that in a given case the acceptance of a sentence is required by the rules of meaning because he looks upon the contrary behaviour (i.e. the rejection of this sentence) as a violation of the meaning-assignment of the language. The acceptance of sentences according to rules of meaning is characterized by strict self-evidence and an unquestioned definitiveness.[4]

5. Deductive, Axiomatic and Empirical Rules of Meaning

We now list several kinds of rules of meaning which occur in actually existing languages. Without any claim to completeness, I believe I can specify three such kinds; these I designate as (1) deductive; (2) axiomatic; and (3) empirical.

Our previous rule of meaning based on *modus ponens* exemplifies a deductive rule of meaning. That rule ran: Only that person connects with expressions of the English language the meaning coordinated with them in that language who is prepared to accept the sentence 'B' as soon as he accepts sentences of the form 'if A, then B' and 'A'. Other examples of deductive rules of meaning stem from definitions. We have already noted one of them. For another example, suppose that in the language of arithmetic '2' is defined as '$1 + 1$'; then in this language, the following deductive rule of meaning holds: only that person connects with the signs of arithmetic the meaning coordinated with them by that language who is prepared to accept a sentence Z containing the sign '2' if he accepts a sentence which differs from Z only in that the sign '$1 + 1$' occurs in place of the sign '2'.

Each deductive rule of meaning of a language puts a requirement on anybody who wants to use the words and expressions of this language in accordance with its meaning-specification. The requirement has this form: that the person be prepared to draw from premisses of a certain type a conclusion in a particular way. Thus, speaking more generally, a deductive rule of meaning correlates with a sentence of a certain type (as premiss) a sentence of another definite type (as conclusion). (Of course, if the meaning-rule required the drawing of a conclusion from several premisses, we would say: the deductive rule of meaning correlates with a *class* of sentences of certain types (as premisses) a sentence of another definite type (as conclusion).) Hence it is clear that a deductive rule of meaning determines a sentence-to-sentence relation (or a sentence-class-to-sentence relation); and moreover that this relation is characteristic of the deductive rule of meaning. Let us refer to the domain, the range and the field of this characteristic relation as the 'domain', 'range' and 'field' respectively of the deductive rule of meaning. In particular, we define the 'scope' of a deductive rule of meaning to be that set of ordered pairs of sentences (or that set of ordered pairs whose first elements are sentence classes and whose second elements are sentences) such that an ordered pair belongs to the set if and only if the characteristic relation of the meaning-rule holds between the first and second elements of the pair.

Turning to what we call 'axiomatic' rules of meaning, we find these best illustrated in the languages of axiom-systems. There, again, an unconditional demand is made of anybody who wants to use the words of an axiom-system in the meaning coordinated with them by the language of the system: that the person be prepared to accept without further ado the sentences set up as the axioms of the system. I believe that analogous rules apply to everyday languages, too, e.g. it seems to be required of anybody who attaches to the words 'every' and 'is' of English the meaning coordinated with them by that language that he be prepared to accept without further ado any sentence of the form 'every A is an A'. In general, all sentences that are (as is said) evident a priori relate to an axiomatic meaning-rule which enjoins those who would not violate the meaning-specification of the language to accept such sentences. And just as a deductive rule of meaning determines a unique characteristic relation between sentences, so an axiomatic rule of meaning determines a unique characteristic set of sentences, viz. precisely those sentences whose acceptance is enjoined by the axiomatic rule of meaning. This characteristic set of sentences we call the 'scope' of axiomatic rule of meaning.

The empirical rules of meaning constitute our third class. These rules are characterized by the fact that the situations they involve (in which readiness to accept a sentence is required by the meaning-specification of the language) consist either exclusively or partly in experiencing a perception. One apparently proceeds according to such a rule when he accepts the sentence 'it hurts' upon experiencing a toothache. If ever we meet a situation in which someone experiences what for us is the normal reaction to a severely irritated nerve, and in spite of this the person is not ready to accept the sentence 'it hurts' but rather rejects this sentence or even accepts the sentence 'it feels good', then as already explained we see in this situation a proof that he does not attach to the sentences 'it hurts' and 'it feels good' the same meanings that we do.

We distinguish two kinds of empirical rules of meaning: *simple* and *compound*. An empirical rule of meaning is called 'simple' in case it declares: Only that person does not violate the meaning-specification of a language who is prepared to accept such and such a sentence upon experiencing such and such a perception. An empirical rule of meaning is called 'compound' in case it requires a readiness to accept such and such a sentence upon the fulfilment of certain conditions including inter alia, the experiencing of such and such a perception. The totality of such conditions, together with individual perceptions, we term 'data of experience'. These can comprise, for example, perceptions and inarticulate judgments by which a situation is interpreted as 'normal'. We also permit compound empirical rules of meaning to require the acceptance of certain sentences in the context of a series of sequential perceptions and certain other data. Such, it seems, is the case with the so-called 'statements about the external world'. Perhaps it is a hopeless enterprise to seek in familiar everyday languages for clear cases of empirical meaning-rules which are not simple and by which we govern our statements regarding the so-called 'external world'. If so, the reason would appear to lie in the fact that the familiar everyday languages are not languages in the strict sense: their meaning-specifications are fluid and fluctuating (see the last section of this paper).

Words whose usage is controlled by empirical rules of meaning we call 'words with empirical meaning'. Words with empirical meaning divide into words with compound empirical meaning or words with simple empirical meaning, according as the empirical rules of meaning controlling usage are all compound or involve at least one simple one. Words which name external objects or their properties usually seem to have compound empirical meaning. Only names of psychic entities or their properties would seem to have simple empirical meaning. In everyday languages, the name of properties of external objects and the names of psychic entities are often the same, e.g. 'red' is said of a rose and of a perception. Epistemologists who do not give the distinction sufficient attention become involved in difficulties and paradoxes which lead them to deny so-called 'sense qualities' to external objects. I only remark this here, intending to go into the matter more deeply in another connection.

Deductive and axiomatic rules of meaning together we call 'discursive rules of meaning'. Languages whose rules of meaning are exclusively discursive (e.g. the languages of pure logic and of pure mathematics) are termed 'discursive languages'. Languages whose rules of meaning include empirical rules are termed 'empirical languages'.

As in the case of deductive rules of meaning (which, because they correlate sentences − or sentence classes − with sentences, give rise to characteristic relations), so for empirical rules of meaning we can define characteristic relations between data of experience and sentences. The domain of such a relation consists of perceptual data and its range of sentences. The scope of an empirical rule of meaning is the set of all ordered pairs of the form (perceptual data, sentence) whose elements satisfy the characteristic relation of that empirical rule of meaning.

6. *Terminology*

Suppose a particular sentence is either: (1) a member of the *scope* of an axiomatic rule of meaning or (2) a member of the domain of a deductive rule of meaning (or of a sentence-class belonging to the domain of a deductive rule of meaning); or (3) a member of the *range* of a deductive rule of meaning, or of the *range* of an empirical rule of meaning. Then we say that the appropriate rule of meaning 'encloses' this sentence.

Suppose a sentence is enclosed by a certain rule of meaning. Then of any expression which is a component of this sentence we say: the rule of meaning 'concerns' the expression.

A rule of meaning R is 'inessential' for an expression A if and only if: either rule R does not concern expression A; or the scope of R is unchanged when, in all sentences enclosed by R, expression A is replaced by an arbitrary expression A' of the same logical type as A, and A' (wherever it occurs in those sentences) is similarly replaced by A. Rule R is 'essential' for expression A if and only if R is not inessential for A. (By way of illustration, consider the aforementioned axiomatic rule of meaning: only that person connects with the expressions 'every' and 'is' of English the meaning coordinated with them by that language who is prepared to accept without further ado any sentence of the form 'every A is an A'. This axiomatic rule is essential for the word 'every' and also for the word 'is'. That such is the case may be seen if e.g. in all sentences of the form 'every A is an A' we replace 'is' by 'loves' and any occurrence of 'loves' by 'is' — presupposing, of course, that 'loves' is of the same logical type as 'is'. It then appears that the scope of our axiomatic rule is changed. By the same token, our axiomatic rule is inessential for any name which can be introduced in place of 'A'.)

It is evident that if a rule of meaning is inessential for an expression A, then that rule is inessential for all expressions of the same logical type as A.[5]

If two expressions, A and A', occur simultaneously in the same element of the scope of a meaning-rule of language S, we say: in the language S there exists between A and A' a direct (immediate) meaning-relation. On the other hand, of two expressions A and B we say that in the language S there exists between A and B an 'indirect (mediate) meaning-relation' if there can be formed a finite sequence of (at least three) expressions which begins with A, ends with B, and between any two successive members thereof a direct meaning-relation obtains.

Here also we should remark briefly that the meaning-rules of a language concern not only expressions, but syntactical forms as well. The matter could be made precise in the same way that it was for expressions. Further, one could distinguish between syntactical forms for which a rule of meaning is essential and those for which it is inessential. And finally, just as above, one could specify a meaning-relation between expressions and syntactical forms. We shall not delay over these matters, however.

7. *Concerning the Determination of the Rules of Meaning by Meaning*

Now let us turn to the question: Does the alteration of a rule of meaning of a language necessarily entail an alteration of the meaning-specification of this language? We asserted previously that the meaning-rules of language are uniquely determined by the meaning-specification of the language. Which, it would seem, answers our question. But to believe this is to misunderstand the original assertion. It does not claim that the rules of meaning of a language are determined individually by the meaning-specification of the language. What it does claim is that in a sense the totality of meaning-rules is determined uniquely by the meaning-specification of the language.

Let us be a little clearer on this. As said earlier, to each rule of meaning corresponds a unique scope. So long as the individual rules of meaning are of the same logical type, their scopes can be summed. These sums, clearly, can remain constant even though their components (i.e. the scopes of individual meaning-rules) are formed in various ways. In other words, two systems of meaning-rules may differ and nevertheless the scope-sums of these systems be identical. In asserting that the meaning-specification determines the meaning-rules, we intend to assert only this – that the scope-sums of all the rules of meaning are determined by the meaning-specification of a language.

For illustration, consider a language with only three rules of meaning. Suppose these rules are axiomatic. Let the scope of the first comprise the sentence '$2 \times 2 = 4$'; the scope of the second, the sentence '$1 + 1 = 2$'; and the scope of the third, the sentence '$1 \times 1 = 1$'. The sum of the scopes of these rules is then a set comprising the three sentences as members. Now, instead of these three rules, take a new system of only two rules such that the scope of the first comprises both '$2 \times 2 = 4$' and '$1 \times 1 = 1$', and the scope of the second comprises '$1 + 1 = 2$'. The scope-sum of the two-rule system is the same as that of the original three-rule system. Because these scope-sums are the same, we would say that the indicated alteration of the meaning-rules did not necessarily entail an alteration of the meaning-specification of the language.

Let us, for convenience, designate the set of scope-sums of all rules of meaning by 'the total scope of the rules of meaning' – even though this manner of speaking is a little misleading.

Considering now the alteration of the total scope of the meaning-rules, we see that such alteration may occur either (1) by the total scope receiving elements which involve expressions not previously in the language; or (2) without new expressions entering the total scope. When we referred above to an alteration of the total scope consequent upon alteration of the meaning of an expression, we had in mind such alterations of the total scope as come about without the introduction of new expressions. Before taking up the other sort of alteration of the total scope, and the effect of such alteration on the meaning-specification of the language, we must first make certain distinctions between languages.

8. *Closed and Open Languages*

Take two languages, S and S', and associate with each word and expression of S like-sounding word or expression of S' (but not vice versa).[6] Consider the corresponding expressions of the two languages to be translations of each other. Now suppose that an expression A' of the richer language S' has a translation A in S and also is in direct meaning-relation with another expression A_i' of S'. If expression A_i' has no translation in language S, we say language S is 'open' with respect to language S'. Instead of saying a language is open respecting another language, we may simply say 'the language is open'. If a language is not open, we call it a 'closed' language.

The choice of 'open' is suggested by the fact that an open language can have its vocabulary of expressions augmented without altering thereby the meaning of expressions already occurring in it. More precisely, by augmenting its vocabulary of expressions an open language S can be carried over into a language S' without any alteration in the meaning of expressions occurring in S. This is not always possible for a closed language.

In an open language, some rules of meaning are contained more or less latently in the meanings of its expressions. The meaning of expression A is already so adapted to the meaning of the translation of A_i' (as yet lacking in language S) that when this translation is added to the vocabulary of expressions of S, expression A enters into suitable meaning-relations with the translation without undergoing a modification of its meaning. This latent capacity of A to adapt to the other meaning is not manifest in the use of language S because of the poverty of S. The reverse is true for closed languages, for in these all possible moments are contained in the meanings of their expressions and are revealed in the use of the languages.

Now we are able to resolve the problem which was posed — but left unsettled — at the end of the previous section: does an alteration of the total scope of the meaning-rules by the introduction of new expressions necessarily entail a change in the meaning-specification of the language? The problem must be treated separately for closed and open languages; we begin with the closed.

Assume that language S is closed; and that, in augmenting its vocabulary of expressions by any expression W, it goes over into a richer language S_W. Language S_W thus contains all expressions of S and the expression W as well. The total scope of the meaning-rules of S_W contains, apart from the expressions of S (hereinafter referred to as the 'old' expressions in S_W), also the expression W. Our question is: Do the old expressions in language S_W have the same meaning they had in language S?

We distinguish two cases: either W has a direct meaning-relation with the old expressions in S_W, or it does not. Suppose it does. Then the old expressions in S_W cannot have their original S-meaning, for if they did either S would be an open language, or W would have the same meaning as one of the old expressions and therefore would have an old expression as a translation. Hence the old expressions of S_W maintain their S-meaning only if W does not have a direct meaning-relation with any old expression in S_W or if W has the same meaning as some one of them.

If, however, W is not in direct meaning-relation with any of the old expressions, then likewise W is not in indirect meaning-relation with any of them.

Now let us designate as a 'part of the language' any non-empty subclass of the class of expressions of that language; and, further, as an 'isolated part' any part whose elements are meaning-connected with no expression in the remainder of the language. If no part of a language is isolated, we call the language 'connected'.

Our preceding considerations thus furnish the following conclusion. If to a closed language S is added a new expression W (not identical in meaning with any old expression), and if in the richer language S_W the old expressions retain the meaning they had in S, then the language S_W is not connected.

Turning to open languages, let us ask again: If new expressions are added to such a language, i.e. if the total scope of the meaning-rules of the language is thus altered, does this necessarily entail a change in the meaning of any original expression? From the notion of an open language, it follows that an open language can be augmented with new expressions without altering the meaning of its old ones or without suffering disconnection. This actually happens when, upon introduction of new expressions, the language is transformed into a new language with respect to which the initial language is open. Such a transformation yields a richer language whose meaning-rules have a total scope that properly includes the total scope of the meaning-rules of the poorer language.

We now recapitulate. Whatever alteration of the total scope of the meaning-rules follows the introduction of new expressions necessarily changes the meaning-specification of the language insofar as the new meaning-specification comprises coordinations between the new expressions and their meaning, as well as coordinations between the old expressions and their meaning. However, no alteration of the meaning-coordination of the old expressions occurs only in case either (1) the new language is disconnected; or (2) the newly-introduced expression is identical in meaning with an old expression; or (3) the original language is open respecting the new.

If by the introduction of one or more expressions, a language S goes into a language S' with respect to which S is open, then we say: language S' 'closes to' language S' and, reciprocally, language S' 'opens to' language S. If a language S closes to the language S', and if S' itself is a closed language, we say: language S 'completely closes to' language S'.

Can an open language S close to different connected languages? This is quite possible, unless the addition of a single expression completely closes S. For then, by adding to the open language S an expression W or expression V or both, we partially close S to S_W or to S_V or to $S_{W,V}$, etc. Eventually, by such extensions with constantly new expressions, we arrive at a completely closed language.

Is this the only way we can close an open language to a connected one? If so, for each open language there is just one closed connected language to which the open language can close. But this in turn leads to paradoxical results, as we shall now show. Assume that, upon introducing several expressions (among them W_1 and W_2), the open language S completely closes to a language S'; and further, that the meaning-specification of S' coordinates meaning d_1 with W_1 and meaning d_2 with W_2. Now consider another language S'' which differs from S' in just one respect, viz. the meaning-specification of S'' coordinates meaning d_2 with W_1 and meaning d_1 with W_2. Clearly, it is just as possible for the open language S to close to S'' as to S'. Otherwise, in such an open language as that of the sentential calculus based on the primitive signs '$\supset$' and '$\sim$' (but having no defined signs) the signs '$\vee$' and '.' could be introduced with their usual meanings, but could not be introduced with their meanings interchanged.

This result so radically contravenes our general understanding of meaning that we rule out the originating situation and maintain that an open language can completely close to two different connected languages.

Now let us examine the relation between two different closed connected languages S' and S'' if there is an open language S which completely closes to both S' and S''. In the case studied above, S'' was obtained from S' by interchanging the meanings of expressions W_1 and W_2; hence we were concerned with languages which translate into each other. We call language S' a 'translation' of language S'' in case the expressions of S' can be coordinated univocally with the expressions of S'' in such a way that coordinate expressions have the same meaning. Thus the question arises: if an open language S completely closes to two distinct closed connected languages S' and S'', are S' and S'' necessarily translations of each other?

To answer this question, we must give closer attention to the notion of translation.

9. *Synonyms and Translations*

First we state a necessary condition for the identity of meaning – or synonymity – of two expressions A and A' of the same language S. The condition runs as follows: If in S expressions A and A' have the same meaning, then in the total scope of the meaning-rules of S expressions A and A' behave as isotopes, i.e. the total scope of the meaning-rules is not altered if, in all its members, occurrences of A are replaced by A', and those of A' by A.

This last means: (1) if there is an axiomatic meaning-rule which requires acceptance of sentence Z forthwith, then there is also another axiomatic meaning-rule which similarly requires acceptance of the sentence obtained from Z by replacing A by A' and A' by A; (2) if there is a deductive meaning-rule which requires inference from a sentence (or sentence-class) Z_1 of the sentence Z_2, then there is also another deductive meaning-rule which requires inference from the sentence (or sentence-class) obtained from Z_1 by exchanging A and A' of the sentence obtained from Z_2 by exchanging A and A'; and (3) if there is an empirical meaning-rule which on the basis of certain data requires acceptance of sentence Z, then there is also another empirical meaning-rule which on the basis of the same data requires acceptance of the sentence obtained from Z by replacing A by A' and A' by A.

It should be remarked here that the identity of meaning of two expressions is not the same as the equivalence of two expressions. We say two expressions A and A' are equivalent in case to each true sentence containing A there corresponds another true sentence which is like the first except that A has been replaced by A' and A' by A. Two expressions can be equivalent in this sense without having the same meaning, however, e.g. while the expressions '$a \supset b$' and '$\sim a \vee b$' are equivalent in the Russell-Whitehead logistic, they do not have the same meaning there because the logistic provides a deductive rule of meaning for '$a \supset b$' (viz. the rule requiring inference of 'b' from '$a \supset b$' and 'a') and does not provide an analogous rule of meaning for '$\sim a \vee b$'.

By abstraction from the definition of the equivalence of two expressions, we secure a definition of the 'valence' of an expression. In the case of names, for example, this yields a definition of the scope of a name (in Mill's terminology, the denotation of a name).

We should not leave unmentioned certain consequences of our original necessary condition for the indentity of meaning of two expressions of the same language. These appear in connection with the question: Do two expressions A and B have the same meaning when they are made equal by definition? The answer to this question depends on how such a definition is construed.

If the definition is conceived as a rule of inference (e.g. a rule which permits acceptance of the sentence secured from a previously-accepted sentence by replacement of A by B or vice versa), then expressions A and B need not have the same meaning. To see how this follows from our necessary condition for the identity of meaning, consider a language with an axiomatic meaning-rule whose scope contains the sentence '$F(a)$'. Suppose this language does *not* have an axiomatic meaning-rule whose scope contains '$F(b)$'. And suppose the language has a deductive meaning-rule based on a definition which, in the way suggested above, sets 'a' equal to 'b'. Clearly whenever the rules of meaning of this language lead mediately or immediately to the acceptance of a sentence '$\varphi(a)$', they also lead (by the cited rule of meaning based on the definition '$a = b$') to the acceptance of '$\varphi(b)$'. In short, the meaning-rule based on the definition permits a free exchange of 'a' and 'b'. Despite this, however, 'a' and 'b' do not satisfy our original condition for the identity of meaning. While there is an axiomatic meaning-rule requiring unqualified readiness to accept '$F(a)$' as an axiom, there is no such rule requiring instant acceptance of '$F(b)$' as an axiom – even though '$F(b)$' follows deductively from '$F(a)$' and is thus a thesis in its own right because '$F(a)$' is an axiom.

If the definition is conceived not as a rule of inference but rather as a proposition *about* axioms and rules of inference, then an altogether different answer is given to our question, whether two expressions satisfy the necessary condition for identity of meaning when they are set equal by definition.

The definition which makes 'A' and 'B' identical may be thought of as a proposition which declares: "From now on, each rule of inference should assert of 'B' the same thing it asserts of 'A', and to each axiom '$\varphi(A)$' which holds for 'A' should correspond a sentence '$\varphi(B)$' which holds for 'B' and which likewise is an axiom". When the definition is so conceived, the equated expressions 'A' and 'B' satisfy the necessary condition for identity of meaning (at least in the discursive languages).

It seems that in deductive systems, at least, definitions are never conceived in the second way, i.e. as propositions about the axioms and rules of inference. Rather, they are held to function either as rules of inference or as assertions of the system (this last occurring but rarely). Our necessary condition for identity of meaning thus *cannot* be satisfied by two expressions which are definitionally equated in a deductive system. We have been careful to note this consequence, because it may perhaps be considered an invalidation of our asserted necessary condition. That (possibly dubious) condition can be altered without difficulty into a form which does not lead to the consequence just mentioned. One would simply take our original necessary condition as one alternative and definitional identity as the other.

Now let us take up the matter of the identity of meaning of two expressions which belong to different languages. If expression A in language S has the same meaning as expression A' in language S', then we call expression A' a 'translation' of A from language S into language S'. The relation 'is a translation of' is reflexive, symmetric and transitive.

Assume that an expression A' is a translation of expression A from language S into language S'. Suppose further that in language S expression A enters into a multitude of direct meaning-relations with other expressions

$A_1, A_2, ..., A_n$; relations with certain syntactic forms; and even relations with certain data of experience. Now the following assertion seems entirely compatible with the usual notion of translation: If A' is a translation of A from language S into language S'; and if in S, moreover, A has direct meaning-relations with expressions $A_1, A_2, ..., A_n$, which latter expressions likewise have translations $A'_1, A'_2, ..., A'_n$ into language S'; then in language S', expression A' must have with $A'_1, A'_2, ..., A'_n$ direct meaning-relations which severally are analogous to those A has with $A_1, A_2, ..., A_n$ in language S.

This assertion, for example, justifies the following remarks. Suppose an axiomatic meaning-rule prescribes the instant acceptance of a sentence made up from expression A and other expressions A_1 and A_2 according to a syntactic form K. Suppose that S' is a translation of A. Then, if there are also translations A'_1 and A'_2 of A_1 and A_2, and a translation K' of the syntactic form K, the language S' must validate a meaning-rule which requires instant acceptance of the sentence made up from A', A'_1 and A'_2 according to the syntactic form K'. (The syntactical forms admitted by a language – forms of expressions which comprise more than one word – are determined by the rules of syntax of the language and are as peculiar to that language as its vocabulary. Thus these forms undergo translation just as words do.)[7]

Our last example involving an axiomatic meaning-rule is typical. If an expression of a language is to be translatable into another language, the meaning-rules of the former must be coordinated with analogous meaning-rules of the latter.

We have one more observation to make before giving the original assertion a more precise formulation. We stated above, as a condition for expression A' to be a translation of A from S into S', that if A has direct meaning-relations with $A_1, A_2, ..., A_n$, then A' must have analogous meaning-relations with translations of $A_1, A_2, ..., A_n$ (in case expressions $A_1, A_2, ..., A_n$ have translations into language S'). Now the restriction of this condition by the proviso 'in case expressions $A_1, A_2, ..., A_n$ have translations into language S'' is necessary only if we do not confine our attention to closed languages, but consider open languages as well. Indeed, from the definition of a closed language S' it follows at once that if there is a translation of expression A from S into S', then likewise there are translations from S into S' of all those expressions in S with which A has direct meaning-relations. Were our attention confined to closed languages only, we could omit the proviso which is at present part of the restriction.

Now recall our original assertion, to the effect that if an expression A of language S has direct meaning-relations with expressions $A_1, A_2, ..., A_n$, the translation of A from S into S' must have analogous meaning-relations with the respective translations of $A_1, A_2, ..., A_n$. Meaning-relations are reflected in the scopes of meaning-rules, and thus in their total scope. Hence, by restricting ourselves to closed languages, we may reformulate our assertion as follows: If S and S' are closed languages, and if A' is a translation of A from S into S', then all those members of the total scope of the meaning-rules of S' which contain A' must be constructible from those members of the total scope of the meaning-rules of S which contain A, the construction to be such that A is represented everywhere by A', and the other expressions and syntactical forms of S which are involved are similarly represented by their translations.[8]

Let us contrast languages which are translatable into one another with languages which are not so translatable. (In this connection, we consider only literal or faithful word-for-word translations and not – as might also be the case – faithful sentence-for-sentence translations.) Two languages are called 'translatable' into each other just in case to each expression of one language there corresponds one or more expressions of the other which are its translations from the one language into the other, and conversely.

We make the following claim. If S and S' are both closed and connected languages, and if in language S' there is an expression A' which is a translation of an expression A from language S into language S', then S and S' are translatable into each other.

Suppose this claim were not true. Then there would be an expression A_n in S with no corresponding translation in S', or vice versa. But if an expression of one closed language is not translatable into another such language, then all expressions of the first language directly meaning-connected with the given expression also are not translatable. Consider an expression A_x directly meaning-related to A_n. If A_n cannot be translated from S into S', then A_x likewise cannot be translated. The reason is that if A_x had a translation in S' (assumed to be closed), so would all expressions of S (among them, A_n) which are directly meaning-connected with A_x; and this last contradicts our presupposition that A_n has no translation.

Similarly, the A's directly meaning-connected with A_x are not translatable; and so on. All these latter expressions indirectly meaning-relate with A_n in one or more steps. Hence if A_n is not translatable, all expressions which indirectly or directly meaning-connect with A_n are likewise not translatable.

Now, let 'S_1' designate the set of those expressions of language S which are meaning-connected with A_n; and 'S_2' the set of remaining expressions of S. Set S_1 consists exclusively of untranslatable expressions; hence it does not contain expression A, which by assumption is translatable. Set S_2 therefore is not empty. Further, no expression in S_2 can be meaning-connected with any expression in S_1, for otherwise such an expression would meaning-relate with A_n and so belong to S_1. Thus, A being translatable and A_n not, it follows that the totality of expressions of language S divides into two non-empty sets with no meaning-connections whatever between expressions in different sets. Language S is therefore not connected, in contradiction to our original assumption regarding S.

We have proved: If S and S' are closed connected languages, and if an expression of one translates into the other, then *all* expressions of the one language translate into the other.

Finally, now, we can take up the question whether an open language can close to two different languages which themselves are closed and connected and not translatable into each other. The preceding discussion makes clear that this is impossible. If it were, there would be two closed connected languages, each having some expressions which translate into the other (viz. those expressions the two languages have in common with the open language) and some expressions which do not so translate. Our previous result makes this situation impossible.

From the investigations above, it follows that every meaning occurring in a closed connected language also occurs in *every* language which is reciprocally translatable with it, and does *not* occur in any other closed connected language. In other words, the system of all meanings occurring in a closed connected language overlaps with no other such system. We call that system of meanings a 'conceptual apparatus' Anyone who uses a language which simultaneously involves meanings from two different conceptual apparatuses is thereby committed to using a non-connected language.

10. *An Attempt at a Definition of 'Meaning'*

The discussion to this point has relied not on a definition of 'meaning', but on the common understanding of this term. We made certain assertions regarding the subject of meaning and (after defining several technical terms) drew from these assertions further conclusions.

Now we propose to define 'meaning'. The definition will be such that from it all our previous assertions can be rigorously derived.

We do not intend to 'validate' this definition, i.e. to show its conformity with the generally accepted notion of meaning. Indeed, because the 'generally accepted notion of meaning' is so vague, it is not possible for a precise definition to reflect such an imprecise common notion. And if we want a precisely defined concept — as we do — it is not even desirable to have our definition conform entirely to the popular notion of meaning. Nevertheless, we shall try to arouse within the reader the feeling that our definition does justice to the most essential significations of the ordinary word 'meaning'.

Two remarks are in order at the outset. The proposed definition will be made sketchily and with no claim to completeness. Again, when we speak of 'languages' in what follows, we shall be referring only to closed connected languages. Closed connected languages alone deserve the designation 'language', for the so-called 'open' languages are really but fragments of closed languages; and non-connected languages are merely loose conglomerations of several connected languages.

We begin by sketching some preliminary definitions. The term 'language' refers to a construct which is uniquely determined by a class of signs and a matrix elaborated out of these signs and possibly also out of perceptual data. (This matrix corresponds to the total scope of the meaning-rules.) Members of the sign-class co-determining a language are called 'expressions of the language'.

The matrix of a language is a table consisting of three parts. The first part corresponds to the sum of the scopes of all axiomatic meaning-rules; the second, to the sum of the scopes of all deductive meaning-rules; and the third, to the sum of the scopes of all empirical meaning-rules.

The first part of the matrix may be envisaged as a vertical array of horizontal lines. To each of these lines corresponds a different member (i.e. a sentence) of the scope of some axiomatic meaning-rule of the language. Each line is a finite sequence of expressions; and the sequence comprises all the expressions which appear in the corresponding sentence or axiom. The constituent expressions of any such sequence are ordered according to their syntactical arrangement in the corresponding axiom-sentence. This principle of syntactic order might be phrased as follows: first, the entire sentence; second, the designation of the main functor of the sentence; third, the first argument of this main functor; fourth, its second argument, etc. Each argument is then replaced by a sub-sequence constructed according to the same principle, and so on until no composite arguments remain. Two examples may serve to illustrate this ordering principle.[9] The conjunction 'Jack loves Mary and Joe loves Annie' yields the following sequence: (1) 'Jack loves Mary and Joe loves Annie', (2) 'and', (3) 'Jack loves Mary', (4) 'loves', (5) 'Jack', (6) 'Mary', (7) 'Joe loves Annie', (8) 'loves', (9) 'Joe', (10) 'Annie'. The equivalence '$p \vee q . \equiv . \sim p \supset q$' yields the sequence: (1) '$p \vee q . \equiv . \sim p \supset q$', (2) '$\equiv$', (3) '$p \vee q$', (4) '$\vee$', (5) '$p$', (6) '$q$', (7) '$\sim p \supset q$', (8) '$\supset$', (9) '$\sim p$', (10) '$\sim$', (11) '$p$', (12) '$q$'.

The second part of the matrix – the part related to the deductive meaning-rules – again may be envisaged as a vertical array of horizontal lines. To each line corresponds a member of the scope of some deductive rule of meaning. But now, each line is an ordered pair of sequences of expressions. The first sequence of the pair is derived from the first element of the corresponding member of the scope of a deductive meaning-rule, the derivation being identical with our previous one for producing the sequences associated with axioms. The second sequence of the pair is derived in similar fashion from the second element of the corresponding member.

The third part of the matrix is also a list of ordered pairs. Each of these ordered pairs has for its first element a datum of experience, and for its second element a sequence of expressions which is derived (as above) from the sentence coordinated with this datum by some empirical rule of meaning.

We cannot illustrate the notion of a matrix by exhibiting the matrix of an actual extant language; this would be too difficult. However, we can illustrate the notion by inventing a language with a small number of expressions. Suppose we make up a language with, say, just eleven expressions (designated by the first eleven letters of the alphabet). Let us narrow to three (say 'α', 'β', 'γ') the number of experiential data necessary for this language. The matrix of this language might then appear as follows:

The axiomatic part:
$$\begin{cases} a\,b\,c \\ d\,k\,a\,b\,c\,e\,f\,g \end{cases}$$

The deductive part:
$$\begin{cases} a\,b\,c, & e\,f\,g \\ d\,k\,a\,d\,c\,e\,f\,g, & i\,j\,b \\ e\,f\,g, & h \end{cases}$$

The empirical part:
$$\begin{cases} \alpha, & h \\ \beta, & e\,f\,g \\ \gamma, & h \end{cases}$$

This table makes it plain that there are only five sentences in our invented language, viz. a, d, e, h, i. Sentence a contains the expressions b and c. Sentence e contains the expressions f and g. Sentence h consists of a single word. Sentence d connects a with sentence e by the functor sign k. And finally, sentence i contains the expressions j and b. The whole matrix also implies: (1) that the scope of the axiomatic meaning-rules consists of two sentences, viz. a and d; to avoid violating the meaning-specification of our invented language, one must be prepared to accept these two sentences unconditionally; (2) that one must be ready to infer e from a, i from d, and h from e, in accordance with the deductive meaning-rules, if the meaning-specification of the language is not to be violated; and (3) that one must accept both sentence h (in view of experiential data α and γ) and sentence e

(in view of the experiential datum β), according to the empirical meaning-rules, if again the meaning-specification of the language is not to be violated.

Now let us define the 'translatability' of two languages in which, for simplicity, synonyms are supposed not to occur. (A definition accounting for languages which do contain synonyms is introduced in the small print below.) We say S and S' are translatable into each other by R if and only if: both S and S' are languages; R is a one-to-one correspondence which associates with each expression of S an expression of S', and vice versa; and the correspondence R is such that under it (i.e. by the replacement of expressions of one language with their R-associates in the other language) the matrix of S transforms into the matrix of S' and the matrix of S' transforms into the matrix of S.

Two expressions of a language are called 'synonymous' in case they are isotopic respecting the matrix of the language (i.e. in case the matrix is unchanged, apart from the order of its lines, when the two expressions are exchanged in it).

To account for languages which contain synonyms, our definition of translatability would be rephrased as follows. We say S and S' are translatable into each other by R if and only if: (1) both S and S' are languages, and for each separately the totality of its expressions can be partitioned into two subclasses in such a way that the first class is free of synonyms (i.e. no two of its member-expressions are synonymous) and the second class — which could be empty — contains only expressions having synonyms in the first class; (2) R is a one-to-one correspondence which associates with each expression of the first subclass of S an expression in the first subclass of S', and vice versa; and (3) the correspondence R is such that under it (i.e. by the replacement of expressions of the first subclass of one language with their R-associates in the first subclass of the other language) the transform of the S-matrix differs from the transform of the S'-matrix at most with respect to isotopic expressions.

One matrix is said to be differentiated from another 'at most with respect to isotopic expressions' in case both matrices transform into the same matrix under the following operation. From *each* set of isotopic expressions, choose one (say, a); now strike from the matrix all lines which contain an expression isotopic with a, retaining those lines which contain a but no expression isotopic with a.

At this point, we define: A in S is identical in meaning with A' in S' if and only if both S and S' are languages; A is an expression of S and A' an expression of S'; and there is a correspondence R such that S and S' are translatable into each other by R, and the relation R holds between A and A'.

The relation of meaning-identity defined above is an equivalence relation, i.e. it is reflexive, symmetric and transitive. On the basis of this relation, therefore, one can by abstraction define 'meaning' for expression. A loose definition of this property would perhaps run as follows: The meaning of A in S is such a property of A in S that it also attaches to A' in S' if and only if A' in S' is identical in meaning with A in S.

All languages translatable into one another have matrices which map onto one another. Of such matrices we can say that they have the same structure, i.e. are isomorphic.

The notion of matrix-structure is made clearer if we adopt a numerical designation of the places occupied by expressions in a matrix. Let us accept the following conventions. Using arabic numerals and beginning at the top with '1', number down consecutively the sequences which comprise the vertical array of horizontal sequences in the first (axiomatic) part of the matrix. Do the same thing for the second (deductive) part, with this modification: since each horizontal line is now an ordered pair of sequences, give *one* prime to the number to indicate its reference to the first sequence of the pair, and *two* primes to the number to indicate its reference to the second sequence of the pair. For the third (empirical) part, use roman numerals and, beginning at the top of this verbal array with 'I', number the horizontal sequences consecutively. By these agreements, so to speak, we fix the vertical location of a place in the matrix. The horizontal location in any particular sequence is fixed by beginning at the left with the arabic numeral '1' and numbering consecutively the constituent expressions of the sequence. This last agreement has one exception; the experiential datum which stands at the head of a horizontal sequence in the third part shall always be assigned the horizontal coordinate '0'.

These agreements enable us to specify any position in a matrix unambiguously by means of an ordered pair of the form '(a, b)', where 'a' designates the sequence containing the position (i.e. 'a' is the vertical coordinate) and 'b' the location of the position in sequence a (i.e. b is the horizontal coordinate). Thus (II,0) locates the experiential datum which heads the second sequence in the third (empirical) part of a matrix. Again, e.g. all the locations of expression e in the matrix proposed above in our invented language are specified by the following list:

$$(2,6), \quad (1",1), \quad (2`,6), \quad (3`,1), \quad (II,1).$$

Hereafter, we shall refer to such number-pairs as 'positions' of a matrix.[10]

Now suppose we tell someone (who understands our number-pair scheme for specifying the positions of a matrix) just what positions are to be filled by the same expression. We might do this as follows. Divide the positions of the matrix into classes in such a way that the positions of a particular class are all filled in the same way and two positions of different classes are filled in different ways; and then tell the individual what these classes are. Further, suppose we tell this individual what data of experience he is to put in the '(roman numeral, zero)'-places. At this point our subject is in a position to select from all possible matrices those which suit the given information. The matrices he selects will differ at most in word-sounds and will transform into each other under one-to-one dictionary substitutions. I.e. on the basis of the information we have given him, the individual can discard the matrices of languages not translatable into a given language. Our information consisted in all and only that which is *common* to the matrices of all languages translatable into a given language; it properly omitted mention of just those properties which differentiate one individual matrix from another.

Let us look more closely at what our information specified, i.e. at the feature (called the 'structure') common to the selected matrices. Our information specified the classes of positions which are to be filled by the same expressions (hereafter, for brevity, we call these classes 'equivalence classes of positions'), and it specified coordinations between certain data of experience and '(roman numeral, zero)'-places. Thus we can say: The system[11] consisting of all equivalence classes of positions and of coordinations between experiential data and '(roman numeral, zero)'-places constitutes the structure of the matrix.

We have called the 'meaning of A in S' that property which A in S has in common with all and only those A' in S' which have the same meaning as A. It appears from the above that this property amounts to filling one of the positions of an equivalence class of positions in a matrix of given structure. A particular meaning is therefore determined unambiguously by the specifying of a structure for a matrix and an equivalence class of positions. One thus would be inclined to equate meaning with the couple 'equivalence class, structure' on the ground that when a matrix-structure is specified so also is specified the aggregate of all 'equivalence class, structure'-couples, and hence the class of *all* meanings proper to the expressions of a language of this structure; and conversely. Recalling our earlier term 'conceptual apparatus' (which we introduced as a designation of the class of all meanings attaching to the expressions of a closed connected language), we can reformulate this last observation as follows: a matrix-structure determines a conceptual apparatus, and conversely.

The question now arises, what kind of matrices would someone select if he were given the equivalence classes of positions and – instead of the coordinations between experiential data and '(roman numeral, zero)'-places – merely classes of '(roman numeral, zero)'-places to be filled in the same way. Matrices selected on the basis of such information would be differentiated not only with respect to the wording of their expressions but also with respect to what experiential data appear in what '(roman numeral, zero)'-places. Hence the selected matrices would not be the matrices of languages translatable into each other. These languages, however, would be differentiated at most with respect to their empirical rules of meaning; they would agree in respect to their discursive rules of meaning (recall that 'discursive' means 'non-empirical').

We call the set of all equivalence classes of positions the 'discursive structure' of a language; and similarly, the set of all classes of '(roman numeral, zero)'-places the 'empirical structure' of a language.

Because no empirical rules of meaning apply in them, the structure of the languages of purely mathematical systems (e.g. geometry) is coextensive with their discursive structure. Every language which possesses an empirical structure and which has a discursive structure identical with that of some mathematical system constitutes an empirical interpretation of the language of that mathematical system.

11. *On the Customary Notion of a Language*

Many of the assertions which underlie the conclusions of this paper will seem false to a reader who understands by 'language' what one thinks of when referring to '*the* German language' or '*the* French language' or '*the* Polish language', etc. Consider, e.g. one of our first theses, the one claiming that two persons do not use the same language if they attach a different meaning to the same expression. Suppose two individuals speak English without violating either English phonetics or English syntax. Suppose their meaning-specifications agree respecting all words, with one exception: by the word 'star', one of them understands fixed stars only while the other understands both fixed stars and planets. Would it be said of these individuals that one of them speaks English and the other does not? Hardly. If two people use the same sounds with different meaning, we would say they did not speak the same 'language' only when their respective meaning-specifications become decidedly different. If their meaning-specifications are very similar, though somewhat different, we would say they speak the same 'language' (taking the word 'language' in its usual sense, of course).

It follows that the customary notion of '*a* language' is vague to the same degree as 'very similar'. For this reason, the customary notion of a 'language' is about as useless for the semasiological investigations we have undertaken here as 'hot' and 'cold' would be for physics or 'big and 'little' for mathematics. Our strict concept of a language has the same relation to the customary notion of a language as the chemist's concept of water has to the popular notion of water.

Our concept 'language' requires for its unequivocal characterization not a more or less determinate coordination between word and meaning, but rather a completely explicit meaning-specification. If we maintain this strict conception of a language, we cannot say there is *one* English language. We would assert, rather, that there are many English languages; and that, while they may actually use the same sounds and words, these various English languages are differentiated by the coordination of word and meaning (even though their differences may be slight). Indeed, we can enumerate several English languages in common use which (apart from different dialects and historical phases) employ the same words and sounds: a medical English language, a physical English language, etc., etc.

The epistemologist forgets — and often the oversight is fatal — that a language is not *a* language in our sense of the term, but rather, strictly speaking, a multiplicity of languages. According to our terminology, no ambiguous words can occur in a language because a language is unambiguously determined only when there is an unambiguous coordination between expression and meaning. A single ambiguous word points to the existence of two languages whose sounds and words are the same and whose coordinations between word and meaning differ at *one* point only.

By keeping in mind the distinction between the strict concept designated 'language' and the customary notion going by the same name, we probably can vacate the arguments against the assertion that in each language certain rules of meaning are unambiguously determined. In what is *customarily* called a 'language', the meaning-specification is not absolutely fixed and so the rules of meaning (in which the meaning-specification manifests itself) are not unambiguously determined. Such languages have rules of meaning which are as flexible as the meaning-specifications. But this is not the case in what is *strictly* called a 'language', i.e. when the meaning-specification is exactly determined. Consider, e.g. the languages of rigorously deductive systems and the languages of symbolic logic. The meaning-rules of these languages can be determined easily and precisely by means of their axiom and inference schemata. Thus, e.g. the language of a logistic system is a language in the strict sense, although it is almost always an open language.

NOTES

[1] [See the present volume p. 67 — Editor]
[2] E. Husserl, *Logische Untersuchungen*, vol. II, Part I (2nd. revised edition, Niemyer, Halle, 1913), Section 1: *Ausdruck und Bedeutung*.
[3] In my paper *0 znaczeniu wyrazeń* (*On the Meaning of Expressions*), Commemorative Volume of the Polish Philosophical Society, 12.2.1904 — 12.2.1929, Lwów, 1931), I attempted to set up such a definition. A definition somewhat different from this will be proposed later in the present paper.
[4] Carnap has recently called attention to the connection between the meaning of an

expression and the criteria of sentences in which it occurs. (Cf. Carnap, 'Überwindung der Metaphysik durch logische Analyse der Sprache', *Erkenntnis* 2 (1931), 219–241.) There Carnap refers to analogous views in Wittgenstein's *Tractatus logico-philosophicus* (Kegan Paul, 1922); "the meaning of a sentence lies in its truth-criterion".

[5] Regarding a sentence Z of a language S, suppose there is no rule of meaning of S which is essential for Z. Is Z decidable in principle? We call a sentence of a language 'decidable in principle' if it is either positively or negatively decidable in principle. Further, we say of a sentence of a language that it is 'positively decidable in principle' if: either it is a member of the scope of an axiomatic rule of meaning; or it is a member of the range of an empirical rule of meaning; or it is the second element of an ordered pair which is a member of the scope of a deductive rule of meaning and which has as its first element one of a class of sentences that are themselves positively decidable in principle. (The apparent circularity of this definition can be removed by reformulating it recursively, i.e. as a *Ketten-Definition*.) Finally, in case the denial of a sentence is positively decidable in principle, we say of the sentence that it is 'negatively decidable in principle'.

Now suppose sentence Z, for which its language S has no essential rule of meaning, is nevertheless decidable in principle. In this case every sentence of S must be positively decidable or else negatively decidable, according as Z is positively or negatively decidable. Such is the case because then all the meaning-rules of S which concern Z would be inessential for it, and as such would say the same thing about Z as about all other sentences of S. Languages in which all sentences are decidable in the same direction are self-contradictory if they contain negation. Let us exclude every language in which all sentences are decidable in the same direction. Then we must say that *a sentence for which no rules of meaning are essential is undecidable in principle*. The converse of this assertion is not valid, however. It may happen, e.g., that neither an axiomatic nor an empirical rule of meaning is essential for a sentence and yet that a deductive rule is, in the sense that the deductive rule simply involves the sentence in its domain and there treats the sentence distinctively. Such a sentence would be undecidable in principle, although a rule of meaning is actually essential for it. Let us say of a sentence of which no meaning-rule of its language is essential that it is 'void of meaning'. (We call an expression 'meaningless' if in general no rule of meaning concerns it; in such an event, the expression does not belong to the language.) Then we should state: *every sentence which is void of meaning is undecidable in principle, but not every sentence which is undecidable in principle is void of meaning*.

With decidability in principle we contrast decidability in fact. The latter, we hold, should be relativised to a prescribed set of perceptual data. Referring to a set G of data of experience, we would define a 'decidable in fact' sentence just as we did a 'decidable in principle' sentence, with only the following difference. Instead of 'it is a member of the range of an empirical rule of meaning', we now would say 'it is the second element of an ordered pair belonging to the scope of an empirical rule of meaning, the first element of which pair is a datum in G'.

[6] From now on 'expression' refers to simple words as well as composite expressions.

[7] In some logistic languages of sentential calculus, certain sentence functions are so written that the function sign stands in the middle, the first argument being to the left of the sign and the second, to the right (e.g. '$p \supset q$'). In other logistic languages, such formulations do not occur; rather, sentence functions appear with the function sign first, followed by its first argument and then by its second (e.g. Lukasiewicz's notation 'Cpq' – see his 'Philosophische Bermerkungen zu mehrwertigen Systemen des Aussagenkalküls', *Comptes Rendus des Séances de la Société des Sciences et de Lettres de Varsovie, Classe III*, 23 (1930), 51–77, Warszawa. One formulation translates into the other, i.e. 'pFq' is a translation of 'Fpq'.

[8] In this paper, we are taking 'translation' to refer to complete or literal (word) translation. One could speak, of course, of an incomplete translation, i.e. a sentence translation

which does not necessarily involve separate translation of the sentence's individual constituent words. To comprehend the latter type of translation within our study, we would have to relax somewhat our previous condition for one expression to be a translation of another. We would no longer want to demand that *all* meaning-relations holding for an expression in S be mirrored in the language into which the expression translates. The condition would be phrased rather in terms of a limited number of meaning-relations only (which, in turn, would require more accurate specification). We cannot go into the details of the programme here.

[9] [A more elaborate description of the scheme of syntactic ordering appears in Section 4 of Ajdukiewicz's paper *Syntactic Connexion*, supra. Cf. the present volume p. 122. (For the sake of clarity, this paragraph has been somewhat amplified over that of the original text.) Translator]

[10] [Some parts of this and the previous paragraph depart a little from the original text. Translator]

[11] We prefer the looser term 'system' to 'class', because, a coordination (logically, an ordered pair) not being of the same logical type as a class, there is no class which can contain both classes and coordination as its members. Instead of a 'system' we might use 'relation', having in mind here a relation whose domain is a unit class containing just the set of all equivalence classes of positions and whose range is a unit class containing just the set of coordinations described in the text.

3. THE WORLD-PICTURE AND THE CONCEPTUAL APPARATUS*

(1934)

1. *Purpose of the Investigation*

The principal thesis of ordinary conventionalism (as represented for example by Poincaré) is contained in the following statement:

> Some problems cannot be solved by appeal to experience without the introduction of a convention; it is only when experiential data are combined with convention that the problems become solvable.

According to this thesis, the judgments constituting such a solution are not imposed on us by experiential data alone. The acceptance of those solutions is in part a matter of our discretion, since by arbitrarily changing the convention which co-determines the solution we arrive at other judgments.

The purpose of this paper is to generalize and radicalize the thesis of ordinary conventionalism. Specifically, we wish to establish the assertion:

> Of all the judgments which we accept and which accordingly constitute our entire world-picture, *none* is unambiguously determined by experiential data; every one of them depends on the conceptual apparatus we choose to use in representing experiential data. We can choose, however, one or another conceptual apparatus which will affect our whole world-picture.

Otherwise put: only so long as an individual uses a *fixed* conceptual apparatus, will experiential data compel him to accept these judgments. He might employ another conceptual apparatus, on the basis of which the same experiential data would no longer compel him to accept these judgments, for in the new conceptual apparatus, the original judgments do not occur at all.

This, briefly and inexactly, is the principal thesis of the present work; it will be formulated precisely later on in the paper. Our view, which might be

* Translated from the German by John Wilkinson. First published in *Erkenntnis* IV (1934), 259–87. *Język i Poznanie*, I, 175–195. Reprinted here by kind permission of the publishers of *Erkenntnis* and the University of Chicago Press. Copyright © 1951 by University of Chicago Press.

referred to as 'radical conventionalism', is probably related to the views of the French philosopher LeRoy and perhaps to others.

We spoke above of judgments as of something which occurs in a conceptual apparatus. This reference is not to all judgments, but only to a class of judgments we call 'articulated judgments'. The significance of this term was explained in our paper 'Language and Meaning'.[1] The term 'conceptual apparatus' was also defined there. Our present study is based in general on the results obtained in that paper, and presupposes a knowledge of it.

At this point let us review briefly the most important concepts and results of the previous article which we need here.

First of all, it was claimed that the specification of the vocabulary and syntax is not sufficient to determine a language unequivocally, but that there is needed in addition the meaning-specification (coordination) of the language, i.e. the way in which meaning is coordinated in this language with its words and expressions. Then it was established that one can discover whether a person attaches to a certain sentence of a language the meaning coordinated with it in this language by putting the person into a situation (chosen with the sentence in mind) and noting whether he is prepared to accept the sentence in this situation, e.g. if a person, while in a situation where he genuinely experiences pain, is nevertheless not willing to accept the sentence 'it hurts', we are entitled to conclude that he does not attach to the sentence 'it hurts' the meaning coordinated with it by the meaning-specification of the English language. Thus rules can be set up, of which perhaps the purport might be: Only that person uses the sentences of a language in the meaning coordinated with them by the meaning-specification of S who is invariably prepared to accept a sentence of type T when he is in situation L.

We referred to such rules as *rules of meaning* (or meaning-rules) of the language. We distinguished three kinds of meaning-rules, to wit: (1) axiomatic rules of meaning (which specify the sentences whose rejection — irrespective of the situation of the rejector — indicates a violation of the meaning-specification of the language); (2) deductive rules of meaning (which specify of sentences of such a sort that a person, if he accepts the first, must be prepared to accept the second on pain of violating the meaning-specification of the language); and (3) empirical rules of meaning (which coordinate with certain experiential data certain sentences that — in view of the experiential data — one must be prepared to accept if he would avoid violating the meaning-specification of the language).

We maintain that the meaning-rules of a language are characteristic of that language. E.g. suppose an axiomatic meaning-rule holds in a language S whose vocabulary of words and expressions is identical with that of another language

S'; and further suppose this rule provides that he who rejects a certain sentence Z violates the meaning-specification of language S. Now if such a rule of meaning does *not* hold for language S', then the meaning-specifications of the two languages are different. For the same behaviour (i.e. the rejection of Z) violates the meaning-specification of S, but not the meaning-specification of S'.

Next, the following terminology was introduced. We call two expressions 'immediately (directly) meaning-related' if either (a) both occur simultaneously in one and the same sentence dictated by an axiomatic meaning-rule; or (b) both occur simultaneously in one and the same sentence-pair specified by a deductive meaning-rule; or (c) both occur simultaneously in one and the same sentence coordinated with an experiential datum by an empirical meaning-rule. A language is called connected in case its vocabulary of expressions is not decomposable into two non-empty classes such that no expression of one class is immediately meaning-related to any expression of the other class.

Further, we differentiated open and closed languages. A language is open in case there is another language containing all the expressions of the first and imparting to them their original meaning, which second language however contains expressions *not* occurring in the first (as regards either sounds or meanings) and at least one of these expressions is immediately meaning-related to an expression of the first language. A non-open language is called closed.

Open languages can have added to them new expressions (not synonymous with any of those already present) which are immediately meaning-related to expressions already present, without thereby altering the meaning of the expressions already present. Closed languages, on the contrary, become disconnected when there is added a new expression not synonymous with any of those already present.

It was shown that if both S and S' are closed and connected languages and if a certain expression of one language has a translation in the other, then both languages are translatable into each other (i.e. each expression of one has a translation in the other).

The set of all meanings which attach to the expressions of a closed and connected language was called the conceptual apparatus. Thus two conceptual apparatuses are either identical or entirely disjoint. It was asserted that every meaning is an element of some conceptual apparatus.

Finally, that notion of language with which we were concerned in our investigation was contrasted with the popular notion embodied in references to 'a German language' or 'an English language' or 'a Polish language', etc.

It was shown that, from our point of view, what one usually calls, e.g. the German language is not *a* language but a multiplicity of languages which differ at least in their meaning-specifications. For if two people use the same German sounds but attach slightly different meanings to them, one would still say (speaking popularly) that they speak the same language; according to our precise notion of the term 'language', however, these two would not be speaking the same language — to do so it is necessary that they attach to the same sounds *exactly* the same meaning.

2. *Hypotheses, Theories, and Factual Reports*

From what has been said, it follows that it is quite easy to pass from one language to another without leaving the basis of a particular so-called 'language'. The meaning attaching to the words undergoes alteration in this transfer, often without our conscious knowledge. Such a thing happens in ordinary life, but even oftener in the sciences as they develop. Let us take an example of it from the sciences.

Despite the retention of words and sounds unchanged, we can detect a change of language by employing as a criterion the alteration of the meaning-rules. If, e.g. there can be exhibited a sentence whose rejection at one time does not signify a violation of the meaning-specification of a language, but whose later rejection does signify such a violation, then we regard this event as evidence that a new axiomatic meaning-rule came into operation. Our point may be clarified in the following example.

Before Newton, the proposition 'A body upon which an uncompensated force acts, alters its velocity' was probably accepted. This proposition was based entirely on induction. The word 'force' had an anthropomorphic meaning; and the proposition was obtained by generalizing from individual cases. However, like any other inductive generalization, this proposition was at most a well-confirmed conjecture. If, at that stage of development of the language of physics, one had rejected the proposition instead of accepting it, the rejection would not have signified a violation of the meaning-specification specific to that physical language. Indeed, one would have rejected the proposition without compunction upon the occurrence of a single contrary instance. But today, so far as I can judge, no physicist would reject this proposition; and of anyone who does not accept it, it is said that he does not understand the word 'force' as the physical language bids him to.

This example indicates that the language of physics, while its words and sounds remain the same, has nevertheless changed in respect to meaning-specification. At one time it was possible to reject the proposition stated above; nobody would have seen in this rejection a violation of the language, which is to say, there was then no axiomatic meaning-rule requiring the acceptance of this sentence. In the later stage of the language, however, the situation has completely changed for our proposition: the meaning of the words used in it is now such as to demand unconditionally an acceptance of the sentence. We would describe this alteration of the language in our terminology by saying that in the later stage there had begun to hold for the language an axiomatic meaning-rule whose scope includes the proposition; and that this axiomatic meaning-rule did not hold in the first stage of the language.

More than one example could be given of this process, which in essence is that of raising what are initially inductive generalizations to the level of axioms. The process itself is evidence that an alteration has occurred in the meaning-specification of the language, and hence in the language. Perhaps it would be well to designate as *principles* those sentences which were once only provisionally accepted inductive generalizations, but which later — through alteration of the language — became theses accepted as axioms; and to reserve the designation *hypothesis* for those inductive generalizations whose rejection is not forbidden by the meaning-rules of the language (i.e. whose rejection is not a violation of meaning).[2]

I believe that many propositions of Euclidean geometry (considered as a branch of physics and not as a mathematical discipline), which today are regarded as self-evident, were at one time merely very probable inductive suppositions. Subsequently a change of language occurred whereby new axiomatic meaning-rules began to hold. These rules demanded a readiness to accept those geometric sentences without qualification. The sentences thereby became axioms.

Among the sentences accepted within a particular language a contradiction can arise. If the contradiction occurs between a sentence whose acceptance is required by a meaning-rule (and whose rejection is therefore forbidden) and another sentence which is accepted although its acceptance is not required by any meaning-rule, the contradiction may readily be removed without leaving the original language base. One simply abstains from accepting the sentence which is not dictated by a rule of meaning. This situation arises whenever an inductive hypothesis which has not been raised to the status of a principle comes into contradiction with sentences which stem from empirical and deductive meaning-rules. The contradiction is removed by renouncing the hypothesis. The case is different when the contradiction is between two sentences which are both dictated by meaning rules. Here the difficulty can be resolved only by leaving the language base whose meaning-rules compel acceptance of the two mutually contradictory sentences.

Such a case arises when, e.g. a sentence adopted as a principle and a sentence dictated by empirical meaning-rules (in conjunction with experiential data) lead by deduction to a contradiction. To free ourselves of the contradiction we must give up the language base in which the conflict arose and go over to another language. The transition, of course, cannot lead us into a language translatable into the original; for if the meaning-rules of the original language in conjunction with the experiential data have issued in a contradiction, then the meaning-rules of every language translatable into the original must also lead to a contradiction on the basis of the same experiential data — a contradiction which differs at most with respect to its phonetic or graphic appearence. To avoid having such contradictions forced on us by meaning-rules and perhaps experiential data, we must move to another language untranslatable with the first, i.e. we must forsake the conceptual apparatus of the first language and have recourse to some other conceptual apparatus. This change can preserve in the new language all phonetic features of one — or even both — of the two sentences which mutually contradicted themselves in the first language. But the meaning possessed by those two sentences in the first language must be lost to both of them. The meaning of a sentence having been called a judgment, clearly we retain in a transition from one conceptual apparatus to another neither the empirical judgment nor the judgment expressed in the principle-sentence of the first language.[3]

3. *Radical Conventionalism*

Now we have arrived at the principal thesis of our study:

> No articulated judgment is absolutely forced on us by the data of experience. Experiential data do indeed force us to accept certain judgments if also we are based in a particular conceptual apparatus. However, if we change this conceptual apparatus, we are freed of the necessity of accepting these judgments despite the presence of the same experiential data.

This formulation of our thesis is somewhat figurative, and will not satisfy anyone who likes strictly precise formulations. Those who are not so demanding may omit the sections immediately following between two asterisks.

* It is reasonable to ask what it means to say "A judgment is not forced on us by experience". How is the word 'forced' to be understood here? If it is a case of causal constraint, the negative part of our thesis simply seems trivial and the affirmative part (in which it is admitted that experience forces us to accept certain judgments if also we are based in a particular conceptual

WORLD-PICTURE AND CONCEPTUAL APPARATUS   73

apparatus) seems to be false. For clearly when experiencing a datum of experience, however sharply it may obtrude itself on our consciousness (as happens, e.g. during a tooth-extraction) we need not make any articulated judgment, i.e. a judgment adequately expressed in words; nor do we have to make one when we are 'tuned', so to say, to a given conceptual apparatus.

Such a view of our thesis we must reject entirely. In it we may have referred figuratively to a constraint, but we did not have in mind any causal constraint. We used 'constraint' only as a turn of phrase to lighten somewhat the all-too-heavy style of our exposition; we used it in the sense of a hypothetical relation.

Let us state our meaning more exactly, though not yet with complete precision. When we say "the experiential data E force us, if we are based in the conceptual apparatus B, to accept the judgment U" we mean "In the conceptual apparatus B there is a decision question (i.e. a question of the type 'yes, or no?') such that the only possible answer to it in the presence of experiential data E is the positive assertion of the judgment U; nothing else would qualify as an answer to this question". On the other hand, the phrase "The experiential data E force us absolutely (i.e. irrespective of the conceptual apparatus) to accept the judgment U" we take to mean "In every conceptual apparatus there is a decision question such that in the presence of experiential data E, the only admissible answer to it is the positive assertion of the judgment U".

This formulation can be further amplified if we remember that a decision question is one which admits of two answers only, one the positive assertion − and the other, the negative − of one and the same judgment. (This is why instead of 'decision question' we often say 'question posing a judgment as a problem'). For instance, the question asked in the interrogative sentence 'Is Europe a continent?' is such a decision question. To say that there is a decision question in a conceptual apparatus is to say that the judgment which this question concerns is present in the conceptual apparatus. One gives a solution of a decision problem if and only if one makes a judgment with either positive or negative assertion. Hence we can simplify our previous clarification as follows: "The experiential data E *force* a person who is based in the conceptual apparatus B to make the judgment U with positive assertion" means "In the conceptual apparatus B there is such a judgment X that if a person in the presence of data E does make the judgment X with positive or negative assertion, he thereby makes judgment U with positive assertion". If from our 'force'-phrases we remove the relativization to a conceptual apparatus and so say "The experiential data E force us (irrespective of the conceptual apparatus) to make the judgment U with positive assertion", this means "In each conceptual apparatus there is such a judgment X that if a person in the presence of the data E does make the judgment X with positive or negative assertion, he thereby makes the judgment U with positive assertion".

Radical conventionalism admits that experiential data 'force' us to make certain judgments, but only relative to a given conceptual apparatus. It denies, however, that experiential data force us, independently of the conceptual apparatus in which we are based, to any particular judgment whatever. In the light of the above, the meaning of the two statements is now clear.

The explications given suggest that the positive thesis needs proof. That thesis asserts: For certain experiential data E there is such a judgment U and such a conceptual apparatus B that in B occurs a judgment X such that if a person in the presence of the data E makes judgment X with positive or negative assertion, he thereby makes judgment U with positive assertion. Suppose there is a conceptual apparatus B proper to language S. Suppose there holds for S an empirical meaning-rule according to which only that person does not violate the meaning-assignment of S who in the presence of data E is prepared to accept the sentence Z (hence in the presence of E at least does not reject sentence Z). Let U be the meaning of Z in S. If all this be granted, we claim that the experiential data E force anyone based in the conceptual apparatus B to accept the judgment U, i.e. we claim that there exists in B a judgment X such that the positive or negative assertion of X in the presence of E is equivalent to the positive assertion of U. Now U itself is such a judgment X. For, first, U belongs to the conceptual apparatus B. Second, note that if a person in the presence of E makes judgment U with positive or negative assertion, he makes judgment U with positive assertion. In the presence of E, a judgment made with negative assertion could not be an assertion of U, i.e. it could not have U for its content. To make a negative judgment of content U, the person would have to proceed by rejecting a sentence W whose meaning in a language S' is formed from U (we are considering here only verbal judgment-processes) without violating by this rejection the meaning-specification of S'. But if W in S' has the meaning U, then W is a translation of Z from S into S'. Since it was presupposed that whoever in the presence of E rejects Z violates the meaning-specification of S, nobody in the presence of E can reject Z in S or a translation of Z from S into S' without thereby violating the meaning-specification of S or of S'. Hence in the presence of E one can make no negative judgment of content U. If, therefore, in the presence of E one makes the judgment U with positive or negative assertion, he can make it only with positive assertion.

It has been shown that under the specified presuppositions there is in the conceptual apparatus B such a judgment X that if one makes this judgment with positive or negative assertion one makes the judgment U with positive assertion. As we have indicated, U itself is such an X. Hence it has been established that there are judgments to whose acceptance anyone is forced by certain experiential data when he is based in a conceptual apparatus, provided only the presupposition of the proof above holds, i.e. if it is the case that there is a language with an empirical meaning-rule. Of course, we hold this last to be assured (at least for the simple empirical meaning-rules).

Now let us turn to the second thesis, which denies the absolute 'forcing' by experiential data of the acceptance of a judgment. The assertion is: For no judgment U and no experiential datum E does there exist in every conceptual apparatus a judgment X such that if a person in the presence of E makes judgment X with positive or negative assertion, he thereby makes judgment U with positive assertion.

Assume there is such a judgment X in the conceptual apparatus B. Then no such judgment can exist in another distinct conceptual apparatus B'. Otherwise, there would be in B such an X, and in B' such an X', that the positive or negative assertion of X in the presence of E would be equivalent to the positive assertion of U, and the positive or negative assertion of X' in the presence of E would also be equivalent to the positive assertion of U; and thus an assertion of X would necessarily be equivalent to an assertion of X'. In short, a judgment-process of content X is necessarily equivalent to a judgment-process of content X'. If two judgment-processes are equivalent, their contents are identical; thus X is necessarily identical with X'. Now X belongs to the conceptual apparatus B, and X' to the conceptual apparatus B' which is by assumption distinct from B. But two different conceptual apparatuses (considered as classes of all meanings of two closed connected untranslatable languages) have no common elements. Hence X must be different from X'. If, therefore, the positive assertion of U is equivalent, in the presence of E, to the decision made in regard to the question 'Whether X?', then it cannot be equivalent to the decision made in the presence of E regarding the question 'Whether X'?' whenever X and X' belong to distinct conceptual apparatuses.

We have now established the negative thesis of radical conventionalism, provided only it be agreed that there are two different conceptual apparatuses. This last matter is easily supported. One need simply allude to the conceptual apparatus of a strictly deductive system on the one hand, and on the other to that of a language equipped with empirical meaning-rules. Those two conceptual apparatuses cannot be identical, since one contains no 'empirical' meanings whereas the other does. Indeed, I believe it would not be difficult to show that there are two distinct 'empirical' conceptual apparatuses. In my opinion, e.g. the conceptual apparatus of classical physics and that of relativistic physics are instances in point. To justify this claim, however, one would have to write a special memoir. *

Before going further, we might eliminate a misunderstanding which could eventually arise. Perhaps someone might so construe our assertion as to understand that if a transition is made from one language to another untranslatable with the first (this, of course, involves a transition to a different conceptual apparatus), it might happen that while a certain sentence was true in our language, in the other language a sentence of the same meaning would be false. In other words, by the hocus-pocus of changing languages, one could contrive that the sentence 'This paper is white' would be true in one language whereas its translation in another language would be false. This would be a complete misapprehension. Up to this point, we have said nothing whatever about truth and falsity. Furthermore, while someone based in language S may be bound to accept a sentence Z in the presence of certain experiential data, we have not asserted that by appropriately choosing another language S' we can secure justification for rejecting the translation of Z from S to S' despite the presence of the same experiential data. This is certainly not our view. What we do assert is simply this, that by a change of language it can be brought about that while a person in the presence of certain experiential data may have been forced on the basis of some language to accept a certain sentence, in the changed language he no longer finds a sentence of the same meaning and thus does not violate the meaning-map of this new language if he refrains from accepting the original sentence and its translations.

One should not think, however, that this transition to another language, freeing us from the necessity of accepting a certain sentence, consists in moving to a new language too poor in words to verbalize the judgment which was the meaning of the sentence dictated to us by experiential data on the basis of the meaning-rules of the original language. This would be the case if the transition were effected by opening the first language: after the first language was opened, we might perhaps lack only words to express the judgment originally accepted. However, the transition we have in mind does not consist in opening the original language. The transition we have in mind is from one language to another which is in principle untranslatable with the first; and the opening of a language always leads to another language which is in principle translatable with the first.[4] The transition we have in mind consists not so much in a change of the words or in an impoverishment of the conceptual apparatus as in the choice of a new conceptual apparatus which in no single point coincides with the former conceptual apparatus. We consider this matter further below.

4. *Ordinary Conventionalism*

Now let us consider some objections which might be raised against our thesis. One such objection might be based on the distinction between sentences which report facts and sentences which interpret facts; let us call them report-sentences and interpretation-sentences, respectively. This distinction between sentences is found among the ordinary conventionalists, who hold that if a contradiction occurs between an accepted sentence (e.g. a hypothesis) and an interpretation-sentence, a person in the presence of fixed experiential data can maintain the accepted sentence and renounce the interpretation; but that if a contradiction occurs between any sentence and a report-sentence, the person cannot maintain the former at the expense of the latter.

Let us look a little closer at what the conventionalists understand by report-sentences and interpretations, e.g. the sentence 'The rod A is as long as rod B' is a report-sentence if it is accepted in a situation in which the person accepting the sentence actually sees both rods coincide, i.e. sees them in immediate congruence. However, the sentence 'The rod C is as long as the rod D' is not a report-sentence if the person accepting it does not see the two rods in immediate congruence; in this case, the acceptance of the sentence would constitute an interpretation. For the conventionalists hold it impossible (indeed, impossible in principle) to decide about this last sentence without assuming some convention regarding the comparison of rods not immediately adjacent to one another. On the other hand, they claim no convention is needed for deciding on the equality in length of two rods which coincide; that decision can be made without any convention.

The difference between a report-sentence and an interpretation-sentence consists in this, that for a decision regarding a report-sentence certain primitive criteria suffice, whereas for the decision concerning an interpretation-sentence these primitive criteria do not suffice, but further criteria are necessary, the selection of which depends on us. Thus, depending on the choice of additional criteria, it is allegedly possible to make different decisions regarding interpretation-sentences, but not in the case of report-sentences.

Let us grasp somewhat more clearly this difference between report-sentence and interpretations. What characterizes the difference is the way one arrives at a decision about them. Both are empirical sentences; experiential data are requisite to the decision about them. The difference consists only in this, that criteria which suffice for the acceptance of a report-sentence on the basis of certain experiential data are insufficient for a decision (i.e. an acceptance or a rejection) regarding the interpretation-sentence, no matter what experiential

data may be at our disposal. Thus, for empirical decisions regarding interpretation-sentences, new criteria must be added.

What are these criteria we have been talking about? I believe them to be a
matter of empirical rules of meaning. The criterion which suffices for
deciding the report-sentence quoted above is nothing but the empirical rule
of meaning which declares that whoever is not prepared seeing what is called
the coincidence of the two rods, A and B to accept the sentence 'Rod A is as
a long as rod B', does not attach to the expressions that meaning which is
coordinated with them by the language. According to the conventionalist,
these meaning-rules are insufficient for a decision regarding a sentence of the
interpretation type, whatever experiential data may be at our disposal.

The preceding discussion seems to justify the following definitions of
report-sentence and interpretation-sentence. A sentence is called a 'report-
sentence' if the empirical meaning-rules of one of the ordinary languages of
daily intercourse suffice in the presence of certain experiential data for a
decision about this sentence. Contrariwise, a sentence is called an 'interpretation-sentence' if in the presence of experiential data none of the meaning-
rules of ordinary language suffice for a decision regarding it, but, once certain
new meaning-rules have been added to those of ordinary language, there are
experiential data in whose presence the enriched system of meaning-rules
leads immediately or mediately (i.e. in one or more steps) to a decision about
this sentence. These additional meaning-rules are called 'conventions',
'coordinative-definitions', etc. (A convention is called a 'coordinative-defini-
tion' in case it is an empirical meaning-rule. However, conventions also can
be deductive meaning-rules and axiomatic meaning-rules.)

In view of the analysis above of the conventionalist distinction between
report-sentences and interpretation-sentences, can the priority of the first
be maintained? If our conception of report- and interpretation-sentences is
correct, then the only difference between them is this, that the rules of
meaning of an ordinary language suffice for decision regarding report-sentences
but do not suffice for any decision regarding interpretation-sentences, these
last however being empirically decidable on the basis of the meaning-rules
enriched by conventions. However, report-sentences would have a claim to
precedence over interpretation sentences only if the meaning-rules of the
ordinary language were more worthy of being observed than were the added
conventions. If someone in the presence of fixed experiential data submits
that he can free himself of certain interpretations by replacing one convention
by another, he should not be unaware of the fact that he can just as readily
free himself of report-sentences by altering the meaning-rules of his ordinary
language.

Thus the only differences between report-sentences and interpretation-sentences is that the former are decided in languages which are part of our upbringing, whereas the latter are decided in languages in whose construction we have consciously participated. From this point of view, the meaning-rules which enable us to decide about report-sentences appear at first glance to be unexceptionable, whereas the conventions necessary to a decision about interpretation-sentences seem to be alterable arbitrarily by us since we introduced them by willing them so.

Our point of view is significantly more radical than that of the conventionalism just discussed. We see no essential difference between a report-sentence and an interpretation-sentence. In our opinion, experiential data by themselves cannot force us to accept either one. We can avoid accepting such sentences (either as themselves or as translations) if we are willing to choose a conceptual apparatus in which their meaning does not occur. Thus, and it seems with some justification, we designate our point of view as that of a *radical conventionalism*.

5. *Rejection of the Tendency towards Universality*

Let us take up here another consideration which can be raised against our principal thesis. In this thesis we asserted that one can avoid the compulsion (stemming from certain experiential data) to accept a certain sentence of a language by going over to another language in which that particular sentence of the first language has no translation. As was mentioned earlier, this transition does not consist simply in opening the first language, i.e. the new language does not differ from the old simply in respect to the richness of its vocabulary of expressions (so that, after transition, we merely lack words to express the judgment which we found ourselves forced to accept on the basis of the first language). We said that the transition (in which the vocabulary of expressions may or may not be altered) is to lead us into another universe of meaning where the meaning of the initial sentence does not occur.

Now the question is, does the apparent success of this transition stem from the fact that thereby we rebase ourselves in too poor a universe of meaning?

Let us call the class of all meanings coordinated with the expressions of a language the 'universe of meaning' of the language. Suppose that the language in which as a basis we were forced by experiential data to accept the judgment U, was a connected but not necessarily closed language. The transition freeing us from the compulsion by experience to accept judgment U consists in the transition from the universe of meaning Σ_1 (which contains U and is part of a conceptual apparatus B_1) to the universe of meaning Σ_2 (which is part of a conceptual apparatus B_2 different from B_1). Such a transition has been characterized as one leading from one language to another language in principle untranslatable with the first. The conceptual apparatus B_2, being different from B_1, does not contain U; hence, *a fortiori*, Σ_2 does not contain U. Therefore, so to broaden Σ_2 to Σ_2' that U would occur in Σ_2' requires that Σ_2' consist of two universes of meaning which belong to different conceptual apparatuses. This in turn means that S_2', the language whose expressions are coordinated to the meanings comprising Σ_2', must consist of expressions which can be so divided into two classes that expressions of the first class belong to a closed connected language G_1, that expressions of the second class belong to a closed connected language G_2, and G_1 and G_2 are not translatable into each other. But such a language S_2' must be disconnected. Otherwise, a person could add to one of G_1 or G_2 the expressions of the other whose meanings are foreign to it without thereby disconnecting the first language or changing the meaning of its own expressions. This is impossible, however, as we showed in 'Language and Meaning'.

The discussion to this point makes clear that if one, in avoiding the necessity of accepting a certain judgment, moves from a language in which this judgment can be expressed to another in principle untranslatable with the first, he can enrich this new language by the expressions of the original judgment only at the expense of disconnecting the second language. And one ought to be very clear as to what it means to have a disconnected language.

In a non-connected language it is impossible, e.g. to utilize generally the formulas of logic. The use of these formulas depends on the rule of substitution, which permits us, e.g. on the basis of the formula '$p \supset p$' to accept a sentence of the form '$A \supset A$', where A is an arbitrary sentence. To the scope of the substitution meaning-rule, which corresponds with the substitution inference scheme, would belong all sentence-pairs of the form '$(p \supset p, A \supset A)$' where A is an arbitrary sentence. If such a rule holds in a language, then all the sentences of that language which can appear in place of A are in mediate meaning-relation with the formula '$p \supset p$' and hence stand in mediate meaning-relation to each other. Such a language would have to be connected, at least provided that each of its expressions occurs in some of its sentences (languages which do not satisfy the last condition are not considered here). A non-connected language would have to have a multiplicity of logics; these logics would have no relation to one another, and each would apply to a different universe of sentences provided there were logical formulas for each universe of sentences.[5] A universe of meaning which corresponds to a disconnnected language would comprise judgments which fall into various universes having between them no logical relations at all.

Let us call a language in which every judgment can be expressed a 'universal language', and the universe of meaning corresponding thereto a 'universal universe of meaning'. It follows from our previous remarks that a universal language is necessarily a disconnected language whose universe of meaning is a loose assemblage of conceptual apparatuses. We do not think that the development of science shows a tendency to a universal language or to a universal universe of meaning. Science seems, rather, to be developing towards a connected world-picture; and this is not consistent with a tendency to universality. If this is so, then it must be admitted that science proceeds as if it were putting blinkers on its eyes by including in its system just those judgments which belong to a single conceptual apparatus and leaving to one side judgments belonging to other conceptual apparatuses; and further, when a certain conceptual apparatus does not suit, by replacing it with one better suited to the goals of science without bothering about judgments which belong to the abandoned conceptual apparatus.

We have spoken above of how empirical meaning-rules depend not alone on experiential data, but on the chosen conceptual aparatus as well. Our remarks were confined to empirical meaning-rules, but they could have been made of non-empirical meaning-rules just as well. Thus a logic to which we defer at a particular stage seems necessary to us only because we are based in a certain conceptual apparatus; by changing the conceptual apparatus, we change the logic into another one. Herein lies the generalization of the thesis of radical conventionalism presented in the foregoing paragraphs.[6]

6. *The 'Truth' of Various World-Pictures*

We have spoken of the possibility of choice in the selection of a conceptual apparatus in which to express our world-picture. Assume that two men, Jack and Pete, each use a closed connected language, and that these two languages are not translatable into one another. Each of them expresses a world-picture, but the two world-pictures are different. No judgment accepted by Jack is accepted by Pete, and conversely; however, no judgment accepted by Jack is rejected by Pete, and conversely. The two world-pictures are different, but they do not collide with one another. The question arises, are both world-pictures true, or does only one of them deserve to be called true?[7]

Let us not discuss this question ourselves (since predication of the attribute 'true' is open to various antinomies, e.g. the antinomy of Eubulidus), but rather pass the investigation on to someone else — to an epistemologist whom we call '*E*'. About *E* we presume the following. *E* speaks a connected language S_e in which occur the elements of the language of the present paper. Further, in the use of the words of this language, *E* is guided by the same rules as we are; and in addition he has the word 'true' at his disposal. His use of 'true' is controlled by, among others, the following meaning-rule: only he does not violate the meaning-specification of language S_e who, having accepted a sentence Z of S_e, is on that basis prepared to accept the sentence 'Z in S_e is true'.

I believe that epistemologists who predicate the attribute 'true' of sentences are ready to submit to this meaning-rule leading from the acceptance of a sentence Z to the acceptance of the sentence 'Z is true in my language'.

If someone states with conviction the sentence 'The Vistula is a river', then additionally he is ready to state with conviction the sentence " 'The Vistula is a river' is true in my language". If a person does not behave this way, we consider it conclusive evidence that he does not understand by the word 'true' what is generally understood by it.

The addition 'in my language' is essential, because 'true' is here predicated of a sentence (not a judgment), and this sentence can occur in various languages, being perhaps 'true' as a sentence of one language and contrariwise not 'true' as a sentence of another language.

It should not be thought that an epistemologist who acknowledges this meaning-rule lays down thereby a claim to infallibility. Such a claim would consist rather in the declaration 'If I accept a sentence, then this sentence is true'. Acknowledgment of the indicated meaning-rule amounts to a different declaration, viz. 'If I accept a sentence, then additionally I am prepared to predicate of this sentence that it is true'. This readiness to designate as 'true' any sentence stated with conviction comports well with the modest doubt whether everything which I state with conviction and accordingly designate as 'true' is true.

The indicated meaning-rule permits our epistemologist E to make pronouncements about truth only with regard to sentences of his own language. We believe we can ask E to control the word 'true' with yet another meaning-rule, a rule which permits him to assign the attribute 'true' to sentences of languages other than his own. This meaning-rule runs: Only he does not violate the meaning-specification of language S_e who, having simultaneously accepted the premise 'Z is a translation of the sentence Z_x from language S_x into S_e' and the sentence Z, is on that basis prepared to accept the sentence 'Z_x in S_x in true'. According to this rule, e.g. one must characterize as true the sentence '*Die Sonne ist grösser als die Erde*' if one knows that the sentence 'The sun is larger than the earth' is a translation of the first sentence from the German language into the English language and if one states this English sentence with conviction.

Equipped with these meaning-rules, E now can face the problem of the 'truth' of sentences of his own language, and of those sentences of other languages of which he believes himself to know into what sentences of his own language they are to be translated. Let us assume moreover that E is as rich as possible in experience, and so is aware of all experiential data which in general men apprehend.

Suppose we ask E to decide in his language S_e a question which makes problematic a sentence dictated by an axiomatic meaning-rule of the language S_e. His decision must be to accept this sentence, for otherwise he would not speak language S_e. Next, at the very moment E experiences a datum D (to which, in a known way, an empirical meaning-rule of S_e coordinates sentence Z), we might ask him to decide a question which makes Z problematic. E's decision, if he makes one, must be to accept Z, for otherwise he would not speak language S_e. Again, holding before E several sentences Z_1, already accepted by him, we might ask him to decide a question which makes sentence Z_2 problematic (where, in a known way, Z_2 is coordinated as a conclusion to the Z_1 as premises by a deductive meaning-rule of S_e). Here, too, E will accept Z_2, for otherwise he would not speak S_e. From all this it is evident that one can, in principle, bring E eventually to accept every individual sentence of S_e which belongs to the linguistic world-picture of E's universe of meaning (of course, E must not die beforehand). E is forced to this on the basis of his conceptual apparatus (as we explained in Section 3 of this paper).

To illustrate the procedure just described, suppose E is asked to decide the question 'Is every A an A?', i.e. either to accept or reject the sentence (an axiom in S_e) 'Every A is an A'. On the assumption that E speaks S_e, it is clear that he must accept this sentence, since otherwise he would be violating the meaning-specification of S_e (which is to say, he would not be speaking language S_e).

As soon as E accepts a sentence which belongs to the world-picture of his language, we put to him the question: 'Is this sentence in S_e also true?'. E must answer this question affirmatively if he is to avoid violating the first of the meaning rules given above for the word 'true', i.e. if he is to speak the language S_e. In this fashion E is brought to characterize as 'true' each of the totality of sentences which comprise the world-picture of his language.

The same result follows if we ask E about the truth of the sentences which make up the world-picture of another language, different from S_e but translatable into S_e. He will translate these sentences into S_e and (in conformity with the second of the two mentioned rules governing 'true') pronounce them 'true'.

The two mentioned meaning-rules governing 'true' do not, of course, enable E to decide the truth of sentences untranslatable into his own language. If, while grounded in S_e (i.e., while based on the corresponding conceptual apparatus), E is able to pronounce 'true' or 'not true' of sentences untranslatable into his own language, it must be that he is conforming to a meaning-rule for 'true' which does not refer to the meaning of these sentences (since this meaning does not occur in his conceptual apparatus). It must be a meaning-rule enabling him to pronounce 'true' of sentences on the basis, e.g. of the external form of these sentences. It is doubtful whether anyone can institute for 'true' a meaning-rule which (like the one just suggested) makes no reference to meaning. In all likelihood no epistemologist would consider such a rule as squaring with his conception of 'true'.[8]

If we imagine another epistemologist E' who speaks a language S_e' untranslatable into S_e (in S_e' there occurs also the sound 'true' — or some other such — governed by meaning-rules analogous to those governing 'true' in S_e), then our second epistemologist E' would again characterize as 'true' those sentences of S_e' comprising his world-picture; but now the 'true' of S_e' no longer means the same as the 'true' of S_e.

To make the moral of this section clear, we shall speak loosely for a moment; we ask the reader to indulge us by not holding us accountable for every word. If an epistemologist would judge articulately (i.e. express his judgments in some language or other) then he must employ some conceptual apparatus and submit himself to the meaning-rules of a language coordinated with this conceptual apparatus. He cannot speak without speaking some language; he cannot articulate judgments without grounding himself in some conceptual apparatus. If he does in fact conform correctly to the meaning-rules of a language, then he will be compelled to accept all sentences to which the meaning-rules of the language (in combination with experiential data) lead; and, further, he will be compelled to declare these sentences 'true'. Of course, he can change his conceptual apparatus and his language. But when he does this he is compelled to make other judgments, and to accept other sentences and declare them 'true', although this second 'true' no longer has the same meaning as the first. In any case, we see no possibility for our epistemologist to take the neutral attitude of adopting no conceptual apparatus at all. He is stuck in some skin, even though he can change his skin like a chameleon.

7. *Evolutionary Tendencies of Conceptual Apparatuses*

Should we infer from what has been said that all conceptual apparatuses and world-pictures presented in them are equally good? Let us put this question off to the end of the paper; and once more (in what follows) ask the reader's indulgence in the matter of exact expression and rigorous proof.

'Good' (with the possible single exception of moral 'good') is a relative characterization meaning good for something. If one wants to distinguish the good, better and best among conceptual apparatuses, one must prepare for the question. To what end? For the biological welfare of the human species? To satisfy our desire for knowledge? Or some other desire? Here pragmatism is relevant as our last remarks suggest.[9]

To us, the most natural view is an evolutionary one. Thus we might put the question as follows: What conceptual apparatus is closer to the goal toward which science does in fact develop? When we speak here of the goal towards which science develops, we do not understand 'goal' anthropomorphically as something consciously striven for. We take the goal of science to be an idealized end stage to which the several stages of science approach closer and closer, much as the terms of a series approach its limit. Presumably this end stage can be determined from tendencies now apparent in the development of science.

Let us note briefly at this point some of what appear to us to be main tendencies in the development of science; and let us agree to call that conceptual apparatus 'better' in which these tendencies are realized to a greater degree.

For myself I discern four main tendencies in the development of science. The first appears in the fact that we promptly discard a language (or a conceptual apparatus) if it turns out to be contradictory. This appears not only in the modifications of scientific theories but also in the development of the ordinary languages of daily use. (From this standpoint, the difficulties encountered by the traditional theory of knowledge with the question of the so-called 'reality' of sense qualities are pretty well resolved.)

The second tendency (we call it the 'tendency toward rationalization') consists in this: so to choose the conceptual apparatus that as many problems as possible are solvable without recourse to experiential data. The tendency to transform hypotheses into principles seems to be a special case of our second tendency.

The third tendency (we call it the 'tendency toward perfecting the conceptual apparatus') appears in the change from languages in which certain problems are unsolvable in principle to languages in which such problems are rarer and rarer. An example of this tendency might be the introduction of conventions or coordinative definitions, as pointed out by the conventionalists; this permits decisions about 'interpretation-sentences' which otherwise would go unsolved.

Our fourth tendency (called the 'tendency toward increased empirical sensitivity of the conceptual apparatus') cannot be described without some preliminary discussion. Let us say that in passing from language S_1 to language S_2 we attain an empirically more sensitive conceptual apparatus in case: (1) to each of the experiential data, which are necessarily responded to with sentences according to the meaning-rules of S_1, the rules of S_2 also coordinate sentences; (2) whenever a distinction between experiential data is reflected in S_1, it is also reflected in S_2; and lastly (3) either there is an experiential datum for which the meaning-rules of S_1 specify no response (in the form of the acceptance of a sentence) while the meaning-rules of S_2 do, or else there are two distinct experiential data D_1 and D_2 whose difference is inessential for the meaning-rules of S_1 but is essential for the meaning-rules of S_2. The tendency toward increased empirical sensitivity then consists in this, that we prefer conceptual apparatuses which ignore as few experiential data as possible and which treat distinct data as differently as possible. This tendency is not to be confused with the 'tendency toward universality' referred to earlier.

It should be understood that we regard these four evolutionary tendencies as tentative, that we have made no attempt to ground them or formulate them rigorously, and that in no sense do we claim them to be exhaustive.

If now we would rank the various conceptual apparatuses in terms of their goodness, we would do so according to the degree in which these tendencies are realized in each of the apparatuses. The different tendencies would not have equal weight, however.

8. *Conclusion*

We conclude our remarks with a characterization of the point of view implicit in them.

Earlier we called this point of view 'radical conventionalism'. It differs from the usual conventionalist ones not only by its radical nature, but also in its *not* asserting (by contradistinction to Poincaré) that principles freely adopted as axioms and interpretations based on conventions are neither true nor false but simply useful (commodes). On the contrary, we are inclined to characterize these principles and interpretations as true so long as they occur in our language.

Moreover, our position does not forbid us to assume this or that as fact although we have pointed to the dependence of empirical judgments on the conceptual apparatus selected and not alone on the raw material of experience. On this point our view is close to the Copernican idea of Kant, according to which knowledge of experience depends not only on the material of experience but also on the apparatus of categories used in working up this material. However, in Kant's philosophy this apparatus of categories is rigidly connected with the nature of man (though the possibility that it can change is not excluded). For us, on the contrary, this conceptual apparatus is a rather plastic affair. One alters it continuously, either involuntarily and unconsciously or voluntarily and consciously. But so long as a man practises articulated knowing, he must stick to some such conceptual apparatus.

There is another essential difference between the Kantian conception of knowledge and the one proposed by us. Here we can only indicate this difference figuratively. In Kant's philosophy, part of the world-picture which emerges from our process of knowing consists of perceptual data formed by the pure forms of the intuition and the categories. So to speak, perceptual data are the colours in which the world-picture is painted, the painting itself of course being done in strict accordance with the patterns of the forms of the intuition and the categories. To us, however, the world-picture which constitutes the product of the knowing activity is not a coloured picture, if experiential data be colours. Our world-picture consists rather in just the meaning of the expressions; and in these experiential data are not contained. The world-picture is constructed entirely of abstract elements. The role of perceptual data consists only in this: the conceptual apparatus having already been selected, in terms of it, perceptual data determine which of the elements in the conceptual apparatus are to enter the world-picture.

That science is not simply worked up out of experience, but itself produces the very 'facts of science' by working them up linguistically and conceptually from raw empirical material, is a notion also to be found in the philosophy of LeRoy.[10] LeRoy combines Bergsonian intuitionism with the view of radical conventionalism, in the sense that he maintains the existence beyond scientific knowledge (which has to do with artificial constructs) of philosophical knowledge (which has to do not with mere human constructions but with 'real reality'; and it gets at 'real reality' by a method quite different from that of the sciences).

We bring our whole discourse to a close with a final — this time apologetic — remark. Some perhaps might consider that what we have here treated as 'language' is quite out of this world. So much, it might be said, is demanded of a structure for it to be called a 'language' that nothing can possibly be found which could be called a 'language' (with the possible exception of the languages of logistic systems). As a matter of fact, we have even declared that so-called 'ordinary languages' and 'ethnic languages' are not languages in our sense; and the same might safely be said of the 'language' of almost all the sciences as well. Hence what we have said may be correct and interesting as a conceptual game, but it can scarcely receive application in epistemology and methodology — which have nothing to do with idealized fictions.

In meeting this objection, let us remark at the outset that almost all the sciences exhibit this 'tendency toward idealization'. Physics, e.g., sets up theses about ideal gases, although it is well known that no such gases exist. Again, in mechanics, the concern is with motions which run their course under conditions never actually realized. Physics does this, we submit, because it is the only possible way for knowledge to approach reality. First of all, one sets up laws which hold rigorously only for ideal gases; for real gases, they hold only to within a rather larger error of approximation. Only after the first step are we in a position to transform these laws with a view toward reducing the initial error of approximation. To begin by instantly demanding an absolute agreement between the laws and reality is to set much too difficult a problem for ourselves. We claim the same sort of extenuation for our procedure. We begin by considering an ideal case which agrees only approximately with reality. Maybe this is the first step which will be followed by others diminishing the errors of approximation.

NOTES

[1] In the present volume p. 35.

[2] I believe that Poincaré had this difference in mind when he wrote: "*Quand une loi a reçue une confirmation suffisante de l'expérience ... on peut l'ériger en principle en adoptant des conventions telles, que la proposition soit toujours vrai ... Le principe n'est plus soumis au contrôle de l'expérience*" (*La valeur de la science*, Paris, Flammarion, 1929, p. 235).

[3] I should like to discuss here briefly a rather subtle objection which may be raised against what has been said in the text. What are we to understand by two sentences immediately contradicting one another? The following answer may be given to this question: two sentences of a language immediately contradict one another if and only if one of them results from the other by prefixing it with a function symbol which is a translation of the logical symbol '~' (the sentence which is conjoined to this symbol is then its argument). Two sentences are said to be mediately (indirectly) contradictory, if, although they are not themselves immediately contradictory, they yield two immediately contradictory sentences on application of deductive meaning rules.

If this definition is adopted then one has to admit that immediately contradictory sentences exist only in those languages in which there is a translation of the logical symbol '~'. Such languages are either intertranslatable or else have intertranslatable closures. If in a language it is possible to form two contradictory sentences, then it is not possible to form such sentences in another language, non-translatable with the former.

However, one may define two contradictory sentences in such a way that it will be possible to form contradictory sentences in either of two, mutually non-translatable languages. The following definition will do: Two sentences S and S_1 of language L are immediately contradictory if in L there is a deductive meaning-rule according to which one of the two sentences has to be rejected whenever the other is accepted. The present definition requires, however, that there should be in L not only rules demanding readiness to accept sentences but also rules demanding readiness to reject them. This would necessitate modifications in what we have said about the scope of a meaning rule and about the matrix of a language.

to reject them. This would necessitate modifications in what we have said about the scope of a meaning rule and about the matrix of a language.

[4] Two languages are in principle intertranslatable if either they are intertranslatable or may be made such by closure.

[5] The language of Whitehead and Russell's *Principia Mathematica* is similar to the one just described: 'systematic ambiguity' of the symbols of the propositional calculus and multiplicity of propositional calculi result in it from the distinction of various logical types of sentences.

[6] The universalist tendency critizised in the text has nothing in common with what R. Carnap discussed in his 'Die physikalische Sprache als Universalsprache der Wissenschaft', *Erkenntnis* **2**, Nos. 5 and 6.

[7] A class of sentences will be referred to as the linguistic picture of the world associated with a meaning-universe (or conceptual apparatus) if and only if all and only those sentences belong to it which satisfy the following two conditions: (1) They are elements of one and the same language with which the universe of meaning in question is coordinated, (2) as sentences of such a language they are factually positively decidable with respect to any experiential data (See 'Language and Meaning', notes to section 6, p. 65). By a world-picture of a language S we mean a world-picture of the meaning-universe of S expressed in the sentences of S. This shows that to the meaning-universe belong several linguistic world-pictures which, however, consist of sentences translatable one into another. The class of judgments which form the meaning of sentences of one of the linguistic world-pictures is the same for all world-pictures of the meaning-universe and we shall call it simply the world-picture of the meaning-universe.

[8] This does not imply that there is no structural property which only true sentences possess. It is doubtful, however, that in ordinary speech there exists a suitable meaning-rule.

[9] Cf. e.g. G. Simmel: 'Über eine Beziehung der Selektionstheorie zur Erkenntnistheorie', *Archiv für systematische Philosophie* **1**, (1895), 35ff.

[10] "Every fact is the result of a collaboration between nature and us; every fact symbolizes a point of view adopted in order to look at reality"; LeRoy, 'L'organisation scientifique', *Revue de Métaphysique et de Morale*, September, 1899; our quotation is from a reprint under the title *'Qu'est ce que la science?'* in *Cahiers de la nouvelle journée*, No. 5 (1926) Paris, p. 148. See also Poincaré, where (in *La valeur de la science*, the section entitled 'La science, est-elle artificielle? ') he contrasts his own view with that of LeRoy, formulating the latter's thesis in the proposition "the scientist creates the fact".

4. ON THE APPLICABILITY OF PURE LOGIC TO PHILOSOPHICAL PROBLEMS*

(1934)

I should like to discuss the problem formulated in the title of this paper[1] using as an example the relationship between logical extensionalism and the problem of the identity of mental and physical phenomena.

The identity problem is concerned with the question whether mental phenomena are or are not identical with the physical phenomena which are invariably associated with them. Our problem is not whether every mental phenomenon is identical with some physical phenomenon, i.e. whether for every mental phenomenon there exists an inseparable physical phenomenon. The question we are asking is whether if a mental phenomenon is invariably accompanied by a physical phenomenon, the two phenomena are identical.

Let us first emphasize the ambiguity of the term 'phenomenon'. One may use the term 'phenomenon' to refer to the fact that I am speaking here now. On the other hand one may also use this term to refer to speaking in general. If the term 'phenomenon' is applied to the fact that I am speaking here now, then by 'a phenomenon' is meant a state of affairs consisting in the fact that an individual located in a determinate place and time has the property of speaking. If, on the other hand, I use the term 'phenomenon' for speaking in general, then I apply this term to that property whose possession by an individual in a determinate place and time I referred to before as a phenomenon. In the rest of this analysis we shall use the term 'phenomenon' only in the second of the two mentioned senses; the term 'phenomenon' in the first of the two meanings will be replaced by the term 'occurrence'.

Owing to the ambiguity of the term 'phenomenon', there are two, rather than one, theses concerning the psycho-physical identity, depending on whether the claim concerns the identity of mental and physical occurrences (states of affairs) or the identity of mental and physical phenomena (i.e. properties).

The distinction made here is not the only possible one. We have made it on the assumption that man is an 'object' in Whitehead's sense and that

* Translated by Jerzy Giedymin. First published in *Przegląd Filozoficzny* **XXXVII** (1934), 323–327. Translation based on the text reprinted in *Język i Poznanie*, I, 211–214. Reprinted here by kind permission of PWN.

physical and mental phenomena are not of the same logical type as man. It is possible, however, to see man as an 'event' in Whitehead's sense, i.e. as a four-dimensional spatio-temporal solid. Then one might regard also physical and mental phenomena as 'events'. They would then be spatio-temporal cross-sections of the 'event'-man and would be of the same logical type. If, therefore, man conceived as an 'event' were to be of the lowest logical type, i.e. an individual, his physical and mental phenomena would also have to be individuals. On this conception of man and his phenomena, no relationship may be established between extensionalism and the problem of psycho-physical identity. We shall ignore here, however, this rather artificial approach and adopt the previously mentioned one.

In turn it should be noted that there exist more than one thesis of extensionality, some of them ontological, others semantical. One of the ontological theses of extensionality may be written down using logical symbols as follows:

$$\varphi x \underset{x}{\equiv} \psi x \, . \supset . \, F\varphi \underset{F}{\equiv} F\psi$$

On the assumption of the Leibnizian definition of identity it is equivalent to the following sentence:

$$\varphi x \underset{x}{\equiv} \psi x \, . \supset . \, \varphi = \psi$$

The latter formula is usually paraphrased in everyday language as follows: two coextensional properties are identical. The second of the ontological theses of extensionality may be formulated in the following way:

$$p \equiv q \, . \supset . \, Fp \underset{F}{\equiv} Fq$$

If the definition of identity is extended to sentences, then the above formula may be transformed into another one: $p \equiv q \, . \supset . \, p = q$, which in verbal translation claims that two equivalent states of affairs are identical.

From the above ontological theses of extensionality one should distinguish the semantical thesis according to which all functors of a particular language are symbols of extensional functions, i.e. functions which satisfy some ontological thesis of extensionality. In the formulation of the semantical thesis one should, of course, make it explicit which language it concerns.

If one considers the ontological theses of extensionality, or rather their verbal paraphrases, it appears at first sight obvious that the two theses of psycho-physical identity are special cases of those ontological theses of extensionality. For if two co-extensional properties are always identical, then a property which is a mental phenomenon is identical with the property invariably accompanying it, i.e. with the physical property co-extensional with it.

The same relation holds between the second of the theses of extensionality, concerned with the state of affairs or sentences, and the second thesis of psycho-physical identity, concerned with occurrences (in contrast to phenomena). The identity of mental and physical occurrences is implied by the thesis of extensionality. (The latter implies more, viz. the identity of all factual occurrences whatever).

These comments seem clearly to imply that the thesis of extensionality has among its consequences the thesis of psycho-physical identity, though one may deny the thesis of extensionality and yet accept the thesis of psycho-physical identity.

The problem of extensionality arose within contemporary formal logic, known also as mathematical logic or logistic. For it turned out that the at first sight very plausible admission of intensional functions, i.e. functions which do not satisfy the thesis of extensionality, generates far-reaching complications in the construction of some parts of logic. As a result, most contemporary logicians have opted in favour of extensionalist logic.

If a system of logic is characterized as extensionalist, this may mean one of two things. Firstly, this may mean that in the language of the system there are only functors which denote extensional functions. Secondly, we may want to say that among the asserted sentences of the system there are also ontological theses of extensionality.

Let us ask now whether a philosopher who is in favour of extensionalist logic may appeal to the thesis of extensionality when solving problems formulated in ordinary language? We believe that this would not be appropriate. For if the extensionality of the system of logic in question consists in the fact that there are no intensional functors in the language of the system, then this does not imply at all that in the ordinary language in which the philosopher formulates his problems no intensional functors exist.

If, on the other hand, the philospher's system of logic is extensionalist in the sense that the thesis of extensionality is among its theorems, then he must not replace the functor variables in that thesis by the expressions of ordinary language. In other words: though our philosopher may favour a logical system among whose theorems the sentence '$\varphi x \equiv \psi x \,.\, \supset \,.\, \varphi = \psi$' occurs, he is not permitted to replace the variable 'φ' by the word 'thinks', the variable 'ψ' by the word 'speaks' and in this way conclude "If x thinks if and only if x speaks, then thinking and speaking are identical". Our philosopher may not employ the theorems of logic in this way without altering their meaning. Contemporary logic is pure and not applied. In other words: for the variables which occur in logical theorems one may substitute as their values only such expressions which can be constructed from logical constants and variables exclusively. It follows that from the theorems of pure logic one may legitimately derive by substitution only such consequences which result from those theorems by substitution of expressions constructed exclusively from logical constants and variables. The expressions 'speaks' and 'thinks' may in no way be regarded as constructed from logical constants and variables alone, hence they may not be substituted for variables in the theorems of pure logic. From the logical thesis of extensionality one may not derive the thesis of psycho-physical identity.

The above comments concern all theorems of pure logic. These theorems must not be applied outside their proper area of applicability. Even a specific syllogism like 'If all men are morta! and Socrates iș a man, then Socrates is mortal', cannot claim validity on the basis of pure logic.

The apparent use of logic in solving philosophical problems formulated in natural language does not consist, therefore, in the deduction from logical theorems by legitimate substitution of conclusions which contribute to the solution of those problems. The procedure which has all the appearances of such application in fact consists in the construction in a natural language of sentences whose structure is isomorphic with the structure of logical theorems, i.e. in paraphrasing logical sentences into sentences with variables ranging over different domains of substitution than logical variables. It is only from such paraphrases that one may derive by substitution consequences relevant to philosphical problems formulated in a natural language. There is no doubt that the construction of such a system of sentences is desirable, for it would constitute the logic of ordinary language. However, those sentences, as paraphrases of universal logical sentences, require a validation which the existing contemporary logic is unable to supply.

They could be validated as analytic sentences through a meaning analysis of the expressions of ordinary language. In the search for this validation one might use the phenomenological method. Alternatively, they could be justified by elevating them to the rank of postulates which − disregarding the meanings expressions have in ordinary language − would fix those meanings arbitrarily. This second method is more promising, it seems, than the phenomenological one which should be tried nevertheless.

One must not forget, however, that if the second of the two methods is used the expressions of the language may acquire meanings different from those they had previously. Hence the same verbal formulations might not express the same problems. However, this need not necessarily be regrettable.

NOTE

[1] *Actes du VIII Congrès International de Philosophie*, Prague 1936, pp. 170–174 ('Über die Anwendbarkeit der reinen Logik auf philosophische Probleme').

5. ON THE PROBLEM OF UNIVERSALS*

(1935)

The indeterminateness of everyday language is apparent not only from its considerable departures from so-called 'standard language', e.g. standard English (in speech and writing), or in its vague assignments of meanings to expressions but also in the indeterminateness of its variety of syntactical forms. By syntactical forms I mean so-called semantical categories. The concept of semantical categories, originally introduced by E. Husserl, has been precisely elaborated by S. Leśniewski, not however in relation to natural languages but with respect to the symbolic language of his system of logic. In doing so Leśniewski was able to give a purely structural definition, i.e. in terms of purely external properties which two expressions always and only have if they belong to the same semantical category. When one wants to apply the basic idea of that classification to the expressions of everyday language, one cannot be satisfied — in view of the ambiguities in which that language abounds — with a purely structural definition and one has to appeal, in addition, to the meaning of the classified expressions. To familiarize readers with the term 'semantical category' it is convenient to begin by clarifying the term 'sentence'. Now, from the logical point of view an expression taken in some of its senses is a sentence if — taken in that sense — it is either true or false. Hence the term 'sentence' has in logic a narrower extension than in grammar since interrogative sentences, commands, etc. do not belong to it but only expressions in which something is either asserted or denied. Having this concept of 'sentence' in mind one may introduce the concept of a semantical category in the following way: expressions A and B, taken in sense a and b respectively, belong to the same semantical category if and only if every sentence Z_A containing expression A in sense a upon replacement of A by B taken in sense b (the meaning of all other expressions and their interconnections remaining unaltered) is transformed into an expression which is also a sentence, and if vice versa: every sentence Z_B upon replacement of B by A (with analogous qualifications) is also transformed into a sentence. So, for example, expressions 'Socrates' and 'Plato', when used in

* Translated by Jerzy Giedymin. First published in *Przegląd Filozoficzny* **XXXVIII** (1935), 219–234. Translation based on the text in *Język i Poznanie*, I, 196–210. Reprinted here by kind permission of PWN.

their normal sense, belong to the same semantical category since from every sentence which contains one of these expressions we obtain again a sentence upon replacement of that expression by the other one. By contrast the words 'stands' and 'Socrates' do not belong to the same semantical category, since the sentence 'Socrates stands' is not transformed into another sentence upon replacement of 'stands' by 'Socrates'.

Now, as has been said before, the question of specifying the semantical categories of everyday speech is indeterminate. In particular, it is possible to indicate a class of expressions of everyday language with respect to which one cannot decide whether all expressions in that class belong to one semantical category or to several. Such a class is, for example, the class of terms (names) of everyday language. It can be characterized approximately as that class of expressions each of which belongs to the same semantical category as a noun when used in its normal nominal sense. In other words, a term in everyday language is an expression which is either a noun or else has the property that one can find a noun such that every sentence containing that expression is transformed into another sentence upon replacement of that expression by that noun. It follows that the question whether or not all terms of everyday language belong to the same semantical category depends on whether or not all nouns of that language constitute one semantical category. This question, however, cannot be uniquely decided one way or the other.

Let us try, for example, to decide whether or not the terms 'Socrates' and 'man' belong – given their usual sense – to the same semantical category. Consider for that purpose the expression 'every man is mortal', which without doubt is a sentence when expressions which occur in it are used in their usual sense. Let us replace in that sentence the term 'man' by 'Socrates'. The outcome is the expression 'Every Socrates is mortal' with respect to which it is difficult to decide unequivocally whether it is a sentence or a meaningless expression. For if we take the term 'Socrates' in its normal sense which somehow implies the uniqueness of the object named by it, then one would regard the phrase 'every Socrates ...' as somewhat unnatural. Some logicians, e.g. W. E. Johnson, divide terms (names) into general and singular, one of the criteria for the distinction being that general terms may be meaningfully connected with expressions such as articles, demonstrative pronouns and words like 'some', 'every', etc.[1] According to Johnson's view, not all terms can occur significantly in the sentence 'Every man is mortal' in place of 'man'; only general terms can. This would imply that not all terms belong to the same category, that they fall at least into two distinct categories.

On the other hand, one may claim that the expression 'Every Socrates is a man' is a meaningful sentence, though of somewhat unnatural construction. At any rate, one is not as clear about the nonsentential character of that expression as about the expression 'Every let us after is a man' which, given the usual meaning of the expressions involved, is obviously nonsensical. This is why there are logicians who are prepared to classify all terms as belonging to one and the same category, and do not see any reason why one should distinguish general from singular terms as different semantical categories. These logicians distinguish the following semantical categories: (1) sentences, (2) terms and (3) an unlimited hierarchy of semantical categories of functors, i.e. expressions which combined with other expressions form composite expressions with uniform sense. Apart from sentences they distinguish sentence-forming functors of one argument (i.e. 'stands'), of two arguments (e.g. 'loves'), name-forming functors of one argument, etc. Such is also the hierarchy of semantical categories in the language of Leśniewski's logic. Apart from numerous categories of various functors and the category of sentences, there is in his language only one further category, viz. the category of terms (names). T. Kotarbiński's interpretation of the variety of syntactical forms in everyday speech is modelled on the paradigm of Leśniewski's symbolic language. According to Kotarbiński all expressions of everyday speech (when taken in the literal sense) which are neither functors nor sentences belong to one semantical category of names.

It is difficult to decide categorically which of these two views of the syntactical forms of everyday speech is intuitively more plausible. It seems that everyday speech is vague on this point allowing either one or the other interpretation. It is possible that there are differences in this respect between different languages. It may be that Kotarbiński's view is more adequate from the point of view of the Polish language, while Johnson's is more adequate from the point of view of the English language. Neither of these two interpretations seems, however, to be clearly incompatible with the spirit of e.g. the Polish language.

It seems that the view that not all terms of everyday speech belong to one semantical category was part of Aristotle's doctrine. This is what Kotarbiński writes on this subject: "Already Aristotle believed that one can significantly predicate of Socrates this or that, but that one cannot predicate Socrates of anything significantly; for according to Aristotle there are 'primary beings' as Socrates and 'secondary beings' as man: one may predicate something of the former but they cannot be predicated of anything; the latter – on the other hand – can be predicated of the former (and of the latter as well)". Here Kotarbiński refers to Aristotle's *Categories* (chaps. 2 and 3) and continues as follows: "If in these Aristotelian assertions we separate semantical ideas (by semantics is meant a discipline concerned with the meaning of linguistic expressions) from ontological trappings (Aristotle writes as if he were classifying not words with respect to their meaning but various kinds of being) then the result will be the claim that proper names cannot function significantly as predicates and that in the sentence-structure '*A* is *B*' a proper name may only occur in place of *A*, i.e. as a grammatical subject while the place of *B* must be taken by a general name. Generality here consists not in having several designata but in having the character of a predicate ...". "... A singular name is a term which may be used only as a subject (*A*), a general name is a term which may also be used as a predicate. According to Aristotle general terms may also function as grammatical subjects; however, subtler analysis shows that then the whole structure of the type '*A* is *B*' has a derivative role, hence we arrive at the view that a general name may be used only as a grammatical predicate (*B*). From this point of view the use of a singular term (e.g. 'Warsaw') in place of a predicate or the use of a general term (e.g. 'city') in place of a grammatical subject in the structure '*A* is *B*' understood in the fundamental sense, would result in nonsense just as if we were to say 'help yourself is a capital city' or 'Warsaw is a help yourself'.[2]

We shall not be concerned here whether or not Kotarbiński is right in attributing those views to Aristotle. What we are interested in is to look at another view concerning the variety of semantical categories of everyday speech. According to this view terms (names) in everyday speech do not all belong to the same semantical category for — according to this view — if the term 'man' is replaced in the sentence 'Socrates is a man' by 'Socrates' (leaving the meaning of 'is' unaltered), then the result will no longer be a sentence but will be syntactically nonsensical.

One can try to see the point of this view. To do this one should clarify for example the sense of the word 'is' in the sentence 'Socrates is a man' as follows: by saying 'Socrates is a man' I intend to communicate that Socrates is one of men. This is apparent in those languages which make use of articles as e.g. the German language in which one would say '*Sokrates ist ein Mensch*'. If this is to be the meaning of the word 'is' in the sentence under discussion, then no term whose meaning implies uniqueness of its designatum may occur in place of a predicate; since 'Socrates' is such a term, it cannot significantly be used as a grammatical predicate together with 'is'. Conversely, when I say 'Socrates is a man' I predicate the being of a man of a particular object. The name of that object must be such that its meaning implies the uniqueness of its designatum; the term 'man' is unsuitable since its meaning does not direct its intention to a specific object. These comments were meant to help our intuitive understanding of Aristotle's position and did not pretend to make it precise. One may stimulate and help understanding in various ways, for example by reciting poems with musical accompaniment, with the use of drugs, etc. not necessarily with the help of responsible language.

The above approach to Aristotle's view appeals to a linguistic intuition which many will find unconvincing. Kotarbiński, as we have said already, is one of them. There is no doubt, however, that many others found it convincing and in conformity with their linguistic intuition. This is another example of the vagueness associated with everyday speech, which makes it impossible to establish unequivocally the varieties of semantical categories of that language: one can do it in a number of ways. Philosophers and scientists by choosing one interpretation or another make their own language to some extent more explicit but they do it in different ways. Indeed, the language of Aristotle differs from the language of Kotarbiński with respect to the multiplicity of syntactical forms, or – in another terminology – with respect to semantical categories. In Kotarbiński's language there are only three categories: that of functors, that of sentences and that of terms. In Aristotle's language, apart from the categories of functors and sentences, there are at least two categories of terms: the category of terms which may function only as grammatical subjects and the category of terms which may function as predicates.

This affects the variety of functors in both languages. Consider the word 'is' in its ordinary sense. The only undisputable restriction on that word in ordinary languages is that it can form sentences exclusively in combination with terms. If, however, we see the terms of ordinary speech in the light of Kotarbiński's position as expressions which belong without exception to one semantical category, then the word 'is' as a sentence-forming functor of two arguments will always be a sentence-forming functor whose both arguments belong to the same semantical category. If, on the other hand, we see everyday speech in the light of Aristotle's position, then – the usual restriction on its ordinary use notwithstanding – this word may serve as a sentence-forming functor whose two arguments will belong to two different semantical categories though it may also serve – if used in a different sense – as a sentence-forming functor whose arguments belong to one category. In general, in Kotarbiński's language there can be only one semantical category of sentence-forming functors of two name-arguments while in Aristotle's language sentence-forming functors may belong to various semantical categories.

Let us agree, for convenience's sake, to indicate the semantical category of a word with the help of a suitable index. Let us use single letters as indices of semantical categories which are not categories of functors and let the index of any functor-category have the form of a fraction, such that in its denominator there will be successive indices of the semantical categories of the functor's arguments and in its numerator there will be the index of the whole expression formed by the functor together with its arguments. Let, for example, in Kotarbiński's language 'z' be the index of sentences and let the letter 'n' be the index of the only category of names in that language. Similarly, let 'z' be the index of sentences in Aristotle's language and letters 'i' and 'g' be respectively the index of subject-terms and the index of predicate-terms which in Aristotle's language form two distinct categories. The word 'is' which in Kotarbiński's language is a sentence-forming functor of two name-arguments will be assigned the index $\frac{z}{nn}$ with a symmetrical denominator. By contrast, in Aristotle's language the word 'is' will perform two functions: firstly, it will occur as a sentence-forming functor whose first argument is a subject-term (with an index 'i') and whose second argument is a predicate-term (with an index 'g'), hence 'is' itself will in this case be assigned an index $\frac{z}{ig}$; secondly, it will occur as a sentence-forming functor whose first and second arguments are predicate-terms, hence 'is' in this role will be assigned an index $\frac{z}{gg}$. For example, in the context 'Socrates is a man' 'is' occurs with the index $\frac{z}{ig}$ while in the sentence 'Dog is an animal species' the word 'is' occurs with the index $\frac{z}{gg}$.

It is not our aim to give a precise definition of 'is' in either of the two languages. Those languages have been discussed as two possible reconstructions of everyday speech whose understanding among our readers we may assume. We have limited ourselves to attempts at stimulating an understanding of various senses of 'is' with the help of – so to say – verbal propaganda and examples. We cannot be sure that in this way we have achieved our aim. One could use a more radical method to familiarize the reader with the two languages or at least with their relevant parts; such a radical method would be axiomatization, i.e. specification of the axioms and inference rules of the two languages. This would not be difficult in the case of Kotarbiński's language since it is modelled on the language of Leśniewski's logic whose axioms we would have to paraphrase into everyday speech. An axiomatization of Aristotle's language would be more difficult. We shall not attempt it here. We shall have to take the risk that not all readers will understand the languages of Kotarbiński and Aristotle. Nevertheless they will be able to follow with understanding that part of our argument in which referring to both languages we shall claim that in Aristotle's language one can define a concept which is not definable in the language of Kotarbiński. An understanding of Aristotle's language is only necessary in order to check whether the concept in question is identical with the historically given concept of *'universale'*.

Kotarbiński[3] has given in his language a critique of universals whose fundamental idea is based on comments made on this problem by S. Leśniewski in 'Critique of the Logical Law of Contradiction'[4], as well as in 'On the Foundations of Mathematics'[5]. In the book from which we took our quotations Kotarbiński gives two definitions of a 'universal' or *'universale'*. We shall consider the second of these definitions. It runs as follows: '*P* is a universal for the designata of the term *N* if and only if *P* is an object which possesses only the properties common to all the designata of *N*'. Making explicit some of the consequences of this definition Kotarbiński shows that "if something were a universal it would be an inconsistent object", in other words − from the assumption that universals exist we get absurd consequences. Kotarbiński's argument has to be qualified to some extent. For one obtains a contradiction from this definition not on the basis of the assumption that there are universals but from the assumption that there are universals for at least two distinct designata of a term *N*, i.e. from the assumption that there exist universals which are exemplified by more than one object. If this minor defect is disregarded (which, by the way, cannot be found in Leśniewski's more careful critical discussion of universals), then Kotarbiński's proof is quite valid within his own language. However, Kotarbiński then proceeds to consider a possible objection to the effect that "given alternative definitions reporting also some of the intended meanings of the word ('universal') in its historical use (under discussion is the Greek term *'to katholu'* or the Latin *'universale'*) no contradictions would arise." "We have to say [so Kotarbiński continues] that no such definitions *are known to us* (provided that we disregard obscure ones"[6]. Nor are *we* familiar with such a definition expressible in Kotarbiński's language. One should remember, however, that the historical concept of *'universale'*, inherited from Aristotle's writings, had been formulated in Aristotle's language different from Kotarbiński's. In Aristotle's language, with its two distinct semantical categories of terms, a definition of *'universale'* (unattainable in Kotarbiński's language) is possible. Indeed one can model it for Aristotle's language on Leśniewski's definition of 'object' quoted by Kotarbiński for his own language. The definition of 'object' is as follows:

$$\text{``}x \text{ is an object if and only if for some } z, x \text{ is } z\text{''}$$

$$n \quad \frac{z}{nn} \quad n \qquad\qquad n \; n \; \frac{z}{nn} \; n$$

One can paraphrase the above definition as follows:

  "An object is that which is something".

Both the quoted definition and its paraphrase are formulated in Kotarbiński's language; hence 'is' belongs to the category $\dfrac{z}{nn}$.

Now it is possible to construct in an analogous way in Aristotle's language a definition of the term 'individual', the only difference being that the word 'is' used in it will belong — in accordance with its function in Aristotle's language — to the category $\dfrac{z}{ig}$. The definition is as follows:

$$x \text{ is an individual if and only if for some } z, x \text{ is } z$$

$$i \quad \frac{z}{ig} \quad g \qquad\qquad g \; i \; \frac{z}{ig} \; g$$

Now we are able to define the word *'universale'* in Aristotle language in the following way:

$$x \text{ is } universale \text{ if and only if for some } z, x \text{ is } z$$

$$g \quad \frac{z}{gg} \quad g \qquad\qquad g \; g \; \frac{z}{gg} \; g$$

It should be noted that 'is' as used in this definition is the second of the two 'is's' in Aristotle's language, viz. it belongs to the category z. So we have given a definition of *universale* which is in conformity with its 'historical usage' and does not imply a contradiction within the language of Aristotle.

Let us consider now the problem of the existence of universals within the language of Aristotle. The word 'exists' can also be defined by paraphrasing the definition which Kotarbiński (following Leśniewski) gives for his language. In Kotarbiński's language *'a* exists' means 'for some x, x is a'; of course, in conformity with Kotarbiński's language 'is' belongs here to the category $\dfrac{z}{nn}$. In Aristotle's language the expression 'exists' is used in two different ways. In conformity with everyday speech, from which Aristotle does not depart, 'exists' is a sentence-forming functor of two term-arguments. Since, however, terms in Aristotle's language belong to two different semantical categories, the word 'exists' will also occur in two meanings, viz. as a sentence-forming functor with a subject-term argument and as a sentence-forming functor with a predicate-term argument. When used in the first of the two senses it will have the index $\frac{z}{i}$, when used in the second sense it will have the index $\frac{z}{g}$. Now the phrase 'x exists' in which 'x' is of the i-category, may be definitionally identified with 'x is an individual'. Thus we get the following definition:

$$x \text{ exists if and only if: for some } z, x \text{ is } z$$

$$i \quad \frac{z}{i} \qquad\qquad\qquad g \; i \; \frac{z \; g}{ig}$$

The definition of 'exists' in the second sense, i.e. as a functor of the category $\frac{z}{g}$ may have exactly the same wording as Kotarbiński's:

$$\text{"}x \text{ exists if and only if for some } z, z \text{ is } x\text{"}$$

$$g \quad \frac{z}{g} \qquad\qquad\qquad g \; g \; \frac{z \; g}{gg}$$

In accordance with this definition:

$$\text{universals exist if and only if for some } z, z \text{ is } \textit{universale}$$

$$g \qquad \frac{z}{g} \qquad\qquad\qquad g \; g \; \frac{z}{gg} \qquad g$$

Upon replacement in this definition of the phrase:

$$\text{'}z \text{ is } \textit{universale}\text{'}$$

$$g \; \frac{z}{gg} \qquad g$$

by the definitionally equivalent expression:

$$\text{'for some } y, z \text{ is } y\text{'}$$

$$g \; g \; \frac{z \; g}{gg}$$

we get:

universals exist if and only if for some z, for some y, z is y

$$g \qquad \frac{z}{g} \qquad\qquad g \qquad\qquad g\ g\ \dfrac{z}{gg}\ g$$

If, therefore, in Aristotle's language in which (as in ordinary speech) the usual laws of logic hold, there is a true sentence of the form

z is y

$$\frac{g\ z\ g}{gg}$$

e.g. the sentence:

man is a species

$$g \quad \frac{z}{gg} \quad g$$

then the following sentence will also be true:

for some z and some y, z is y

$$g \qquad\qquad g\ g\ \dfrac{z}{gg}\ g$$

hence the sentence:

universals exist

$$g \qquad \frac{z}{g}$$

will also be true. It seems that in Aristotle's language the sentence 'Man is a species' is true, hence the sentence 'Universals exist' is also true in it.[7]

In general philosophers use in their deliberations ordinary language. As we have observed already, vagueness is characteristic of that language. When they make expressions more precise for their purposes, philosophers enter — without violating ordinary language — one of the lanes left open by that language. The decision to make linguistic expressions more precise in one or another way results in the choice of one of possible conceptual frameworks (apparatuses) which are potentially available in the system of admissible meanings of the expressions in ordinary language. Having selected one specific among the many possible conceptual frameworks, a philosopher may construe and express in his language (a variant of ordinary speech) a concept which another philospher, operating with another conceptual framework implicit in ordinary language, is unable to construct in *his* conceptual framework and unable to express in *his* language. Under these circumstances, the second of our two philosophers devises a different concept, constructible in *his* conceptual apparatus, a concept which for some reason seems to him very close to the conception used by the first philosopher in the other framework, then he associates with that new concept a word identical with the corresponding word used by the first philosopher and proves the concept to be absurd. Moreover, if he is careless, then he believes and announces that he has proved the absurdity of the conception of the first philosopher; or, if he is careful, he honestly admits that what is absurd is the conception constructed by himself. However, he also declares that he is not aware of any other concept similar to the one used by the first philosopher and not 'burdened with obscurity'. In speaking thus he can provoke in the minds of uncritical people the impression that the conception of the first philosopher was either absurd or obscure.

The problem of universals is related to the problem of the number of so-called ontological categories. There are languages obtained as possible interpretations of ordinary speech in which the latter problem cannot be formulated in the material mode. We shall, therefore, consider its semantical counterpart. In the semantical problem we are concerned with the question of the number of so-called maximally universal terms in ordinary language. By a maximally universal term we mean a term 'N' of a natural language (i.e. a noun) which for some sense of the word 'is' satisfies the following condition:

$$x \text{ is } N \text{ if and only if for some } z, x \text{ is } z \qquad (0)$$

where 'is' in both its occurrences has the same meaning. A term satisfying this condition is maximally universal because every term which may occur as a subject in a true sentence of the form 'x is z' (the word 'is' having the same meaning given which the term 'N' satisfies the condition (0)) falls under the term 'N', i.e. satisfies a sentence of the form 'x is N' when substituted for 'x'. Now, the problem of the number of ontological categories is concerned with how many non-equivalent maximally universal terms (names) there are.

It is clear that the answer to this question depends on how one explicates (makes more precise) vague expressions of ordinary language. If, for example, with Kotarbiński we decide to use 'is' in one sense only, then we shall have just one ontological category, or – to put it more precisely – one maximally universal term (together perhaps with its synonyms).

The thesis of Kotarbiński's reism can be formulated using the concept of 'a maximally universal term' as follows: 'Every maximally universal term is equivalent with the term 'thing''. To make this thesis unambiguous it is necessary to specify the language in which this thesis is to hold. If it is claimed that the thesis holds in every language obtainable as a more precise reconstruction of ordinary language, then this claim seems to me false. If, on the other hand, it is claimed that the thesis holds for Kotarbiński's language, then indeed the consequence of the thesis to the effect that there are no non-equivalent maximally universal terms, is true for that language. A separate issue concerns the claim that the only maximally universal term in Kotarbiński's language is co-extensive with the term 'thing'. This claim amounts to saying that in Kotarbiński's language the following sentence is valid: 'All things and only things are objects'. To say that a sentence is valid in a language means here the same as to say that the language in question is based on acceptance rules (i.e. rules governing the acceptance of sentences) such that if a speaker made a sufficiently extensive and consistent use of them and, moreover, had at his disposal sufficient empirical data, then he would have to accept that sentence. Now, in Kotarbiński's language the sentence 'All things are objects' is valid in this sense. But is also the sentence 'All objects are things' valid? Kotarbiński's language is based on the rules of Leśniewski's ontology translated into ordinary language as well as on the rules of ordinary language. Neither the former nor the latter seem to us sufficient for a decisive answer to the question: 'Is every object a thing?'. The only way to decide that question appears to be a further strengthening of the rules of ordinary language. This would result in making the problem decidable a priori or on empirical grounds. At any rate, by enriching the rules which govern the acceptance of sentences one makes the meaning of expressions more precise. Hence the decidability of the question: 'Are all objects things?' is again a matter of making more precise the meaning of expressions of ordinary language in one way or another.

Until such an operation is performed, the reistic thesis 'All objects are things' is an example of bad metaphysics just as the sentence 'The essence of the universe is will', since both are sentences which can neither be justified nor falsified. The reistic thesis cannot even aspire to that status of 'a hypothetical credo' (as Kotarbiński would like it to have). For this status may be granted only to those sentences whose consequences are in principle decidable, i.e. such that given a sufficiently long, persistent and consistent application of the language rules and given sufficient empirical data can be decided one way or the other. However, what would a dispute be like between a defender and an opponent of the reistic thesis if the opponent of the thesis attempted its refutation with the help of suitable counterexamples?

They both would be using ordinary language made precise to the extent that 'is' would belong to the category $\frac{z}{nn}$ and that the definitions and axioms of Leśniewski's ontology would apply. The critic of the reistic thesis might perhaps argue as follows: "The sky is not a thing, since it is neither something extended and subject to inertia, nor something experiencing" (for this is how Kotarbiński defines 'thing'). "But the sky is blue, hence for some y, the sky is y, hence (by definition of 'object'), the sky is an object. *Ergo* not every object is a thing". The defender of reism, on the other hand, would deny the premiss 'The sky is blue' (literally understood) and in this way would reject the criticism. Can this controversy indeed be settled within ordinary language (however modified along the lines of Leśniewski's system)? In my view this dispute is just as hopelessly undecidable as the question whether a twenty-five year old man is young. These are examples of problems which cannot be solved, following the rules of ordinary language, as long as the latter are not made more precise in one way or another.

Consequently, I believe that in order to be entitled to assert the thesis of reism Kotarbiński would have to explicate vague expressions of ordinary language in such a way as to introduce conventionally into that language rules in virtue of which the thesis of reism would become either an axiom, or a consequence of axioms or − at least − an empirically decidable sentence. I believe, however, that without violating the established meanings of the expressions of ordinary language and even observing the rules of Leśniewski's ontology, one could − by convention and with equal right − make precise those expressions in such a way that a sentence formally inconsistent with the thesis of reism would be valid.

If ordinary language is interpreted in such a way that two syntactically distinct 'is'-words (both as sentence-forming functors of two name-arguments, just as in the language which we have conventionally called Aristotle's language) are distinguished in it, then one obtains two non-equivalent maximally universal terms, viz. 'individual' ('particular') and *'universale'*.[8]

Another interpretation of ordinary language might be seen, for example, in such a reading of simplified Russellian logic in which sentence-forming functors of one or more arguments occur as arguments of '$\in$'. Consider the formula '$R \in Rel$' read as 'R is a relation'. On this interpretation symbols 'R' and 'Rel' which are sentence-forming functors will be read with the help of terms (names) while the functor '$\in$' which in this context is a sentence-forming functor with functor-arguments will be read with the help of the word 'is' from ordinary language; whatever the vagueness of ordinary language 'is' is used in it exclusively to combine terms (names) into sentences.

One may like or not this reading of logical formulae: one may condemn it, if one sees a tremendous gap between functors and names. If, on the other hand, one adopts a suitable view of the role of names, then one may regard this reading as admissible. For one may take the position that in ordinary language a term (name) does not differ from a functor as belonging to a different semantical category but is simply an inflectional variant of a functor, a variant which occurs when a functor (without its arguments) is itself an argument of another functor in a sentence. So, for example, the word 'divisibility' in the sentence 'Divisibility holds between 4 and 2' would differ from the verb 'divides' in the sentence '2 divides 4' as the word 'man' differs from 'men' in the sentence 'Every man belongs to the class of all men'.[9] 'Divisibility' and 'divides' would be 'one and the same word' in two inflectionally different forms which do not affect its meaning. This view, as most other semantical claims concerning ordinary language, can neither be justified nor refuted. One may either favour it or dislike it. It is one of possible interpretations of ordinary language. If one adopts it, then one may regard as admissible the way of reading logical formulae mentioned before, in which functors are rendered through names while the sentence-forming functor '∈' with functors as arguments is read as 'is'.

On this interpretation of ordinary language a great number of maximally universal terms would be distinguished in it, each belonging to a different semantical category. This would make it possible to find such interpretations of 'is' and 'exist' on which sentences like 'There exist relations of n-th order' would be true.

On account of the vagueness of the expressions of ordinary language which we have just discussed, disputes of ontological nature conducted in ordinary language in the material mode, are bound to result in confusions. Different authors who adopt different ways of making ordinary language more precise arrive at ontological theses which appear to be mutually incompatible. One of them may proclaim, for instance, 'Only things exist', another one: 'There exist universals which are not things' (in Aristotle's language this may be a meaningful sentence since in it 'thing' and *universalia* belong to the same semantical category), still another 'There exist relations, properties, classes, etc.'. The confusion arises from the illusion that all these authors using the same ordinary language indeed speak the same language, hence that they are using expressions – in particular the word 'exist' – in the same sense; the illusion persists as though these different authors proclaimed mutually incompatible theses. In fact those theses belong to different, not inter-translatable languages. One should be aware of the differences between these languages and – having chosen one out of a multiplicity of languages permitted by ordinary speech — one must not claim that all those others are in error who in their own languages assert theses which appear incompatible with the theses accepted in our own language.

NOTES

[1] "... we may point out that a universal characteristic of the general name is its connection with the article — the use of the grammatical term 'article' being extended to include this, that, some, every, etc. All terms of this kind ... might more properly be called applicatives or selectives. Now a general name is distinguished as that to which any applicatives can be significantly prefixed" (W. E. Johnson, *Logic*, Cambridge, 1921, Part I, p. 97). "The consideration that to the general name any applicative can be prefixed distinguishes it from the singular name ..." (ibid., p. 99).

One must not confuse general terms with universal terms, nor singular with individual. The difference between universal and individual ones concerns the number of objects they denote; this is a different criterion from the one on which the distinction between general and singular terms is based. The two classifications are not co-extensive either.

[2] T. Kotarbiński, *Elementy teorii poznania, logiki formalnej i metodologii nauk (Elements of Epistemology, Formal Logic and Methodology of Science)*, Lwów, 1929, pp. 16, 17.

[3] Ibid., p. 42.

[4] *Przegląd Filozoficzny* XVI (No. 2 and 3), 317–320.

[5] *Przegląd Filozoficzny* XXX, 183–184.

[6] Ibid., p. 43.

[7] In the language used above one could not reasonably define '*universale* of universals', i.e. 'second order *universale*'. To make it possible one would have to have apart from 'is' with the index $\frac{z}{ig}$ and 'is' with the index $\frac{z}{gg}$ also 'is' with the index $\frac{z}{gg_1}$ as well as 'is' indexed $\frac{z}{g_1g_1}$, thereby distinguishing within the class of terms three semantical categories. One can go as far as one wants in this proliferation of semantical categories of terms making it possible to define universals of arbitrary order.

[8] In Aristotle's language it is possible to formulate the problem of the number of ontological categories in the material mode; this is so because each of the two 'is'-words occurring in it combines as a predicate with words of the same semantical category. One can put the following definition:

$$K \text{ is } \overbrace{\text{an ontological category}} \text{ if and only if}$$

$$\underset{\frac{z}{gg}}{g} \qquad\qquad \underset{g}{}$$

either (i) x is K iff for some z, x is z

$$\underset{\frac{z}{ig}}{i}\ g \qquad\qquad g\ \underset{\frac{z}{ig}}{i}\ g$$

or (ii) y is K iff for some z, y is z

$$g\ \underset{\frac{z}{gg}}{}\ g \qquad\qquad g\ g\ \underset{\frac{z}{gg}}{}$$

On the basis of this definition one may ask meaningfully: How many non-identical ontological categories are there? The answer will be that there are two ontological categories, viz. individual and *universale*.

[9] [The example used in the text is 'Every man is a man'. In Polish the second occurrence of 'man' differs inflexionally from the first. Translator.]

6. THE SCIENTIFIC WORLD-PERSPECTIVE

(1935)

In the following, a line of thought is sketched which, though lacking rigor of formulation, is perhaps suitable as it stands for initiating a discussion of certain questions which constantly confront us as we work in our circle of problems, and which questions can be brought nearer solution by a thorough airing.

Every scientific judgment and every scientific question is composed of concepts. These concepts are linguistically pinned down, and constitute the meaning of language expressions. Now, the meanings of the expressions of a language involve certain criteria to which one must conform in accepting or rejecting sentences composed of the expressions if one is not to do violence to these meanings. We shall call these criteria meaning-rules of the language. (In this connection, see 'Language and Meaning', present volume, pp. 35–66.)

A rule of this kind for the English language demands, for example, that one be ready to accept without further ado every sentence of the form 'Every A is an A'. Should anybody reject a sentence of this form, should he, for example, say with conviction 'Not every man is a man', this would be an infallible indication that though the person in question made use of English syllables, he does not attach to them *the* meaning which belongs to them in the English language. Another meaning-rule of the English language states that anyone who has accepted as true a conditional sentence of the form 'If a then b' together with the antecedent 'a', and bearing this acceptance in mind rejects the consequent 'b' as false, can only do this if he does not attach to the connective 'if, then' its assigned English meaning. A final example: if anyone has a sharp toothache and simultaneously denies with conviction the sentence 'It hurts', he can only do this if he does not attach to the sentence 'It hurts' the meaning which belongs to it in English.

That there exist such meaning-rules seems to me to be perfectly evident. Furthermore we tacitly make use of these rules as premises when we note

* Translated from the German by Wilfrid Sellars. First published in *Erkenntnis* V (1935), 22–30. *Język i Poznanie*, I, 215–21. Reprinted from *Readings in Philosophical Analysis* (1949), pp. 182–8, by kind permission of Professors Herbert Feigl and Wilfrid Sellars and of Prentice-Hall, Inc. Copyright © 1949 by Appleton-Century-Crofts Inc.

that somebody misuses words, that is, employs them otherwise than in their prescribed sense. If we suspect somebody of a misuse of a given word, we induce him to answer on certain suppositions (or even without these) a question in answering which he will use this word. If the answer to this question takes — as we see it — a turn contrary to sense, we see in this fact an infallible indication that the person in question has used words in other than the prescribed meaning.

There are three kinds of meaning-rules. To the first kind belong those which demand an unconditional readiness to accept certain sentences. This is what was done, for example, by the first of the meaning-rules we have cited. Meaning-rules of the first kind I call *axiomatic meaning-rules*, since by them are specified the sentences in a language which have the status of axioms.

Meaning-rules of the second kind demand a readiness to accept certain sentences, not unconditionally, but only on the supposition that certain other sentences are accepted. Such meaning-rules I call deductive meaning-rules, as by them the modes of deductive inference are determined. In the language of symbolic logic, detachment and substitution are examples of these modes of inference involved in the meaning of symbols.

The third kind of meaning-rule demands the readiness to accept certain sentences in the presence of certain data of experience. I call such rules *empirical meaning-rules*, as by them are specified sentences which can be established with certainty, in a purely empirical way.

The totality of meaning-rules of a language in conjunction with certain data of experience sets apart certain sentences of this language together with the judgments which constitute their meaning. In the first place, there are the sentences which are to be accepted according to the axiomatic meaning-rules, and which are set apart by the fact that one cannot reject them as false if one attaches to them the meaning which they possess in the language in question. In the second place, there are the sentences which are set apart by the empirical meaning-rules and the data of experience as those which cannot be rejected in the face of those data of experience, without violating the meaning which belongs to them in that language. The third class of sentences which are set apart is constituted by the totality of those sentences which are derivable in accordance with the deductive meaning-rules from the sentences thus set apart by axiomatic and empirical meaning-rules.

The totality of all sentences in a given language which are set apart in one or the other of the three ways indicated above by the meaning-rules of that language together with certain data of experience, we call the *world-perspective (corresponding to those experiential data) of that language.*

We shall call the totality of the judgments which make up the meaning of those sentences which belong to the world-perspective of a language (which world-perspective corresponds to certain data of experience) *the world-perspective (corresponding to these data) of the conceptual apparatus* out of which is built the meaning of the expressions of the language in question.

Sentences which belong to the world-perspective of a language constitute (ultimately, with certain qualifications) the indubitable component of the knowledge of anyone who makes use of that language. The sentences dictated by the axiomatic meaning-rules can under no circumstances be rejected as long as they are used in the sense prescribed by the language. The sentences dictated by the empirical meaning-rules can often be rejected without violating their meaning; this, however, only when the corresponding data of experience are not present. In the presence of such data of experience, the rejection of these sentences is possible only if one attaches to them a meaning other than assigned them in the language in question. Those sentences belonging to the world-perspective of a language at which one can arrive from the axiomatic or empirical sentences in accordance with deductive meaning-rules can also often be rejected without doing violence to their meaning. If, however, one accepts exactly those sentences which a deductive meaning-rules coordinates as premises with these sentences as conclusions, the latter cannot be rejected without doing violence to their meaning.

In a given language the world-perspective coordinated with a set of data of experience is thus made up of sentences which at least potentially constitute the unshakeable component of the knowledge which can be achieved by making use of this language or its corresponding conceptual apparatus. This knowledge, however, need not be restricted to those sentences already gained in accordance with the meaning-rules of the language; for it can also include sentences which are accepted, although, on the basis of the hitherto achieved portion of the world-perspective and the hitherto enjoyed data of experience, they are not demanded (nor forbidden) by any meaning-rule of the language. To this class of cognitions belong all sentences accepted on the basis of inductive inference. With its help, we attempt to piece together by way of anticipation the as yet unknown parts of the world-perspective.

The world-perspective is a function of two factors. On the one hand, it depends on the material of experience, which is its foundation; on the other hand, it depends on the conceptual apparatus, and the meaning-rules that are bound up with it. The first part of this assertion is obvious. The second, however, is no less clear. A change in conceptual apparatus is reflected in a change in the problems which one solves on the basis of the same data of experience. Different sciences make use of different conceptual structures which can only partially coincide. But even one and the same science changes its conceptual apparatus in the course of its historical development. This change, however, is often concealed by the fact that while the concepts are changed, the words remain the same.

As long as one makes use of a limited conceptual apparatus, which does not exclude an enrichment, one can only arrive, however completely one exploits the material of experience, at a world-perspective, and never at a complete world-picture. Thus, if anyone limits his conceptual apparatus, and rejects certain modes of enriching it, he is putting on blinkers and deliberately neglects certain portions of the world-picture; that is to say, he contents himself with the contemplation of a selected world-perspective.

Now it seems to us that science as a whole is taking this course. It chooses its conceptual apparatus along certain lines, and rejects every enlargement which runs counter to these lines. We shall give examples to back up this assertion.

The conceptual apparatus is determined by the establishment of the meaning-rules. Now, meaning-rules can be so chosen that by following them on the basis of enjoyed data of experience, or, in other cases, immanently, that is without reference to data of experience, we are led to contradiction. We can determine concepts by laying down axiomatic and deductive meaning-rules. The building of concepts in formalized deductive systems proceeds in this manner. However, a conceptual apparatus can be constructed along these lines which is associated with meaning-rules which lead to contradiction. Science rejects such a building of concepts, and seizes upon different prescriptions (for example the theory of types) in order to protect itself from such conceptual structures which lead to contradiction. This, however, is a deliberate restriction of conceptual apparatus.

The empirical portion of the scientific conceptual apparatus has arisen in a natural way out of the conceptual apparatus of everyday life. The latter has, in the course of its development, gone through phases in which its employment in relation to the actual data of experience led to contradictions which are known under the name of the illusions of sense. Once there were empirical meaning rules which assigned the sentence 'This is bent' to the optical data of experience which one has when one looks at a bent stick. There was also an empirical meaning-rule which assigned the sentence 'This is straight' to certain tactual data. Now the following of these rules in the case of a stick half immersed in water led to mutually incompatible sentences. The rules were therefore discarded, in that these concepts, bound up with the rules, were put aside. People, therefore, freed themselves from the illusions of sense by restricting the conceptual apparatus, as a consequence of which one part of the complete world-picture was left out of account.

The above can perhaps be generalized by saying that we have to do with so-called illusions of sense either when the following of certain empirical meaning-rules in the presence of certain data of experience leads directly to contradiction, or when such a contradiction is derivable from the sentences dictated by the data of experience with the help of axiomatic and deductive meaning-rules — often also with the help of inductive hypotheses. In the latter case, the contradiction could be avoided by the rejection of the hypothesis without the need of any narrowing of the conceptual apparatus and empirical meaning-rules. If, however, in such cases one sees no *instantia contraria* against the hypothesis, but speaks instead of "sensory illusion", this shows that in these cases one had decided for a change of empirical meaning-rules, and therefore of conceptual apparatus.

Still another lesson is to be drawn from illusions of sense. There we have to do with two sentences arrived at from the data of experience in accordance with empirical meaning-rules, which in view of other meaning-rules, and, finally, of certain hypotheses, lead to contradiction. If one removes the contradiction by annulling the authority of the empirical meaning-rules, this is usually done in such a way that after the change of meaning-rules, one of the two empirical sentences is discarded and the other retained. Which of the two is retained depends on which fits better in the totality of sentences already accepted either on the basis of meaning-rules, or as hypotheses.

This continual and continuous reciprocal accommodation of "facts to theories" has set our entire original use of language, which at first was connected in a simple and naïve way to the material of experience, to fluctuating. One would soon find oneself in difficulties if he attempted to specify the empirical meaning-rules in accordance with which a certain person oriented himself in his use of language. This, however, by no means implies that a language, which in accordance with the very concept of a language must be unambiguously determined by its dictionary, its syntax and its meaning stipulations, might have no empirical meaning-rules. The impossibility of specifying the empirical meaning-rules which hold for the language used by an individual, shows merely that this language usage vacillates between different languages.

From what we have said it becomes clear, when we consider the human effort to gain knowledge, that instead of man being placed, so to speak, in front of a heap of factual material with the task of encompassing it by a theory, he is rather in the position of hunting for a conceptual apparatus, for it is this alone which can give rise to empirical sentences — and with its help he obtains only an excerpt of the entire world-picture, obtains, that is to to say, a world-perspective, which is to satisfy certain conditions. We have suggested consistency and systematic order as two such conditions, to which undoubtedly many others should be added. What we have said relates as well to every-day as to scientific knowledge.

We have thus asserted that science deliberately restricts its conceptual apparatus, and among many possible conceptual structures aspires to one of a special sort, whereby science renounces a complete world-picture and aims instead at only one world-perspective besides which are many others.

Why does science seek exactly this and not another conceptual apparatus? Why does science prefer exactly this world-perspective to the others? Perhaps it does this on the ground that only those judgments which constitute the world-perspective at which it aims are true, and the judgments which belong to the other world-perspectives are to be rejected as false? To reject a judgment as false can signify one of two things: (1) that the same judgment is made with negative assertion, (2) it can mean, however, the predication of falsity of the rejected judgment. Now it seems to be clear that one can only make a judgment if one makes use of the conceptual apparatus corresponding to this judgment. From this it follows that one can only reject as false a judgment which belongs to a different conceptual apparatus by making a judgment about this judgment in which one predicates falsity of it. It is indeed very doubtful whether one can predicate falsity of a judgment if the conceptual apparatus of that judgment is foreign to us, if, that is to say, we cannot translate the sentence formulating the judgment into our own language. We cannot, however, exclude this as impossible. It may therefore be the case that one who employs conceptual apparatus B_1 can predicate falsity of judgments which belong to the world-perspective of a foreign conceptual apparatus B_2. This predication, however, occurs either at random, or else it belongs to our own world-perspective, and as such it derives its entire value and status from the value and status of our own world-perspective.

We must take into consideration, however, that in opposition to our own unfavorable judgment of the sentences of a foreign world-perspective there stands a conflicting positive judgment on the part of one who makes use of the conceptual apparatus corresponding to that world-perspective. For it can be shown that any one who employs conceptual apparatus B, provided only that the data of his experience are sufficiently rich, and that he has a sufficiently sharp deductive insight, must accept as true every judgment which belongs to the world-perspective of his conceptual apparatus and to which he takes any stand at all. For should he reject a sentence of his language the meaning of which is constituted by such a judgment, he would be running counter to meaning-rules of his language, that is to say, would be rejecting with that sentence, not the judgment in question, but rather another. In so far, however, as he accepts the judgments of his world-perspective as true, he will also, in accordance with the meanings of the words 'true' and 'false', reject the predication of falsity with respect to these judgments. (See in this connection 'The World-Picture and the Conceptual Apparatus', present volume, pp. 67–89.)

Thus there would stand over and against one another two opposed judgments of the truth of a world-perspective. Each of them is itself part of a world-perspective. Now the epistemologist takes upon himself the role of an impartial umpire. To which of the two world-perspectives shall he concede the advantage with respect to truth? Is, however, the epistemologist truly an impartial umpire? Is he not also imprisoned in a conceptual apparatus which dictates to him his world-perspective? Even the epistemologist cannot speak without a language, cannot think without a conceptual apparatus. He will thus make his decision as to truth in a way which corresponds to his world-perspective.

The epistemologist therefore is not suited for the role of an impartial umpire in the struggle between two world-perspectives for the title of truth. Consequently, he should not push forward to assume this role. Instead of this he should set himself another task. He should give his attention to the changes which occur in the conceptual apparatus of science and in the corresponding world-perspectives, and should seek to ascertain the motives which bring these changes about. Perhaps this sequence of world-perspectives permits of being conceived as a goal-directed process which advances as though someone consciously wished to achieve the goal by means of the sequence. The task involved in such a conception of the history of science constitutes the sound kernel of the *geisteswissenschaftlichen* (culture-theoretical) understanding of the evolution of science.

7. SYNTACTIC CONNEXION*

(1936)

1. The discovery of the antinomies, and the method of their resolution, have made problems of linguistic syntax the most important problems of logic (provided this word is understood in a sense that also includes meta-theoretical considerations). Among these problems that of syntactic con-nexion is of the greatest importance for logic. It is concerned with the speci-fication of the conditions under which a word pattern, constituted of meaning-ful words, forms an expression which itself has a unified meaning (consti-tuted, to be sure, by the meaning of the single words belonging to it). A word pattern of this kind is *syntactically connected.*

The word pattern 'John loves Ann', for instance, is composed of words of the English language in syntactic connexion, and is a significant expression in English. However, the expression 'perhaps horse if will however shine' is constructed of meaningful English words, but lacks syntactic connexion, and does not belong to the meaningful expressions of the English language.

There are several solutions to this problem of syntactic connexion. Russell's theory of types, for example, offers a solution. But a particularly elegant and simple way of grasping the concept of syntactic connexion is offered by the theory of semantic categories developed by Professor Stanislaw Leśniewski. We shall base our work here on the relevant results of Leśniewski,[1] adding on our part a symbolism, in principle applicable to almost all languages, which makes it possible to formally define and examine the syntactic con-nexion of a word pattern.

2. Both the concept and the term 'semantic category' *(Bedeutungskategorie)* were first introduced by Husserl. In his *Logische Untersuchungen*[2] Husserl mentions that single words and complex expressions of a language can be divided into classes such that two words or expressions belonging to the same class can be substituted for one another, in a context possessing unified meaning, without that context becoming an incoherent word pattern and

* Translated from the German by Horst Weber. First published in *Studia Philosophica* I (1936), 1—27. *Język i Poznanie*, I, 222—42. Reprinted from Storrs McCall (ed.), *Polish Logic 1920—1934* (1967), pp. 207—31, by kind permission of PWN and Oxford University Press. Copyright © 1967 by Oxford University Press.

losing unified sense. On the other hand, two words or expressions belonging to different classes do not possess this property. Take the sentence 'the sun shines' as an example of a context having a coherent meaning. If we substitute for the word 'shines' the word 'burns' or the word 'whistles' or the word 'dances', we obtain from the sentence 'the sun shines' other true or false sentences which have coherent meaning. If we replace 'shines' by 'if' or 'green' or 'perhaps' we obtain incoherent word patterns. Husserl terms these classes of words or expressions semantic categories.

We want to define this concept a little more precisely. The word or expression A, taken in sense x, and the word or expression B, taken in sense y, belong to the same semantic category if and only if there is a sentence (or sentential function) S_A, in which A occurs with meaning x, and which has the property that if S_A is transformed into S_B upon replacing A by B (with meaning y), then S_B is also a sentence (or sentential function). (It is understood that in this process the other words and the structure of S_A remain the same.)

The system of semantic categories is closely related to the simplified hierarchy of logical types − although ramified to a much higher degree than the latter − and basically constitutes its grammatical semantic counterpart.[3]

Among all semantic categories two kinds can be distinguished, *basic categories* and *functor categories*. (The term 'functor' derives from Kotarbiński; that of 'basic category' is my own.) Unfortunately we are unable to define these terms with any tolerable precision. An understanding, however, of what is meant by them can be reached easily. A 'functor' is the same as a 'functional sign', or an 'unsaturated symbol' with 'brackets following it'. Functor categories are the semantic categories to which functors belong. I shall call a semantic category a basic category when it is not a functor category.

From the above definition of a semantic category it follows at once that any two sentences belong to the same semantic category. Sentences are, of course, not functors, consequently the semantic category of sentences is among the basic categories. Besides the sentence category there can also be other basic categories. Leśniewski has only one basic category besides the sentence category: the name category, to which belong singular as well as general names. If one compared the simplified theory of types with the theory of semantic categories, the sentence type and the proper-name type would have to be counted among the basic categories. All other types would belong to the functor categories. It seems that not all names form a single semantic category in ordinary language. In our view, at least two semantic categories can be distinguished among names in ordinary speech: first, the semantic category to which belong the singular names of individuals, and the general names of individuals in so far as these are taken *in suppositione personali*; secondly, the semantic category of general names in so far as they occur *in suppositione simplici* (i.e. as the names of universals).

If the concept of syntactic connexion were to be defined in strict generality, nothing could be decided about the number and kind of basic semantic and functor categories, since these may vary in different languages. For the sake of simplicity, however, we shall restrict ourselves (like Leśniewski) to languages having only two basic semantic categories, that of sentences and that of names. Apart from these two basic semantic categories, we shall assume, again in accordance with Leśniewski, an unbounded and ramified ascending hierarchy of functor categories characterized in two ways: first by the number and semantic category of their arguments taken in order; second by the semantic category of the whole composite expression formed by them together with their arguments. Thus, for example, the functors which form a sentence with *one* name as argument would represent a distinct semantic category; the functors which form a sentence with *two* names as arguments would form a different semantic category, and so forth. Functors that form a *name* with one name as their argument would again constitute a different semantic category. Also, sentence-forming functors which allow a sentence as their only argument (e.g. the '∼' sign in mathematical logic) would be assigned to a separate semantic category, and so forth.

3. We assume that the semantic category of a single word is defined by its meaning. We shall give single words an index according to their semantic category, viz. the simple index 's' to single words belonging to the sentence category; the simple index 'n' to words belonging to the category of names. To single words belonging not to a basic category but to functor categories we shall assign a fractional index, formed of a numerator and a denominator. In the numerator will be the index of the semantic category to which the whole expression composed of the functional sign plus its arguments belongs, while in the denominator appear, one after the other, the indices of the semantic categories of the arguments, which together with the functor combine into a significant whole. For example, a word forming a sentence with two names as its arguments gets the fractional index s/nn. In this way each semantic category receives a characteristic index. The hierarchy of semantic categories would be reflected in a series of indices (far from being complete) of the following form:

$$s, n, \frac{s}{n}, \frac{s}{nn}, \frac{s}{nnn}, ..., \frac{s}{s}, \frac{s}{ss}, \frac{s}{sss}, ..., \frac{s}{ns}, \frac{s}{sn}, ...,$$

$$\frac{s}{\frac{s}{n}}, \frac{s}{\frac{s}{n}\frac{s}{n}}, ..., \frac{n}{n}, \frac{n}{nn}, \frac{n}{sn}, ..., \frac{\frac{s}{n}}{\frac{s}{n}}, \text{ etc.}$$

To illustrate this index symbolism with a proposition from mathematical logic, e.g.

$$\sim p \supset p \,.\, \supset .\, p$$

we add indices to the single words and obtain:

$$\sim p \supset p \,.\, \supset .\, p$$

$$\frac{s}{s} \quad \frac{s}{ss} \quad \frac{s}{ss} \quad \frac{s}{ss} \quad s$$

If one applies this index symbolism to ordinary language, the semantic categories which we have assumed (in accordance with Leśniewski) will not always suffice, since ordinary languages apparently are richer in semantic categories. Furthermore, the decision to which semantic category a word belongs is rendered difficult by fluctuations in the meaning of words. At times it is uncertain what should be considered as *one* word. In simple and favourable cases, however, the index apparatus cited above will be quite suitable for linguistic use, as is illustrated by the following example:

The lilac smells very strongly and the rose blooms.

$$\frac{n}{n} \quad n \quad \frac{s}{n} \quad \frac{s}{\frac{s}{n}} \quad \frac{s}{\frac{s}{n}} \quad \frac{s}{ss} \quad \frac{n}{n} \quad n \quad \frac{s}{n}$$

4. In every significant composite expression it is indicated, in one way or another, which expressions occur as arguments, and to what expressions, appearing as functors, they belong. Whenever the functor has several arguments, it must be indicated which of these arguments is the first, which is

the second, etc. The order of arguments plays an important role; the difference between subject and predicate, or between antecedent and consequent of a hypothetical proposition, are special cases of the important differences made by the order of arguments. Generally speaking, this order is not identical with the sequence in which arguments occur in expressions. In fact, the order is not a purely structural, i.e. purely external affair, but is based on the semantic qualities of the whole expression. Only in symbolic languages and in some ordinary languages does the order of arguments correspond to their sequential ordering.

In order to indicate the manifold interrelationships of the constituents (or parts) of an expression, symbolic languages use conventions concerning the 'scope' of various functors, as well as employing brackets and making use of word order. In ordinary speech these interrelations are indicated by means of word order, inflexion, prepositions, and punctuation marks. A semantic pattern in which these interrelations are not indicated at all, or only incompletely, is devoid of any coherent meaning.

In every significant composite expression the relations of functors to their arguments have to be such that the entire expression may be divided into constituents, of which one is a functor (possibly itself a composite expression) and the others are its arguments. This functor we call the *main functor* of the expression. (The concept of the main functor and the basic notion of its definition we owe to Leśniewski.) In the logical example given above, the second implication sign is the main functor of the whole proposition; in the example taken from ordinary language, the word 'and' is the main functor. When it is possible to divide a composite expression into a main functor and its arguments, we call such an expression *well articulated*. The main functor of an expression and its arguments we call *first-order constituents* of this expression. If the first-order constituents of an expression *A* either consist of single words, or, being composite, are themselves well articulated; and if, descending to the constituents of constituents, and to the constituents of constituents of constituents, etc., i.e. to the *n*th order constituents, we always meet with single words or well articulated expressions, we call the expression *A well articulated throughout*.

It should be mentioned that ordinary language often admits elliptical expressions, so that sometimes a significant composite expression cannot be well articulated throughout on the sole basis of the words explicitly contained within it. But a good overall articulation can be easily established by introducing the words omitted but implicit. The difficulties are greater if the language e.g. German, admits separable words. In this case the criterion for a *single word* cannot be stated structurally.

5. Good articulation throughout is a necessary but not sufficient condition for a composite expression's having a unified sense, and hence being a meaningful expression. This condition must be supplemented by others. In order that an expression which is well articulated throughout may be meaningful, all its constituents of the same order (which are related as functor and arguments) must fit together. That is, to each constituent of the nth degree, which occurs as the main functor either of the entire expression or of an $(n-1)$th-order constituent of it, and which requires — according to its semantic category — so-and-so many arguments belonging to certain semantic categories, there must correspond as arguments just this number of constituents, of the nth degree and of the required semantic categories. To a main functor of the semantic category with the index s/ns, for instance, two arguments have first of all to correspond. Secondly, the first argument must belong to the semantic category of names, and the second to that of sentences. An expression well articulated throughout, and complying with both the above-mentioned conditions, we shall call *syntactically connected*.

These conditions can be formulated in another way, and more precisely, by means of our index symbolism. For this purpose we introduce the concept of the *exponent* of an expression, and illustrate this with an example. If we take the expression

$$p \vee p \, . \, \supset . \, p$$

and add indices to each word, we obtain

$$p \vee p \, . \, \supset . \, p \tag{A}$$

$$s \quad \frac{s}{ss} \quad s \quad \frac{s}{ss} \quad s$$

We arrange the constituents of this expression according to the following principle. First we write down the main functor of the entire expression, and then, successively, its first, second (and if necessary third, fourth, etc.) arguments. We thus obtain:

$$\supset, p \vee p, p \tag{B}$$

$$\frac{s}{ss} \quad s \quad \frac{s}{ss} \quad s \quad s$$

If any constituent, appearing in this sequence, is still an expression composed of a main functor and its arguments, we separate this constituent into constituents of the next higher degree and order them by the same principle, putting first the main functor and then its first, second, etc., arguments. Hence we obtain:

$$\supset, \vee, p, p, p \tag{C}$$
$$\frac{s}{ss} \frac{s}{ss} \ s \ s$$

Any composite constituent left in this sequence is decomposed according to the same principle, and this procedure is continued to the point where only simple, single words appear as constituents of the sequence. A sequence ordered in this way, and consisting of the words of an expression, we call the *proper word sequence* of the expression. In our example the proper word sequence has already been obtained with the second step, i.e. (C) is the proper word sequence of (A). If we now separate the indices from the words of the proper word sequence of an expression, writing down the indices in the same order, we obtain what is called the *proper index sequence* of the expression.

The proper index sequence of expression (A) takes the following form:

$$\frac{s}{ss} \frac{s}{ss} \ s \ s \ s. \tag{1}$$

We now see whether we can find in this index sequence, reading from left to right, a combination of indices with a fractional index in the initial position, followed immediately by exactly the same indices that occur in the denominator of the fractional index. If we find one or more of these combinations of indices, we cancel the first one (again reading from left to right) from the index sequence, and replace it by the numerator of the fractional index. The new index sequence obtained by this procedure we call the *first derivative* of the proper index sequence of the expression *A*. It looks like this:

$$\frac{s}{ss} \ s \ s. \tag{2}$$

This first derivative consists of a fractional index followed directly by the same index combination that forms the denominator of the fractional index. We can therefore transform it once more in the manner described above, forming its second derivative, which consists of the single index

$$s. \tag{3}$$

This we shall call the final derivative, as no further derivations are possible.

The final derivative of the proper index sequence of an expression we call the *exponent* of the expression.

Let us now determine the exponent of the ordinary language proposition given on page 121. Its proper index sequence and its successive appear as follows:

$$\frac{\dfrac{\dfrac{\dfrac{s}{n}}{\dfrac{s}{n}}}{\dfrac{s}{ss}}\ \dfrac{\dfrac{\dfrac{s}{n}}{\dfrac{s}{n}}}{\dfrac{s}{n}}\ \dfrac{\dfrac{s}{n}}{\dfrac{s}{n}}\ \dfrac{s}{n}\dfrac{n}{n}\ n\ \dfrac{s}{n}\dfrac{n}{n}\ n}{}\quad\text{(proper index sequence)}$$

$$\frac{s}{ss}\ \frac{\dfrac{s}{n}}{\dfrac{s}{n}}\ \frac{s}{n}\frac{n}{n}\ n\ \frac{s}{n}\frac{n}{n}\ n \qquad\qquad\qquad \text{(1st derivative)}$$

$$\frac{s}{ss}\ \frac{s}{n}\frac{n}{n}\ n\ \frac{s}{n}\frac{n}{n}\ n \qquad\qquad\qquad\qquad \text{(2nd derivative)}$$

$$\frac{s}{ss}\ \frac{s}{n}\ n\ \frac{s}{n}\frac{n}{n}\ n \qquad\qquad\qquad\qquad\quad \text{(3rd derivative)}$$

$$\frac{s}{ss}\ s\ \frac{s}{n}\frac{n}{n}\ n \qquad\qquad\qquad\qquad\qquad \text{(4th derivative)}$$

$$\frac{s}{ss}\ s\ \frac{s}{n}\ n \qquad\qquad\qquad\qquad\qquad\quad \text{(5th derivative)}$$

$$\frac{s}{ss}\ s\ s \qquad\qquad\qquad\qquad\qquad\qquad\quad \text{(6th derivative)}$$

$$s \qquad\qquad\qquad\qquad\qquad\qquad\quad\ \text{(7th and final derivative)}$$

We are now able to make a definition. An expression is *syntactically connected* if, and only if, (1) it is well articulated throughout; (2) to every functor that occurs as a main functor of any order, there correspond exactly as many arguments as there are letters in the denominator of its index; (3) the expression possesses an exponent consisting of a single index.[4] This index may take the form of a single letter, but it may also be a fraction. For instance, the expression

$$smells \quad very \quad strongly$$

$$
\dfrac{s}{n} \qquad
\dfrac{\dfrac{s}{n}}{\dfrac{s}{n}} \qquad
\dfrac{\dfrac{s}{n}}{\dfrac{s}{\dfrac{s}{\dfrac{s}{n}}}}
$$

which has the proper index sequence

$$
\dfrac{\dfrac{s}{n}}{\dfrac{s}{\dfrac{s}{\dfrac{s}{n}}}} \qquad
\dfrac{\dfrac{s}{n}}{\dfrac{s}{n}} \qquad
\dfrac{s}{n} \, ,
$$

has as its exponent the fractional index

$$\dfrac{s}{n} \, .$$

As an example of an expression not syntactically connected, consider the following word pattern:

$$F \ (\phi) \ : \ \equiv \ : \ \sim \ \phi \ (\phi)$$

$$
\dfrac{s}{\dfrac{s}{n}} \quad
\dfrac{s}{n} \quad
\dfrac{s}{ss} \quad
\dfrac{s}{s} \quad
\dfrac{s}{n} \quad
\dfrac{s}{n} \, .
$$

Its proper index sequence and its derivatives are:

$$
\dfrac{s}{ss} \quad
\dfrac{s}{\dfrac{s}{n}} \quad
\dfrac{s}{n} \quad
\dfrac{s}{s} \quad
\dfrac{s}{n} \quad
\dfrac{s}{n}
$$

$$
\dfrac{s}{ss} \quad
s \quad
\dfrac{s}{s} \quad
\dfrac{s}{n} \quad
\dfrac{s}{n} \, .
$$

The first derivative, being also the final one in this instance, forms the exponent, which patently consists of several indices. Therefore the expression is not syntactically connected. (The word pattern examined in this last example forms the well-known 'definition' which leads to Russell's antinomy of the class of classes not containing themselves as members.)

The exponent of a syntactically connected expression gives the semantic category to which the whole composite expression belongs.

6. A symbolism which appended indices to single words would need no parentheses or other means to show the articulation of its syntactically connected expressions; i.e. to denote the mutual relations of functors and their arguments. A strict adherence, in ordering words, to the same principle that governs the order of indices in the proper index sequence of an expression would suffice. That is, the words of each composite expression would have to be arranged in such a way that the sign for the main functor would always be followed by its first, its second, etc., arguments. The proposition, for example, which reads in Russell's symbolism:

$$p \cdot q \cdot \supset r : \equiv : \sim r \cdot q \cdot \supset \sim p \tag{A}$$

would be written by this principle as follows:

$$\equiv \supset \, . \, p \, q \, r \supset \, . \sim r \, q \sim p \, . \tag{B}$$

We call a functor n-adic, when the denominator of its index contains n indices. Then we can say, the expression A is the kth argument of the n-adic functor F in the expression B, if and only if, (i) an uninterrupted constituent T, following directly to the right of F, can be lifted out of the expression B, the exponent of T being the same as the denominator of the index of F; (ii) this part T can be completely decomposed into n uninterrupted subconstitutents in such a way that the exponents of the subconstituents are, taken successively, the same as the indices contained in the denominator of the index of F; (iii) A is the kth of these subconstituents; and (iv) F together with T constitutes either the entire expression B or a constituent of B.

(Strictly speaking, this explanation should be replaced by a recursive definition.)

For example, according to this explanation, the constituent of expression
B designated as 3 is the first argument, and that designated as 4 the second
argument, of the implication sign designated as 5 in expression B. For (i) the
uninterrrupted constituent 1, following directly to the right of 5, and having
an exponent identical with the denominator of the index of 5, can be lifted
out of the expression B; (ii) constituent 1 can be completely reduced to two
uninterrupted subconstituents, their exponents being, in order, the same as
the indices contained in the denominator of the index of 5; (iii) 3 is the first
of these subconstituents, 4 the second; and (iv) 5 together with 1 constitutes
a constituent of B.

The advantage of the index symbolism, which makes parentheses dispensable, may perhaps seem insignificant if one considers only examples
from the propositional calculus. In fact, for the propositional calculus
Łukasiewicz has introduced a symbolism that needs no parentheses or other
signs in order to signify the articulation of syntactically connected expressions, and which involves no indices.[5] The possibility of dispensing with
parentheses without introducing indices is explained by the fact that the
propositional calculus is concerned with only very few (in practice only
three) semantic categories. All variables belong to one semantic category, and
the number of constants is limited, thus making it possible to indicate the
semantic category of an expression by the form of the symbols themselves.
In this case, the rules of formation are easily enumerated. But in the case of
a large, theoretically unlimited number of different semantic categories some
systematic mode of differentiation like our index symbolism has to be employed.

So far our inquiries have concerned only expressions containing no
operators (see below, Section 7). We will now consider expressions that contain them.

II

7. It has been assumed above that any word of a language can be assigned to
a certain semantic category by its meaning, and can consequently be furnished
with an index. Composite expressions may be analysed according to the
pattern, 'functors and their arguments', only if this assumption holds. For
some languages it may hold; it does not, however, seem to be applicable to
certain symbolic languages. We are referring here to languages that make use

of what are called operators. By this term we understand such signs as the universal quantifier in logic, '(Πx)', or '(x)', which is also called the all-operator (cf. Carnap, *Abriss der Logistik* (Vienna 1929), p. 13); the existential operator '$(\exists x)$'; the algebraic summation sign

$$\sum_{k=1}^{10} \ ;$$

the product sign

$$\prod_{x=1}^{100} \ ;$$

the definite integral sign $\int_{0}^{1} dx$, etc.

All these signs have the property of applying to an expression that contains one or more variables, and reducing one or more of these variables to the role of an apparent variable. For instance, when an operator is applied to an expression which contains only one variable, a composite expression of constant value is created. Thus the expressions '$(\exists x) . x$ is human' and

$$\sum_{x=1}^{10} x^2$$

have constant values, although variables occur in them. These variables are reduced to apparent variables by the operator; or, in other words, they are 'bound' by the operator.

The analysis of an expression that contains an operator, e.g. the general proposition '$(\Pi x) . fx$', into functors and arguments with appropriate semantic categories, seems to meet with insuperable difficulties.

Disregarding the inner structure of the composite operator '(Πx)', we shall first reject the obvious interpretation of the syntactical structure of the general proposition '$(\Pi x) . fx$'; to wit, that which implies that in a proposition of this kind the operator '(Πx)' plays the role of the main functor and the propositional function the role of its argument. If this were the correct syntactical analysis of a general proposition, the universal operator '(Πx)' would have to be counted among the functors which form a sentence with one sentence as their argument, and hence belong to the $\frac{s}{s}$ category. But, on the other hand, it is to be considered that an $\frac{s}{s}$ functor must be a truth functor in an extensionalistic logic. Therefore it has to correspond to one of the following four tables.

p	$f_1 p$		p	$f_2 p$		p	$f_3 p$		p	$f_4 p$
0	0		0	1		0	1		0	0
1	1		1	0		1	1		1	0

In other words, if the universal operator were an $\frac{s}{s}$ functor, the proposition '$(\Pi x) . fx$' would have to be either (1) equivalent to 'fx'; or (2) equivalent to '$\sim fx$'; or (3) always true, independent of 'x'; or (4) always false. All these cases are, however, excluded. Hence, in an extensionalistic logic, the '(Πx)'-operator may not be interpreted as an $\frac{s}{s}$ functor. Yet, since it forms a proposition with the proposition 'fx', it cannot be any other kind of functor.

The thought, however, comes to mind that the syntactical structure of a general proposition

$$(\Pi x) . fx$$

could also be interpreted in a different way. Perhaps 'Πx' is not the main functor in this proposition and 'fx' not its argument, but the 'Π'-sign might be the main functor and 'x' its first, 'fx' its second argument. Then the general proposition would have to be written in the following form in order to be correct:

$$\Pi(x, fx).$$

Since 'x' can belong to different semantic categories, 'Π' would have to be of various types. If, for example, 'x' belongs to the name category and 'f' to the $\frac{s}{n}$ category, Π would have to belong to the $\frac{s}{ns}$ category. But if 'x' belonged to the category of sentences, and 'f' to the $\frac{s}{s}$ category, 'Π' would have to belong to the $\frac{s}{ss}$ category for '$\Pi(x, fx)$', to be a proposition. In this latter case, 'Π' would have to be a dyadic truth functor in an extensionalistic logic; it would therefore correspond to one of the sixteen known tables for dyadic truth functors. But is is easily demonstrated that this too is incompatible with the meaning of the general proposition '$(\Pi x) . fx$'.

Thus both the first and the second way of interpreting the syntactical structure of general propositions as composed of functors and arguments have proved unsuccessful.

8. Nothing may be substituted for a variable, in a legitimate proposition, which is bound by an operator (assuming that the latter is not a universal operator forming a main part of the entire proposition). This is the meaning of the 'apparency' or 'boundness' of the variables. Functors, on the other hand, behave in the opposite way in this respect. If, therefore, functors are conceived of as non-binding and operators as binding, it becomes evident that an operator may not be counted as a functor. As a secondary difference between a functor and an operator, it should be noted that a functor can appear as the argument of another functor, while an operator can never be the argument of a functor.

Despite these differences, there is a similarity between an operator and a functor. An operator can form a composite, coherent whole with the expression to which it applies, just as a functor can with its arguments. Therefore, one would also be able to assign indices to operators. These would have to be different from the indices assigned to functors, as they cannot be treated in the same manner as the functor indices in determining the exponent of an expression. Since an operator can never be an argument, its index must not be combined with an index preceding it in the proper index sequence or its derivatives, but must always be combined with the indices following it. We therefore propose for operator indices a fraction with a vertical dash to its left. The universal operator '(Πx)' would thus receive the index $\left|\frac{s}{s}\right.$, since it forms a sentence out of a sentence.

We assign *one* index to the entire operator, although the operator appears to consist of several words. By this we do not abandon the principle that from the start an index should be assigned only to a single word, and that indices of composite expressions are considered to be their exponents (i.e. the final derivatives of their index sequences). For an operator must not be treated as an expression composed of several words. An operator is basically a single word composed of several letters. There are ways of writing operators which make this clear. Professor Scholz, for instance, writes '$\tilde{x}$' for '(Πx)'. And the usual notation '(x)' instead of '(Πx)', or 'Π_x' instead of '(Πx)', makes the single-word character of operators evident.

9. The exponent of an expression containing an operator has to be determined in a way other than the one given above. If we proceeded with operator indices as with functor indices, it might happen that the operator index was combined with an index preceding it, and this, as we have seen, is not permissible.

Let us take the following expression as an example:

$$F \ . \ \Pi x \ . \ x \ . \tag{A}$$

$$\cfrac{\dfrac{s}{n}}{\dfrac{s}{s}} \qquad \left| \dfrac{s}{s} \ n \right.$$

If we formed its exponent by the rule given earlier, we would obtain the following derivatives:

$$(1°) \ \cfrac{\dfrac{s}{n}}{\dfrac{s}{s}} \quad \left| \dfrac{s}{s} \, n, \quad (2°) \ \dfrac{s}{n} \, n, \quad (3°) \ s. \right.$$

According to this the exponent would prove to be a sentence index, although the expression (A) is obviously syntactic nonsense.

Our new rule for the formation of the exponent of an expression requires that the part of its proper index sequence which begins with a vertical dash on the extreme left must be treated separately. For this part, which contains a dashed index only at the beginning, the final derivative must be determined by the original method. In this process the dashed index is treated exactly like an undashed one; thus, for example,

$$`\left| \dfrac{s}{s} \, s \, ` \quad \text{as well as} \quad `\dfrac{s}{s} \, s \, `$$

is replaced by the index 's', and similarly in other cases.

When the final derivative of this partial index sequence has been determined, it is substituted for the partial index sequence in the complete index sequence. Two possibilities must now be distinguished. Either the initial dashed index of the partial index sequence has disintegrated in the course of determining its final derivative (i.e. in forming the nth derivative from the $(n-1)$th, the initial dashed index, together with the indices following it, was replaced by its numerator); or it has remained intact.

In the second case, where the dashed index heading the partial index sequence remains intact, we stop and declare the complete index sequence (which results from replacing the separated partial index sequence by its final derivative) to be the final derivative, i.e. the exponent, of the original proper index sequence of the expression.

In the first case, where the dashed index heading the partial index sequence disintegrates, its vertical dash disappears from the whole index sequence, diminishing the number of vertical dashes by one. In this case the procedure is repeated, and continued either until some dashed index does not disintegrate, or until all dashed indices have vanished and we have arrived at an index sequence without dashes and with no further derivatives. The index sequence obtained is taken as the final derivative of the proper index sequence of the original expression, and hence as its exponent. We shall demonstrate this new procedure by the following example:

$$(\Pi fg): . (\Pi x) . f \ x \supset g \ x : \supset : (\Pi x) . f \ x . \supset . (\Pi x) . g \ x. \qquad (A)$$

$$\left|\frac{s}{s} \quad \right|\frac{s}{s} \quad \frac{s}{n} \quad \frac{n}{ss} \quad \frac{s}{n} \quad \frac{s}{} \quad \frac{n}{} \quad \frac{s}{ss} \quad \right|\frac{s}{s} \quad \frac{s}{n} \quad \frac{n}{} \quad \frac{s}{ss} \quad \right|\frac{s}{s} \quad \frac{s}{n} \quad n$$

The proper index sequence of this expression is

$$\left|\frac{s}{s} \quad \frac{s}{ss} \quad \right|\frac{s}{s} \quad \frac{s}{ss} \quad \frac{s}{n} \quad n \quad \frac{s}{n} \quad n \quad \frac{s}{ss} \quad \right|\frac{s}{s} \quad \frac{s}{n} \quad \right|\frac{s}{s} \quad \frac{s}{n} \quad n. \qquad (I)$$

First we form the final derivative of the part to the right of the last vertical dash:

$$(1) \quad \left|\frac{s}{s} \quad \frac{s}{n} \quad n, \qquad (2) \quad \right|\frac{s}{s} \quad s \qquad (3) \quad s.$$

We now replace in (I) this part by its final derivative, thus reducing the number of dashes by one:

$$\left|\frac{s}{s} \quad \frac{s}{ss} \quad \right|\frac{s}{s} \quad \frac{s}{ss} \quad \frac{s}{n} \quad n \quad \frac{s}{n} \quad n \quad \frac{s}{ss} \quad \right|\frac{s}{s} \quad \frac{s}{n} \quad n \ s. \qquad (II)$$

Proceeding with (II) in the same manner as with (I) we get

$$\left|\frac{s}{s} \quad \frac{s}{ss} \quad \right|\frac{s}{s} \quad \frac{s}{ss} \quad \frac{s}{n} \quad n \quad \frac{s}{n} \quad n \quad \frac{s}{ss} \quad s \ s. \qquad (III)$$

which is again to be dealt with in the same way. What must be determined is the final derivative of the part separated by the last dash. Since this is a lengthy procedure, we demonstrate it here:

$$\left|\frac{s}{s} \quad \frac{s}{ss} \quad \frac{s}{n} \quad n \quad \frac{s}{n} \quad n \quad \frac{s}{ss} \quad s \ s \qquad (1)$$

$$\left|\frac{s}{s} \quad \frac{s}{ss} \quad s \quad \frac{s}{n} \quad n \quad \frac{s}{ss} \quad s \ s \qquad (2)$$

$$\left|\frac{s}{s} \quad \frac{s}{ss} \quad s \ s \quad \frac{s}{ss} \quad s \ s \qquad (3)$$

$$\left|\frac{s}{s} \quad s \quad \frac{s}{ss} \quad s \quad s \right. \tag{4}$$

$$\left|\frac{s}{s} \quad s \quad s \right. \tag{5}$$

$$s \quad s \tag{6}$$

We replace the part separated by the last dash in (III) by this quantity and obtain

$$\left|\frac{s}{s} \quad \frac{s}{ss} \quad s \quad s. \right. \tag{IV}$$

The final derivative of the remaining index sequnece (IV) we determine without difficulty to be

$$s.$$

This final derivative of the original index sequence is the exponent of the expression (A).

As another example we shall examine a case in which not all dashed indices disintegrate. Take for instance the expression

$$(\Pi x) . f \ x : \supset : (\Pi x) . g \ (x, z). \tag{B}$$

$$\left|\frac{s}{s} \quad \frac{s}{n} \quad n \quad \frac{s}{ss} \quad\right| \frac{s}{s} \quad \frac{n}{nn} \quad n \ n$$

Its proper index sequence is

$$\frac{s}{ss} \quad \left|\frac{s}{s} \quad \frac{s}{n} \quad n \quad\right| \frac{s}{s} \quad \frac{n}{nn} \quad n \ n. \tag{I}$$

Forming the final derivative of the part separated by the last dash we obtain

$$\left|\frac{s}{s} \quad n. \right.$$

Since the dashed index has not disintegrated, the last dash is not omitted, and the final derivative of (I), which is also the exponent of (B), takes the form of

$$\frac{s}{ss} \quad \left|\frac{s}{s} \quad \frac{s}{n} \quad n \quad\right| \frac{s}{s} \quad n.$$

Hence the expression (B) does not have a single index as exponent.

We have now become familiar with the method of forming the exponent of expressions containing operators. Clearly the earlier method for operator-free expressions is contained in it as a special case. (In its formulation mention would merely have to be made of possibly appearing dashed indices.) We could now repeat word for word the definition of syntactic connexion given earlier; it would now also apply to expressions containing operators.

10. The syntactic connexion of operator-free expressions coincides with their syntactical correctness. However, besides being syntactically connected, expressions containing operators have to comply with a further condition. This condition stipulates that to each variable contained in the operator there must correspond, in the argument of the operator (i.e. in the expression to which the operator applies),[6] a variable of the same form which is not bound within this argument. Only when this condition has been fulfilled will a syntactically connected expression containing operators be syntactically correct.

III

11. We have taken the binding role of operators to be their characteristic property, distinguishing them from functors. Binding one or more variables is a property common to all operators, although some operators distinguish themselves by playing other roles as well. There is, however, one species of operator which is confined to binding one or more variables, to which category the circumflex sign '$\hat{}$', introduced by Whitehead and Russell, appears to belong. Russell employs the circumflex in order to distinguish between what he calls the 'ambiguous value of a function' and 'the function itself'. If 'fx' symbolizes the ambiguous value of a function, '$f\hat{x}$' denotes the function itself. Closer examination reveals that Russell's 'ambiguous value of a function' is identical with what is commonly termed 'value of the dependent variable'. What Russell calls 'the function itself' is, on the other hand, not a variable, but a constant. A further study of the explanations by which Russell clarifies the notion of 'the function itself' leads us to surmise that by this term he means what we would call the objective correlate of a functor. Therefore $f\hat{x}$ is the same as f and the symbols '$f\hat{x}$' and 'f' denote the same thing. If this supposition is correct the circumflex sign can be counted as an operator, for its function is to 'cancel' or 'bind' a variable. In addition it should be mentioned that several variables can be bound simultaneously in an expression by the circumflex sign. Thus '$f\hat{x}\hat{y}$' represents the functor 'f' of two arguments.

In the simplest cases, where the circumflex sign is placed over all the arguments of the main functor of an expression, as in the schematic examples '$f\hat{x}$' or '$f\hat{x}\hat{y}$', the circumflex sign has the same effect as a stroke cancelling the circumflexed variable, which is thus eliminated. If, however, not all arguments of the main functor of the whole expression are circumflexed, the role of the circumflex sign can no longer be compared to that of an ordinary cancellation mark. For example, '$\hat{p} \supset . a . {\sim}a$' ('$a$' being a constant proposition) represents an $\frac{s}{s}$ functor 'f', for which the following equivalence holds:

$$fp . \equiv . p \supset . a . {\sim}a$$

But it is obvious that the negation sign will do in place of the 'f' of this equivalence. Therefore '$\hat{p} \supset . a . {\sim}a$' means the same as '$\sim$'; while '$\supset . a . {\sim}a$', which is the same as '$p \supset . a . {\sim}a$' with 'p' cancelled, is not an $\frac{s}{s}$ functor, and is in fact not even a syntactically connected expression.

12. If an entire expression, in which the circumflex sign is applied to a variable, belongs to the category of sentences, we find in Russell's symbolism another sign with which the circumflex sign can be equated. This is the prefix ($\hat{x}$) used in class symbols, or the prefixes ($\hat{x}, \hat{y}$), used in symbols for relations. If 'fx' stands for a propositional function, and if we disregard certain complications arising from the admission of intensional functions, dropped in any case by Russell in the second edition of *Principia*, the symbol '($\hat{x}$) . fx' designates the same thing as the functor 'f', and hence the same thing as '$f\hat{x}$'. The same is true with regard to the symbols '($\hat{x}\hat{y}$) . fxy' and '$f\hat{x}\hat{y}$'.

We wish also to employ the prefixes ($\hat{x}$) or ($\hat{x}\hat{y}$) when the expression to which they refer does not belong to the category of sentences, so that we may then in general write '($\hat{x}$) . fx' for '$f\hat{x}$'-symbols and '($\hat{x}\hat{y}$) . fxy' for '$f\hat{x}\hat{y}$'-symbols. This revised notation for the circumflex operator has the advantage of allowing the whole expression to which the circumflex operation applies to be clearly marked. This was not possible with the previous notation, and could lead to ambiguities in complicated cases. Apart from this, the new notation permits us to apply the circumflex operator several times successively to the same expression. Thus we may write '($\hat{x}$) : ($\hat{y}$) . fxy', which is not the same as '($\hat{x}\hat{y}$) . fxy' (previously written '$f\hat{x}\hat{y}$'). The operational character of the circumflex symbol is also made more evident by the new notation.

13. In our index symbolism the circumflex symbols ($\hat{x}$), ($\hat{x}\hat{y}$), etc., are assigned, as operators, a dashed index. Since, however, circumflex operators can be applied to expressions of various semantic categories, and can also transform

them into expressions of various semantic categories, circumflex symbols do not always receive the same dashed index.

The general definition of the (monadic) circumflex operator would be the following. An operator '$(\hat{x})$' referring to a variable X in an expression A is a circumflex operator, if, together with this expression, it forms a functor, and if the functor, with the variable X as its argument, forms an expression equivalent to the expression A. This can be illustrated by the following example, in which the expression A takes the form 'fx', and the variable X the form 'x':

$$(\hat{x}) . fx : x . : \equiv . fx.$$

From the above it is clear that, if the expression A to which the operator refers has the exponent 'E_1', and the variable X has the index 'E_2', the operator must have the dashed index

$$\left| \frac{\dfrac{E_1}{E_2}}{E_1} \right.$$

Depending on the indices to be substituted for 'E_1' and 'E_2', the dashed index of the circumflex operator will assume various forms. Many-place circumflex operators behave similarly.

It was mentioned above that circumflex operators appear to be restricted to binding variables only. Other operators, however, have wider roles. We have seen that the main difference between a functor and an operator lies in the fact that an operator plays the role of binding while a functor does not. This suggests that it might be possible to divide in two the role of those operators not restricted to binding alone; thus the part of binding could be performed by the circumflex operator, the other by a functor. Let us, for example, introduce the functor 'Π', to which we assign the index

$$\frac{s}{\dfrac{s}{n}}$$

Syntactically speaking, 'Π' is a sentence-forming functor with an $\frac{s}{n}$ functor as its argument. In addition we make the following definition of this functor: '$\Pi(f)$' is satisfied by all and only those $\frac{s}{n}$ functors (in the place of 'f') which form a *true* proposition with every name. Thus we have:

$$\Pi(f) . \equiv . \Pi(x) . fx .$$

We shall call such a functor a universal functor. We can now replace the universal operator by the universal functor in all cases where, in place of the propositional function to which the universal (Πx) operator applies, we can specify a functor which, with x as its argument, forms an expression equivalent to the original propositional function. But this the circumflex operator always permits us to do. For '$(\hat{x}) . fx$' is just the functor sought for the propositional function 'fx', no matter what form this propositional function may take. We may therefore always-write '$\Pi((\hat{x}) . fx)$' for '$(\Pi x) . fx$'. Thus the role of the universal operator can be filled by a combination of the roles of the universal functor and the circumflex operator. We need not stress the fact that there will be not just *one*, but several universal functors, differing from each other by their semantic category, according to the semantic category of the functors which they take as their arguments.

Owing to the equivalence

$$\Pi(f) . \equiv . (\Pi x) . fx ,$$

the universal functor can be easily defined with the assistance of the universal operator. Its definition meets, however, with insurmountable difficulties if one does not want to make use of the universal operator. Nevertheless, in our opinion, a substitute for the definition of the universal functor might be found in a statement of those rules of inference which pertain to its deductive use. This would introduce the 'Π' symbol openly into logic as a primitive sign, which would then have a clearer place in the system of this science than the smuggled-in universal operator, which belongs neither to the defined nor to the primitive signs of logic.

However, either the circumflex operator must be defined, or else it must be smuggled into logic in the manner of the universal operator. We shall refrain from resolving this dilemma here. Should, however, it be decided to smuggle the circumflex operator in, we would permit ourselves the suggestion that this subterfuge might well pay, for it is possible that all other operators (of which there are many in the deductive sciences) might be replaced by the circumflex operator and by corresponding functors. It would be a great advantage, in our opinion, if the employment of operators could in all cases be restricted to one kind, that of circumflex operators.

NOTES

[1] Stanisław Leśniewski, *Grundzüge eines neuen Systems der Grundlagen der Mathematik*. (Reprinted from *Fundamenta Mathematicae* 14 (Warsaw, 1929), pp. 13 ff., 67 ff.) We

borrow from Leśniewski only the basic idea of semantic categories and their type. Leśniewski cannot be held responsible for the wording of the definitions and explanations we offer, nor for the details of the content we assign to this term, since his definitions are not general, but apply only to his special symbolism, in a quite distinct, highly precise, and purely structural sense.

[2] Edmund Husserl, *Logische Untersuchungen*, vol. ii, part 1 (2nd. rev. ed. Halle/S., 1913), pp. 294, 295, 305–12, 316–21, 326–42.

[3] R. Carnap, *Abriss der Logistik* (Vienna 1929), p. 30; A. Tarski, *Projęcie prawdy w językach nauk dedukcyjnych* (The Concept of Truth in Formalized Deductive Sciences) (Warsaw 1933), p. 67.

[4] Compliance with the first and third conditions alone does not guarantee syntactic connexion. For example,

$$\sim (\phi, x)$$
$$\frac{s}{s} \quad \frac{s}{n} \quad n$$

is not syntactically connected, although the expression is well articulated throughout, and its exponent, which we find by the following procedure:

$$\frac{s}{s} \quad \frac{s}{n} \quad n$$

$$\frac{s}{s} \quad s$$

$$s$$

is a single index.

[5] *Cf.* Jan Łukasiewicz, 'Philosophische Bemerkungen zu mehrwertigen Systemen des Aussagenkalküls', *Comptes rendus des séances de la Société des Sciences et des Lettres de Varsovie* 13, Cl. iii (Warsaw 1930). ['Philosophical Remarks on Many-Valued Systems of Propositional Logic', *Jan Łukasiewicz; Selected Works*, ed. by L. Borkowski, North-Holland, 1970, pp. 153–178.]

[6] Strictly speaking one should not speak of the 'argument' of an operator, but perhaps use the word 'operand'. Our earlier remarks about 'good articulation' of an expression must obviously be extended to the operator-operand relationship.

8. A SEMANTICAL VERSION OF THE PROBLEM OF

TRANSCENDENTAL IDEALISM*

(1937)

The remarks contained in the present paper are connected with the second
of the two main problems proposed for discussion by the Organizing Com-
mittee of the Congress.[1] I intend to demonstrate here the great importance
of contemporary logic for a satisfactory formulation and solution of central
issues handed down to us by philosophical tradition. This paper will consist
of two parts. In the first part, I will try to explain in general terms why the
results of logic may be of use in solving philosophical — in particular,
epistemological — problems. In the second part, I will give an example of such
application of logic. I will show, namely that by using the concepts developed
in modern logic the problem of transcendental idealism can be formulated
precisely and solved in an elementary way.

Let us begin the first part of the paper by surveying the disciplines which
form part of contemporary formal logic or so-called logistic. There are three
main branches of logic: so-called sentential calculus, theory of classes and
relations and meta-logic with meta-mathematics, i.e. the theory of deductive
systems. The sentential calculus is of relatively minor importance for philosophy. The significance of the theory of classes and relations is incomparably
greater. It realizes in a precise and scientific fashion a sizable part of the
programme of Aristotle's "first philosophy" — "the general theory of being".
The name 'ontology' given by Professor Leśniewski to that part of his logical
system which corresponds to the theory of classes and relations is therefore
most appropriate. The formal schemata developed in this theory enable us to
give an adequate construction of the fundamental concepts used in everyday
life and in science and whose oversimplified treatment has often been the
source of errors and confusions in philosophy. The magnificent construction
of the realm of mathematics, given by Frege, Russell, Whitehead and others,
with the help of the concepts of the theory of classes and relations, is the
most powerful evidence of the great importance of that theory for solving the
constructive problems of ontology. How primitive intellectually are the
endeavours of philosophers of the past concerned with the problems of

* Translated by Jerzy Giedymin. First published in *Przegląd Filozoficzny* **XL**, (1937),
271–87. Translation based on *Język i Poznanie*, I, 264–77. Reprinted here by kind
permission of PWN.

numbers in comparison with the philosophy of numbers based on logic. The construction of the real world, with the help of the concepts of the theory of classes and relations given by Whitehead, Russell, Nicod, Carnap, and in this country by Tarski and Mehlberg, is in sharp contrast with the activities of philosophers who — lacking this invaluable instrument — were unable to conceptualize precisely the results of their often perceptive and subtle intuitions. It should be expected that the conceptual apparatus of the theory of classes and relations will be suitable for the explication of many fundamental concepts of humanities, e.g. the concepts of whole, type, etc. In this area also certain results have been achieved. One may mention here Carnap's construction of the world of the so-called objective mind, my own definition of 'meaning', Hempel and Oppenheim's analysis of the concept of psychological type.

No less important is the third of the three main branches of logic, viz. meta-logic which seems now to be the focus of attention. Its role in investigations of epistemological nature, which we shall discuss presently in greater detail, is of particular significance. The subject matter studied in epistemology is knowledge. The term 'knowledge' is ambiguous; one may understand it either in the psychological or in the logical sense. Knowledge, in the psychological sense, consists of thought processes, namely of the processes of judging, representing, inferring, etc. From the logical viewpoint knowledge consists of 'Sätze an sich', 'Begriffe an sich' in Bolzano's sense, which are referred to by some as the "products" of the processes of thinking, by others as the expressions of the objective mind, etc.

One can characterize them simply as the meanings of statements and of terms with the proviso that 'meaning' is taken here not in the psychological sense as an individual's understanding of an expression but rather in the sense of linguistic or ideal meaning (meaning relative to a language) which is regarded as invariant when several people independently use the given expression in a way appropriate to the given language.

The theory of knowledge (epistemology) deals in some of its branches with knowledge as a psychological process, in others, with knowledge in the logical sense. The fact that knowledge in the logical sense consists of meanings relative to language implies that for any sentence about judgments or concepts (in the logical sense) there exists an equivalent sentence about sentences or terms whose meanings are those judgments and concepts. So, for example, sentences about the relation of consequence or about the relation of inconsistency, etc. between judgments are equivalent with sentences asserting suitable relations between the sentences whose meanings are those judgments. This circumstance is made use of in a certain recently developed approach to the theory of knowledge, viz. the semantic theory of knowledge in which epistemological problems are programmatically studied from the point of view of language as a system of expressions endowed with meaning. Its theses are formulated in such a way that they concern expressions, i.e. sentences and terms, but sentences and terms of a definite language which endows them with meaning.

In this way the semantic theory of knowledge makes use consciously of the only method which enables one to make assertions about certain cognitions with determinate content. For it is impossible to name a given concept or judgment except by characterizing them as the meanings of certain terms or sentences. *Prima facie,* the contrary appears to be the case, namely that one does not have to study concepts and propositions indirectly through language. For to refer to certain determinate cognitions (with definite content) one uses such phrases as, for example, 'the concept of a triangle', 'the proposition that $2 \times 2 = 4$', etc. In such phrases one does not mention – or so it appears – any expressions whose meanings would be those cognitions. This is an illusion, however. In a phrase like 'the concept of a triangle', provided it is to serve as a singular name of a determinate concept, the word 'triangle' is not being used in the usual way as, for example, in the sentence 'a triangle is a plane figure', where 'triangle' denotes a class of geometrical figures; in the phrase 'the concept of a triangle' the word 'triangle' occurs *in suppositione materiali*, i.e. as its own name. For if we were to regard 'the concept of a triangle' as containing 'triangle' in the normal supposition, i.e. as a name of triangle, then that expression would have, from this point of view, the same syntactic structure as, for example, 'John's father'. 'John's father' denotes the only object, which stands in the fatherhood-relation to John. Similarly, other expressions of the same structure, provided they are singular names, denote a unique object which stands in a certain relation to the object denoted by the term in the genitive case. The relation in question is indicated by the noun in the nominative case. (In Russell's logical symbolism, so-called descriptive function '$R'x$' corresponds to expressions of this sort.) One may say, therefore, that John's father is identical with the (unique) object which stands in the relation of fatherhood to John. Now if the 'concept of a triangle' were to be regarded as having the same syntactical structure as 'John's father', then one would have to say that 'the concept of a triangle' denotes the only object which stands to triangle in the relation of being its concept or – in other words – that the concept of a triangle is identical with the only object which stands to triangle in the relation of being its concept. By analogy, if we consider in a similar fashion 'the concept of a trilateral figure' one would have to say that the concept of a trilateral figure is identical with the only object which stands to the trilateral figure in the relation of being its concept. However, a triangle is the same as a trilateral figure. If, on the other hand, a is identical with b, then whatever the relation R, the only object which stands in the relation R to a is identical with the only object which stands in the relation R to b. Therefore, the only object which stands to a triangle in the relation of being its concept, i.e. the concept of a triangle, would be identical with the only object which stands to a trilateral figure in the relation of being its concept, i.e. the concept of a trilateral figure. This is not the case, however; the concept of a triangle is not identical with the concept of a trilateral figure (*nota bene*, if the expressions used here, 'the concept of a triangle', and 'the concept of trilateral figure' are to serve as singular names of certain determinate concepts and not as universal terms denoting classes of concepts which correspond to the symbolic schema '$\vec{R}$'x').

In order to talk about a determinate concept of a triangle, we must not use 'the concept of a triangle' as if the term 'triangle' in the normal supposition (as the name of triangle) occurred in it. Rather we ought to understand that term as containing the word 'triangle' in the material supposition, i.e. as the name of itself. Accordingly, expressions like 'the concept of a triangle' – if they are to be singular names of determinate concepts – ought to be used as abbreviations of expressions such as 'the concept which constitutes the meaning of the term 'triangle' ', i.e. as expressions each characterizing its designatum as an object which is the meaning of the term 'triangle'. If we want to name a determinate concept we ought, therefore, to write either 'the concept which constitutes the meaning of the word 'triangle' ', or – briefly – 'the concept of 'triangle' ', keeping in mind that the word 'triangle' is used here in *suppositione materiali*, i.e. as the name of itself. This does not mean that 'the concept of a triangle' with 'triangle' in the normal rather than material supposition, is not a grammatically correct expression. It is; one has to bear in mind though that then it is not a singular name of a determinate concept, but rather a universal term to whose extension belong all concepts which constitute the meanings of the terms co-extensive with the term 'triangle'.

The semantic theory of knowledge is thus intentionally on the same path which had been followed by the epistemologists (without their realizing it) whenever they talked about certain determinate concepts, judgments, etc., or, which should have been followed by them had they expressed their ideas more precisely.

Up till now we have argued that the theory of knowledge, in so far as its subject is not knowledge in the psychological sense but objectivized knowledge, i.e. knowledge in the logical sense, may be practised as a discipline whose statements are concerned with the expressions of a language, endowed by that language with definite meanings.

We shall see now that there is a close relation between the semantical theory of knowledge whose statements concern languages as systems of expressions with determinate meanings on the one hand and meta-logic, i.e. the theory of deductive systems, on the other hand. In order to see the nature of this relation, we shall first discuss deductive systems.

A deductive system is uniquely characterized, firstly, by the rules which determine the class of its expressions, secondly, by the rules which select certain sentences as its axioms and, finally, by the rules which determine when a given sentence is a direct consequence of other sentences (or, of a class of other sentences). These three determinants of a deductive system may, however, be reduced to two, viz. the rules which define the class of its expressions and the rules which define the direct consequence relation. This may be achieved by using a suitably broad concept of direct consequence. One may adopt, for instance, the convention that axioms are sentences which are direct consequences of any class of sentences. We shall see in a while that there are several arguments, apart from practical ones, in favour of such a convention. The convention in question will provide, apart from the rules which specify certain sentences as direct consequences of certain specified classes of premises, also rules which state of certain sentences that they are direct consequences of any class of premises; the axioms of the system will be identified, in accordance with the adopted convention, by the rules of the latter type. Having so extended the rules of direct consequence one may say that to characterize uniquely a deductive system it is sufficient to specify the rules which define the class of its expressions and the rules which define the relation of direct consequence. The following definition of a deductive system may then be accepted: a deductive system is a system of expressions for whose sentences the relation of direct consequence has been defined.

After this discussion of the essential properties of deductive systems which are studied in meta-logic, let us concentrate now on the essential properties of a language, conceived as a system of expressions with determinate meanings and which is the subject investigated in the semantical theory of knowledge. If a language is understood in this way, then in order to characterize it uniquely it is necessary and sufficient to specify the class of its expressions together with the meanings coordinated in that language with its expressions. Now, we shall see that by specifying the meanings of expressions we determine thereby the relations of direct consequence which hold between them.

To demonstrate this, let us, first of all, examine one of the methods which may be used in order to show that a speaker is not using the expressions of the given language in the sense which they have in that language. Let us begin with examples and assume that a person while pointing at a figure and affirming with conviction the sentence 'this figure is a square' at the same time in all seriousness rejects the sentence 'this figure is an equilateral parallelogram whose all angles are equal among themselves'. Having ascertained the behaviour of that person, would we not regard it as a conclusive proof that he does not associate with the sentences in question the meanings they have in English? Or, to choose another example. Assume that someone seriously accepts the sentence 'John is older than Peter' while denying sincerely at the same time the sentence 'Peter is younger than John'. Surely this person's behaviour would also show beyond doubt that he did not use the sentences in question with meanings which they have in English. One could give as many such examples as one likes. In all of them the rejection of certain sentences accompanied by the acceptance of certain other sentences (sentences of a determinate class) indicates that the speaker does not associate with the sentences meanings appropriate to them in the given language.

There exists another method of showing that a speaker does not use the sentences of a language in conformity with the meanings which they have in that language. There are, namely, in a language sentences whose rejection under all circumstances, no matter what other sentences one accepts, indicates that the meanings they have in the given language have been violated. For example, whoever rejects the sentence 'A triangle has three angles', shows thereby that he is not using the expressions in that sentence with meanings which they have in English, no matter what other sentences he would accept. Similarly, if I came to the conclusion that someone has seriously denied the sentence 'All men are men', I would be sure that he does not understand the expressions involved in the way they usually are understood in English, no matter what other sentences might be accepted by him.

Our analysis of the methods of discovering that a speaker is not using the expressions of a language in the sense they have in that language, implies that as soon as the meanings of the expressions of a language are determined, certain relations between the sentences are also established with the effect that the rejection of some sentences accompanied by simultaneous acceptance of other sentences results in the violation of their meanings. Now, those relations are exactly the relations of direct consequence holding between sentences. For to say that sentence B is a direct consequence in the language L of a class of sentences A amounts to saying that the rejection of B and simultaneous acceptance of the sentences in A violates the meanings which those sentences have in L. If so, the results of our previous analysis may be formulated by saying that the determination of the meanings of the expressions of a language also determines the relations of direct consequence holding between its sentences. Those relations are of two types. The meanings of the expressions of a language determine which sentences are consequences of certain specified classes of premisses as well as which sentences are consequences of any class of premisses, i.e. which sentences are — according to the previously accepted convention — the axioms of the language.

Since determinate meanings of the expressions of a language establish the relations of direct consequence between its sentences, a language conceived as a set of expressions having determinate meanings is also a set of expressions for whose sentences the relation of direct consequence has been determined. Now we had previously defined a deductive system as a set of expressions such that the relation of direct consequence has been determined for its sentential expressions. We can, therefore, conclude that a language conceived as a set of expressions with determinate meanings is a deductive system. This is not intended to imply that a language is nothing but a deductive system, that this is its only function. Besides being a deductive system a language may have several other properties: it may be used as a means of suggesting ideas, emotions, moods, of conveying commands, etc. Apart from all this it is a deductive system and it performs this role as a system of expressions endowed with meanings which are judgments and concepts.

If this is realized it becomes clear why meta-logic as a theory of deductive systems may have great importance for epistemological investigations, in particular when epistemological problems are approached through the study of language, i.e. when we engage in semantic epistemology. For, as we said before, epistemology developed in this way is a theory whose statements concern the language as a system of expressions endowed with determinate meanings. Since a language so conceived is a deductive system, one should expect that semantic epistemology may be able to make use of the results of meta-logic, i.e. of the theory of deductive systems. I am not claiming that we have shown this dependence to be necessary. The established identity of the subjects studied by the two disciplines need not imply the dependence of one of them on the other. Scientific disciplines concerned with the same domains may investigate those domains from different points of view and attempt problems which are not logically interrelated. Our claim is that the affinity between the domains investigated by the two disciplines under discussion allows one to expect that one of them may profit from the results of the other. That this is so in fact has yet to be shown and this is the task of the second part of this paper now to follow.

In this part of our paper we will attempt to show that one of the fundamental problems of the classical theory of knowledge, viz. the problem of transcendental idealism, when translated into the semantical meta-language turns into a problem whose solution on the basis of meta-logic is almost trivial. In order to show this, we shall first answer a certain metalogical question and then use this answer in our solution of the problem of transcendental idealism.

Let a deductive system be given, characterized by its formation rules and the rules of direct consequence relation between its sentences. Among the latter rules let there be two types, firstly, the rules which specify which sentences are direct consequences of an arbitrary class of premisses; secondly, the rules stating which sentences are direct consequences of specified classes of premisses. The former we shall call axiomatic rules and use the term 'axioms of the system' for the sentences specified by them as direct consequences of an arbitrary class of premisses. Rules of the second type will be referred to as deductive rules, since in accordance with them the theorems of the system will be deduced from the axioms. Let us designate as the theorems of the system both its axioms and the sentences which can be linked to the axioms with the help of the relation of direct consequence in a finite number of steps. Let us now consider the problem whether every true sentence of the language of the deductive system under discussion is a theorem of the system, i.e. is either its axiom or a sentence derivable from the axioms in the sense just explained. The answer to this question will depend on the way we choose to interpret the expression 'true sentence'. An analysis of the sense of the term 'true sentence' has been recently given by Dr Tarski in his treatise *The Concept of Truth in Formalized Languages*.[2] In his treatise which exemplifies in an excellent way the importance of metalogical investigations for the theory of knowledge, Dr. Tarski deals with the mentioned problem and solves it in an extremely simple way. Using Dr Tarski's comments and without engaging into a detailed analysis of the sense of 'true sentence', we may assert the following: If the term 'true sentence' is used in such a way that the metalogical law of excluded middle is valid, then − if the deductive system is incomplete − not all true sentences in the language of the system under consideration are its theorems. A system is incomplete if in its language there is a sentence such that neither that sentence nor its negation is a theorem of the system. The metalogical law of excluded middle states that of two contradictory sentences one is true. If this principle is accepted then for any incomplete system we shall have to conclude that not all its true sentences are its theorems. For if a system is incomplete then there will be in its language two contradictory sentences, neither of which is a theorem of the system and yet − according to the metalogical principle of excluded middle − one of them is true.

This is the simple answer to our metalogical question. And now let us resume our discussion of the problem of transcendental idealism. Transcendental idealism whose origins may be found in the philosophy of Kant and which played such an important role in the philosophy of German Romantics, surviving until recently in the Marburg and Baden schools, must be distinguished from subjective idealism exemplified mainly in the works of Berkeley. According to subjective idealism, physical objects which may be perceived by our senses, are nothing but correlates of the representations or thoughts of individual minds. This is not the view of transcendental idealism. According to it, the real world, both physical and mental, is a correlate of consciousness. However it is not a correlate of the consciousness of individuals but of the consciousness in general (*Bewusstsein überhaupt*), not a correlate of the mental subject but of the transcendental subject. The terms 'consciousness in general', 'transcendental subject', introduced by Kant, do not have – so far as I know – a quite clear sense. The transcendental subject is, so to say, the repository of categories and principles of pure reason. Furthermore, it is characterized by that mysterious unity which is reflected in the unity of the objects intuited by the perceiving mind. The personifying term 'transcendental subject' and the unity inherent in it have suggested to later philosophers mythological conceptions of some superhuman being in which individual human subjects participate just as individual objects participate in platonic ideas. In the historical development of this conception the mysterious person of the transcendental subject has been pushed into the background leaving the foreground – if I may put it so – to its function. It ceased to play the role of a superindividual mind, of a superindividual mental substance and became – like Hume's substantive individual self – a complex or system of ideas and judgments. Except that those ideas and judgments are no longer mental phenomena but concepts and judgments in the logical sense. According to transcendental idealism, the real world is thus nothing but a correlate of certain judgments in the logical sense, i.e. of ideal meanings of certain sentences and not of someone's thinking processes. The outlined conception of transcendental idealism may be found in the writings of neo-Kantians who were members of either the Marburg or Baden school. Cohen believes that the world of mathematics consists exclusively of systems of objects constituted by the axioms and theorems of mathematics. He holds a similar view of the whole of reality. It is, according to him, a correlate of a system of statements (similar to mathematical theories) which we approximate asymptotically through a series of developmental stages, i.e. successively accepted systems of scientific theories. This evolutionary conception was rejected by Rickert, the leader of the Baden school. In his view, there exist certain norms, so-called transcendental norms, which have absolute validity. The truth of our asserted statements depends on the conformity with those norms. Our judgments are true if and only if they conform to those norms. Nevertheless one cannot regard reality as a correlate of human judgments made in conformity with transcendental norms. Human judgments are not the only ones dictated by the norms. Norms distinguish a certain set of judgments in the logical sense not all of which become the content of human cognitive processes. Now the universe of all truths is identical only with the set of all judgments (in the logical sense) dictated by transcendental norms. It is that set of judgments (in the logical sense) dictated by transcendental norms that constitutes the transcendental subject whose correlate, according to idealism, is reality.

This is roughly Rickert's conception of the transcendental subject and his doctrine of transcendental idealism associated with it. Since to my mind his formulation of that doctrine is easier to understand than any other found in literature, I shall rely on it in the rest of my analysis. The claim that reality is nothing but a correlate of judgments (in the logical sense) dictated by transcendental norms as well as the equivalent claim that a judgment is true if and only if it is dictated by transcendental norms, involve a concept of those norms which, unfortunately, has not been sufficiently clarified by Rickert. Presumably, among those norms are rules of logic which to some statements assign others as their consequences, forbidding the rejection of the latter if the former are accepted. There will also be norms which elevate some statements to the status of axioms whose rejection is forbidden no matter what other beliefs one has. Rickert's examples indicate that the rules forbid the rejection of some statements in circumstances in which one has certain perceptions; those statements would be of empirical nature.

Now if we correctly conjecture what kind of norms Rickert had in mind, it will not be difficult to give a semantical paraphrase of Rickert's transcendental idealism. In this paraphrase the rules of direct consequence of a language will correspond to Rickert's transcendental norms. The language in question will be the language of natural sciences, in particular of physics, since knowledge is identified by philosophers with natural science. It is clear, that the axiomatic rules of direct consequence will correspond to the norms which dictate the axioms while deductive rules will correspond to the norms of logic. One can only be in doubt as to the possibility of paraphrasing norms which dictate empirical statements into some rules of direct consequence. There is, however, no difficulty in this case either. In my previously published articles I have distinguished, apart from axiomatic and deductive language rules, also so-called empirical rules which I have recently succeeded in characterizing in such a way that they are a special kind of axiomatic rules.[3] Since axiomatic language rules may be treated as rules of direct consequence, so can the empirical rules.

If Rickert's norms are paraphrased as rules of direct consequence specific to the language of natural science, then the transcendental subject, i.e. the judgments dictated by those norms, is paraphrased as the theorems of the axiomatic system constructed from the expressions of the language of natural science and determined by the rules of direct consequence of that language. In this semantic paraphrase the main doctrine of transcendental idealism, according to which a statement is true if and only if it is dictated by transcendental norms, will be translated into the claim that in the language of natural science a statement is true if and only if it is dictated by the rules of direct consequence specific to that language, i.e. if it is a theorem of that language.

As we said before, if the metalogical principle of excluded middle is accepted as valid, then the question whether the paraphrased idealist claim is acceptable or not will depend on whether the deductive system reconstructed for the language of natural science is complete or not. Now, as we know, even axiomatized arithmetic cannot be made complete. Since the language of natural science contains as its part the language of arithmetic, it is obvious that the language of natural science cannot be made complete, i.e. there will be in it pairs of contradictory sentences such that neither sentence of a pair is a theorem. Nevertheless, in accordance with the law of excluded middle, one of those sentences is certainly true.

I conjecture that in this way one solves the problem which was at the heart of the disputes between philosophers over the so-called question of transcendental idealism. I cannot be sure of this, however. For neither am I an experienced scholar of transcendental idealism nor do I believe that anyone could give a precise interpretation of their vague and unclear doctrines without having doubts as to whether that interpretation matches the intended meaning. At any rate it seems to me that my own interpretation of the problem of transcendental idealism is close to their intuitions. It turns out that as soon as the vague ideas have been expressed with the help of the conceptual apparatus of meta-logic, the problem which transpires through the mist of intuitive formulation becomes solvable in an elementary way. It is only then that one may try to distinguish several more subtle shades of the problem. In our paraphrase we have taken from meta-logic a finitistic conception of a theorem in the sense of a sentence which is either an axiom or is derivable from the axioms in a finite number of steps. There is another concept of a theorem in meta-logic, which is infinitistic. These two different concepts of theoremhood are associated with two different conceptions of completeness. Languages may be incomplete in the finitist sense but complete in the infinitist sense. For such a language the relation between truth and finitist theorems will be different from the relation between truth and infinitist theorems. We shall, however, be satisfied here with merely mentioning this difference.

In our outlined solution of the problem of transcendental idealism an essential role was played by the metalogical principle of excluded middle which with regard to an incomplete language makes it possible to prove that not every true sentence in such a language is its theorem. Now it is worth mentioning that the application of that principle to incomplete languages results in paradoxical effects. We shall discuss these presently.

Incomplete languages are those which contain so-called vague terms. One usually says that vague terms have extensions imprecisely defined, or that the boundaries of their extensions are blurred. These are terms such as 'young', 'old', 'bald', 'rich', etc. When using them we are able to decide of some objects that they belong to the extensions of those terms, of others that they do not; there are objects, however, of which neither the one nor the other can be decided no matter how much experience one has at one's disposal or how effective one's mind is in drawing conclusions or finding premises. To put it more precisely: a term is vague if and only if its use in a context decidable in virtue of the rules of language will make the context undecidable in virtue of those rules. The meta-law of excluded middle, however, requires that such contexts be regarded as true or false sentences. This consequence of the meta-law of excluded middle may seem paradoxical.

Let us consider a specific example. Let us introduce into English a neologism 'abra' in such a way that the following sentences are new axioms of the language: 'All abras are men', 'Adam is an abra'. The introduction of this expression into English extends the class of its theorems only by those two axioms and their consequences. The term 'abra' introduced in this way is a typical term with a vague meaning whose extension has blurred boundaries. Of its extension we know that it is included in the class of men and that Adam is definitely one of its elements. But what about Eve? Is Eve an abra or not? Which of these sentences is true? This is a question undecidable by the rules of the language. They do not sanction either the assertion that Eve is an abra or that she is not. And yet the meta-law of the excluded middle requires that either the one or the other of the two sentences is true. Does not this verdict of the meta-law of the excluded middle seem paradoxical? Are we not rather inclined to believe that neither of these contradictory sentences is true? How can a sentence which classifies Eve as an abra or a sentence which excludes her from the extension of that term be true, if the meaning acquired in our language by the term 'abra' is so deficient that it does not determine the term's extension! Surely the term 'abra' endowed with such imperfect meaning seems semi-nonsensical! Since the meta-law of the excluded middle is inapplicable to expressions of sentential form which involve meaningless components, ought one not to restrict its applicability in the case of sentences with vague terms which are, as it were, semi-meaningless?

The objections which we have just tried to formulate, in a way falling much short of any precision, are directed against the meta-law of the excluded middle. This meta-law, given the classical interpretation of the term 'true', is equivalent with the logical law of the excluded middle (this has been shown by Tarski in his treatise referred to before). Therefore the objections raised against the meta-law of excluded middle indirectly apply to the logical law of excluded middle if the classical conception of truth is used. If, in view of the objections presented here, one were to decide to reject the meta-law of the excluded middle, one would have to abandon either the logical law or to give up the classical conception of truth, replacing it by the concept of a theorem of the language. The latter solution would be tantamount to the acceptance of the doctrine of idealism. I make these remarks in a rough form, fully aware of the fact that the problems involved merit a deeper analysis which will not be undertaken here.

To conclude our investigation let us consider whether the meta-law of the excluded middle which we have used as a premiss in our argument refuting the fundamental claim of transcendental idealism, cannot be also used against conventionalism. It would seem at first sight that it can. For conventionalism points out that there are numerous problems which are unsolvable either on a priori or on empirical grounds and declares that we can solve those problems by convention, guided by the considerations of convenience, usefulness, simplicity, etc., hence in a way which has nothing to do with logical validation. Now it may appear that this exemption from the requirement of justification which is dispensed by conventionalism in case of unsolvable problems, may – in virtue of the meta-law of the excluded middle – result in our granting to falsehoods the status of accepted statements of science. If, namely, in accordance with the meta-law of the excluded middle, of two contradictory sentences one is always true and the other false, even though neither can be validated, then our conventional decision to accept one of them may result in our accepting exactly the false sentence. And this is sanctioned by conventionalism. In other words: if neither of the two contradictory answers to a question can be justified, then conventionalism allows us to solve the problem in an arbitrary way. But surely only one of such answers is true, the other being false. By permitting the choice of either of them, conventionalism gives its sanction to falsehoods.

Now, in spite of appearances to the contrary, this argument is not correct. When conventionalism sanctions arbitrary solutions of problems which are not soluble with the help of procedures of rational justification, it permits the choice of one of the answers to the given question on condition that the selected answer is elevated to the status of an axiom (postulate). The meaning of the sentence which forms the answer to the question is, however, altered through this procedure. Taken in its previous meaning, it was not an axiom. Its previous meaning was not such that the rejection of the sentence would violate the meaning. As soon as the sentence is raised to the status of an axiom its meaning is such that the rejection of the sentence does violate the meaning. Therefore, the meaning of the sentence as an axiom must be different from its meaning before it had been raised to the status of an axiom. As a consequence, the conventionalist solution of a question for which no justified answer could be given is — strictly speaking — not a solution of the same problem; it is a solution of an homomorphous question whose meaning has been changed. Nor is there any need to fear that our conventional decision will result in the acceptance of a false sentence. As an axiom, the sentence is a theorem of the language and as such it is certainly true in the given language, for every theorem is true. These brief comments on the issue must suffice here, although — again — I am aware that a more detailed discussion would be required.

In the present paper I have tried to show using a specific example that among the classical problems of philosophy there are some whose solution was made intractable by the imprecise conceptual apparatus used for their formulation; I have also tried to show that the conceptual apparatus of contemporary logic makes the solutions of those problems simple. I shall be glad if my arguments prove convincing and if they encourage others to approach classical problems of philosophy in a similar manner.

NOTES

[1] The Third Congress of Polish Philosophers held in Kraków in 1936. This article is a slightly extended version of a paper read on September 25, 1936 at the plenary session of the Congress.

[2] A. Tarski, *Pojęcie prawdy w językach nauk dedukcyjnych*, *Towarzystwo Naukowe Warszawskie*, Warszawa 1933.

[3] K. Ajdukiewicz, *Sprache und Sinn* (Language and Meaning), *Erkenntnis* **IV**, (1934), 133ff, present volume pp. 35–66; also K. Ajdukiewicz, *Empiryczny fundament poznania* (The Empirical Foundation of Knowledge), *Sprawozdania Poznańskiego Towarzystwa Przyjaciół Nauk*, No. 1 (1936), p. 27ff.

9. INTERROGATIVE SENTENCES*

(1934/1938)

PROPOSITIONAL FUNCTION

Let us replace the word 'John' in the sentence 'John is a man' by the letter 'x' which has no meaning. The resulting expression will be 'x is a man'. Since 'x' has no meaning, this expression is neither true nor false, hence it is not a sentence. It is, however, a formula from which a true or false sentence may be obtained, provided for the letter 'x' we substitute suitable meaningful expressions, viz. suitable terms. An expression which in place of a word contains a meaningless letter or letters and which turns into a sentence when for those letters suitable meaningful words are substituted, is known as a propositional formula or a propositional function. The meaningless letter which occurs in a propositional function is a variable. The following are examples of propositional functions: 'x is a man', 'John R Peter', '$x + 5 = 7$', etc. It is obvious that the first of these expressions will be transformed into a sentence on replacement of 'x' by suitable names, the second will turn into a sentence on substitution of suitable functors for 'R' (sentence-forming functors like 'likes', 'beats', 'saves', etc.), the third on replacement of 'x' by numerals.

THE STRUCTURE OF INTERROGATIVE SENTENCES

The idea of a propositional function will enable us to discuss more precisely interrogative sentences which play such an important role in teaching. An interrogative sentence is, of course, not a sentence in the logical sense, since no interrogative sentence is either true or false. While sentences in the logical sense may be characterized as expressions which are either true or false, no such simple characteristic of interrogative sentences can be given. We shall stipulate here only that we use here 'interrogative sentence' in the sense in which it is used in grammar.

An interrogative sentence is always coupled with a set of sentences in the logical sense which are its answers.

* Translated by Jerzy Giedymin. First published in Logiczne Podstawy Nauczania, *Encyklopedia Wychowania*, Warszawa 1934, reprinted 1938. Translation based on *Język i Poznanie*, I, 278–286. Reprinted here by kind permission of PWN.

Among the answers to a given interrogative sentence we shall distinguish proper and improper ones. We shall first consider proper answers. For this purpose we have to analyze more closely the structure and varieties of interrogatives. In every interrogative sentence there is, as its part, either a whole sentence in the logical sense or at least a fragment of such a sentence. Besides, an interrogative sentence will contain an interrogative particle in the form of either an interrogative pronoun or adverb, possibly with a qualifying expression or a question mark, or both. In the sentence 'Is the Earth spherical?', there is a complete sentence in the logical sense 'The Earth is spherical' and the question mark.[1] In the sentence 'Who has discovered America?', there is the interrogative pronoun 'who', the question mark and a fragment of a sentence in the logical sense (an incomplete sentential expression) '... has discovered America'.

DATUM QUESTIONIS

Let us concentrate on those interrogative sentences which apart from an interrogative particle and the question mark contain only a fragment of a sentence (in the logical sense), e.g. the sentence 'Who has discovered America?'. Which sentences in the logical sense would qualify as (proper) answers to this question? The following, for example: 'Columbus has discovered America', 'Magellan has discovered America', 'Caesar has discovered America', 'Napoleon has discovered America', 'Socrates has discovered America'. Among these answers there are true and false sentences. It is easy to see that all those sentences which qualify as answers to the question 'Who has discovered America?' fall under the same schema, i.e. may be obtained from the propositional function 'x has discovered America' by the substitution of suitable names for the variable 'x'. If one has understood an interrogative sentence, one does not know yet what its true answer will be, one does know, however, the answer's structure, viz. one does know that the true answer will be a substitution instance of the propositional function 'x has discovered America', uniquely determined by the interrogative sentence itself. The relevant propositional function is determined partly by the fragment of the sentence in the logical sense contained in the interrogative sentence, and partly by the interrogative particle which indicates where the incomplete sentential expression is to be supplemented by a variable to yield a propositional function as a schema of answers to the question. For example, the interrogative pronoun 'who' in the sentence 'Who has killed Caesar?' indicates that the incomplete expression '... has killed Caesar' is to be supplemented with the variable 'x' in such a way that it replaces the subject term; the pronoun 'whom' in the sentence 'Whom has Brutus killed?' indicates that the variable 'x' is to occur in the place of the object, 'Brutus has killed x', etc. The propositional function coordinated in this way with an interrogative sentence and forming the schema Polish of its answers is called *datum questionis*, which literally means 'the given of the question'. The variable (or variables, if there are several interrogative particles in the interrogative sentence) which occurs in the *datum questionis* will be referred to as the *unknown of the question*.

An interrogative particle together with its complements indicates not only the place in the incomplete sentential expression where the variable is to be inserted in order to obtain the *datum questionis*; usually it also distinguishes only some from among the values which turn the *datum questionis* into a true or false sentence when substituted for the unknown. So, for example, the interrogative pronoun 'who' in the sentence 'Who has discovered America?' distinguishes the names of persons from among all terms which turn the propositional function 'x has discovered America' into a true or false sentence when substituted in it for the variable 'x'. In the sentence 'Who among Polish 18th century leaders was fighting in the American War of Independence?' the interrogative pronoun 'who', together with a qualifying expression, distinguishes the names of Polish 18th century leaders. The set of those values of the unknown of the question distinguished by the interrogative pronoun or adverb will be called the *range of the unknown*.

Up till now we have discussed interrogative sentences which consist of an interrogative particle and of a fragment of a sentence in the logical sense. Is what we have said about them also applicable to those interrogative sentences in which whole sentences are governed by an interrogative particle? Is such a sentence also coordinated with a *datum questionis* in the form of a propositional function which serves as the schema for its answers? Let us consider, for example, the sentence 'How do lamps shine?' which − apart from the particle 'How' − contains a complete sentence in the logical sense 'lamps shine'.[2] Its *datum questionis*, i.e. the schema of its answers will be the propositional function 'lamps shine x' where the range of 'x' will be the set of adverbs like 'brightly', 'adequately', 'poorly', etc. A *datum questionis* is, therefore, coordinated also with an interrogative sentence in which the interrogative particle governs not an incomplete sentence but a complete one.

DECISION AND COMPLEMENTATION QUESTIONS

Certain difficulties in finding the *datum questionis* are presented by questions[3] which [in some languages (e.g. Polish) consist of the interrogative particle followed by a complete sentence in the logical sense, in others (e.g. English, German, etc.) are constructed from a sentence in the logical sense by inverting the order of words in it in such a way that its verb (or an auxiliary verb) is at the beginning of the sentence.] These are so-called *decision questions* in contradistinction to all others which are *complementation questions*.[4] Questions 'Does the sun shine?', 'Are whales fish?' are examples of decision questions. Questions discussed before, e.g. 'Who has discovered America?', 'How do this lamps shine?', etc. are complementation questions. Peculiar to a decision question is the fact that it has only two proper answers which are mutually contradictory sentences. For example, the sentences 'Yes, whales are fish' and 'No, whales are not fish' are proper answers to the question 'Are whales fish?'. The *datum questionis* in this case would have to be a propositional function whose values are these two contradictory sentences or sentences synonymous with them. So it is possible to find (somewhat artificially) a *datum questionis* for a question of this type also.

To demand clarity of formulation in the case of an interrogative sentence means to require also — apart from other conditions to be satisfied by all clearly formulated sentences — that it should indicate unambiguously the *datum questionis* and the range of the unknown. Unless these are given, the person to whom the question is addressed does not understand the question.

THE ASSUMPTION OF A QUESTION. SUGGESTIVE QUESTIONS

In reply to a question not always a proper answer is given. Before we consider various types of improper answers we have first to explain what is meant by the 'positive' and 'negative assumption of a question'.

By the *positive assumption of a question* is meant the claim that at least one proper answer to the question is true; this claim is equivalent to the disjunction of all proper answers to the question. By the *negative assumption of a question* is meant the claim that at least one of the proper answers to the question is not true; this is equivalent to the disjunction of the negations of all proper answers to the question. The positive assumption of the question 'Who has discovered America?' will be the claim 'Somebody has discovered America', its negative assumption — 'Somebody has not discovered America'. We use here the term 'assumptions', since it seems that anyone who seriously poses a question may be assumed to believe that some proper answer to his question is true and does not believe that all are true. A question whose positive or negative assumption is false is an *improperly formulated question*. Decision questions are always properly formulated since each of them has exactly two proper answers which are mutually contradictory, i.e. one of them is true and the other false.

In view of the fact that a question expresses the questioner's belief in its positive and negative assumptions, interrogative sentences may be used to communicate information. If I am asked 'When did John get married?' and I did not know before anything about John's marriage, then this interrogative sentence informs me that John has indeed got married just as well as if I were told 'You know, John got married'. The ability of interrogative sentences to communicate information expressible by their assumptions is utilized when we ask so-called *suggestive questions*, i.e. questions asked in order to communicate to another person information which they do not possess. So, for example, our question will be suggestive if we address it to someone who still does not know whether its assumptions are true and we do this in order that he accepts those assumptions on the basis of the confidence he has in us. For since he believes in the truth of our beliefs and hearing our question addressed to him accepts that we believe in its assumptions, he will himself believe in those assumptions on the basis of the confidence in us.

Otherwise any question may be suggestive if it is uttered with the use of such words and gestures from which the answer desired by the questioner may be gathered. Decision questions are particularly suitable for this purpose; since they admit only two answers 'yes' and 'no', it is easy to indicate the desired answer with the help of intonation or gestures. A suggestive question may be malicious if the questioner's intention is to suggest to the respondent a false answer. Similar to malicious suggestive questions are trap-questions, i.e. such that the intention of the questioner is to elicit an answer which implies – without the respondent being aware of it – something that contradicts other statements made by the respondent or something he wants to conceal.

IMPROPER ANSWERS

We have defined proper answers to a question as any sentence which is obtained from the *datum questionis* by substituting for the variable(s) some value(s) from the range of the unknown. Not always, however, is a proper answer given in reply to a question. Sometimes in reply a sentence is given which is not a proper answer to the question but which satisfies some of the expectations of the questioner. Such sentences may also be regarded as answers to the question but will be distinguished here as *improper answers*.

Among both proper and improper answers it is useful to distinguish complete and partial answers. An *answer* is *complete* if it is a sentence which implies (possibly in conjunction with the positive assumption) one or more proper answers to the question. Every proper answer is, of course, complete. We shall refer to them as *direct complete answers* to distinguish them from complete but *indirect answers*, i.e. answers which are not proper but which imply a proper answer. So, for example, the sentence 'Whales are mammals' is a complete indirect answer to the question 'Are whales fish?'. For though it is not itself a proper answer to the question, it implies one, viz. 'Whales are not fish'.

By a *partial answer* we shall mean a sentence which does not imply any proper answer but which excludes some of the proper answers, i.e. which in conjunction with the positive assumption implies a disjunction of some (not all) proper answers. The sentence 'An Italian has discovered America' is a partial answer to the question 'Who has discovered America?'. When, in reply to the teacher's question 'Who shouted?' — addressed to one of the pupils in the class — the pupil answers 'I did not', he has given a partial answer to the teacher's question.

We shall distinguish complete *answers* from *exhaustive* ones. An answer is called exhaustive if it is a true sentence and if it implies every true proper answer to the question. Any other answer is not exhaustive. Obviously, every exhaustive answer is complete but not vice versa. A proper answer is exhaustive only if it is the only true answer to the question or if it implies every proper true answer. It is desirable so to formulate questions that some proper answer to it should be also exhaustive.

Among improper *answers*, finally, there are *answers refuting the positive assumption of the question*. By an answer refuting the positive assumption of the question we mean a sentence which contradicts the positive assumption of the question or which implies a sentence contradicting the assumption. If in reply to the question 'Who was Copernicus' son?' the answer given is 'Copernicus did not have a son', then this answer refutes the assumption (of this question) that someone was Copernicus' son. We have said that a question, one of whose assumptions is false, is an ill-formulated (improperly posed) question. If the positive assumption of the question is not true, then it is not possible to give either a complete or partial true answer in reply to it. If we want to give in reply to it a true answer, then it has to be one refuting the positive assumption. If the negative assumption of the question is not true, i.e. if all proper answers to the question are true, then the only exhaustive answer to such a question will be one refuting its negative assumption. The latter will always be a complete indirect answer. Since in the case of decision questions both assumptions are always true, it is not possible in reply to any such question to give a true answer refuting any of the assumptions.

We have produced the following classification of answers:

I.   (a) proper answers
     (b) improper answers
II. (a) complete answers (i) direct, (ii) indirect
     (b) partial answers
III. (a) exhaustive answers
     (b) inexhaustive answers

THE PSYCHOLOGICAL MEANING OF AN INTERROGATIVE SENTENCE

Like any other expression, interrogative sentences have their psychological and linguistic meanings. The psychological meaning of an interrogative sentence, i.e., the thought expressed by it for the speaker or listener, is usually the state of mental tension, similar to thirst, experienced by a person, and directed towards the acquisition of a belief (information) which may be expressed by a proper answer to this question. The individual experiencing that psychological state – which we call the questioning-state – normally endeavours to acquire information; not any information, however, but one determined in advance to some extent. The information the questioner is after is confined within the limits set by those sentences in the logical sense which may be obtained from the *datum questionis* of the interrogative sentence expressing his questioning-state. Whoever seriously asks the question 'Who has discovered America?' endeavours to acquire information which is not arbitrary but expressible with the help of a sentence of the form 'x has discovered America'.

When we say here that the questioning-state of the questioner is a state of mental endeavour, directed towards the acquisition of information, we do not mean to say that the questioner desires that information. What one desires is also the object of one's relevant thoughts. Now, in asking the question the questioner does not think about the information he will acquire; his thoughts are concerned with what information will be about. So, for example, if one asks 'What colour is an emerald?', one is concerned in one's thinking only with emeralds and their colour, not with one's future knowledge of the colour of emeralds. By saying that the questioning-state is a state of endeavour directed towards the acquisition of information we merely want to say that the inquiring attitude, i.e., the questioning-state, is an aspiration that is satisfied as soon as the information has been acquired.

A seriously experienced questioning-state is a particular form of interest or attention. The state of being interested (in something) in contrast to the disposition to be in such states, is also a state of mental tension directed towards the acquisition of information of a certain kind. Its direction may be more or less precisely determined. If it is determined so precisely that it is focussed on items of information expressible by sentences which are substitution instances of a *datum questionis*, the state of being interested turns into a question. However, one's interest may be insufficiently crystallized with respect to its direction to be expressible with the help of an interrogative sentence. Until then the state of being interested is not yet a questioning-state. The latter is a crystallized (or well-defined) interest.

The psychological meaning of an interrogative sentence is not always identical with the state of mental tension directed towards certain items of information. Among the psychological meanings of interrogative sentences one should make distinctions analogous to those we have with respect to the psychological meanings of sentences in the logical sense, or judgments (conceived as mental phenomena). Among the latter we have distinguished beliefs and suppositions. By analogy among the psychological meanings of interrogative sentences we should distinguish questions seriously asked from those only entertained in thought. If someone searching for his lost umbrella says 'Where is my umbrella?', he is seriously in a questioning-state. On the other hand, another man who happens to hear that sentence and is not at all interested in finding the umbrella may understand the interrogative sentence; that sentence also has for him a psychological meaning but it is not a state of tension directed towards acquiring a suitable item of information. Such a disinterested bystander does not aim at finding out where the umbrella is and yet experiences a thought which constitutes his understanding of the interrogative sentence he heard. This thought is not a question seriously asked but a question merely entertained.

DIDACTIC QUESTIONS

The psychological meaning of an interrogative sentence used by a teacher in school is usually not a seriously asked question but one merely entertained. For a teacher usually puts to his pupils interrogative sentences the answers to which are already known to him; he cannot, therefore, express with their help the aim of acquiring information which he already has. The psychological meaning of the same interrogative sentence for the pupil may, however, be a question taken seriously. The teacher may also sometimes ask a genuine question, for example, when he asks a pupil conducting an experiment 'What temperature does your thermometer read?' without seeing the thermometer. In general, however, a teacher does not ask genuine questions; he does not, for example, when he examines a pupil or when he uses the erothematic method. The interrogative sentence 'Who succeeded Kazimierz the Great as King of Poland?', addressed to a pupil during an examination by a teacher, does not express the latter's genuine question. From the teacher's point of view it is not even a complete expression but an elliptic one. The examiner's complete thought would be expressed by the command: 'Tell me who suc-ceeded Kazimierz the Great as King of Poland', or perhaps the interrogative sentence 'Do you know who succeeded Kazimierz the Great as King of Poland?'. The latter sentence would express a genuine question.

The same is the case when the teacher uses heuristic questions as part of the erothematic method. This includes, apart from so-called principal questions, also so-called leading or cue-questions. A question is principal for a teaching unit (lesson, part of a lesson, or a series of lessons) if one of the main aims of the given unit is for pupils to find a correct and justified answer to that question. A question is with respect to the given unit of teaching a leading one if to find a correct and justified answer to it is not among the main aims of the unit but is only a means of finding a correct and justified answer to one of the principal questions. The qualifications 'principal' and 'leading' are, therefore, relative. The same question may be, with respect to a smaller unit, a principal one whereas with respect to a larger unit it may serve merely as a leading question. Such heuristic interrogative sentences adressed to pupils do not express the teacher's genuine questions. Nor are they shorthands for commands demanding that the pupil should answer the question, or else for interrogative sentences asking whether the pupil knows the fact with which the sentence is concerned. It seems that the mental state of the teacher expressed by an heuristic question is similar to the state expressed by an actor on the stage when he speaks his part in the play. The teacher seriously acts the role of a questioner but he does not seriously ask genuine questions; he places himself in the role of a man who does not know the answer to the question and 'acts' accordingly. On the other hand, the pupil who hears the heuristic question is in fact a person whom the teacher him-self pretends to be; accordingly, for him the heuristic questions are serious (genuine) ones, i.e. their psychological meaning for the pupil are genuine questions.

We have devoted a lot of attention to interrogative sentences and their meanings because interrogative sentences and questions expressed by them play an important role in teaching and yet they have been very rarely analyzed from the logical point of view.

NOTES

[1] [In Polish the interrogative sentence 'Is the earth spherical?' consists of the interrogative particle 'whether' (used, however, both in direct and indirect speech), followed by the declarative sentence 'the earth is spherical'. In English, of course, the latter sentence is contained in the interrogative sentence only if one inverts the order of the verb and the noun. Cf. also 'Decision and complementation questions' in the present article. Translator.]

[2] [If the subject of the interrogative sentence is in the singular, e.g. 'How does the lamp shine?', then a complete declarative sentence 'the lamp shine(s)' is obtained from it by transferring the ending 's' from the auxiliary verb 'does' to the main verb 'shine'. The same must be done to obtain the *datum questionis* of this interrogative sentence. No such operation is necessary in Polish interrogative sentences used in the original text. Translator.]

[3] [The first sentence of this paragraph has been modified to take into account the syntactical differences (mentioned in the previous two notes) between interrogative sentences in Polish and in other languages, e.g. English. Translator.]

[4] [Decision questions are also known as whether-questions and complementation-questions as which-questions. Translator.]

10. LOGIC AND EXPERIENCE*

(1947)

I

1. Logic is the discipline that for the longest period of time has been successful in withstanding the attacks of empiricism which in the course of history invaded one after another the bastions of so-called *a priori* knowledge. However, radical empiricists aim at subordinating to experience even logic itself. In their view the truth of the laws of logic is decided by no other criterion than experience.

Appeal to experience is used by some in order to attack the laws of logic established by agelong tradition, such as the law of contradiction or the law of the excluded middle.[1] According to others, experience is to decide the choice of one or another of the numerous many-valued logics which can be constructed.[2] It might seem that these empiricist claims are mere illusions and that the sanctions from which the laws of logic derive their right to the status of scientific statements are entirely different from the test of experience. The aim of the present article is to examine this problem.

2. There are two forms of empiricism, radical and moderate. Characteristic of radical empiricism is the thesis according to which only empirical sentences may have scientific status. Moderate empiricism, on the other hand, grants such status not only to empirical sentences but also to sentences which are valid in virtue of the meanings of expressions occurring in those sentences. According to moderate empiricism no appeal to experience is necessary to grant scientific validity to sentences such as 'every square is a quadrilateral' or 'all radii of a circle are equal to one another', since the meaning of the words 'square' and 'quadrilateral', 'circle', and 'radius', respectively, is sufficient to guarantee the truth of the sentences in question. The laws of logic are classified by moderate empiricism as statements of just this type, i.e. as statements whose truth is ensured by the meaning of expressions alone.

3. Before we proceed to analyse in detail the positions of both radical and

* Translated by Jerzy Giedymin. First published in *Przegląd Filozoficzny* **XLIII** (1947), 3−21. Present translation based on *Język i Poznanie*, II (1965), 45−60. Reprinted here by kind permission of PWN.

moderate empiricism outlined above, we shall explain in a few words the term 'empirical sentence' which plays an essential role in the formulation of the thesis of empiricism. Empirical sentences, i.e. sentences based on experience, may be divided into sentences directly and indirectly based on experience. Those directly based on experience are known as perceptual sentences. They are usually characterized as sentences which report what one sees, hears, feels, etc. This will suffice only as a rough description. Attempts to give a more precise definition of sentences founded directly on experience give rise to a vast range of problems recently discussed by epistemologists in the controversy over protocol sentences. For our purposes it is not necessary to dwell on this matter, although an analysis of the nature of perceptual sentences and of the role played by the conceptual apparatus used to formulate them is not without significance for our criticism of radical empiricism. The present article, however, is not concerned with a detailed discussion of the thesis of empiricism but only with one particular question, namely, whether the view that logic should also be based on experience is right or not.

Nor is it easy to give a precise definition of sentences based indirectly on experience. Making no claim to a precise treatment of this problem we shall be satisfied with a rough outline of such a definition, aware that it will be in need of many qualifications and corrections. As a first approximation we might say, then, that sentences based indirectly on experience are: (1) hypotheses verified by experience, (2) non-perceptual sentences derived by deduction either from perceptual sentences, or from verified hypotheses or from both.

A sentence is a verified hypothesis if it is not itself a perceptual sentence but is an essential component of a conjunction of sentences from which in accordance with the laws of logic some perceptual sentences have been derived, none of them contradicting any already accepted perceptual sentence. By saying, that a sentence is an essential element of a set of sentences which yields consequences in agreement with experience, we mean that the same consequences cannot be derived if the given sentence is eliminated from the set, in other words, that in the set the sentence in question is indispensable for deriving those consequences.

As a rule, verified hypotheses themselves are not logically derivable from perceptual sentences. Apart from such hypotheses, however, among sentences based indirectly on experience there are non-perceptual sentences derived by deduction from perceptual sentences. Finally, there are also those which have been deduced, according to the laws of logic, from verified hypotheses alone, or from such hypotheses and perceptual sentences.

II

1. Our definition of sentences based indirectly on experiences implies that in their acceptance laws of logic play a certain role. Hypotheses are tested in accordance with the laws of logic, consequences are derived from perceptual sentences also in accordance with the laws of logic. What is, however, the status of the laws of logic according to radical empiricism? Their structure alone makes it impossible to regard them as perceptual. They would have to be classified, from the radical empiricist's point of view, as sentences based indirectly on experience.

Such a view of the status of the laws of logic might appear, at first sight, to involve a vicious circle. For we have seen that every sentence indirectly based on experience is either a hypothesis and then, before it is accepted, some consequences have to be derived from it in accordance with the laws of logic and confronted with experience, or it is itself derived from other sentences in virtue of the laws of logic. It would appear, accordingly, that the acceptance of any sentence indirectly justified by experience, presupposes the acceptance of the laws of logic which seem to be indispensable assumptions for any logical derivation. If so, the acceptance of the laws of logic on the ground of indirect justification by experience, would involve a vicious circle. For in order to justify the laws of logic indirectly by experience we would have to perfom first a logical derivation, a deduction, which already presupposes laws of logic.

2. To see whether the criticism just outlined is correct, let us examine (1) what role is played by the laws of logic in any deduction, (2) what is a vicious circle.

By laws of logic one may mean either logical tautologies or logical rules of inference. As an example of a logical tautology may serve the syllogistic mood *Barbara*, formulated as a conditional: 'If every M is P and every S is M, then every S is P'. This logical theorem should be distinguished from the logical rule of inference which may be referred to as the syllogistic rule *Barbara*. Logical rules are formulated in various ways. Sometimes they are statements saying that sentences of one form imply a sentence of another form. On other occasions rules declare that if sentences of one form are theorems, then so is a sentence of a certain form. The most common way of phrasing rules is as licences to accept a sentence of a certain form if one accepts other sentences of certain forms. The rule *Barbara* may be formulated similarly, for example as the rule that anyone who accepts a sentence of the form 'Every M is P' and a sentence of the form 'Every S is M', may accept a sentence of the form 'Every S is P'.

The difference between the syllogistic mood *Barbara* and the rule *Barbara* consists, above all, in that the latter mentions sentences of certain form and employs names of those sentential forms, while the logical tautology bearing the same name neither refers to sentential forms nor employs the names of those forms but directly employs those sentential forms. This is why rules have to be part of the methodology (or theory) of science or, in any case, of a science of science. On the other hand, logical tautologies are part of a theory which does not treat of any other science and may themselves be the object of metascientific research. Were we to make the rules of logic the object of our investigation, this would have to be done on a still higher level of theory, viz. one concerned with investigating a metascience.

The thesis of empiricism might belong to any of the levels just mentioned starting with the second one, since it makes an assertion about the statements of science. It seems most natural to regard it as a thesis concerned with sciences not yet engaged in methodological reflection, i.e. as belonging to the second level. If so, those sentences to which the thesis refers will have to belong to level one. Therefore the laws of logic which the thesis of empiricism requires to justify by experience will have to be logical tautologies and not rules of logic.

Having clarified that issue let us see what role is played in any deduction by logical tautologies. Logical tautologies may function in deductions either as premisses or as conclusions. Deductions in which logical tautologies function as both premisses and conclusions may be found, primarily, in logic itself. They are very rare outside logic. However, apart from functioning as premisses or as conclusions logical tautologies may perform in deductions another role. Let us consider, for example, the deductive sequence in which from the fact that all mammals are vertebrates and that all dogs are mammals one deduces that all dogs are vertebrates.

In the deduction under consideration no logical tautology occurs as either a premiss or as conclusion. Nevertheless a certain role is performed in it by the syllogistic mood *Barbara*. The deduction in question namely has the form exhibited by the mood *Barbara*. This means that the conditional whose antecedent constitutes the conjunction of the premisses of the deduction under discussion and whose consequent is its conclusion, results by substitution from *Barbara*. In fact the conditional: 'If all mammals are vertebrates and all dogs are mammals, then all dogs are vertebrates' is a substitution of the syllogistic mood *Barbara*: 'If all M's are P's and all S's are M's then all S's are P's'. The role played by the mood *Barbara* in the deduction under discussion may be characterized by saying that *Barbara* is the principle of this deduction. In general: a logical tautology L is the principle of a one-step deductive chain D if and only if the conditional whose antecedent consists of the conjunction of the premisses of D and whose consequent is its conclusion results by substitution from L.

Apart from appearing as a premiss or the conclusion of a deduction a logical tautology may, therefore, also form the principle of that deduction. Let us add that a deduction is called logical or based on the laws of logic if and only if for every step in the deductive sequence there is a logical tautology which is the principle of that step.

We argued before that in order to give a statement the status of a verified hypothesis it is necessary that from that statement in conjunction with additional assumptions one should logically deduce conclusions confirmed by experience.

In the light of our previous comments this amounts to saying that for the acceptance of a hypothesis a deduction is necessary whose every step may be associated with a logical tautology as its principle.

3. Let us recall now under what circumstances an argument commits the vicious circle fallacy.

An argument is circular if a premiss, which is not yet a validly accepted statement, occurs also in the given or in a later step of the argument as a conclusion. Apart from such explicit vicious circles there are implicit ones. Whether or not an inference is implicitly circular depends on (1) what premisses one is allowed to accept without a proof, (2) what types of argument are regarded as valid. Provided both these conditions are fixed, an argument is circular if − given the argument types regarded as valid − some of its steps would be valid only if its conclusion or the conclusion of some of the later steps were among the previously validated statements. So, for example, an enthymematic argument is circular if one of its suppressed premisses also occurs later as conclusion. Thirdly, an argument is implicitly circular if one accepts illegitimately a premiss without deriving it from other statements and if its legitimate derivation − given the types of argument regarded as valid − would involve an explicit circle.

4. After these preliminary clarifications let us consider whether the view that the laws of logic are indirectly based on experience is bound to involve a vicious circle. We shall restrict ourselves to examining whether attempts to test the laws of logic in the way hypotheses are tested are necessarily circular.

The testing of hypotheses consists in their more or less provisional acceptance on the basis of perceptual sentences and additional assumptions; it is, therefore, a kind of argument or inference if the latter terms are understood in the broad sense of any procedure in which some sentences are accepted on the basis of others. Let us use the term reductive argument to refer to the kind of argument used in inferring hypotheses from perceptual sentences. A reductive argument consists in the acceptance of a hypothesis H on the basis of the acceptance of perceptual sentences S and of some additional assumptions Z, provided that those perceptual sentences S had been deduced in virtue of the rules of logic from the conjunction of H and Z and none of so deduced sentences turned out to be in conflict with any accepted perceptual sentence. The premisses of such argument are the perceptual sentences S and the assumptions Z; the deduction involved is not a premiss but a condition which has to be satisfied if the argument is to be admissible. In order, therefore, to infer the hypothesis it is necessary to carry out the deduction according to the laws of logic but it is not necessary to assert that the deduction had been effected in conformity with the laws of logic.

Now let us assume that someone has reductively inferred a law of logic L as a hypothesis. For this to be possible he would have first to deduce, in virtue of the laws of logic, some perceptual sentences S from the conjunction of L and some assumptions Z; afterwards he would have to infer L from sentences S and Z. Such an argument is not explicitly circular; since this is a one-step argument, it would be explicitly circular if the conclusion occurred among the premisses. However, the conclusion does not occur among the premisses. The latter consist of perceptual sentences S — the logical law L is not one of them — and of additional assumptions Z. Those additional assumptions are other perceptual sentences as well as other hypotheses previously verified. (Additional assumptions must not contain any hypothesis which had not yet been tested, i.e. auxiliary hypotheses. If in testing a hypothesis auxiliary hypotheses are also used, what is tested in fact is not that hypothesis alone but the given hypothesis in conjunction with auxiliary hypotheses.)

If therefore the justification of a law of logic L with the help of a reductive argument is to be circular, the circularity would have to be implicit. The first of the forms of circularity of arguments distinguished by us occurs if the conclusion has been accepted incorrectly on the basis of premisses and if in order to make the argument correct one would have first to accept the conclusion. A reductive argument from the acceptance of sentences S and Z to the acceptance of L is correct if, firstly, sentences S had been previously deduced in accordance with the laws of logic from L and Z and, secondly, if none of the deduced sentences contradict any already accepted perceptual sentence. It is here that the charge of circularity appears to have some ground. One may think, namely, that in order to effect valid deduction it is necessary to accept in advance those logical tautologies which constitute the (logical) form of the deduction. This is not so, however. In order to deduce a sentence B from another sentence A in conformity with the laws of logic it is necessary and sufficient that for every step of the deductive chain there exist a logical tautology which is its principle basis. In other words, in each step it is necessary to match the conclusion with the premisses in such a way that the conditional with the conjunction of the premisses as its antecedent and the conclusion as its consequent should be a substitution of a logical tautology. This is enough to effect the deduction. It is not necessary to be familiar with the logical tautology in question nor is it necessary to *know* that one's inference conforms to it. It is enough that the inference does *in fact* conform to it. The charge of implicit circularity, viz. the claim that in order to infer correctly by reductive argument the law L from perceptual sentences S and assumptions Z one would have first to accept the logical law L, is not justified in this case. The illusion that it is justified originates from the mistaken belief that to perform any deduction it is necessary to accept in advance suitable laws of logic.

The illusion of circularity may also originate from a conception of reductive argument different from the one outlined before. According to this other conception whenever one accepts a hypothesis H in the process of a reductive argument one infers H not only from perceptual sentences S and assumptions Z but also from the claim that the hypothesis H explains on the basis of Z the facts described in sentences S, i.e. from the claim that S is logically implied by H and Z. Since such a claim is not a sentence that could be justified directly, one has to produce its proof. To prove that a sentence is logically implied by other sentences amounts to showing that the conditional with the conjunction of the latter sentences in the antecedent and with the former sentence as its consequent, is a substitution of a logical tautology.

Now it seems that familiarity with the laws of logic is necessary to produce such a proof.

The conception of reductive argument now under consideration would require from every scientist testing a hypothesis to engage in metascientific reflection, viz. to examine whether certain statements are logically implied by certain other statements; it would require, therefore, that every scientist be familiar with the laws of logic. Let us see on the basis of an example how scientific hypothesis is tested. As our example let us choose the testing of the hypothesis of electrolytic dissociation. Electrolytes are characterized by twice as large a depression of the freezing point as is implied by Raoult's law. According to the latter, the depression of the freezing point of a solution (below that of pure solvent) is proportional to the number of molecules of the solute in a given quantity of the solvent. Let us express this using the formula $t = ki$ where k is a constant and i is the number of molecules of the solute in 100 g of the solvent. Now experience shows that if i molecules of e.g. salt are dissolved in 100 g of water, then the depression of the freezing point will be given by the equation $t = 2ki$. A physicist would argue as follows: If we assume that each molecule of salt breaks in water into two parts, then the number of those parts in water will be equal to $2i$. Hence according to Raoult's law the depression of the freezing point ought to be given by $t = k\,2i$. This is confirmed by experience. Therefore on the basis of this evidence (the observational statements S) and of Raoult's law (the auxiliary assumption Z which in our case is a previously verified hypothesis) the physicist will accept the hypothesis H according to which when salt is dissolved in water each of the molecules of salt breaks into two parts.

If we examine the physicist's argument we shall see that it accords completely with the characterization of reductive arguments given by us before. From the hypothesis of electrolytic dissociation being tested in conjunction with Raoult's law (which is the auxiliary assumption) the physicist derives a statement confirmed by experience. Having made this deduction he proceeds to accept the hypothesis of the dissociation of salt in water on the basis of the evidence of experience and of Raoult's law. We do not find in the physicist's procedure anything that would correspond to the second conception of reductive arguments. He does not assert that the observed depression of the freezing point of the salt solution is logically implied by the hypothesis of dissociation and Raoult's law. Since he merely derives certain sentences from others and does not assert the logical implication between them, he need not prove that the relation of implication holds.

Our analysis of one example of the testing of hypotheses shows, it seems, convincingly that the second conception of reductive argument is far from reflecting its actual nature. Hence the charge of circularity associated with that conception ought to be regarded as without foundation. It applies to a fiction and not to an actual attempt at inferring the laws of logic from experience with the help of reductive arguments.

III

1. Against the principal thesis of radical empiricism holding that only assertions directly or indirectly based on experience have a right to be admitted in science, the following argument may be put forward. Radical empiricism seems to overlook the fact that every sentence and therefore also every

perceptual sentence is formulated in a certain language. But every language is bound by certain rules concerning the acceptance of sentences. These rules are called by some authors rules of transformation, rules of language or rules of meaning.[3] Two classes of these rules may be distinguished. Rules belonging to the first class allow to accept certain sentences irrespective of experience and without regard to what other sentences are accepted. The rejection of those sentences would indicate that they are not being understood in the sense associated with them in the given language. In everyday English such a sentence is, for example: 'Every square has four sides' or 'No mountain is higher than the highest one'. It seems that indeed anybody rejecting these sentences, i.e. being sincere in saying 'not every square has four sides' or 'there exists a mountain higher than the highest one', would show that he does not attach to these sentences the meaning associated with them in everyday English. The second class constitute rules which permit the acceptance of certain transformations of previously accepted sentences. In ordinary English such a rule is for instance that which allows to accept the sentence 'Peter is younger than John' on the basis of the accepted sentence 'John is older than Peter'. Here again anybody acting differently, namely accepting the sentence 'John is older than Peter' while denying the sentence 'Peter is younger than John', would show that he does not understand these sentences in the sense which is appropriate to them in the English language.

We refer to the rules of the first kind as axiomatic, of the second – as deductive rules. Axiomatic rules permit the acceptance of certain sentences irrespective of any circumstances, and thus irrespective also of what other sentences are accepted simultaneously and of what one experiences at the same time, etc. Sentences which according to axiomatic rules may be accepted in any circumstances are those which it is impossible to reject if they are understood in the sense attached to them in a given language. Deductive rules, on the other hand, do not permit to accept certain sentences in all circumstances but only if certain other sentences are accepted as premises. Deductive rules, therefore, join sentences into groups consisting of two or more sentences and distinguish in each group sentences which constitute premises and a sentence which forms the conclusion. In natural languages we deal with such groups in cases where a given sentence is related with certain other sentences in such manner, that its rejection and simultaneously acceptance of those other sentences would violate the sense which all these sentences have in a given language.

Whoever accepts rules of both these kinds thereby rejects the main thesis of radical empiricism. For, firstly, he permits the acceptance of certain sentences, those namely which are distinguished by axiomatic rules, irrespective of any circumstances and, therefore, also without referring to experience. Let us designate those sentences as the axioms of the language. Secondly, he permits the acceptance of sentences which may be inferred from the axioms in accordance with deductive rules. Both the axioms (defined as above) and the sentences which may be inferred from them in accordance with deductive rules might be designated as analytic sentences. Such a definition of these sentences seems to express better the intention which induced Kant to introduce the notion of analytic sentences than his own which, as is well known, can be applied only to affirmative subject-predicate sentences and which is, therefore, not general enough. It also seems that the above definition of the term 'analytic sentence' is more in accord with Kant's intentions than the somewhat different definition proposed by Carnap.

2. The doctrine according to which apart from empirical also analytical and only analytical sentences have the right to a place in science might be called moderate empiricism. To any epistemological doctrine which grants this status also to other non-empirical sentences we might apply the term apriorism.[4]

If non-empirical sentences occurring in science are called a priori sentences and non-analytical sentences are identified with synthetic sentences, we may characterize empiricism, apriorism and their variants with the help of the following formulations: Empiricism does not grant the status of scientific statements to synthetic sentences a priori. Radical empiricism grants this status only to empirical sentences. Moderate empiricism grants it to both empirical and analytical sentences. Apriorism admits into science synthetic sentences a priori. Moderate apriorism admits moreover empirical as well as analytical sentences. Radical apriorism refuses to empirical sentences a place in science. The following diagram represents the above:

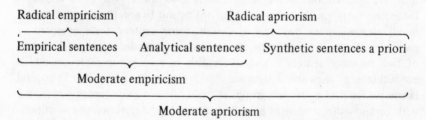

3. Moderate empiricism, though allowing a place in science to analytical sentences, tries to lessen their importance by calling them contemptibly tautologies and by claiming even that these sentences do not convey anything about reality. Let us consider whether this view — if taken literally — is

correct. What does it mean to say that a given sentence conveys information about this or that? The sentence 'the Mont Blanc is a mountain' pronounces something about the Mont Blanc and about mountains. Likewise, the sentence 'the Earth is a planet' tells us someting about the Earth and about planets. In general, a given sentence conveys something about objects named in that sentence. In this sense it is difficult to agree with the statement claiming that analytic sentences convey nothing about reality. The sentence 'no mountain is higher than the highest mountain on earth' is an analytic sentence and yet it speaks of Mount Everest, i.e. of something real.

The claim that analytic sentences convey nothing about reality might be interpreted differently, namely, that what these sentences assert does not exist in reality. This, however, would mean that these sentences are false and surely no empiricist would want to maintain such a statement.

It seems that when empiricists claim that analytic sentences convey nothing about reality they wish to imply that these sentences assert no connections between objects based on experience and that they remain true irrespective of what experience will show. If the claim is understood in this way one cannot but agree with it though it will be difficult to see why it should undermine the importance of analytic sentences.

4. If there are sentences in a language whose rejection would violate the meaning attached to them, it would be pointless to insist upon the condition of their being confirmed by experience before they are asserted. It would be pointless because *ex definitione* these sentences cannot at all be rejected if they are understood in their normal meaning and therefore they cannot be refuted by experience either. For example, could experience induce us to reject the sentence: 'every square is a quadrilateral'? It would have to show us an object to which we would apply the name 'square' while denying it at the same time the name 'quadrilateral'. If, however, we denied the name 'quadrilateral' to an object, i.e. if we stated of an object that it is not a quadrilateral, we surely would never attach the name 'square' to that object as long as we use these terms in their normal sense. In other words, were we to assert of an object 'this is a square although it is not a quadrilateral', we might do so only if we understood this sentence in a different way from that prescribed by the English language. Hence, as a sentence of ordinary English 'every square is a quadrilateral' is not in danger of ever being refuted by experience. Therefore, there seems to be no good reason why in the case of this sentence we should follow the recommendation of radical empiricism and refrain from accepting it until it is confirmed by experience. The same applies also to the sentence 'no mountain is higher than the highest one' or

to the sentence 'every sparrow is a bird' and in general to all analytic sentences.

5. According to moderate empiricism the laws of logic are classified as analytic sentences. Some of them are given the status of axioms, i.e. of sentences governed by axiomatic rules, hence sentences whose rejection would constitute a violation of their meaning; other laws of logic are treated by the moderate empiricist as sentences deduced from the axioms in accordance with deductive rules.

In everyday language, for instance, we are inclined to regard the law of contradiction as an axiom, i.e. as a sentence which it is impossible to reject without changing the meaning of the words involved. The law of contradiction proclaims: 'it is never the case that something is the case and at the same time is not'. Indeed, it seems that anybody rejecting this principle and stating: 'it may happen that something is the case and at the same time is not' could do this only if he used the term 'not' in a meaning different from that attached to it in the English language.

What is involved here is not at all a psychological law but something else. The meaning of a word determines the manner or method of using it. A person who does not understand a given word, e.g. the word 'pentahedron', will be at a loss to know what principles he should follow in answering questions in which this word occurs. When he grasps the meaning of that word, for example by being told that 'pentahedron' means the same as 'five-sided polyhedron', he will be in possession of a certain method concerned with the use of that word. He will then know what to do in order to answer the question 'is this object a pentahedron?', namely, to find out whether the object is a five-sided solid or not. The question 'has every pentahedron five sides?' which he was unable to deal with as long as he did not understand the term 'pentahedron', is now easy for him to answer without resorting to further information or to the test of experience. In short, having understood a given word, having correlated it with a certain meaning, provides the person in question with certain methods, peculiar to the given meaning, of verifying the sentences which contain that word. It is only when one has learned how to use a word in a manner appropriate to its meaning, that one has grasped the meaning of the word correctly. Until one has learned this, one does not understand the word properly. For to understand a word in a manner dictated by its meanings, *means* to understand it so as to be prepared to use it in a certain way appropriate to that meaning.

The reason, therefore, why the sentence 'every square has four sides' (if understood in its usual meaning) cannot be rejected is not that the structure of the human mind makes it impossible to reject it. The sentence in question cannot be rejected without changing its usual meaning because to use the sentence in its usual sense *means* to observe certain ways of usage which are determined by that meaning.

Nor is it because the human mind is incapable of doing so that one cannot reject the law of contradiction and assert that something may be the case and at the same time not be the case when the word 'not' is understood in its normal sense. It cannot be rejected because to understand the word 'not' in its proper meaning in the English language, *means* to understand it so that a certain definite way of using it is determined by that understanding.

Now it seems to us that the proper way of using the term 'not' in its usual sense (in English) requires, among other things, exactly that no sentence should be asserted simultaneously with its negation. In other words, it seems that anyone asserting that something is the case, and at the same time that it is not the case, would violate the meaning of the word 'not' just as a person asserting with conviction that some squares are not quadrilaterals would violate the meaning of relevant terms.

6. We have thus before us two opposed views concerning the nature of the laws of logic. One, represented by radical empiricism, considers them as sentences based on experience and grants them the status of statements of science only as long as they are claimed to be 'based on experience'. The other, represented by moderate empiricism, regards the laws of logic as analytic sentences and allows them to be accepted as scientific statements irrespective of the test of experience. Which of these views is correct?

In spite of appearances to the contrary, it seems that there is no incompatibility between these two views. It seems that each of them may be correct but each in relation to a different language. The thesis of radical empiricism. according to which only empirical sentences may be accepted as scientific statements does after all make a claim about sentences, and sentences are always sentences of some language. The thesis of radical empiricism may therefore be correct in relation to one kind of language, whereas the thesis of moderate empiricism – permitting to accept some sentences (i.e. analytic sentences) irrespective of experience – may be correct in connection with another kind of languages.

All languages known to me whose logical theory has been developed are languages with axiomatic and deductive meaning-rules, i.e. languages in which analytic sentences may be accepted without appeal to experience. It seems that to this category belongs also everyday language. With respect to such languages, radical empiricism is untenable. In those languages there are sentences which may be accepted without recourse to experience but which cannot be denied if they are used in the appropriate sense. Logical tautologies belong to this category of analytic sentences.

Although in intentionally constructed languages (viz. artificial languages whose logical syntax has been developed) as well as in everyday speech, there are analytic sentences, languages without analytic sentences are possible. To show this, it is sufficient to build a language in which there are no axiomatic meaning-rules but in which deductive rules are retained. Such a language will have no axioms (i.e. sentences governed by axiomatic rules) but it will be possible to make deductions in it since it contains deductive rules. However, by means of deductive rules alone it is not possible to obtain analytic sentences, for by deduction one may only generate analytic sentences from other analytic sentences. For languages without axiomatic rules, therefore, the thesis of radical empiricism will be valid: no non-empirical sentence may be accepted in them.

In such languages the laws of logic will also have to assume empirical status if they are to be validly accepted statements.

7. The question now arises how it is possible for the laws of logic to be founded on experience in languages without axiomatic rules. It is difficult to see what consequences testable by experience could be derived from logical laws alone. Hence it is difficult to see in what way they could be tested empirically as hypotheses.

It seems that this would be possible if the theorems of logic were treated as auxiliary hypotheses verified not in isolation but jointly with certain scientific hypotheses. Some modest deductive rules would be valid in the language we are considering, e.g. the rule of detachment, the *modus tollens* rule, the rule corresponding to de Morgan's laws and the rule of substitution. The system of logical theorems would play the role of auxiliary hypotheses which, when assumed, would justify further rules derivative with respect to those logical theorems and primary rules.[5] With regard to their scope, these derived rules would comprise all the methods of inference usually referred to as logical methods of inference (i.e. methods based on logical theorems). However, the derived rules would not have the character of the rules of the language (meaning-rules), since they could be transgressed without the meaning of the expressions of the language being thereby violated. They would be valid only as long as the hypothetical logical theorems are accepted. The procedure of verifying logical theorems or of rejecting them would take the following course. From scientific hypotheses consequences would be drawn by applying not only the primary deductive rules of the language, but also rules derived from the former and from logical theorems treated as auxiliary hypotheses. Should these consequences be in conformity with experience this result could be regarded as a confirmation (verification) of the conjunction composed of the hypothesis and hypothetically assumed logical theorems. If, however, these consequences were not in accordance with experience the ensuing difficulty could be overcome in one of two ways: one could retain logical theorems (thus accepting the completed deduction as correct) and reject the scientific hypothesis; alternatively, one might retain the hypothesis in spite of this contradiction with experience and reject some of the logical theorems which played the role of auxiliary hypotheses; finally, and with the same effect, one might regard the deduction as formally incorrect, i.e. question the correctness of those steps of the deduction which were based on the rule derived from the rejected logical theorem.

8. Such a flexible approach to logical theorems as hypotheses similar to scientific hypotheses may prove useful in natural sciences. Some physicists have conjectured that ordinary logic is incompatible with the fundamental principles of quantum theory (the principle of complementarity) and are inclined to reject some laws of logic while retaining the physical principles. The issue has not yet been sufficiently clarified to allow one to take a stand. At any rate, the above conception of language without analytic sentences in which also the laws of logic would be reduced to the rank of hypotheses opens a way for this kind of approach.

However, this is not the only solution. Logic may be changed even though its theorems are analytic sentences of the language. In that case the replacement of some logical theorems by others constitutes a transition from one language to another. For if logical theorems are analytic sentences, then the rejection of one of these sentences must be, or, at least must lead, to a violation of some axiomatic or deductive rules; such a violation will in turn produce a change of the meaning of the words and therefore a change of the language.

9. The proposed compromise resolution of the conflict between the radical empiricist and his opponent will presumably satisfy neither the radical empiricist nor the apriorist, who in addition to analytic sentences admits also synthetic sentences a priori.

To the radical empiricist axiomatic rules in whatever language are unacceptable. These rules allow the acceptance of certain sentences unconditionally and therefore also irrespective of the test of experience. But what is precisely meant by 'allow'? What is meant, it seems, is that whoever admits such rules grants the status of accepted statements of science or (to express this more explicitly) asserts as the statements of science sentences governed by the rules even though these sentences have not been deduced from other sentences or supported by the test of experience. The radical empiricist, however, does not regard such sentences as part of science. He will not agree therefore to employ in science a language with axiomatic rules, as this would be inconsistent with his fundamental thesis.

One may ask, however, why such languages should be avoided or — to formulate the problem more emphatically — why should only empirical sentences be asserted as statements of science? Is it because only such sentences convey information about reality? This argument has been dealt with before. Is it because only such sentences are true? Whoever accepts as valid that of two contradictory sentences one must be true, can surely conclude that true non-empirical sentences exist. For it is enough to take any non-empirical sentence and its negation. Of two such sentences one will be true *ex hypothesi* although neither need be an empirical sentence. Or is it perhaps because only empirical sentences should be regarded as sentences (the term 'empirical sentence' is now understood in a different sense, namely, as referring to sentences which in principle can be tested by experience although they may not yet have been subjected to such control)? I believe that those who adopt this view use the term 'sentence' in a non-standard way, namely, they use 'sentence' and 'empirical sentence' as synonyms. In that case the argument that only empirical sentences can be asserted in science because only empirical sentences are sentences, is not at all convincing. Finally, the reason why only sentences based on experience are allowed to be accepted may be that there exists no other method of justifying statements than the test of experience, in other words, that only experience is the criterion of truth.

It may well be that this is the actual motive prompting radical empiricists to grant the right of place in science only to sentences based on experience.

But whatever motive induced radical empiricists to take their view, they would have to produce arguments in support of their thesis in order to convince their opponents of its truth. In doing so they would have to use the notions of a validated scientific statement and of validation acceptable to their opponents. Otherwise the dispute would be based on a verbal misunderstanding.

However, the viewpoint adopted by radical empiricists may also be regarded as a programme for doing science. In that case one must not expect them to prove the truth of their view since programmes are neither true nor false, they can be only reasonable or unreasonable. In order to be reasonable they must be purposeful and practicable. The aim of this paper was to find out whether in principle the programme of radical empiricism can be put into effect. The result of our considerations is positive. Whether this programme also serves a purpose can only be shown by actual scientific practice. However, the actual course of science up till now does not seem to be consistent with the programme of radical empiricism.

NOTES

[1] Adam Schaff, 'The Principle of Contradiction in the Light of Dialectic Logic', *Myśl Współczesna* **3–4** (1946), 328ff.

[2] Jan Łukasiewicz, 'What Does Philosophy owe to Modern Mathematical Logic?", *Przegląd Filozoficzny* **4** (1936), 325–329.

[3] Cf. K. Ajdukiewicz, 'Sprache und Sinn', *Erkenntnis* **IV** (1934), 100ff, and R. Carnap, *Logische Syntax der Sprache*, Wien 1934, 120ff.

[4] I propose to use the term 'apriorism' to refer to the doctrine opposed to empiricism and discard the term 'rationalism' in that context. The term 'rationalism' ought to be reserved for the doctrine opposed to irrationalism.

[5] To say that the rule R is derivative with respect to rules D and theses T means that every sentence which may be derived from arbitrary sentences Z according to rule R can be derived from the sentences Z and the theses T according to rules D.

11. EPISTEMOLOGY AND SEMIOTICS*

(1948)

I. The importance of epistemology for our world-view consists primarily in the conclusions drawn from its results, conclusions which concern the world as the object of our cognition. One such conclusion, for example, drawn from epistemological considerations is that of metaphysical idealism which claims that the world given in our knowledge does not have an 'independent existence' and is merely a 'correlate of thought' (understood either in a psychological or logical sense).

The purpose of the present article is to consider whether it is legitimate to draw metaphysical conclusions from epistemological considerations. We shall make use here of an analogy between epistemology and the theory of language, i.e. semiotics. For in semiotics a problem analogous to the one we intend to consider here has been solved at least to some extent. I have in mind the problem whether and under what conditions from sentences about a language one may draw conclusions concerning extralinguistic objects. In semiotics this problem has been clarified in the process of studying the conditions necessary for an adequate definition of 'truth' or for an adequate definition of 'denotation'.

By an adequate definition of a true sentence we understand a definition of 'a true sentence' which has among its consequences such sentences as e.g. 'the sentence "the sun is shining" is true if and only if the sun is shining'; 'the sentence "John is older than Peter" is true if and only if John is older than Peter', etc.

By an adequate definition of 'denotation' we mean a definition which has among its consequences sentences such as 'the term "man" denotes x if and only if x is a man'.

An adequate definition of 'truth', just as an adequate definition of 'denotation', makes it possible from sentences about expressions to infer sentences about things which those sentences concern. For example, on the basis of an adequate definition of 'true' from the fact that the sentence 'the sun is shining' is true we can infer that the sun is shining. This is possible, however,

* Translated by Jerzy Giedymin. First published in *Przegląd Filozoficzny* **XLIV** (1948), 336–47. Present translation based on *Język i Poznanie*, II, 107–16.

only on the condition that we have suitable means for the construction of adequate definitions of concepts such as 'a true sentence' or 'denotes'.

Now in order to construct an adequate definition of 'truth' and of 'denotation' we must have at our disposal a language in whose vocabulary there are not only names of expressions of the language under consideration but also those expressions themselves. The language used in the theory of language (i.e. the language which contains the names of the expressions under investigation) is usually referred to as the meta-language; the language under investigation, on the other hand, is usually known as the object-language. The necessary condition for adequate definitions of 'truth' and 'denotation' mentioned before, may therefore also be expressed by saying that the meta-language, in which the definitions are to be constructed, should contain the object-language as its proper part. The branch of the logic of language (semiotics) in which we use a meta-language containing the object-language as its proper part, is known as semantics; the branch of the logic of language in which one uses a meta-language not containing as its part the object-language, is called syntax. One can, therefore, construct adequate definitions of 'truth' and 'denotation' in semantics but not in syntax. Similarly, only in semantics but not in syntax from sentences about linguistic expressions one can infer sentences about extralinguistic objects which those sentences concern.

By analogy we obtain the following conjecture concerning epistemology: In epistemology from sentences about thoughts one may infer sentences about things, which those thoughts are concerned with, only on the condition that throughout one uses a language containing not only names of thoughts but also expressions for things which those thoughts are about.

In the light of this analogy between semiotics and epistemology, philosophers engaged in epistemological investigations are confronted with the following alternatives: (1) In epistemological inquiries one may start with the language of syntax, in the broad sense, i.e. with the language which contains names of the expressions of the object language or the names of thoughts which are meanings of those object-language expressions, but which does not contain the object-language expressions themselves; if our conjecture concerning epistemology is correct, an epistemologist using a language of this kind will never be able to infer any sentences of the object-language, i.e. any sentences about the object of knowledge which he investigates. (2) In epistemological inquiries one may, however – apart from the language of syntax – also use the object-language. In this case one has to obey the rules of that language; problems formulated in the object-language have then to be solved in accordance with the same rules (criteria) which are obeyed in purely substantive (e.g. scientific) inquiries in which no epistemological analysis is made.

A philosopher who chooses the second approach must be a realist and join scientists in claiming that houses, trees, mountains, etc. exist, under-standing this claim literally, as it is understood by scientists who use the object-language.

On the basis of our analogy between semiotics and epistemology one would expect that a philosopher who chooses to use the language of syntax as his starting point, will not be able to infer validly any sentence of the object-language; he will not be able to infer any sentences about the objects of knowledge, which he subjects to epistemological analysis. In particular, he will not be able to infer either any existential sentences of the object-language, in their literal sense, or negations of such existential sentences. One would expect, therefore, that whichever of the two approaches a philosopher chooses he will not be able to infer negations of any existential sentences normally accepted in the object-language.

Contrary to this expectation, however, idealists do deny such sentences and are prepared to accept them only if their sense is altered. So, for example, Berkeley would accept sentences that mountains, houses, trees exist, only if those sentences were understood as synonymous with the claim that someone has suitable perceptions (of mountains, houses, trees); he rejects them, however, if they are taken literally in the sense in which they are used in the object language, e.g., by scientists when no epistemological reflection is conducted.

We are, therefore, inclined to suspect that the argument used by idealists in support of their position is not valid. For it seems that they start their argument using only the language of syntax (in the generalized sense we have introduced) with no object-language expressions at their disposal; on this basis they construct a *quasi*-object-language which, in fact, remains the language of syntax. In this *quasi*-object-language they formulate certain theses (e.g. "*esse = percipi*") and argue in their support; through an unconscious mystification they identify those theses with sentences of the object-language, though in the latter those theses are obviously false. Hence the paradoxical character of idealist claims which, on the one hand, seem to be uncontestably valid while, on the other hand, seem to contradict our common sense.

II. As an example let us consider Berkeley's reasoning and let us try to see whether it fits the above schema. The base from which Berkeley starts is the world of psychic entities, called by him ideas. His language orginally contains only the names of ideas, i.e. the names of the first elements of the intentional relations. Berkeley's linguistic base is analogous to the linguistic base of the syntax. From the point of view of this analogy we may conjecture that Berkeley will not be able to make the transition to the object-language, i.e. in our case to the ordinary language in which we speak about houses, trees, mountains, stones, in other words, about what in everyday life we regard as real objects or bodies. However, Berkeley introduces by definition the concept of a 'body'. According to that definition a body is nothing but an idea or cluster of ideas. It is obvious that this definition does not lead Berkeley outside the domain of the first elements of the intentional relation and does not constitute a bridge from the language of the syntax (in the generalized sense) to the object-language. Though it introduces a term 'body' homonymous with a term of the object-language, it endows it with a meaning in virtue of which it remains a term of the syntax (in the generalized sense). Indeed the sense given by Berkeley's definition to the term 'body' is such that were we to claim that bodies may exist without anyone being conscious thereof, we would indicate by our claim that we are not using 'body' in Berkeley's sense. For in view of his definition of 'body' to claim that unperceived bodies exist would amount to claiming that there are ideas of which no one is conscious, but for Berkeley ideas are only conscious psychic phenomena. This circumstance alone is sufficient to show that Berkeley uses 'body' in a sense different from the sense this word has in the object-language, which in this case is ordinary language.

The word 'body' has not been introduced into ordinary language by definition; it belongs to those words which we learn through usage. One understands the word 'body' in the sense associated with it in ordinary English, if one uses it in the way prescribed by ordinary English. Were we to use it otherwise, we would show thereby that we do not understand it appropriately. Another word would be synonymous with the word 'body' as understood in ordinary language, if the employment of either word were the same according to ordinary usage. Now, we have seen that in view of Berkeley's definition, to use the word 'body' in his sense it is necessary to accept that *esse* for bodies consists in their *percipi*. But this is not the way we use 'body' in ordinary speech. Those who believe in the existence of unperceived bodies do not thereby violate the rules of ordinary language. Hence 'body' in Berkeley's language has a meaning different from the one it has in ordinary language. By introducing the term 'body' into his original language, Berkeley does not essentially alter that language, he merely makes it a *quasi*-object-language.

This is why Berkeley's idealist thesis according to which *esse* for bodies amounts to *percipi*, far from being a sentence in the object-language, is an apriorist thesis of his *quasi*-object-language. In the object-language one can formulate the problem whether bodies exist without being perceived. If understood appropriately in the object-language this problem is not decidable a priori; only an empirical solution would be acceptable. Indeed we believe that there are unperceived bodies but this belief is a well-corroborated empirical hypothesis. Berkeley's *'Esse = percipi'* does not undermine that hypothesis, if only because it is not concerned with the same problem. It is concerned with the existence of ideas or of clusters of ideas, which Berkeley calls bodies; it is not concerned with the existence of what in ordinary language we call bodies.

The source of Berkeley's mistaken belief that 'body' in his language — if not synonymous — is at least co-extensive with 'body' of ordinary language may be traced to his misconception of 'perceive'. Berkeley's definition according to which a body is an idea or cluster of ideas is based on the assumption that bodies are what we perceive. For Berkeley 'to perceive' means the same as 'to be conscious of'. Now, perception is an intentional relation which from the world of psyche extends to the non-psychological world. To be conscious of is a relation which holds between a conscious subject and the elements of his consciousness; as such it resembles rather the relation between a property and an object which has the property, or — perhaps — the part-whole relation. In order to define a body as something we are conscious of Berkeley did not have to use expressions of the object-language. He did not have them originally in his language and never extended his language to include them, hence his idealist thesis does not at all concern things which we describe using our object-language.

III. Let us now consider logical idealism. I propose to discuss it in the form which twelve years ago was the subject of my article 'A Semantical Version of the Problem of Transcendental Idealism'.[1] The line of argument leading to transcendental idealism begins with the rejection of the classical (or correspondence) definition of truth which is in terms of the correspondence between thought and reality. Various motives were behind this rejection. So, for example, some have claimed that the idea of correspondence essential for that definition, is unclear; for correspondence is neither identity, nor similarity; if the correspondence between the thought and reality cannot be made clear, then the classical definition — so some of its opponents argued — is devoid of any clear content. Hence it should be rejected and replaced by another one. On other occasions the opposition to the classical definition of truth was based on some sceptical arguments according to which thought cannot be directly compared with reality. For to make the comparison we would have to represent reality with the help of another thought; in this way one thought would be compared with another and not with reality: this would be helpful only if we already knew that the second thought corresponded to reality but to know this we would have to compare it with reality and would need for that purpose a third thought and so *ad infinitum*. In other words: truth as correspondence between thought and reality is unknowable. Such arguments formulated (let this be emphasized) in very vague terms, have induced many to abandon the classical conception of truth.

The classical conception was replaced by a different one, allegedly based on the way we in fact use the concept of truth: we actually use the term 'true' in such a way that of any sentence accepted by us we are prepared to say that it is true and conversely, whenever we attribute truth to a sentence we are also prepared to accept it (to assert it). Nevertheless, no one will say that a sentence is true if and only if they believe in it. No one thinks they are infallible and omniscient. We are aware of the fact that we are not omniscient for not all our beliefs are the result of sufficiently careful investigations; some have been obtained with the help of methods which have to yield to higher criteria. If we knew that all our beliefs satisfied criteria from which there is no appeal, whose verdict is final and irrevocable, then we would not hesitate to regard all sentences accepted by us as true. Such criteria are the criteria of truth. So we actually use the concept of truth in such a way that by a true sentence we mean one which satisfies the truth criteria.

This idea of truth as conformity to truth criteria may take various forms, depending on what is taken as the criterion of truth. So, for example on the coherence definition of truth, 'truth' is defined as the 'coherence of thoughts among themselves'; others define truth as immediate (or mediate) self-evidence, or as conformity with the transcendental norm, etc. All these non-classical conceptions of truth fall under the following schema: truth consists in conformity with truth criteria.

Only one step is needed to take us from this definition of truth to idealism. For, using the same obscure and vague language as before, one can continue the argument as follows: whether a sentence is true depends on its conformity with criteria and not on its correspondence with reality. Therefore the world of which true thoughts constitute our knowledge, does not differ from the world of fiction in being real, but rather in being conceived in thoughts which satisfy the criteria of truth; fictions are inventions which do not satisfy those criteria. Nevertheless, the world which we know in our true thoughts is our invention, just as fictions are, and it is at least doubtful if it is something more than that, i.e. if it is real. In Kant's terminology, the world we know in our true thoughts is the world of phenomena, by contradistinction to the world of things in themselves (*Ding an sich*) and with the world of illusion (*der Schein*). The world of phenomena and the world of illusion are both our inventions, they are the worlds of objects which are only intentional, not transcendental. The world of phenomena differs from the world of illusion (fiction) only in that the former is attested by experience, which constitutes the criterion of truth, while the latter is not in conformity with experience.

The essence of logical or objective idealism (in contradistinction to its psychological or subjective counterpart) seems to be the claim that the world we know in our true thoughts differs from the world of fictions not in that the former is real while the latter is not, but merely in that the former but not the latter may be described in judgments which satisfy the criterion of truth. This claim is often expressed by saying, for example, that the world of our cognition does not exist in an absolute sense, that its existence depends on logical factors, i.e. truth criteria, transcendental norms, to which it owes its distinction, its empirical and not transcendental reality, as Kant put it.

We have sketched a line of thought leading to idealism without attempting to formulate ideas more clearly or to argue more precisely than is customary in most philosophical writings. We were concerned with suggesting those intuitions which have guided idealist arguments. We shall now try to reformulate those intuitive ideas a bit more precisely.

For one reason or another philosophers have opted for a definition of truth different from the classical one. For they define: 'a sentence S is true if and only if S satisfies the criterion of truth'. By the criterion of truth is meant a property of sentences which may be characterized in terms concerned with sentences themselves without having to speak about things mentioned in the sentences. For example, the coherence criterion of truth is satisfied whenever the sentence under consideration is consistent with those already accepted, i.e. whenever it does not negate any of the accepted sentences, is implied by them, etc. All these are properties of sentences which we can discuss without using any other terms but names of sentences, of their forms, etc. The criteria of truth so understood can be formulated in the language of syntax; no recourse to the object-language is needed. A definition of truth of this type may be regarded as syntactical. The starting point of an idealist argument is, therefore, the language of syntax and a syntactical definition of truth.

Essential for the type of idealism now under discussion is the fact that its proponents use the language of syntax as their starting point and, having introduced by a syntactical definition the term 'true sentence', proceed to construct their object-language. This they do using an inversion of the semantical definition of truth, i.e. one in which what used to be the *definiens* is now the *definiendum*. In virtue of an equivalence derivable from the semantical definition of truth anyone who is familiar with the object-language but is unfamiliar with the term 'true sentence' is able to translate a sentence involving that term into his object-language; so, for example, the meta-language sentence 'the sentence "the sun is shining" is true' is translatable into the sentence 'the sun is shining'. Our philosophers, however, do not need that equivalence for this purpose. For they have already defined 'true sentence' in syntactical terms. On the other hand, they do not yet possess any object-language and, therefore, use the equivalence to introduce the object-language sentences into their syntactical language. So they define: 'the sun is shining' means 'the sentence "the sun is shining" is true'; 'the earth is round' means 'the sentence "the earth is round" is true', etc. In view of their syntactical definition of truth (as satisfying the criterion), the definitions just given are transformed as follows: 'the sun is shining' means 'the sentence "the sun is shining" satisfies the truth criterion'; 'the earth is round' means 'the sentence "the earth is round" satisfies the truth criterion'.

Accordingly, the claim that reality differs from fiction only in that the sentences which describe the former satisfy the truth criterion (while fictional sentences do not) will presumably amount to the following: If I assert that horses exist while centaurs are fictions, then this means that the sentence 'horses exist' satisfies the criterion while the sentence 'centaurs exist' does not. On the other hand, the claim that both horses and centaurs are nothing but our invention (constructs) may perhaps only be understood as follows: when both the sentences 'horses exist' and 'centaurs exist' are taken in their ordinary sense as used by *non*-philosophers in the object-language (rather than definitionally reduced to syntactical sentences about other sentences satisfying criteria), then neither horses nor centaurs exist. The idealist claim which denies to the objects of the world of our cognition, so-called 'independent existence', presumably amounts to the claim that those objects do not exist in the sense in which they are asserted to exist in the object-language.

If this analysis of the arguments of logical idealism is correct, then it completely confirms our suggestion that they conform to the schema characteristic of any idealist arguments. Logical idealists start with the language of syntax, i.e. with a language which contains only the names of the first elements of the intentional relation (e.g. the names of the expressions of the object-language) and does not contain any expressions of the object-language. In this language they construct a syntactical definition of a true sentence. Then they introduce into their language sentences homonymous with the sentences of the object-language with the help of definitions of the type: 'The sun is shining' means 'the sentence "the sun is shining" satisfies the criterion'. These sentences, though hononyms of the corresponding sentences of the object-language are by no means synonymous with them. For the sentence that S is P if and only if the sentence 'S is P' satisfies the criterion need not be true in general, if the sentence 'S is P' is used as an object-language sentence. For in every suitably rich object-language there will be sentences not decidable from the point of view of the criterion, i.e. such that neither the sentence nor its negation satisfies the criterion. Let us assume that 'A is B' is such a sentence. In accordance with the law of the excluded middle, we may assert that either A is B or A is not B. Hence in one of the equivalences: (1) A is B if and only if the sentence 'A is B' satisfies the criterion, (2) A is not B if and only if the sentence 'A is not B' satisfies the criterion, the left-hand is true, while the right-hand side — in accordance with our assumption — is in both equivalences false. One of the equivalences will, therefore, not be satisfied. Consequently, if 'S is P' is defined as 'the sentence "S is P" satisfies the criteria', then it is taken in a sense different from its sense in the object-language.

Thus sentences introduced by idealists into their syntactical language and homonymous with the sentences of the object-language are, in fact, not sentences of the object-language at all but belong to the *quasi*-object-language which — in spite of appearances to the contrary — is merely a syntactical language. The idealist claim that reality differs from fiction merely by the fact that sentences asserting the existence of real objects satisfy the truth criterion while sentences about fictitious objects do not, is paradoxical only as long as we are deceived into thinking that the sentences of the idealist *quasi*-object-language have the same meaning as the sentences of our object-language.

Idealists, however, go still further and claim that so-called real objects, e.g. trees, houses, horses, etc. do not exist independently of the subject (psychological or transcendental), that they are constructs just as fictions are. I am unable to find for the phrase 'exist independently' any other sense but the one which people not engaged in epistemological analysis associate with the word 'exist'. When in everyday life I say that horses do while centaurs do not exist, then I attribute to horses such an existence independent of the knowing subject, of the criteria, etc. This is why I interpret the idealist claim that reality along with fictions does not possess an 'independent' existence, as the sentence of the object language according to which, e.g. horses do not exist just as centaurs do not exist.

But such an epistemological claim is unjustified. For an epistemologist either uses the language of syntax which does not contain the object-language and within which no object-language sentences may be inferred, or he uses the language of semantics which includes the object-language as its proper part. In the former case he is unable to assert any object-language sentence, hence he is unable to assert, e.g. that horses do not exist. In the latter case, when using object-language sentences he has to obey the rules of that language; if those rules demand the acceptance of the sentence 'horses exist', then he must accept it.

Philosophers often programmatically cut themselves off from the object-language using various devices such as *'epoche'*, *'Einklammerung'*, etc. The use of these devices amounts simply to abandoning the object-language for the duration of epistemological analyses and to restricting one's language to the language of syntax. The thesis argued in the present article is that a philosopher who has so abandoned the object-language, i.e. the language which we normally use in everyday life to describe reality, will be unable to say anything about that reality. If nevertheless he pretends to say something, e.g. if he denies our world full reality and attributes to it some sort of dependent existence, then he does so through an unconscious mystification which replaces our object-language by his *quasi*-object-language.

NOTE

[1] Cf. this volume, pp. 140–153.

12. CHANGE AND CONTRADICTION*

(1948)

1. In the present article I intend to examine critically the correctness of those arguments known to me which have been used to justify the thesis that any change implies a contradiction, i.e. if a sentence stating the occurrence of a change is true, then so must be some two mutually contradictory sentences. I emphasize that this analysis will be concerned only with arguments of this type known to me. It may be that not all arguments of this type will be considered here and that, therefore, my analysis would to be amplified.

The principle of contradiction was attacked already in antiquity by some philosophers most of whom based their objections on the belief that the occurrence of any change whatever is inconsistent with the law of contradiction. Those attacks were often repeated by later philosophers who expressed their agreement with the arguments of ancient critics of the law of contradiction and contributed to the depth and variety of the arguments. However, it should be emphasized at the outset that the campaign against the law of contradiction in many cases originated from misunderstandings. The principle, which logicians know under the name of the law of contradiction, asserts in its semantical formulation that two mutually contradictory sentences (i.e. such that one of them denies what the other states) cannot both be true. Its ontological counterpart may be formulated in the simplest way as the claim that something cannot both be and not be the case. If for an assertion that something is the case we use the letter 'p', then the ontological version of the law of contradiction may be expressed as follows: it is never the case that both p and not-p. Hence to criticize the law of contradiction one would have to produce an argument showing that — contrary to what that law claims — there are two true sentences, one of which asserts what the other denies, or — in other words — that something is so and so and at same time is not so and so, e.g. that an object at an instant of time has a property and at the same time does not have that property. Now many critics believed that one refutes

* Translated by Jerzy Giedymin. First published in *Myśl Współczesna*, (1948), 8/9, 35–52. Translation based on *Język i Poznanie*, II, 90–106. Reprinted here by kind permission of PWN.

the law of contradiction by showing that an object may have elements which are in mutual contrast or 'opposition', e.g. a magnet which has a south and north pole. On other occasions one saw an instance of contradiction in the fact that in a process there may be antagonistic forces or tendencies (e.g. in the case of motion there is friction as well as a moving force). In other words, all forms of so-called 'unity of opposites' were regarded as instances refuting the law of contradiction. This is a misunderstanding, naturally, since the fact, for instance, that a magnet has two poles does not imply any contradiction: to say that a magnet has a north pole is neither tantamount to denying that it has a south pole nor is such a denial implied thereby. Similarly the claim that there are antagonistic forces in all processes leaves the law of contradiction intact for it does not imply that something both is and is not the case. The principle of the 'unity of opposites', or at least many of its particular instances, are in no conflict with the law of contradiction; the appearance that it is otherwise rests in many cases on misunderstandings. It is not my intention to dwell on those misunderstandings. I intend to restrict my attention to those arguments only which attack the law of contradiction without involving any terminological confusion − in particular to those arguments in which it is claimed that contradiction is inseparable from change. I shall try to show that those arguments are not valid and that no one has shown that change implies contradiction (a pair of contradictory sentences).

2. We shall begin by analyzing arguments attributed to Zeno who, as is claimed, attempted to show that nothing changes, in particular that nothing ever moves, by claiming that change implies contradiction.

The first of these arguments may be formulated as follows. If motion occurred, then at an instant t a body C in motion would have to be in a place M and at a subsequent instant t' which differs from t by a finite time interval T it would have to be in some other place M' such that its distance from M along the path of C's motion takes some value l. However, in order to cover the whole distance l, it is necessary first to cover all parts into which it can be divided and from which it can be composed again. But one can divide the distance into infinitely many parts, each of which is of finite length; this can be done, for instance, by first taking the first half of the distance, then taking a half of the remaining half, then a half of the remaining quarter, etc., always dividing the remaining part of the distance into two. The time necessary for travelling over those parts is the shorter the smaller the distance and may become arbitrarily short but will always have a definite duration. However, the time necessary to move over the whole distance l is equal to the sum of the times necessary to move over each of its parts; hence this time is equal to the sum of infinitely many temporal intervals each of which has a definite duration. But a sum of infinitely many temporal intervals, each of which has a definite duration (different from zero), is infinitely great. Therefore, the time necessary to travel over a distance l from a starting point M to any other point M' is infinitely long. In other words, a body cannot be taken from one place to another in a finite time, i.e. a body which at an instant is in some place will not be moved to another place neither in one second, nor in a million seconds nor in any definite (finite) time. But surely it would have to be in a different place after a finite interval of time if it were in motion. Hence, if a body is in motion, then after a finite interval of time it has to be in a different place (this is required by the nature of motion) and it cannot be in a different place after any finite time (as the above argument allegedly shows). To conclude, the assumption that a body is in motion implies a contradiction.

From this contradiction Zeno concluded that motion is impossible, that nothing can be in motion. The fact that this conclusion is in blatant contradiction with experience induced Zeno to reject experience as a source and criterion of knowledge and to adopt apriorism (rationalism), so widespread among ancient philosophers who extolled so-called reason as the only reliable source of knowledge by contrast to the unreliable evidence of the sense. For all those, who believed that Zeno's argument was valid and proved the impossibility of moving from one place to another in a finite time, were henceforth faced with a conflict between alleged 'truth of reason' and the evidence of our senses. The conflict may be resolved in one of two ways: either to accept the principles of 'reason' rejecting the evidence of experience, or to reject the principles of 'reason' and believe in the evidence of the senses. Most Greek authors chose the first of these paths opting for radical apriorism. There were some, however, who chose the other way of resolving the conflict: since the evidence of experience, according to which motion in fact occurs, is contradicted by the principles of 'reason' (according to which motion is impossible) they accepted the results of experience and surrendered the principles of 'reason'. At least they surrendered the law of contradiction according to which two mutually contradictory sentences, i.e. such that one of them denies what the other asserts, are not both true. Indeed the conclusion of Zeno's argument is the claim that a contradiction is implied by the assumption that bodies are in motion. This contradiction must, therefore, be accepted as a fact — urge those who trust experience — and the law of contradiction must be rejected, since according to that law contradictions do not exist. Contradiction is essential to motion, it is claimed, as Zeno has shown already. But motion is a fact, hence contradiction is also a fact, contrary to the law of contradiction. Let us abandon the law of contradiction which may be valid with respect to something that is motionless and fossilized but does not apply to live, moving and changeable reality!

Now, there would be a conflict between experience (which shows that motion exists) and the law of contradiction, if Zeno's argument were valid; if, indeed, the assumption that a body is in motion, implied not only that after a finite time it must be in a place different from its starting point but also that it cannot be in a different place after a finite time. We have seen how Zeno argued in support of this second implication. For some two hundred years now freshmen reading mathematics have been able to show the fallacy in Zeno's argument. The fallacy consists in the claim that a sum of infinitely many time intervals, each of which is of definite length (in this case each successive one is half the length of the preceding one), cannot be finite. According to Zeno the sum

$$\frac{t}{2} + \frac{t}{4} + \frac{t}{8} + \frac{t}{16} + \dots$$

cannot have a finite value. But from elementary theory of infinite geometric series we know that the sum in question is finite and equals exactly t. When this premiss of Zeno's argument is rejected, the whole argument collapses.

Zeno's fallacy was discovered and correctly diagnosed by Aristotle who, without knowing the theory of infinite series, nevertheless saw the relevant point. As Aristotle pointed out, Zeno assumed that a distance of finite length l may be divided into infinitely many parts $\frac{l}{2}, \frac{l}{4}, \frac{l}{8} \dots$, but refused to accept that a finite time-interval is also divisible into infinitely many parts of definite, non-zero length $\frac{t}{2}, \frac{t}{4}, \frac{t}{8}, \dots$. There is no reason, Aristotle continued, to accept that a distance of finite length l may consist of infinitely many parts (each half the length of the preceding one) and yet to reject the claim that a finite time-interval t may consist of (i.e. is the sum of) infinitely many parts (each of them half the length of the preceding one). This comment by Aristotle suffices to refute Zeno's argument for whose validity it is necessary to assume that a finite distance is decomposable into infinitely many parts (different from zero), i.e. that infinitely many such parts put together will form a finite distance, while the sum of infinitely many time segments (different from zero) will not form a time-interval of finite duration. There is no reason why time should here be treated differently from distance.

3. Another of Zeno's arguments, known as 'Achilles and the tortoise', is merely a variant of the argument already discussed and, therefore, subject (*mutatis mutandis*) to the same criticism. I shall disregard it and consider, instead, the third argument known under the name of 'Zeno's arrow'. This one may be formulated as follows: An arrow in flight is in some place at each instant of the duration of flight. However, if something is in a definite place (i.e. does not change its position) in every instant of a time-interval, then it is at rest throughout that time. Therefore an arrow in flight is at rest throughout the duration of the flight.

This argument may be interpreted in two ways and, accordingly, one may see the point of the argument in different ways. I shall first consider a less popular interpretation which — it seems — is less in conformity with Zeno's intended meaning. The argument under discussion may be understood in the following way: (1) If an arrow's flight extends over time T, then for every instant of this time there is a place in which the arrow is located. But (2) if there is a place occupied by the arrow in each instant of the duration of its flight, then the arrow is at rest throughout that time.[1] Hence, (3) if an arrow is in flight during time T, then it is at rest throughout time T, therefore, it is not in flight. From the assumption that an arrow is in flight a contradiction follows; motion implies a contradiction.

The fallacy of this argument is easy to discover. The argument appears to have the form of a hypothetical syllogism, i.e. to be of the form: if I then II and if II then III, hence if I then III. It would indeed have this structure, if the consequent of the first premiss were identical with the antecedent of the second premiss. However, in our formulation the consequent of the first premiss was:

> for every instant of the duration of the arrow's flight there is a place occupied by the arrow at that instant,

on the other hand, the antecedent of the second premiss reads:

> there is a place occupied by the arrow during every instant of its flight.

As we can see, the consequent of the first premiss is not identical with the antecedent of the second premiss. The argument in this formulation has not the form of a hypothetical syllogism; its structure is rather as follows:

> If I then II
> If III then IV
> Hence, If I then IV.

Arguments of this form are valid only in case II implies III, i.e. if the antecedent of the second premiss is implied by the consequent of the first. No such implication holds in our example. From the claim that

II   for every instant of the duration of the arrow's flight there is a place occupied by the arrow at that instant,

it does not follow that

III   there is a place occupied by the arrow in every instant of its flight,

just as from the sentence 'for every human being there is a man who is their father' it does not follow that

'there is a man who is the father of every human being'

or from 'for every number x there is a number y such that $y > x$' it does not follow that

'there is a number y such that for every x, $y > x$'.

In each of the three pairs the first sentence of the pair does not imply its second sentence, for the simple reason that in each of the three pairs its first sentence is true while the second false. A true sentence never implies a false one. Zeno's argument in the present interpretation seems convincing only as long as one believes that the consequent of the first premiss implies the antecedent of the second one; but no such implication holds. The claim to the contrary originates from a logical fallacy known as inadmissible interchange of quantifiers. Zeno's argument in the interpretation we have just discussed is guilty of this fallacy.

4. A different interpretation is usually discussed by philosophers interested in Zeno's paradoxes. Usually the argument is interpreted as follows:

"If a body remains in the same place throughout a period of time, then that body is then at rest. Now an arrow in flight is — as Zeno asserts — in a definite, i.e. one and the same place in every instant of its flight. Hence an arrow in flight is at rest in every instant of the duration of its flight. Since it is at rest in each instant of its flight, then it is at rest throughout its flight. For how could motion result from the composition of states of rest?"

Philosophers who understand Zeno's paradox in this fashion and disagree with its conclusion which denies motion and is incompatible with experience, subject the argument to various criticisms. Bergson, for instance, rejects the premiss according to which a body in motion *occupies* or *is* in each instant of time in a definite, i.e. one and the same, place. For Bergson refuses to identify the concept of an instant of time with a time-point. Time by its nature is duration; a time-point however has no duration; hence, time cannot consist of temporal points for duration cannot result from something that does not endure. Time consists of moments. Therefore, moments are not temporal points, they are time-segments which have duration however vanishingly small. Now, if by a 'moment' we understand a vanishingly small time-segment, then we cannot accept Zeno's premiss according to which a body in motion in each moment of its motion *is* in a definite place. For if the premiss were true, then in every moment of its motion a body would be assigned a definite place. But this is not so, for a moment has duration and a body in motion is in contact with more than one place during that duration; hence, it is not true that in every moment of its motion a body is uniquely assigned a place in the sense that we could say that in the given moment the body actually *is* in that place.

Other critics of Zeno, for example the phenomenologist Reinach, identify the concept of a moment with the concept of a temporal point which has no duration; they distinguish, however, various kinds of relations which may hold between a body and a place in contact with the body in the given moment, when it is in it at rest or in motion. Reinach believes that even if one ignores completely what has happened to a body in the past and what will happen to it in future it is possible to see differences in the relationships between a body and the place with which it is at present in contact, depending on whether it is in that place at rest or in motion. He distinguishes four kinds of contact between a body and a place in a moment of time: a body may be passing (*passieren*) through the place at the moment, it may be reaching (*erreichen*) or just leaving it (*verlassen*), finally it may be staying there (*verweilen*). In the first moment, when motion begins, a body leaves the starting point, in later moments of the duration of motion a body passes through the places on its path, in the final moment of motion, just before coming to rest, a body in motion reaches the end of the path, then stays there until its motion may be resumed again. In the light of these distinctions between various kinds of contact between a body in motion and the places on its path, one may subject Zeno's argument to criticism in the following way: The premiss, according to which a body in motion *is* in each moment of the duration of motion in some definite place, is true provided the word 'is' is taken in the widest sense, which does not specify the kind of contact between the body in motion and the place: whether it stays there, or is just passing through, whether it leaves the place or reaches it. If the word 'is' is taken in this sense, however, then it is fallacious starting from the assumption that a body *is* in every moment in a definite place to conclude that it is in each moment at rest. This conclusion would follow from that assumption only if the meaning of 'is' were narrowed down so that 'is' were identified with 'stays'. Then, however, the premiss according to which a body in motion *is* in a definite place in every moment of the duration of motion, would be false; for it would amount to saying that a body in motion *stays* (is stationary) in every moment of motion in a definite place, which is false. From the point of view of Reinach's distinctions, there is no sense of the word 'is', given which the premiss used by Zeno would be true and the argument valid.

In the light of the mentioned distinctions, one can understand the position, taken e.g. by Plekhanov, which attempts to resolve Zeno's paradox by assuming that wherever motion and change in general are involved either the law of contradiction or the law of the excluded middle cease to be valid. For Plekhanov rejects Zeno's premiss according to which a body in motion *is* in a place in each moment of its motion. But one cannot hold either that it *is not* in a place in every moment of motion. A body in motion both *is* and *is not* in a definite place. As I said before, one may comprehend Plekhanov's claim, provided one interprets him as saying that a body in motion in every moment of motion *is* in a definite place in the widest sense of 'is' (which does not specify the kind of contact), whereas it *is not* in that place in the sense of 'staying' in it. In other words, one may interpret the claim that a body in motion is and simultaneously is not in a definite place, as saying that a body in motion in every moment of motion is in contact with some definite place but does not stay there. So interpreted, Plekhanov's claim does not lend support to the thesis that motion implies contradiction. There is no contradiction in claiming that a body both is in every moment of motion in a definite place and is not, if the word 'is' will be taken in the first part of the claim in one sense while in the second it is taken in another sense.

Let us return, however, to Reinach's critique of Zeno's paradox. Its main point is the suggestion that Zeno confused different meanings the word 'is' may have in contexts of the type 'a body C is at time t in place m'. For he confused the widest sense of 'is' which does not specify the kind of contact between a body and a place with the specific sense in which 'is' is synonymous with 'stays'. The general direction of Reinach's critique seems right, though its details are not satisfactory. Reinach distinguished four kinds of contact between a body at an instant of time and a place on its path. Being a phenomenologist he does not define any of the kinds of contact but is satisfied with stirring our intuition. It appears to him, moreover, that those kinds of contact between place and body may be distinguished irrespective of what had happened to the body before the moment under consideration and irrespective of what will happen subsequently. There seems to be a misunderstanding here. If one considers the present in total abstraction from the past and the future, one loses the ability to distinguish various kinds of contact between place and body and the ability to distinguish motion from rest. If we abstract from past and future, we destroy time. It seems that on this point Bergson was right when he claimed that if an isolated point in time is considered in abstraction from the past and the future, then one is unable to give an account of those concepts which presuppose duration, in particular, one is unable to give a satisfactory account of what is motion and rest. Both the concept of motion and of rest essentially involve the idea of time-segments and one cannot distinguish them properly if time-segments are ignored and one considers only a single time-point. One can define the concept of motion and of rest only by appealing to time-segments in which a temporal point occurs.

One may give definitions of these concepts in various formulations not quite co-extensive. We shall use in these definitions expressions 'a body C occupies a place m at time t' or 'a body C is at t in m' with 'occupies' or 'is' taken in that widest sense in which one merely states that C is in contact with a place m without specifying the kind of contact.

Let us begin with the following definition:

Ia   A body C is at rest at t if and only if there exists a time-interval $(t_1 t_2)$ which contains t (i.e. such that $t_1 \leqslant t \leqslant t_2$) and such that in any two moments chosen from that interval C occupies that same place.

Ib   A body C is in motion at t — if and only if there exists a time-interval $(t_1 t_2)$ such that $t_1 < t < t_2$ and in any two moments from that interval C is in two different places (occupies different positions).

From these two definitions it follows that there exists always a first and a last moment of rest but there is no first or last moment of motion. Without departing from the ordinary meaning of 'motion' and 'rest' we might modify (II) those definitions (by taking the interval inclusive of both end-points in the definition of motion and exclusive of them in the definition of rest) so that they would imply the existence of a first and last moment of motion and the non-existence of a first and last moment of rest. Other modifications (III) are possible (e.g. by taking in the definition of rest the interval inclusive of the left end-point and in the definition of motion inclusive of the right end-point) to imply, e.g. that there exists a first but no last moment of rest and that there exists a last but no first moment of motion. It is also easy to see that definitions Ia and Ib (as well as their modifications) imply that motion and rest exclude one another. However, they do not imply that every body must either be at rest or in motion. So, for example, on the basis of definitions Ia and Ib one could not say of a pendulum reaching its extreme position at time t either that it is at rest at t or that it is in motion. For one cannot find a time interval $(t_1 t_2)$ such that $t_1 \leqslant t \leqslant t_2$ ('t' denotes the moment in which the pendulum reaches the turning point) and such that for every moment in that interval the pendulum were in the same place. Nor is it possible to surround t with an interval $(t_1 t_2)$ such that $t_1 \leqslant t \leqslant t_2$ and for every two moments from that interval the pendulum were in two different places. On the other hand, it is easy to see that according to definition II a pendulum at the moment it reaches the turning point may be said to be in motion.

Other definitions of 'motion' and 'rest' at an instant of time may be based on the concept of instantaneous velocity. By definition (IV) a body will be said to be at rest at time t if its velocity at t equals zero and will be said to be in motion at t if its velocity is not equal to zero. Given these definitions of 'rest' and 'motion', it will turn out that a pendulum is at rest at the time it reaches an extreme position.

All these definitions define motion or rest at an instant as a property which a body has with respect to what happens to it in preceding or succeeding instants. This is obvious in the case of the first group of definitions; the same, however, applies to definitions which make use of the concept of instantaneous velocity which (instantaneous velocity) – as we know – is the limiting value of average velocities for periods containing the moment under consideration. It is apparent, therefore, that the definitions of motion and of rest in terms of instantaneous velocity take into account the behaviour of a body before and after the moment under consideration, that they do not define 'motion' and 'rest' in total abstraction from preceding and subsequent moments.

How in the light of this analysis are we to assess Zeno's paradox of the arrow in its interpretation now under consideration? As we have seen, the starting point of the argument is the premiss according to which an arrow in flight is at each instant of its flight in some definite (one and the same) position. The premiss may also be formulated as saying that for each instant of the arrow's flight one can specify a place at which the arrow is at that instant. From this Zeno concludes that an arrow in flight is at rest at each instant of the duration of its flight. Now from our analysis it follows that an answer to the question whether a body is in motion or at rest at an instant of time cannot be inferred from a premiss which abstracts completely from what happens to the body before or after that instant. For by saying that a body is at rest or in motion at an instant we make a statement concerning the history of the body in the immediate past or future of that instant. Hence, from the fact that a body is in a definite place at an instant it is impossible to conclude — without assuming anything about where it is before or after — whether it is at rest or in motion at that instant. But such a conclusion is drawn by Zeno from his premiss and this is just the fallacy of his argument.

It is easy to see the psychological source of the fallacy. The fallacy arises from failure to distinguish with sufficient clarity between a time-point and an extremely short time-interval. When Zeno declares that an arrow during its flight is in each instant of the duration of the flight in some definite place, he means by an instant a time-point without any duration and not a time-interval of very short duration. For it is only with respect to temporal points that it is apparent that a body is in a definite place. On the other hand, when from the premiss that a body in motion is at every instant in a definite place he concludes that, therefore, the body is at rest in every instant of time, he apparently changes the meaning of 'instant' to 'a very short period' of some, however small, duration. Given this latter meaning of 'instant', from the fact that a body in that instant is (continuously) in a definite place, we can legitimately conclude that it is at rest. For indeed a body which throughout the duration of an arbitrarily short period is in a definite (i.e. one and the same) place, is throughout that time at rest. But if by an 'instant' we mean a time-point without any duration, then from the fact that a body is in a definite place at that instant we cannot derive the conclusion that it is then at rest. For whether a body is at rest or in motion at an instant understood as a time-point does not depend on what we can say about the position of the body in that isolated instant but on what is true about its position in preceding and subsequent instants.[2]

.....

5. Zeno's paradoxes are not the only arguments which have been used to show that change implies contradiction. Let us consider one more argument of this type whose author I do not know. One may argue in the following fashion:

Whenever a body changes its state from A to (a different one) B, there must be an instant t subsequent to every instant in which it still is in state A and preceding every instant in which it is already in state B and such that at t the body under discussion is neither in state A nor in state B. So, for example, between the moments in which a heated body's temperature is 10 °C and the moment in which its temperature equals 11 °C there must be moments in which its temperature is neither 10 °C nor 11 °C but takes some value in between those two. Between the moments when I am at home and the moments I am already in my university office, there must be moments in which I am neither at home nor in the university but on the way from my home to the university. Between the moments in summer when a tree's leaves are clearly green and the moments of autumn when they are distinctly yellow, there must be intermediate moments when leaves are neither green nor yellow but are becoming yellow and hence are greenish-yellow or yellowish-green. The principle whose instances we have just mentioned is very well substantiated by experience.

The principle in question asserts that whenever a body is in an instant in a state A and in a subsequent instant in a state B (different from A), there must be time when the body in question is passing from state A to B and is neither in A nor in B. Let us refer to this principle as the *postulate of transition*. This postulate may be regarded as a consequence of *the principle of continuity* which requires that any change must occur in arbitrarily small steps and not in leaps. For to say that change is continuous is to say that it occurs in such a way that it is enough to choose a sufficiently short period of its duration to make change arbitrarily small. The principle of continuity excludes, therefore, any course of events in which a body would be in state A until time t and in every moment subsequent to t it would be in state B, different from A. If change occurred at a moment in just this way, then however short a period of change we chose beginning at t, the change could never become arbitrarily small for it could never be smaller than the critical change necessary for the switch from A to B. For the same reason the principle of continuity excludes a course of events in which a body after t would already be in state B but in state A in every preceding instant. In other words, the principle of continuity requires that between the moments when a body was in state A and the moments when it will be in state B, there should be moments when it is neither in A nor in B but is just in the transition from the first state to the second. The postulate of transition is thus not only well confirmed by experience but is also logically implied by the principle of continuity.

Now using the postulate of transition one could attack the ontological law of contradiction in the following way: let us consider a piece of ice which melts or sublimates, i.e. is being converted from a solid into a liquid or vapour. From experience we know that some bodies are at first solids and then are converted either into liquids or vapour. From the postulate of continuity it follows that between the period of time when a body was a solid and the period when it was a liquid or vapour there must have been time when it was in transition from one state into the other. During that transition period it was neither solid, nor liquid or vapour. There is no paradox yet unless we assume that these are the only states a body may be in. We know however that this is not so, for there are intermediate states, e.g. liquids at critical temperature are in a state intermediate between liquids and vapour; there are also bodies which may be in a state intermediate between solids and liquids, etc.

But let us look at things more closely. Let us consider the conversion of a solid to a *non*-solid, or − in general − from a state A into a state *non-A*. Any great or small change is of this type; for whenever something is undergoing a change it is first in a state A and subsequently is not in state A. According to the postulate of transition between the moments when a body was in state A and the moments when it will be in state *non-A* there must be a period when it was in the transition from A into *non-A* and, hence, is neither in A nor in *non-A*. However, to say that x is an object which is in state *non-A* amounts to saying that x is not a state A. In other words, to say x is an object which is not in state *non-A* amounts to saying that x is not not in state A, i.e. it is in state A. Therefore, at the time a body is in the transition from state A to *non-A*, it is both not A and is A, hence it has contradictory properties.[3]

.....

We have tried to give a fair account of an argument which seems to be the clearest of those used to support the claim that change implies contradiction. We have also done our best to make explicit the premises of that argument. This will facilitate our criticism of the argument. One could start from a criticism of that part of the argument in which from the premiss that an object is not *non-A* one concludes that it is A. For in order to make this inference valid one would presumably assume those laws of logic which one set out to refute. However, such criticism would be involved and not necessarily convincing. We will, therefore, turn our attention in another direction. As we have seen, the postulate of transition was an essential assumption in the argument purporting to show that any change implies contradiction.

Let us ask on what grounds one could accept that postulate. One of the grounds might be experience, another the principle of continuity. Let us begin with experience. Experience shows indeed that a body's temperature changes, e.g. from 10 °C to 11 °C, that I travel from my house to a university building, etc. But can one appeal to experience to ascertain that a body changes from state A to state *non-A* in the sense that during that change it is neither in state A nor in state *non-A*? We have observed those intermediate states between temperature $10\,°C$ and $11\,°C$ of the body and we have observed my intermediate positions between my being at home and in the university. However, has anyone observed intermediate states between a state A and *non-A*? Surely no one would claim this. Therefore, when we apply the postulate of transition to the case 'A; *non-A*' we extrapolate beyond the evidence of experience. Any such extrapolation is speculative or, at least, conjectural; it is not a result of a rigorous empirical procedure. If the acceptance of such a conjecture results in a contradiction, then it would be unreasonable to accept the contradiction in order to save the conjecture based on nothing but an analogy. On the other hand, one could use the argument under discussion as part of an indirect proof of the claim that the postulate of transition does not apply to the case $(A; non\text{-}A)$. This would amount to the following: From the assumption 'If a body is at a time in state A and subsequently in state *non-A*, then there must have been time when the body was in transition from one state to the other and so was neither in one nor in the other state' a contradiction is derivable; hence the assumption is to be rejected as absurd the more so that it is not confirmed by experience.

Against this an objection may be raised to the effect that the postulate of transition is based on the principle of continuity of change; the former is a logical consequence of the latter, hence the former is at least as acceptable as the latter. In reply one should point out that the principle of continuity is not an a priori truth; it is at best an inductive generalization from experience. Nor is it regarded as universally valid in contemporary science. For contemporary science acknowledges the existence of 'quantum' changes, i.e. non-continuous changes in the processes of emission and absorption of energy. Let us disregard this fact, however, and let us consider whether the principle of continuity is contradicted by the assumption that the change from a state A to *non-A* occurs without a transition from one state to the other during which an object is neither in A nor in *non-A*.

Let us assume, therefore, that the change from a state A to state *non-A* occurs without a 'transition'. In other words, let us assume, for example, that a body up to time t was in state A and that at any subsequent moment it was in state *non-A*. Let us see whether this assumption contradicts the principle of continuity which requires that any change should occur without jumps. As we have seen already, the principle of continuity forbids any case in which a body is up to time t in state A and at any subsequent time in state B for under such circumstances a jump B-A would occur at t. This jump would be the smaller the less state B differs from A. As long as state B is a definite state, the difference between B and A is also definite and as such cannot become arbitrarily small. But the principle of continuity demands that any change should occur through arbitrarily small changes. However, the case of interest to us now is the change from a state *A* to *non-A*. The term 'state *non-A*' is not a singular name of a definite state; it is rather a general term which denotes any change different from *A*. By the same token, 'the difference between state *non-A* and *A*' is not a singular term denoting a definite difference between states; it is a general term denoting any difference between *A* and any state different from *A*. This is essential for our problem. For the question we want answered is whether the principle of continuity is contradicted by the assumption that a body might be in state *A* before *t* and in state *non-A* at any moment subsequent to *t*. There would be a contradiction between them if the difference between states *non-A* (we use plural since 'state *non-A*' is a general term) and state *A* could not possibly be below a *minimum*, i.e. could not be arbitrarily small. Now one of two things might be the case. The set of states under consideration could have, so to say, a grain structure. This would be the case if those states were, for example, 'quantized', i.e. if each of them were a whole multiple of some elementary state. Then a difference between *A* and any of the states *non-A* could not be arbitrarily small, for it could not be less than the quantum of the elementary state. However, this assumption of the 'grain' structure of the set of states is a straightforward negation of the principle of continuity. If the principle of continuity is to be respected, then we have to assume that the set of states under consideration does not have a grain structure, that its structure is continuous in the sense that there are no two states minimally different one from the other, that for any state *A* one may find another state *A'* such that the difference between them is as small as we like.

On this last assumption we shall be able to say that the difference between states *A* and *non-A* is arbitrarily small. If so, however, we do not contradict the principle of continuity by assuming that a body is in state *A* before *t* and in state *non-A* at any moment subsequent to *t*; for we do not introduce thereby any jump into the process of change. Such a jump would occur at a time-point *t* if in every time-interval $(t, t + \tau)$, however small, the change occurring in that interval could not fall below a minimal value, could not be arbitrarily small. But by assuming at *t* state *A* and by further assuming that at any subsequent moment $t + \tau$ one finds a state *non-A*, we do not exclude the possibility that by choosing a suitably short time-increment τ the difference between suitable states *A* and *non-A* may be made arbitrarily small.

Our analysis shows the following: though the principle of transition is implied by the principle of continuity if transitions from a definite state *A* to a definite state B are concerned, it is not implied by it when transitions from a definite state A to not uniquely determined states *non-A* are concerned. One must not, therefore, appeal to the principle of continuity in support of the postulate of transition in an argument in which that postulate is used as an essential premiss to establish the claim that change implies contradiction.[4]

.....

6. I cannot discuss here in detail other arguments that have been used to attack either the law of contradiction or the law of excluded middle in connection with the phenomenon of change. I shall conclude with some brief comments.

One of those other arguments relies on the existence of so-called vague terms. These are terms like e.g. 'young', 'old'; they share the property that while of some objects we are able to decide whether or not the term in question applies to them, of others we are unable to do so. For example, we observe a man throughout his life-time. There is a time when, without hesitation or doubt we would say that he is young; then, there comes a time when also without any doubt we would say that he is no longer young. But surely there will be a period during which neither claim can be easily made. For we lack criteria to decide of a man of a certain age whether he is young or not. This is an unquestionable fact. Some, however, are prepared to conclude from this fact that of an ageing man it is neither true that he is young nor is it true that he is not young.

The fallacy of the above argument against the law of excluded middle consists in the fact that it confuses our inability to decide between two mutually contradictory sentences with the claim that neither of them is true. The circumstance that neither the sentence 'He is young' nor the sentence 'He is not young' is in principle (by contrast to technical difficulties) decidable is no proof that neither of the sentences is true. We shall be satisfied here with this brief comment, although we realize that the question deserves a more detailed discussion.

Finally, a brief comment about another argument purporting to show that change implies contradiction. The argument is as follows: When an object is changing, then it is at first so and so, and afterwards otherwise. For example, Socrates is at first young and afterwards he is no longer young. But it is the same Socrates who is young and is not young. The same object, if subject to change, is such and is not such, contrary to the law of contradiction. − The fallacy of this argument is obvious. Every object in time, hence also every object undergoing changes, has not only spatial but also temporal dimensions. There are many predicates which we can predicate of some of its temporal parts only but not of others, just as there are predicates which we can truthfully predicate of some but not all of its spatial parts. So, for example, of the national flag of Poland we can say that its upper part is white while its lower part is red, hence not white. But this is surely not seen as evidence against the law of contradiction. For sentences 'this flag's upper part is white' and 'this flag's lower part is not white' are not mutually contradictory at all; one does not deny what the other claims. The same applies to the ageing Socrates. We can say of him that in his early years he is young and that he is not young in his later years; or that in his old age he is bald and that he is not bald when young. These sentences attribute a property to some temporal segments of an object known as Socrates and deny it to some other temporal segments of the same object. But they do not refer to the same object, since each refers to a different temporal segment of Socrates. They do not contradict each other. An ageing or balding Socrates cannot, therefore, serve as an argument against the law of contradiction.

7. The fallacy of the last argument is obvious, and our comments concerning it trivial. The same applies, more or less, to our comments concerning other arguments used in support of the view that change implies contradiction. Sometimes, however, even such comments may be useful in that they help avoid undesirable misunderstandings. I hope that the present article will serve this purpose.

NOTES

[1] This is implied by the definition of rest, according to which, a body is at rest at time T if and only if in each instant of time T the body is in the same place, i.e. there is a place in which it is at each instant of T.

[2] [A few sentences summarizing the preceding paragraph have been omitted here in translation. Translator]

[3] [A few sentences summarizing the preceding paragraph have been omitted here in translation. Translator]

[4] [A few sentences summarizing the preceding paragraph have been omitted here in translation. Translator]

13. ON THE NOTION OF EXISTENCE*

Some Remarks Connected with the Problem of Idealism
(1949)

I wish to discuss in the present article two notions of existence, namely, the notion of real existence and that of intentional existence. The results obtained I propose to apply to the interpretation of the idealistic thesis which denies real existence to things we encounter in nature according them only an intentional existence, and to base on this interpretation a criticism of this thesis.

The term 'exists' occurs in logical systems in which it is precisely defined. Such a definition has been given by Russell and Whitehead and also by Leśniewski. Russell's definition is formulated in a manner which allows to apply the term 'exists' only to symbols of classes, relations and descriptions, but its application to proper names is not admissible. This means that an expression consisting of the term 'exists' and a proper name has, in Russell's system, no meaning at all. Leśniewski in whose calculus of names, called ontology[1], proper names belong to the same syntactical category as common names, defines the term 'exists' in such a way that every sentence in which the term 'exists' is conjoined with an arbitrary name, irrespective of whether this is a proper name, a class name, or a description, has a definite meaning. For this reason, as well as because Leśniewski's definition seems closer to everyday language and is better known in Poland, we shall base our considerations on his definition of 'existence'.

To begin with, I shall recapitulate the fundamentals of Leśniewski's terminological conventions taking advantage to some extent of the formulations contained in the account of Leśniewski's ontology included in the *Elements* of Kotarbiński[2]).

The terminology in Leśniewski's ontology is based on the primitive term 'ϵ' (read: is), on the terms of the calculus of propositions and on quantifiers. The primitive term 'ϵ' of ontology is introduced by means of the following axiom:

$$a \, \epsilon \, b \underset{ab}{\equiv} (\Pi x)(x \, \epsilon \, a \supset x \, \epsilon \, b) \, . \, (\exists x)(x \, \epsilon \, a) \, . \, (\Pi x, y)(x \, \epsilon \, a \, . \, y \, \epsilon \, a \supset x \, \epsilon \, y)$$

* Translated by Jerzy Giedymin. First published in *Studia Philosophica* IV (1949/50), 7–22. Translation based on *Język i Poznanie*, II, 143–154. Reprinted here by kind permission of PWN.

The right-hand side of this definition is the logical product of three components for which the following notational abbreviations are introduced:

Def. 1. $a \subset b \equiv (\Pi x)(x \in a \supset x \in b)$ — read: *a sub b* (or: every *a* is *b*) — if and only if for every *x*, if *x* is *a* then *x* is *b*.

Def. 2. ex $a \equiv (\exists x)(x \in a)$ — read: there exist *a*'s — if and only if there is an *x* such that *x* is *a*.

Def. 3. *sol* $a \equiv (\Pi x, y)(x \in a \ . \ y \in a \supset x \in y)$ — read: at most one *a* (or: there exists at most one *a*) —if and only if — when *x* is *a* and *y* is *a* then *x* is *y*.

Taking advantage of these definitions we may formulate the axiom of ontology as follows:

Th. 1. $a \in b \equiv a \subset b \ . \ \text{ex} \ a \ . \ \text{sol} \ a$ — read: *a* is *b* — if and only if — *a sub b*, *a* exists and there exists at most one *a*.

The symbol '*ob*' is now defined:

Def. 4. *ob* $a \equiv (\exists x)(a \in x)$ — read: *obiectum a* (or: *a* is an object) if and only if for some *x*, *a* is *x*.

The definitions of the symbols '*ex*' (there exist) and '*ob*' (is an object) seem to be in agreement with their ordinary meanings. In everyday language they may be formulated as follows:

a's exist if and only if something is an *a*

(e.g. black swans exist if and only if something is a black swan); *a* is an object if and only if *a* is something at all (e.g. Atlantis is an object if and only if Atlantis is something).

It is easy to prove that

Th. 2. *ob* $a \equiv \text{ex} \ a \ . \ \text{sol} \ a$ (i.e. *a* is an object if and only if *a* exists and there is at most one *a*).

Proof: In virtue of Theorem 1 and Definitions 1—3 we may deduce from Definition 4:

(1)   *ob* $a \equiv (\exists x)(a \subset x \ . \ \text{ex} \ a \ . \ \text{sol} \ a)$
(2)   *ob* $a \equiv (\exists x)(a \subset x).(\text{ex} \ a \ . \ \text{sol} \ a)$

However, since from the law of tautology of the propositional calculus we get '$p \supset p$' and Definition 1 implies:

(3) $\quad a \underset{a}{\subseteq} a$

therefore also

(4) $\quad (\exists x)(a \subset x)$

Hence, by omitting this in the product on the right-hand side of formula (2) we get Theorem 2.

From Theorem 2 on the other hand, we get at once

Th. 3. $ob\ a \underset{a}{\supset} ex\ a$

which reads: if a is an object, then a exists.

From this theorem, it seems to follow that one cannot say truly of anything that it is a non-existing object, or, to put it more precisely, that no sentence of the form 'a is a non-existing object' can be true. Some authors, however, believe that such sentences can be true. For example, Twardowski, when justifying his claim that every representation has an object, argues that the object of a representation need not be an object existing in reality. The representation, for example, which corresponds to the name 'Zeus' has an object. This object is, according to Twardowski – Zeus, who admittedly is not a really existing object but is an object nevertheless though only an object in thought. Zeus did not exist in reality but he existed in the minds of the Greeks. This phraseology which distinguishes 'real objects' from 'merely thought-of objects', 'real existence' from 'existence only in thought' is familiar in the whole history of philosophy especially since the Middle Ages when the term *'ens reale', 'ens intentionale', 'esse reale', 'esse intentionale'* were introduced. It plays an important role in the object language (material) mode of formulation of the problems of idealism and realism: moreover this phraseology has penetrated the formulation of many fundamental philosophical problems.

At the present time there is a tendency towards eliminating this terminology. Traditional philosophical problems which used to be formulated in the object-language by means of just that terminology are now translated into the so-called formal (metalinguistic) mode of speech. For example, the problem of subjective idealism which in the material mode of speech was expressed in the form of the question 'do bodies exist in reality or do they exist only in somebody's mind?' is replaced by the metalinguistic question 'are sentences which assert the existence of bodies true or are they merely accepted by men?'.(We are at present not particularly concerned with the point whether these are adequate formulations of the problem of idealism.)

Now, although in principle I am of the opinion that such translation of philosophical problems from the material into the metalinguistic mode of speech is often the only reasonable way of formulating what is essential in the given problem, nevertheless I should like to consider whether it is possible to construct one's own language so as to be able to speak meaningfully of 'real objects' as well as of 'merely thought of objects', of 'real existence' as well as of 'merely intentional existence', etc.

In considering the possiblity of such a language we shall base its construction on the framework of Leśniewski's ontology.

With this in view we must realize that in the language of ontology itself one cannot form any constant name for which it would be possible to prove within ontology a sentence of the form '$a \in b$', containing that name as its subject, or a sentence of the form '$ex\ a$' in which this name would be the argument of the functor 'ex'. The language of ontology is too poor for that purpose. However, we can enlarge that language with new constant terms by adding at the same time to the sentences asserted in ontology new asserted sentences containing these new constant terms. For example, we may enlarge the vocabulary of ontology by adding the names 'Socrates', 'Napoleon', 'man', etc. and by modifying at the same time the rule of substitution so that these names will belong to expressions which may be substituted in the theorems of ontology for variables. Simultaneously the sentences 'Socrates is a man', 'Napoleon is a man', etc. may be added as asserted theses to theses asserted in ontology. Owing to the extension of the rule of substitution it will become possible to include these sentences in the deductive system of ontology and derive from them as consequences 'ob Socrates', 'ob Napoleon', 'ex Socrates', 'ex Napoleon', 'ex man'.

However, the dictionary of ontology may also be enriched by the names 'Zeus', 'Polyphemus', Olympian', 'cyclops', and to the theorems of ontology may be added the following sentences as asserted sentences: 'Zeus is an Olympian' 'Polyphemus is a cyclops'. From these sentences the theorems of ontology will permit to derive the sentences 'ob Zeus', 'ob Polyphemus', 'ex Olympians', 'ex cyclopses'.

This shows that ontology itself does not yield any existential theorems. However, whether we obtain these or other existential theorems will depend upon which sentences of the form '$a \in b$' with name-constants in place of the subject and predicate we conjoin to the theorems of ontology having extended the range of application of the rule of substitution to cover those names. Thus we may be able to assert the sentence 'men exist' but likewise we may be able to assert the sentence 'Olympians exist'.

Let us consider now the language which results from the language of ontology if we enrich the class of its theorems with all sentences which fulfil the following conditions: (1) they may be obtained from sentential functions meaningful in ontology by replacing their variables with appropriate constants; (2) the assertion of these sentences is licensed directly or indirectly by empirical criteria. In the first place perceptual sentences of the form '*a ε b*' or of any other form admissible in the language of ontology will belong here; furthermore, all sentences which according to methods adopted in the sciences (natural or social) may be inferred from those perceptual sentences. Among these sentences might be such as 'Mt. Blanc is a mountain', 'the Vistula is a river', etc. On the other hand, we shall not find among them sentences such as 'Zeus is an Olympian', or 'Polyphemus is a cyclops'.

Now, if in the language so constructed we apply the definition of existence and the definition of object writing

$$ex\ a \equiv (\exists x)\, x \in a,\ ob\ a \equiv (\exists x)\, a \in x$$

we shall assert the existential sentence '*ex a*' if and only if on the basis of experience we arrive at the statement '$(\exists x)(x \in a)$'. Most frequently we get this statement by deducing it from some singular sentence of the form '$x \in a$' asserted on the basis of experience. From the empirical statement 'Mt. Blanc is a mountain' we shall get in this way the assertion of the existential statement 'mountains exist' and likewise of the statement 'rivers exist', etc. We shall, however, not assert the existential sentence 'Olympians exist', or 'cyclopses exist' unless experience confirms a sentence of the form '*x* is an Olympian' or '*x* is a cyclops'.

The same will apply to 'objectivizing' sentences, i.e. to sentences of the form '*ob a*' ('*a* is an object'). We assert such a sentence if and only if in experience we find a basis for stating the sentence '$(\exists x)(a \in x)$'. In the most simple case we do so, when on the basis of experience we are able to state specifically that '$a \in b$'. In this way we shall assert the objectivizing sentence 'Giewont is an object', 'the Vistula is an object', but we shall not assert the sentences 'Zeus is an object' or 'Polyphemus is an object'.

As may be seen, in the language we are discussing here we shall apply the term 'exists' only to those objects which, so to speak, have an empirical exemplification. It seems natural to distinguish the notion of existence occurring in that language as the notion of real existence. For it seems natural to use the term 'real existence' to refer to the notion of existence which is applied on the basis of experience.

It seems also natural to label the notion of object occurring in such a language as the notion of a real object.

We therefore suggest the following terminology: we propose to use 'the notion of real existence' or 'the notion of a real object' for the concepts which are meanings of the terms '*ex*' and '*ob*', respectively, in the extension of the language of Leśniewski's ontology obtained by adjoining to its theorems sentences which, firstly, result from sentences meaningful in ontology by substitution of names for free variables, secondly, are confirmed by experience.

Let us in turn consider a language which is constructed from the language of ontology in a different way. Leśniewski's ontology will be enriched with all those sentences (derived from meaningful sentences of ontology by substituting certain constant names for free variables) which occur (in the form of *oratio recta*) in the English translations of Homer's *Iliad* and *Odyssey*, the rule of substitution of ontology having been extended appropriately. In the language so extended sentences 'Zeus is an Olympian', 'Polyphemus is a cyclops', '*ob* Zeus', '*ex* Olympians', '*ex* cyclopses', etc. occur as asserted sentences.

In view of the fact that in the language discussed at present the rule governing the assertion of sentences of the form '*a* is *b*' is different from that in the language considered before, we must assume that the expression 'is' (just as other expressions of the second language equiform with certain expressions of the first) has different meanings in these two languages. Consequently, the expressions '*ex*' and '*ob*' introduced by means of definitions whose form is taken from ontology will have different meanings in the two languages since the term 'is' to which the expressions '*ex*' and '*ob*' are reduced by definition has a different meaning in each of these two languages. In the language we are discussing at present we have, therefore, notions of 'existence' and 'object' different from those in the first language. Again it seems quite natural to call the notion of object and the notion of existence of the second language, the *notion of intentional object of Homer's epics*, and the *notion of existence in Homer's epics*, respectively.

In order to distinguish the notions corresponding to the symbols 'ϵ', '*ex*', '*ob*', etc. in the first and in the second of the languages under consideration we shall use the subscript '*r*' with these symbols if they belong to the first language, and the subscript '*h*' if they are expressions of the second language. We shall distinguish therefore concepts which are meanings of symbols 'ex_r', 'ex_h', 'ob_r' and 'ob_h'. The notions corresponding to the first members in each of these two pairs (ex_r and ob_r) will be called the notion of 'real existence' and notion of 'real object' respectively, those corresponding to the second members of these pairs (ex_h and ob_h) — the notion of 'intentional existence in Homer's epics' and the notion of 'the object in Homer's epics' respectively.

Before we resume our considerations we have to make certain remarks in order to avoid possible misunderstandings. What has been said in previous paragraphs might be misunderstood as an attempt at defining the terms 'real object', 'intentional object', etc. We might be suspected of having given the following definitions: 1. *a* is a real object if and only if the sentence '*ob a*' is a theorem in the language formed by adjoining accepted empirical statements to ontology. 2. *a* has real existence if and only if the sentence '*ex a*' is a theorem in the language which is an empirical extension of ontology. This interpretation of our analysis must be rejected. We have not given difinitions of the terms 'real object' or 'real existence'. Both the definition of real object and the definition of real existence just quoted are absolutely alien to us. They have a semantic character as they operate with the names of objects as well as with the names of these names whereas our analysis is purely syntactical. We do not speak in it at all of real objects but only of certain expressions such as 'ob_r' and 'ex_r' and propose a certain manner of reading them, namely, as 'real object', and 'real existence.' Consequently, we propose to refer to the meaning of the symbol 'ob_r' as the 'notion of real object' and to that of symbol 'ex_r' as the 'notion of real existence'. We regard the proposed terminology as natural because it seems to correspond with certain intuitions of those familiar with philosophical language. We have been trying to show how that language should be constructed in order that the terms it contains might embody these intuitions.

By defining: '*a* has real existence' means: 'the sentence '*a* exists' is a sentence which fulfils empirical criteria', one presupposes that in the construction of one's language the metalinguistic term 'asserted empirical statement' precedes the object-language expression 'exists in reality'. It is, therefore, a language in which thing-terms occur later than metalinguistic terms and are reducible to the latter. In such a language all object-language sentences (i.e. sentences referring to the world), are reducible to metalinguistic ones which state of those object-language sentences that they fulfil the empirical criteria. In a language of this sort object-language sentences (i.e. sentences referring to the world) would be accepted or rejected depending on what the criteria dictate. This is, it seems, how idealists construct their language. For them the object-language sentence asserting, for example, that bodies exist means only that this sentence fulfils the empirical criteria. Consequently every object-language sentence about the world, if its meaning is specified in accordance with the definition which obtains in a language so constructed, appears to be an expression referring to cognitive criteria or stating the conformity of that same sentence with the criteria. Idealists have this characteristic feature of their language in mind when they assert their fundamental thesis: the world is only a correlate of cognitive criteria and empirical reality differs from fiction only in so far as reality is asserted in sentences conforming with the criteria while fictions are asserted in sentences which violate these criteria.

It is evident that were we to accept the definition according to which 'a exists really' means 'the sentence 'a exists' fulfils the empirical criteria', we would thereby accept idealism (in particular, the so-called objective or logical idealism). This idealist doctrine is just as unacceptable to us as such a definition. We should like to stress this emphatically at this point of our analysis.

The reader might well ask the author what his own definition of a real object is. Before answering this question it will be advisable to ascend to a language of higher level in order to comment on the language of the rest of our inquiry. Now the author has written this article which contains expressions referring to men, houses, trees, mountains, etc. and these material expressions are not reduced to metalinguistic expressions by means of definitions. In uttering his object-language statements the author observes, among other things, empirical rules; he is prepared, for example, to assert the sentence 'this table is round' on the basis of what he perceives right now. He also accepts the basic postulates of ontology and consequently from the above sentence he is prepared to deduce the sentence 'tables exist'. The author accepts Leśniewski's definition 'a exists means the same as: for some x, x is a'. He also accepts Leśniewski's definition of an object, namely the definition 'a is an object means the same as for some x, a is x'. In view of the fact that in asserting sentences the author observes empirical criteria and does not obey the criteria preculiar to languages in which one speaks of intentional objects, we shall identify the notion of an object as used by the author with the notion of a real object. In the material part of the author's language the term 'real object' does not occur at all, but the author could introduce this term as a synonym for the expression 'object'. We repeat once again that the author himself does not use the expression 'object' so as to be able to distinguish 'real objects' and 'intentional objects'. He uses, however, the term 'the notion of an object' in a manner which enables him to distinguish 'the notion of a real object' from 'the notion of an intentional object'.

After this digression whose aim was to avoid misunderstandings, let us return to the main course of our inquiry. In particular, let us clarify the nature of rules peculiar to the language in which the notion of an intentional object of Homer's epics occurs. It seems that a person speaking this language asserts the sentence 'Zeus is an Olympian' if he had previously ascertained that Homer's epics contain the sentence 'Zeus is an Olympian'. He states the presence of this sentence in Homer's texts by means of the criterion of experience just as experience allows him to state the presence of other persons in the room he is himself in. It seems, therefore, that whoever uses a language in which the notion of an intentional object of Homer's epics occurs must also make use of an empirical language. The rules he follows in asserting sentences of the intentional language are, for example, such as: in the intentional language J_h one is allowed to assert the object-language sentence '$a \epsilon b$' if the metalinguistic sentence 'a certain sentence contained in Homer's text has the form '$a \epsilon b$'' is asserted in the empirical language J_r. This rule leads from the assertion of certain metalinguistic sentences in the empirical language to the assertion of certain object-language sentences in the intentional language. No rule which would lead in the opposite direction, from material sentences in the intentional language to metalinguistic sentences in the empirical language, need obtain. For the intentional language has its own immanent logic, i.e. a logic leading from certain sentences in the intentional language to other sentences of that same language. As a result in the intentional language certain sentences may be asserted as inferential consequences of other sentences of that language without any corresponding metalinguistic sentences in the empirical language being asserted. For example, the sentences 'Zeus is an Olympian', 'every Olympian is immortal' may be asserted in the intentional language because these sentences occur in Homer's texts, and from these sentences one may derive and assert in the intentional language the consequence 'Zeus is immortal' even though this latter sentence may not occur in Homer's text.

As already mentioned, whoever speaks the intentional language must also use the empirical language, namely, he must at least use the metalinguistic part of the empirical language as otherwise he will not get to the basic sentences of his own intentional language. In this connection one of two things may happen: the speaker of the intentional language may treat both the empirical and the intentional languages as one language, which means that he will regard as meaningful expressions composed of elements one of which belongs to the empirical language, and the other to the intentional language, e.g. he will treat as meaningful conjunctions, conditional sentences, disjunctions consisting of two sentences, one of which belongs to the empirical, the other to the intentional language. On the other hand, the user of the intentional language may regard it as not forming one language together with the empirical language, just as, for instance, Polish and English do not form one language.

Let us assume that the user of the intentional language regards it as a part of the language whose other part is the empirical language. In other words, let us assume that he is able to make meaningful sentences composed of the elements of the intentional and the empirical languages. It may, of course, happen that using the empirical language he will assert the following: 'the sentence "Zeus is an Olympian" is contained in Homer's works but Zeus is not an Olympian'. In conformity with a rule governing the intentional language he will assert in that language the sentence 'Zeus is an Olympian'. The resulting contradiction will be an apparent one since — as was said before — the word 'is' has different meanings in the empirical and in the intentional language. By marking this ambiguity with the aid of appropriate subscripts we shall be able to write down in the following way this seemingly contradictory statement: $\sim$(Zeus ϵ_r Olympian) and (Zeus ϵ_h Olympian). It is also possible that our intentionalist will assert in the empirical language: 'Zeus does not exist', and in the intentional language: 'Zeus exists'. This, however, will be an apparent inconsistency as the word 'exists' has in each of these languages a different meaning. In view of the fact that the empirical as well as the intentional language are extensions of ontology, whoever speaks a language comprising both these languages will assert that every real object exists in reality and also that every intentional object of Homer exists intentionally in Homer's works. In spite of this, since he will assert in the empirical language that Zeus does not exist in reality ($\sim ex_r$ Zeus), and in the intentional language that Zeus is an intentional object (ob_h Zeus) he will be able to draw the conclusion that some intentional objects do not exist in reality, more precisely : $(\exists x)(ob_h \, x \sim ex_r x)$.[3]

Our analysis up till now was to prepare the ground for answering the question how the language must be constructed in which the idealist asserts his fundamental thesis formulated in the material and not only in the formal mode. His thesis may be formulated as follows: 'objects of experience do not exist really but only intentionally'.

Idealism appears in one of two versions: the subjective or psychological and the objective. They differ from one another in that they relativize intentional existence of the objects of experience to different correlates. Subjective idealism, namely, claims that the objects of experience exist only intentionally with respect to, or for a certain mind; according to objective idealism, on the other hand, the objects of experience are intentional correlates of certain criteria for asserting sentences which determine the correctness of thinking.

The thesis of subjective idealism consists of two parts: objects of experience do not have real existence, they exist only intentionally. The first part of this thesis is expressed in the empirical language, the second in the intentional language.

The subjective idealist who wants to formulate the intentional part of his thesis in the object-language and not only in the meta-language will refuse to identify the statement that objects of experience exist intentionally for perceiving minds, with the meta-linguistic statement that someone believes the statement claiming the existence of the objects of experience. However, he will feel entitled to claim that an object exists intentionally with respect to someone if he has ascertained that someone believes in the existence of that object. In other words, when uttering the sentence that objects of experience exist intentionally with respect to someone he speaks a language with the rule which permits the assertion in that language of sentences, so to say, with a flat ($\flat$) of intentionalism, on the basis of asserting, without that flat, a metalinguistic statement that the sentence has been asserted by someone. The language which the subjective idealist speaks has therefore a similar structure to the intentional language of Homer's epics. In the latter language one is allowed to assert a sentence with a flat of intentionalism if one has asserted in the metalanguage, without this flat, the occurrence of that sentence in Homer's text. In the intentional part of the subjective idealist's language one may assert a sentence with the intentionalist rider if one has asserted in the metalanguage, without that rider, that someone accepts that sentence.

The same applies to the thesis of the objective idealist. It consists of a part expressed in the empirical language which claims that the objects of experience do not exist in reality; and of a part expressed in the intentional language which claims that the objects of experience exist intentionally with respect to criteria. The objective idealist will assert the second part of his thesis claiming the existence of the objects of experience, with the intentionalist qualification, if he asserts without that qualification that the sentence 'objects of experience exist' fulfils the criteria. Generally speaking, the following rule seems to govern the intentional part of the language of the objective idealist: one is allowed to assert a sentence with the intentionalist qualification, e.g. the sentence 'this table is brown', if without the qualification one has ascertained in the metalanguage that the sentence in question fulfils the criteria. This rule is also analogous to the rule of the intentional language of Homer's epics.

In his basic thesis the idealist claims that all things which we encounter in nature, for example trees, do not exist in reality but exist only intentionally. This thesis consists of two parts, one of which belongs to the empirical language and the other to the intentional language. With the help of our two symbols the thesis may be formulated as follows: $\sim ex_r$ trees but ex_i trees.

We are not in a position to reflect upon the truth of this thesis as we ourselves do not speak a language into which the language used by the idealist could be translated. However, knowing the structure of that language we may consider whether a man who thinks consistently and who speaks the language in which the idealist formulates his thesis would be able to assert it. We shall limit ourselves to analyzing the theses of the objective idealist.

The objective idealist, in order to assert the intentional part of his thesis, for example, the sentence 'ex_i trees', will have first to assert in the metalanguage without the intentional qualification that the sentence 'ex_r trees' fulfils the criteria. In this connection two possibilities may occur: the metalinguistic statement that the sentence 'ex_r trees' fulfils the criteria may be true or it may be false.

If this sentence is false, the second part of the idealist's thesis, 'ex_i trees', has been inferred from a false premise and is, therefore, without any foundation.

On the other hand, if the sentence is true, i.e. if the sentence 'ex_r trees' actually fulfils the criteria, then in denying that sentence in the first part of his thesis, namely, in denying the fact that trees exist in reality, he rejects a sentence whose assertion is required by the criteria.

What exactly are those criteria? I am unable to interpret this notion in any other way but by identifying those criteria with what in another place I have called rules of language or rules of meaning. These are, in short, rules prohibiting the rejection of certain sentences on pain of violating the meaning attached to them in the given language. For example, such a rule is the norm proclaiming that should someone reject the sentence 'every rectangle has four sides', he could do so only if he associated with this sentence a meaning different from the one it has in English; or, the norm proclaiming that if someone experienced what is usually felt when the nerve of a tooth is being irritated and, at the same time, sincerely (i.e. without committing a lie) replied 'No' to the question 'does it hurt?', he would thereby prove that he does not associate with the sentence 'it hurts' the meaning which it has in English.

Let us agree to such an interpretation of the term 'criteria' and let us see what consequences should then be drawn for the thesis of the idealist.

We have considered the case when the metalinguistic sentence 'the sentence 'ex_r trees' fulfils the criteria', is true i.e. in fact the rules of language require the assertion of the sentence 'ex_r trees'. Having asserted the metalinguistic sentence the idealist will be quite correct in inferring from it the intentional part of his thesis, viz. 'ex_i trees'. But may he then deny in the first part of his thesis the sentence 'ex_r trees' (trees exist in reality)? If the sentence fulfils the criteria, i.e. if its assertion is required by the criteria, then whoever rejects the sentence will at the same time violate its meaning. In other words, by denying the sentence one would not be denying that trees exist in reality since the rejection of the sentence would change the meanings of the words involved.

Let us recapitulate once more the course of our argument. There are two alternatives: the metalinguistic statement that the sentence 'trees exist' fulfils the criteria is either true or false. If it is false, the idealist asserts without any foundation the second, intentional part of his thesis according to which trees exist in the intentional meaning of 'exist'. If, on the other hand, that metalinguistic statement is true, the idealist cannot assert the first part of his thesis in the language he speaks, i.e. when speaking English he cannot deny that trees exist.

Thus, while expressing no opinion as to the truth of the objective idealist's thesis, which we are unable to translate into our own language, we have concluded that the idealist either asserts his thesis without justification or else cannot assert it at all without violating the language in which he wants to assert it.

NOTES

[1] Stanisław Leśniewski, *Über die Grundlagen der Ontologie, Comtes rendus des séances de la Soc. Sci. Lett. Varsovie*, Classe III, **23**, 111–132.

[2] Tadeusz Kotarbiński, *Elementy teorii poznania, logiki formalnej i metodologii nauk* (Elements of Epistemology, Formal Logic and Methodology of the Sciences), Lwów 1929.

[3] In order to be able to assert this he will have to construct his language so that the term 'Zeus' will have the same meaning in the empirical and in the intentional language. This involves some difficulties. We have said that since different rules govern the assertion of sentences of the form '$a \, \epsilon \, b$' in the empirical and in the intentional language, a sentence of this form has a different meaning in each of these languages. In order to ensure the synonymity of the names occurring as the subject and predicate in these sentences it would be necessary to reduce the entire ambiguity of the sentence '$a \, \epsilon \, b$' to the ambiguity of the term 'ϵ'.

14. CONDITIONAL STATEMENT AND
MATERIAL IMPLICATION*

(1956)

1. From a general lecture course on formal logic students expect to be familiarized with the inferential schemata which underlie arguments in everyday life and in science. They expect that the inference forms presented in the lectures on logic will be applicable to their own thinking. Classical logic did not disappoint such expectations. Categorical syllogisms and so-called hypothetical syllogisms of classical logic were formulated in terms taken from ordinary language without altering the usual meaning of those terms; hence its inferential schemas were indeed 'forms' of actual inferences found in actual thinking. Contemporary mathematical logic seems not to live up to these expectations. The terms which occur in its theorems and inference schemas (so-called logical constants) seem to have meaning which none of the terms of ordinary language have, hence the theorems and inference schemas of contemporary logic appear to be useless for actual thinking in everyday life and in science. This applies above all to the symbol of material implication. It seems that there is no term in ordinary language which would have a meaning identical with that of material implication. The conditional connective 'if ..., then, ...' used in ordinary language has only a similar but not identical meaning with that assigned by contemporary logic to the sign of material implication. This is why, though some theorems and inference schemas of mathematical logic formulated with the help of the sign of implication remain valid when that sign is replaced by the conditional connective 'if ..., then ...' taken in its usual sense (*e.g. modus ponens, modus tollens*, the law of transposition, etc.), others seem to become invalid when the implication sign is replaced in them by the conditional connective 'if ..., then ...'. This applies to those theorems which depend on the fact that implication (i.e. $p \rightarrow q$') is true whenever its antecedent is false or its consequent is true.

A teacher of logic may be faced with this claim of the inapplicability of formal logic to actual thinking unless he has taken the trouble of convincing his students through an analysis of the meaning of the conditional

* Translated by Jerzy Giedymin. First published in *Studia Logica* IV (1956), 117–34. Translation based on *Język i Poznanie*, II, 248–65. Reprinted here by kind permission of PWN.

'if ..., then ...' that their doubts are unfounded since the difference between the meaning of that connective and of the implication sign is not so great as to make some theorems involving material implication invalid for the conditional connective. To achieve this aim it is sufficient to convince students that whenever an implication '$p \to q$' is true so is the conditional 'if p, then q' in its ordinary sense. The truth conditions for implication are given in logic by the matrix:

p	q	$p \to q$
truth	truth	truth
truth	falsity	falsity
falsity	truth	truth
falsity	falsity	truth

according to which material implication is false only if its antecedent is true while its consequent is false, otherwise it is always true. In order to refute the claim of the inapplicability of the laws of formal logic to actual thinking in everyday life and in science, it is necessary to convince students that the truth-table for implication holds also for the conditional in its everyday sense. The same has to be done with respect to the symbol of the logical sum and the connective 'or' as well as to other logical constants of the propositional calculus. For it will then be possible to use the truth-table method of testing the formulae of the logistic calculus in the testing of the formulae of the propositional calculus with suitable constants from ordinary language.

In the present article I will show how in my university lectures I try to convince my audience that the truth-table for material implication is applicable to the conditional understood in its everyday sense and that the truth-table for logical sum is applicable to ordinary sentences with the connective 'or'. It seems to me that what I am going to say here has some merits not only as a didactic method but will also shed some light on the analysis of the meaning of the conditional in its ordinary sense as well as on the analysis of the meaning of expressions in general.

2. The claim that the truth-table for implication holds for the conditional in its ordinary sense is clearly rejected by those who are used only to employing the latter. They reject the contention that the conditional is true whenever either its consequent is true or its antecedent is false. On the other hand, no such objection is usually made against the claim that the truth-table for logical sum is applicable to disjunctive sentences in their usual sense. It is

easy to reach consensus that the sentence 'p or q' is true whenever at least one of its disjuncts is true and that it is false if and only if both disjuncts are false. I take advantage of this consensus in order to convince my audience that the truth-table for material implication holds for the conditional. Having done so I then point out the consequences, e.g. that every conditional statement with a false antecedent and every conditional statement with a true consequence would, therefore, have to be accepted as true. These consequences, especially when illustrated with examples, seem evidently false to my audience. In this way I achieve a paradoxical effect: starting from premisses to which there are no objections and using methods of inference which seem altogether convincing, I derive a conclusion that appears evidently false. Having presented the paradox, I turn to its solution by reconsidering critically the material and formal correctness of the argument on which the paradox rests. In this context I offer an analysis of the meaning of disjunctive sentences and of conditionals in their ordinary sense which yields a solution of the paradox. The solution consists neither in the rejection of the premisses nor in the proof of the invalidity of the argument but in the revision of the objection to the consequences of the paradox. For it turns out that when we object to those consequences we do so not because we think that they are false; we protest against their acceptance for other reasons. The course of my argument which I have just outlined will now be presented in detail.

3. Having reached with my audience consensus on the fact that a disjunctive sentence 'p or q' is true whenever at least one of the disjuncts is true and false whenever both disjuncts are false, i.e. that the truth-table for logical sum is applicable to disjunctive sentences 'p or q' in the ordinary sense, I consider the sentence:

(1)   'not-p or q'

and the sentence:

(2)   'if p, then q.'

By appealing to their ordinary sense I show that

(I)   whenever sentence (1) is true, sentence (2) is also true, and
(II)   whenever sentence (1) is false, sentence (2) is likewise false.

To establish (I), I argue as follows: Whenever sentence (1) is true, i.e. the disjunction 'not-p or q', the sentence 'if not-not-p, then q' is also true, thus also the sentence 'if p, then q' (since double negation is cancelled).

As a rule my audience find this argument convincing and they are persuaded thereby to accept relationship I.

To establish II, the following argument is used: Whenever sentence (1) is false, i.e. the disjunction 'not-p or q' is false, neither of two alternatives mentioned in it occurs, hence their negations 'p' and 'not-q' hold. Then, however, sentence (2) cannot possibly be true, since its truth would exclude p and not-q to be the case.

From the previously accepted premiss that the truth-table for logical sum is applicable to disjunctive sentences in the ordinary sense, these two relationships make it possible to deduce easily the conclusion that the truth-table for implication is applicable to the conditional in its ordinary sense. For since one has agreed that a disjunctive sentence is true when at least one of the disjuncts is true and false when both are false, the sentence

(1)   'not-p or q'

will be regarded as true in the following cases:

> p-true, q-true
> p-false, q-true
> p-false, q-false

and false in one case:

> p-true, q-false.

Since we have shown that sentences (1) and (2) are both simultaneously true or both simultaneously false, we can conclude that sentence (2) i.e. the conditional 'if p, then q' is true in the following cases:

> p-true, q-true
> p-false, q-true
> p-false, q-false,

and false in one case only:

> p-true, q-false,

In other words, the truth-table for implication is applicable to the conditional in its ordinary sense.

Having persuaded my audience to accept that claim I then draw their attention to the fact that it commits them to regard as true every conditional with a false antecedent or with a true consequent, i.e. that it commits them to the acceptance of, for example, the following sentences: 'If the moon is made of cheese, then I shall die on a day with an even number', 'If I die on a day (dated) with an even number, then the moon is a satellite of the earth'. These consequences seem evidently false to my audience. We are thus faced with a paradox and so motivated to subject to critical scrutiny the material and formal correctness of the presented argument.

4. Our scrutiny begins with the starting point of our argument. This was the claim that a disjunctive sentence '*p* or *q*' is true whenever at least one of its disjuncts is true and false only if both disjuncts are false. Let us consider, therefore, whether we were right to accept this claim and let us do it by considering an example. I take two pieces of chalk into my hand and then palm them in such a way that my audience do not see whether I hold both pieces in my right hand or both in my left hand or one of them in my right and the other in my left hand; they see, however, that I·did not let either of the pieces out of my hands. Having done so I ask: "Do I have the chalk either in my right or left hand?". The unanimous answer is 'Yes'. I point out to my audience that there are three possibilities (the chalk is only in my left, only in my right hand or in both) and ask them again whether they accept the disjunctive sentence 'the chalk is in the right or left hand' irrespective of which of them is the case and whether they would regard the sentence as false only if I did not have the chalk in either of my hands; again I receive an affirmative answer. Thus on the basis of a specific example again consensus is reached that a disjunctive sentence in its ordinary sense is true whenever at least one of its disjuncts is true and that it is false only if neither of the disjuncts is true, i.e. there is acceptance of the first premiss of the paradoxical argument. In the specific example used, my audience knew that at least one of the disjuncts was true though they did not know which. At this point of my experiment I open my palms and show my audience that I hold both pieces of chalk, say, in my left hand. I ask them again: "Do I have the chalk either in my right or left hand?". My audience are now far from unanimous in answering this question; they are divided in their views but the majority are of the opinion that under these circumstances when one knows that the chalk is in my left and not in my right hand the answer to my question cannot be in the affirmative. Some will suggest that under these circumstances one cannot say either 'Yes' or 'No' in reply to my question. This semantical experiment shows that we are prepared to accept a disjunctive sentence as long as we know that at least one of its disjuncts is true but we do not know which; as soon as we discover which of the disjuncts is true, we no longer accept the sentence.

Why is this so? Why do we withdraw the acceptance of a disjunctive sentence as soon as we learn which of its disjuncts is true? Is it perhaps because this new information has turned the disjunctive sentence from being true to being false? In order to answer this question let us consider what a disjunctive sentence is concerned with. What is referred to, e.g. by the sentence 'I have chalk either in my right or left hand'? What this sentence concerns is the location of the chalk, i.e. an objective state of affairs, not our knowledge of it. That objective state of affairs has not been affected at all by the change in our knowledge. Since the state of things, referred to in a sentence, has not been changed, the sentence describing it cannot possibly change its truth-value from truth to falsity. Hence, if the disjunctive sentence had been true before we discovered which of its disjuncts is true, it has not ceased to be true afterwards.

Perhaps it will be claimed that a disjunctive sentence, e.g. 'the chalk is in the right or left hand', concerns not only an objective state of affairs (in our example the location of the chalk) but also our knowledge of it, though there is no explicit reference to the latter. The complete content of a disjunctive sentence 'p or q' ought to be stated in the sentence: 'At least one of two alternatives p or q is the case, though I do not know which'. In order to see that this is not so, let us consider the sentence 'For every natural number $x : x$ is even or x is not even'. There is no doubt that this sentence is true. Would it, however, be true were we to regard the disjunctive sentence 'x is even or x is not even' (which follows the quantifier) as synonymous with the sentence that one of the mentioned alternatives is the case though I do not know which? The sentence under discussion would then be: 'For every natural number $x : x$ is even or x is not even, but I do not know which is the case'. As a generalization it will certainly be false if the propositional function under the quantifier turns into a false sentence at least for one of its values. For example, by substituting the value '4' for 'x' in this function we get the sentence '4 is an even number or 4 is not an even number but I do not know which is the case'. This sentence is certainly false, since I do know very well that 4 is an even number, i.e. I do know which of the disjuncts is true. If, therefore, as has been suggested, disjunctive sentences were to concern not only an objective state of affairs but also the subjective state of our knowledge, we would have to regard as false the universal sentence 'For every natural number $x : x$ is even or x is not even'. But this sentence is undoubtedly true. One cannot, therefore, claim that when asserting a disjunctive sentence we make an assertion not only about an objective state of affairs but also about our knowledge of the latter. Hence we were right in claiming that whether or not we know which of the disjuncts is true is irrelevant to its truth or falsity. Therefore, since in the case of a particular disjunctive sentence we have agreed (without knowing the truth-value of its disjuncts) to regard it as true if only the first of the disjuncts or only the second is true, or if both of them are true, and to regard it as false only if neither of the disjuncts is true, we shall not change our position in this respect being now aware of the fact that our knowledge as to which of the disjuncts is true is irrelevant to the truth-value of the disjunctive sentence. Consequently in each particular case we shall consent to the assignment of the truth-value of the disjunctive sentence to the truth-values of its disjuncts in accordance with the truth-table for logical sum irrespective of the fact whether or not we know the truth-values of the disjuncts. Hence the fact that having discovered which of the disjuncts is true we withdraw our acceptance of the disjunctive sentence (i.e. as expressing our belief) does not affect our position with regard to the applicability of the truth-table (for logical sum) to disjunctive sentences in their ordinary sense. We do not withdraw our consensus concerning this applicability.

5. The last sentences of the previous paragraph point out a peculiar fact: there are sentences which — though we regard them as true — we are not prepared to accept, i.e. use to express our beliefs. Quine who also emphasized the same fact sees its explanation in a linguistic habit to the effect that one does not use longer and less informative sentences if one is able to convey more precise information in a more concise way. Why chould we say (so Quine argues) "France is in Europe or the seawater is sweet" if we can be more precise and economical by saying simply "France is in Europe". More examples may be quoted to illustrate this linguistic habit to which Quine draws our attention. One of them is the fact that if we know that every S is P (in the strong sense) then we see some impropriety in asserting that at least some S's are P's, though nobody will deny that since the former is true so is the latter. Similarly improper will appear the statement that in leap-years iron expands when heated, since we know iron to possess this property at all times. Nevertheless it is difficult to agree without qualifications with Quine's claim that one does not use a less informative sentence if one can use a more concise and more informative one, until we clarify what is meant by saying that one sentence is more informative than another. In quoted examples the more informative of the two non-equivalent sentences was always one from which the other was deducible, the other being, of course, less informative. If this were generalized to the effect that of two non-equivalent sentences one of which is deducible from the other, the former is less and the latter more informative, then the linguistic habit mentioned by Quine would amount to the abstention from using logical consequences of those sentences which are themselves available. Such a linguistic habit,

however, would ban any deductive inference since the latter consists in asserting a consequence of premises which may and have been asserted.

Therefore, it will be safer, perhaps, not to employ far-reaching generalizations and restrict oneself to the simple claim that in the case of disjunctive sentences there is a linguistic habit which prohibits one from accepting it if we know which of its disjuncts is true. In view of this habit from the acceptance by a person of a disjunctive sentence one may gather that that person does not know which of the disjuncts is true. In other words, the acceptance by a person of a disjunctive sentence is to anyone familiar with the linguistic habit a sign of the fact that the person in question does not know which of the disjuncts is true; or, to put it still differently, the acceptance by a person of a disjunctive sentence expresses in virtue of the linguistic habit that person's ignorance as to which of the disjuncts is true. For to say that a statement S made by a person P expresses in virtue of a linguistic habit P's state S amounts to saying that the statement S made by P is to anyone familiar with the linguistic habit a sign of P's state S, i.e. the statement S made by P enables anyone familiar with the linguistic habit to gather that P is in state S.

It is useful to distinguish what a sentence *asserts* from what it (indirectly) *expresses*. The sentence 'Paris is in Europe' that has just been uttered by a person P asserts an objective state of affairs, viz. the geographical location of Paris; on the other hand, it expresses P's belief that the state of affairs asserted in that sentence is the case, i.e. the belief that things actually are as claimed in the sentence. In order to acquire information about a state of things asserted in a sentence used by someone it is necessary to accept the sentence as true; on the other hand, to acquire information about the subjective state of the person who uttered the sentence, it is not necessary to believe the sentence, it is enough to hear it, understand and know that it has been used seriously and in accordance with linguistic habits.

Linguistic habit (usage) assigns to sentences states of affairs asserted in them. If the state of affairs asserted in the sentence exists, then the sentence is true; if it does not exist, then the sentence is false. Linguistic habit also assigns to sentences the type of subjective states of the speaker expressed by them. If the speaker is in the subjective state of the type expressed by the sentence in conformity with the usage, then we say that the sentence has been used appropriately; if he is not, then we say that the sentence has been misused. A sentence may be used appropriately without being true. On the other hand, it may be true and yet may have been used inappropriately.

6. The distinction just made between what a sentence asserts from what it   .

expresses and the related distinction between the truth of a sentence and its appropriate use, make it possible to account for the peculiar fact that in some circumstances we refuse to accept sentences which we otherwise know to be true. For the refusal to accept a sentence may be motivated not only by our reluctance to accept a falsehood, it may also be motivated by our unwillingness to use it inappropriately. In other words, the refusal to accept a sentence, i.e. to assert it with conviction may result not only from our unwillingness to assert with its help objective states which do not exist; it may also result from our unwillingness to express subjective states in which we do not find ourselves.

Whether the refusal to accept a sentence is motivated by the unwillingness to accept falsity or by the unwillingness to use it inappropriately, may be gathered, among other things, from the fact that in the former case the refusal to accept the sentence is accompanied by readiness to accept its negation whereas in the latter case it is not.

In the case of the disjunctive sentence whose acceptance we withdrew after we had learned which of its disjuncts was true (though we had accepted it before) our refusal was not motivated by our believing henceforth in its falsity. This is indicated by the fact that after we had discovered which of the disjuncts is true we have not been at all prepared to accept the negation of the sentence. Our refusal was motivated by our unwillingness to use the disjunctive sentence inappropriately. For by using the disjunctive sentence we would have expressed − by virtue of the linguistic usage − that we do not know which of the disjuncts is true whereas in fact we do know it.

7. Let us analyze a bit more what is expressed by a disjunctive sentence in everyday language. A disjunctive sentence expresses (1) our belief that one of the disjuncts is true, (2) our ignorance as to which of the disjuncts is true. Hence, when accepting a disjunctive sentence we shall use it appropriately provided we shall know that one of the disjuncts is true without, however, knowing which. Now, our knowing that one of the disjuncts is true may be due either to the fact that we know which of the disjuncts is true or to the fact that from the negation of one of the disjuncts we are able to infer the other, still without knowing of any of them that it is true. Since, however, the appropriate use of a disjunctive sentence precludes our knowing which of the disjuncts is true, our belief that one of them is true must be due to the fact that from the negation of any of the disjuncts we may infer the other.

To conclude, a disjunctive sentence expresses not only (1) our knowledge that at least one of the disjuncts is true, (2) our ignorance as to which of them is true, but also (3) our readiness to infer either of the disjuncts from the negation of the other. Hence when accepting a disjunctive sentence we shall use it appropriately if we know that one of the disjuncts is true without knowing which and if we are ready to infer (any) one of them from the negation of the other.

8. Through the confusion of what a sentence expresses with what it asserts, the claim that a disjunctive sentence expresses our readiness to infer one of its disjuncts from the negation of the other, has been mistakenly transformed into the claim that a disjunctive sentence asserts a relationship between its disjuncts which permits the inference of one of them from the negation of the other. On this latter claim, which is due to confusion, one has based another argument against the applicability of the truth-table of the logical sum to disjunction in the ordinary sense. According to this argument, since a disjunctive sentence asserts such a relationship to hold between its disjuncts, a disjunctive sentence is true only on condition that this relationship does hold between the disjuncts. If, therefore, one could find a disjunctive sentence between whose disjuncts there is no relationship permitting the inference of one of the disjuncts from the negation of the other, then such a sentence would be false even though one of its disjuncts were true. But examples of such sentences do exist. One of them is the sentence "I shall die on a day (whose date is an even number) or $2 \times 2 = 4$". One of its disjuncts is, admittedly, true but there is no relationship between the disjuncts which would permit the inference of one of them from the negation of the other, therefore the sentence is false. Hence, it is not the case that every disjunctive sentence with at least one true disjunct must be true.

What are we to think of this argument? It is as good as the assumption on which it is based. That assumption, however, is burdened with serious obscurity. It claims that a disjunctive sentence is true if and only if between the disjuncts there is a relationship which permits the inference to one of them from the negation of the other. The expression 'a relationship which permits the inference' is far from clear and requires clarification.

One may understand it in a subjective sense so that 'permits the inference' amounts to 'enables one to infer'. Then, however, a relativization would be necessary to indicate the person whom the relationship enables to make the inference.

The assumption under discussion would then read: "A disjunctive sentence is true if and only if between the disjuncts there is a relationship which enables the person accepting the sentence to infer one of the disjuncts from the negation of the other". It is easy to see that one and the same disjunctive sentence could then be both true and false. It would be true if between the disjuncts there were a relationship enabling a bright person x_1 to make a suitable inference but it would also be false if between the disjuncts there were no relationship enabling a dull person x_2 to make such an inference.

Different difficulties arise if the expression 'permits the inference' is taken in an objective sense in which it is synonymous with 'makes the inference valid'. The interpretative difficulties will then be transferred to the term 'validity of inference' which may be understood variously.

By valid inference one may mean, firstly, conclusive inference, i.e. one which from true premisses never leads to a false conclusion. Now, it is certainly the case that for a disjunctive sentence to be true a relationship between the disjuncts must hold which would make the inference to one of the disjuncts from the negation of the other conclusive, i.e. which would exclude an inference from true premisses to a false conclusion. Such a relationship is asserted, in fact, by a disjunctive sentence for it consists in the fact that at least one of the disjuncts is true. But this relationship is asserted not only by a disjunctive sentence in the ordinary sense but also by logical disjunction, i.e. the logical sum of two sentences. If, therefore, by 'valid inference' is understood 'conclusive inference', then the claim that for a disjunctive sentence to be true the relationship between the disjuncts must ensure the validity of the inference to one of them from the negation of the other, is certainly true. But under this interpretation the claim does not undermine the applicability of the truth-table for the logical sum to disjunctive sentences in the ordinary sense, for if that truth-table is applicable to a disjunctive sentence in the ordinary sense, then the truth of a disjunctive sentence does depend on there being a relationship between its disjuncts which makes the inference to one of them from the negation of the other conclusive.

The validity of an inference may, however, be understood in other ways. By a valid inference one may mean (secondly) a formally correct inference, i.e. one which is based on the laws of logic, or – in other words – one whose conclusion *is logically implied by its premisses*.[1]

Now it is easy to show that for a disjunctive sentence (in the ordinary sense) to be true it is not necessary at all that one of the disjuncts should be logically implied by the negation of the other, i.e. that the inference to one of the disjuncts from the negation of the other should be formally correct. For surely it is true that I shall die either on a day whose number is even or on a day whose number is not even. But the inference that since I shall not die on a day whose number is even therefore I shall die on a day whose number is not even is not formally correct. This inference is enthymematic, its tacit premiss being the sentence that I shall die some day. This example shows that if validity is understood in the sense of formal correctness, then for a disjunctive sentence to be true there is no need for a relationship between the disjuncts which would make the inference to one of them from the negation of the other valid.

By valid inference one may understand, thirdly, any inference whose premisses imply enthymematically its conclusion relative to the knowledge of the person making the inference.[2]

The claim under discussion would, on this interpretation, amount to saying that a disjunctive sentence is true if and only if the negation of one of the disjuncts enthymematically implies the other disjunct relative to the knowledge possessed by the person making the inference. It is not difficult to see that so interpreted the claim yields as disastrous consequences as its subjective interpretation. For the same disjunctive sentence will have to be regarded as both true and false if there are two persons accepting the sentence such that relative to the knowledge possessed by one of them one of the disjuncts enthymematically implies the other, whereas relative to the other's knowledge this is not so.

What are the results of our analysis? It has shown the claim that for a disjunctive sentence to be true a relationship between the disjuncts must hold which permits the inference to one disjunct from the negation of the other, to be correct only if by the mentioned relationship is meant one which makes the inference conclusive. The relationship, however, in virtue of which the inference to one disjunct from the negation of the other is conclusive, consists in the fact that at least one of the disjuncts is true. Therefore, the argument based on the claim that, allegedly, not every disjunctive sentence with at least one true disjunct is true since a relationship between the disjuncts is required to sanction the inference, turns out to be incorrect. Between the disjuncts of a disjunctive sentence whose one disjunct at least is true such a relationship sanctioning the inference always holds, hence it is incorrect to mention this relationship as a requirement which may not be satisfied even though at least one of the disjuncts is true.

The view according to which for a disjunctive sentence to be true it is not enough that at least one of the disjuncts should be true as, in addition, another relationship of a 'dynamic' nature is required, (variously described by saying that the negation of one of the disjuncts should 'cause' the other disjunct, or that from that negation the other disjunct should be 'generated' or in still other metaphorical expressions), is due — I believe — to a misunderstanding or, rather, confusion. A disjunctive sentence does *not assert* (in accordance with established usage) any such dynamic relationship. It only *expresses* (in accordance with established usage in everyday language) the readiness to infer one of the disjuncts from the negation of the other. Whoever accepts a disjunctive sentence and employs it in accordance with usage, must be prepared to make a suitable inference. An inference is a mental process which has, in a sense, a dynamic character. In an inference we accept the conclusion on the basis of premisses; the acceptance of premisses is for us a motive which induces us to accept the conclusion. This dynamic character of the mental state expressed in a disjunctive sentence is attributed wrongly to the relationship between the disjuncts asserted by the disjunctive sentence. Hence the erroneous view that for the truth of a disjunctive sentence it is not sufficient that at least one of the disjuncts should be true since in addition another relationship is necessary, viz. that the negation of one of the disjuncts should 'necessitate' the other disjunct.

9. In our critical analysis of the argument (which resulted in the so-called paradox of implication), we have considered two objections made against the view that a disjunctive sentence in the ordinary sense is true whenever at least one of its disjuncts is true. According to the first objection, a disjunctive sentence asserts not only that one of its disjuncts is true but also our ignorance as to which of the disjuncts is true. According to the second objection a disjunctive sentence asserts not only the truth of one of its disjuncts but also a relationship between its disjuncts which permits the inference of one of them from the negation of the other. A closer scrutiny of these objections has shown, however, that they are due to a confusion: what a disjunctive sentence expresses is confused with what it asserts; as a result the conditions for appropriate use of a disjunctive sentence are confused with the conditions of its truth.

Up till now our critical analysis of the argument which yielded the paradox of implication does not justify any change in our position. We do not withdraw our acceptance of the fundamental premiss of that argument.

In our analysis we ought to check once again that step in the argument in which we asserted that whenever and only if the sentence

(1)　　　'not-p or q'

is true, the sentence

(2)　　　'if p, then q'

is also true. However, this part of the argument is not objectionable at all; we continue, therefore, to regard it as correct.

10. However, one may search for the solution of the paradox in another way.

Since no error has been found in the argument which yielded the paradoxical result, perhaps one may find an error in the line of thought which indicated that result as evidently false. Let us try this approach and subject to scrutiny the line of thought which persuaded us to regard as evidently false the claim that the truth-table for implication is applicable to ordinary conditionals.

We shall preface this scrutiny by additional comments concerning the relation which holds between the sentences

(1)   'not-p or q' and (2) 'if p, then q',

understood in the ordinary sense.

We have stated before that these sentences are equivalent, i.e. whenever one of them is true, so is the other. But these sentences are not only equivalent, they are also equi-expressive or equi-appropriate, i.e. one of them expresses whatever is expressed by the other, hence it is appropriate to use one of them if and only if it is appropriate to use the other.

Indeed, the sentence

'not-p or q'

expresses, firstly, our knowledge of the fact that at least one of the disjuncts not-p or q will be the case, i.e. that not-not-p and not-q will not be the case, or in other words, that p and not-q will not both be the case.

The same knowledge is expressed by the conditional

'if p, then q'.

By asserting it we assert that p will not be the case without q, i.e. that the antecedent will not be the case without the consequent being also the case.

The disjunctive sentence 'not-p or q' expresses, secondly, our ignorance as to which of the disjuncts is true; it expresses the fact that we do not know 'not-p' to be true and that we do not know 'q' to be true, thus it expresses the fact that we do not know 'p' to be false and that we do not know 'q' to be true.

Similarly, the conditional

'if p, then q'

in ordinary speech expresses the fact that we do not know its antecedent 'p' to be false and that we do not know its consequent 'q' to be true. Indeed, a person who has missed a train having left for the station a few minutes too late will never say:

"If I have left a few minutes earlier, I have not missed my train"

for they know that the antecedent of the conditional is false.

Under these circumstances it will be inappropriate to use the conditional in the indicative mood

'if p, then q'

though it will be appropriate to use the so-called counterfactual conditional. For the latter

'were p the case, q would be the case'

by contradistinction to the conditional in the indicative mood, expresses the fact that we know the antecedent to be false. Instead, therefore, of saying "If I have left earlier, then I have not missed my train" we shall say "If I had left earlier, I would not have missed my train". For it is characteristic of the conditional in indicative mood that it expresses the fact that the speaker does not know its antecedent to be false. By contradistinction, it is characteristic of a counterfactual conditional that it expresses the speaker's knowledge of the falsity of its antecedent.[3]

The disjunctive sentence

'not-p or q'

expresses, thirdly, our readiness to infer one of its disjuncts from the negation of the other, i.e. it expresses our readiness to infer 'q' from 'not-not-p', hence also to infer 'q' from 'p'. The same is expressed (in ordinary language) by the conditional

'if p, then q'.

This is why we shall normally refrain from accepting a conditional (understood in its ordinary sense) if we are not prepared to make a suitable inference.

Our analysis has thus shown that in ordinary language the conditional 'if p, then q' is not only equivalent to the disjunctive sentence 'not-p or q' (i.e. asserts the same) but is also *equi-expressive* or *equi-appropriate*.

11. We are ready now to explain what motivated previously our refusal to regard the truth-table for implication as applicable to conditionals (in the ordinary sense) and to show that our refusal was not justified. We regarded the truth-table for implication as inapplicable to ordinary conditionals because we believed that the falsity of the antecedent or the truth of the consequent are not sufficient for the truth of the conditional; for, in addition, a relationship must hold between the antecedent and the consequent which would permit the inference of the latter from the former. Conditionals like 'If the moon is made from cheese, then I shall die on a day with an even

number' and 'If I die on a day with an even number, then the moon is a satellite of the earth' seemed false to us just because there is no such relationship between their antecedents and consequents even though the antecedent of the first conditional is false and the consequent of the second true.

We are now in a position to show that we were mistaken in this line of argument and to indicate the source of the mistake. We have shown, namely, that in ordinary language the conditional 'if p, then q', is equivalent to the disjunctive sentence 'not-p or q'. Hence, they both assert the same; if, therefore, the existence of a state of affairs were necessary for the truth of one of them, it would also be necessary for the truth of the other. In particular, should for the truth of 'if p, then q', a relationship be necessary which would sanction the inference of 'q' from 'p', then such a relationship would be likewise necessary for the truth of 'not-p or q' (or a relationship which would sanction the inference of 'q' from 'not-not-p'). We have tried to convince the reader, however, that for the truth of 'not-p or q' no other relationship is necessary except that at least one of the disjuncts should be true. Similarly no other relationship is necessary for the truth of the conditional 'if p, then q'. The latter is true whenever either 'not-p' or 'q' is true, in other words, whenever either 'p' is false or 'q' is true. To show this we could repeat, *mutatis mutandis*, the same argument which we used in Section 8 with regard to the disjunctive sentence.

The source of the mistaken belief that the conditional asserts a 'dynamic' relationship to hold between its antecedent and consequent and that such a 'dynamic' relationship between its antecedent and consequent is necessary for the truth of the conditional, is to be sought in the confusion of what the conditional asserts and what it expresses. In ordinary language the conditional expresses our readiness to infer its consequent from its antecedent. This is why in ordinary language we are not prepared to accept a conditional if we are not prepared to make a suitable inference. To accept a conditional without having this disposition would constitute an inappropriate use of the conditional, which we shun. Now, our reluctance to accept a conditional from whose antecedent we are not prepared to infer its consequent, due to our reluctance to use sentences inappropriately (i.e. due to our reluctance to express thereby subjective states we are not in), is mistaken for the disposition to deny the conditional, i.e. to regard it as false. This is the psychological explanation of the mistake.

It seems that in this way we have found a solution of the paradox of implication. We have found it not in the discovery of an error in the argument which yields the (allegedly) paradoxical result but in the demonstration that the result is not false at all, though it appeared so at first sight.

12. Our analysis makes it possible now to clarify the relation between the ordinary conditional and so-called material implication. Both assert the same, viz. that things are not such that the antecedent is the case while the consequent is not. No other relationship is asserted by either sentence. There is, therefore, no difference between the ordinary conditional and implication with respect to what they assert, i.e. with respect to truth conditions. On the other hand, they differ with respect to what they express. The conditional (in indicative mood) expresses, among other things, firstly, that the person accepting it does not know its antecedent to be false or its consequent to be true; secondly, that the person accepting it is prepared to infer its consequent from its antecedent. Nothing of the sort is expressed by material implication. This is why speakers may be reluctant to accept conditionals when they would not be reluctant to accept material implication. The reluctance is motivated by the unwillingness to use the conditional inappropriately, i.e. to express with its help the occurrence of subjective states which in fact do not occur and whose presence one might expect in accordance with established usage. Through confusion the reluctance to accept a conditional in such circumstances is mistaken for its rejection.

NOTES

[1] A sentence b is logically implied by a sentence a if the conditional whose antecedent is a and whose consequent is b is a substitution instance of a logical tautology.
[2] A sentence a enthymematically implies another b relative to sentence c if the conjunction of a and c logically implies b but a alone does not logically imply b.
[3] [A footnote on the distinction between *modus realis i irrealis* and *modus potentialis* has been omitted in translation — Translator.]

15. THE PROBLEM OF THE RATIONALITY
OF NON-DEDUCTIVE TYPES OF INFERENCE*

(1958)

1. This article treats a subject which belongs neither to formal logic nor metascience, but to the methodology of science. Since we shall deal with inferences, convictions, and degrees of certainty, the article will be full of psychological concepts. We shall also deal with people who think and act; the whole cognitive process will be considered in connection with the practical life of man and not as an idealized abstraction. The problem raised here is as follows: whether and when we can say that a man acts rationally, if he believes conclusions drawn from true premises in a fallible way, i.e. on the basis of an inference which from true premises may lead to false conclusions. So-called enumerative induction is one such fallible type of inference. Logicians and methodologists have devoted considerable attention to the question known as the problem of justification of induction. However, the nature of this problem i.e. what should be done in order to justify induction has not been clarified. The aim of the present article is to give a clearer sense to the problem of the justification of induction and, at the same time, to make an attempt – unfortunately one without a practical value – at solving this problem.

However, before discussing the problem itself, the terminology must be established and several auxiliary concepts introduced in order to avoid misunderstandings.

2. I shall start by explicating the term 'inference'. By 'inference' we mean a mental process in which on the basis of the acceptance with some degree of certainty of sentences called premises, the acceptance of another sentence, called a conclusion, is reached with some degree of certainty greater than hitherto.

The degree of certainty that accompanies the acceptance of a sentence is a feature of the subjective state of accepting it, i.e. of the belief in what the sentence states. However, subjective degree of certainty may be measured objectively. Reasoning which leads to the establishment of this measure may

* Revised translation by David Pearce. First published in *Studia Filozoficzna* (1958), No. 4 14–29. *Jezyk i poznanie*, II, 282–295. Reprinted here by kind permission of PWN.

be illustrated in the following way: let us suppose that we are confronted with the practical problem of whether or not to start drilling an oil-well in an area. Drilling will give in effect a profit Z, if it is true that there is crude oil in this area, and a loss S, if this is not the case. The ratio of this loss and profit S/Z is the risk we undertake if we start drilling although we do not know whether there is crude oil or not in the area. Now, the greater this risk, the greater our conviction will have to be that the state of affairs is such as will bring profit, if we are to undertake the activity with which this risk is connected. When the risk is small we need only a small degree of certainty that the state of affairs is to our advantage; when the risk is great we shall undertake the activity only if the degree of certainty is high. These and similar considerations should lead us to adopt as measure of the degree of certainty with which we accept sentence A the greatest risk S/Z, which we are willing to take by carrying out the activity. This will bring a profit Z when A is true, and loss S when A is false.

Suppose we are ready to bet that the weather will be good tomorrow and the terms of the bet are that, if the weather is good tomorrow, we receive $2p$ from our betting partner and, if the weather is bad, we pay him $1p$; we refuse to bet under worse terms. The risk of this bet is $1/2$. Adopting the measure of degree of certainty established above, we conclude in this case that the degree of our certainty that the weather will be good tomorrow is $1/2$.

By choosing the level of risk, i.e. the ratio of profit to loss, as a measure of the degree of certainty, we obtain a scale oscillating between zero and infinity. Readiness to act without any risk, i.e. readiness to start activity that will, if a sentence A is true, bring profit other than zero and, if A is false, loss equal to zero, corresponds to zero certainty about A. Infinite certainty about A corresponds to activity connected with an infinitely great risk, i.e. to activity which, if A is true, does not bring any profit at all and, if it is false, entails some loss.

For certain reasons, however, which will become clear later, we prefer to assign numerical values to the degrees of certainty in such a way that this scale does not move from zero to infinity, but from zero to one. We can obtain this by adopting as measure of the degree of certainty the ratio of loss to the sum of profit and loss instead of the ratio of loss to profit.

Now,

if

$$\frac{S_1}{Z_1} > \frac{S_2}{Z_2}$$

then

$$\frac{S_1}{Z_1 + S_1} > \frac{S_2}{Z_2 + S_2} \quad \text{and conversely,}$$

whichever degree of certainty is the greater under one measurement convention, the corresponding degree of certainty will be the greater under the other convention; under either method of measuring, the order of degrees of certainty remains the same.

Thus, we adopt the following definition of the measure of the degree of certainty with which a person X accepts a sentence A:

If a person X is ready to undertake some activity D if and only if this activity brings him at least a profit Z in the case of a sentence A being true, and at most a loss S when A is false, then we assign the measure

$$P_x(A) = \frac{S}{Z + S}$$

to the degree of certainty with which this person accepts the sentence A.

According to the above definition, the degree of certainty for which we are willing to undertake only activities not connected with any risk, i.e. those where the expected profit $Z > 0$, and the expected loss $S = 0$, will be

$$\frac{0}{Z + 0} = 0$$

Conversely the degree of certainty for which we are willing to undertake activities connected with an infinitely high risk, i.e. those where the expected profit $Z = 0$ and the expected loss $S > 0$, will be

$$\frac{S}{0 + S} = 1$$

Suppose that if a sentence A is true, an activity D gives rise to a profit Z, and if A is false, a loss S. Clearly if the sentence not-A is true, D will cause the same effect as if A were false: namely a loss S. Now since every loss can be treated as a negative profit and every profit as a negative loss, we may also say that, if D brings, in the case of a sentence A being true, a profit Z, and, when A is false a loss S, then the same activity will bring a profit $(-S)$ when not-A is true and loss $(-Z)$ when false.

Let us assume that

$$P_x(A) = \frac{S}{S + Z}$$

This means that the person X is ready to undertake an activity which, if a sentence A is true, brings him at least a profit Z, and, if it is false, at most a loss S. Or, in other words, X is ready to undertake an activity which, if the sentence not-A is true, brings at least a profit $(-S)$, and, if it is false, at most a loss $(-Z)$. This means, however, that the degree of certainty with which X accepts the sentence not-A is given by

$$P_x(\text{not-}A) = \frac{-Z}{-S-Z} = \frac{Z}{S+Z}$$

And we have shown that, if

$$P_x(A) = \frac{S}{Z+S}$$

then

$$P_x(\text{not-}A) = \frac{Z}{S+Z} = 1 - \frac{S}{S+Z} = 1 - P_x(A)$$

Let us now assume that the person X is completely undecided as to whether A or not-A is true and in fact, that he believes to the same extent in A and not-A. We then have

$$P_x(A) = P_x(\text{not-}A),$$

i.e.

$$P_x(A) = 1 - P_x(A),$$
$$P_x(A) = \frac{1}{2}.$$

Thus, to a state of complete indecision as to whether A or not-A is true corresponds the value $1/2$. It is apparent that the way of measuring the degrees of certainty we have adopted, leads to a scale similar to the scale of degrees of mathematical probability. It was for just this reason that we passed from the first to the second way of assigning numerical values to the degrees of certainty.

Any attempts of this kind to evaluate the degree of certainty with which a person X accepts a sentence A, according to the level of risk depending on the truth of this sentence, and connected with an activity this person is ready to undertake, may give rise to the following objection: if somebody decides to undertake the activity connected with a certain risk in this way, it depends not only on the degree of certainty with which he accepts the sentence, but also on his financial standing. With the same degree of certainty, a rich person is ready to risk a larger sum of money than a poor person. This objection would be justified, if we wanted to express profits and losses in absolute amounts of money. However, the same sum of money represents a different utility for people of different financial standing and of different needs. Thus, the profit and loss appearing in our definition of the degree of certainty should be expressed not in absolute sums of money, but in units of utility. The concept of utility is widely discussed in mathematical economics. It has also been exhaustively treated by Carnap in § 51 of his work *The Logical Foundations of Probability* (2nd edition, Chicago 1951).

3. I proceed now to terms and concepts concerning inference. I shall begin with the explication of the term 'inferential statement'. An inferential statement results from joining sentences which are the premisses of some inference with a sentence which is its conclusion, by means of the word 'therefore' or some expression synonymous with it. For instance, the statement 'Every human being is mortal, Socrates is a human being — therefore Socrates is mortal' is an example of an inferential statement. Instead of the word 'therefore', I shall use the symbol '~→'.

By substituting in an inferential statement variable symbols in place of one or more constant symbols, we obtain expressions called schemes of inference. I call formal schemes of inference those in which only logical constants occur in the premisses and the conclusion.

If two inferences are expressed in terms of two inferential statements which fall under the same scheme of inference and, if additionally, the same degree of certainty is associated with the acceptance of the premisses and the conclusion, then we say that these inferences are carried out in the same way or that they proceed according to the same *method of inference*.

We shall now introduce the concept of the degree of infallibility of a given scheme of inference as the ratio of the number of variable values or the number of systems of variable values occurring in this scheme, which satisfy both the premisses and the conclusion, to the number of those which satisfy the premisses.

We symbolize the degree of infallibility of the scheme '$P(x)\sim\rightarrow\rightarrow C(x)$' by

$$T[P(x)\sim\rightarrow C(x)]$$

Now, denoting by $N_x[F(x)]$ the number of those values of the variables x which satisfy the sentential formula $F(x)$, we may write

$$T[P(x)\sim\rightarrow C(x)] = \frac{N_x[P(x)C(x)]}{N_x[P(x)]}$$

When for example, natural numbers are the values of the variable x,

$$T[(1 < x < 10) \rightsquigarrow (3 < x < 6)] = \frac{N_x[(1 < x < 10)(3 < x < 6)]}{N_x(1 < x < 10)} = \frac{2}{8}$$

The degrees of infallibility can seldom be computed in this way. Moreover, the concept of the degree of infallibility will not always be significant. For, with schemes of the type $P(x) \rightsquigarrow C(x)$ the fraction $\dfrac{N_x[P(x)C(x)]}{N_x[P(x)]}$, which measures the degree of infallibility, will not have any definite value if the number of values of the variable x which satisfy both the premisses and the conclusion, is infinite. In those cases

$$T[P(x) \rightsquigarrow C(x)] = \frac{\infty}{\infty}$$

In order to guarantee that the concpet of the degree of infallibility of a scheme is also significant in these cases, we would have to use in the definition, the concept of the limit of a sequence. A similar thing occurs in the case of a frequency definition of probability, when moving from finite to infinite sets. This similarity is not surprising. For, our concept of the degree of infallibility of a scheme of inference is exactly coextensive with the frequency concept of the relative probability of conclusions derived, according to these schemes, from adequate premisses.

We have said that the degree of infallibility of schemes of inference often cannot be practically computed. However, it frequently happens that although we cannot compute the degree of infallibility, we are able to compare the degrees of infallibility of various schemes.

Let us take as an example the scheme of inference whose premiss is the statement that at least k objects x being S are at the same time P, and whose conclusion is the general sentence that every S is P. This can be formulated as follows:

(*) $\Sigma_x^k (x \in S . x \in P) \rightsquigarrow S \subset P$

The above scheme may be considered as a form of ordinary enumerative induction. Let us assume for simplicity that P is a constant. Then the degree of infallibility of this scheme will be

$$T(*) = \frac{N_s[\Sigma_x^k(x \in S . x \in P)S \subset P]}{N_s[\Sigma_x^k(x \in S . x \in P)]}$$

The above formula represents the ratio of the number of sets S which have at least k members in P and all of whose members are in P, and the number of those sets S which have at least k members in P. Assuming that the number of sets S is finite it is easy to demonstrate that this ratio increases as k increases i.e. that the greater the number of cases confirming the general conclusion are found in the premise, the more infallible the schemes of enumerative induction become, or, in other words, the less uncertain they are.

It is obvious that the scheme (*) is infallible when $k = 0$, and this means that in inferring according to the scheme of enumerative induction we act less uncertainly than if we stated the general conclusion independently of whether at least one confirming case had been claimed.

4. We now come to the most important concept we shall consider, namely the concept of the rationality of methods of inference. The concept .of rationality is not a specifically logical or methodological concept, but a general praxeological concept. For, we speak not only of a rational or irrational method of inference, but also, more generally, of a rational irrational way of acting.

When do we call human activity rational? We call it rational when it leads to a goal. Thus, the concept of rationality of action requires relativization to some goal. A mode of action may be rational with respect to one goal, but irrational with respect to another. And we do not have to take into consideration only the goals at which man consciously aims. For a person who acts is often not aware of the goal he is aiming at, or *we* may not be aware of his conscious aims. We may then ask whether his activity would be rational, if this or that were his goal.

This is exactly how we shall frame our question concerning the rationality of methods of inferences. Namely, we shall ask when a certain method of inference would be rational, if we assumed it is applied in order to achieve this or that goal. We shall assume in particular that the goal we have in mind is practical in character, viz. that the goal in consideration is to obtain profit and avoid losses. More precisely:

We shall accept as rational from the practical point of view a certain method of inference, if the balance of profits and losses resulting from the activities based on the conclusions obtained in this way from true premisses is not negative in the long run.

5. Let us point out here that by a method of inference we understand a class of concrete inferences characterized not only by a certain scheme of inference, but also by the degree of certainty with which the premisses and conclusions are accepted.

Let us then consider the following method of inference, described firstly, by some scheme of inference $P(x) \sim \to C(x)$, whose degree of infallibility is

k/l, secondly, by the fact that conclusions obtained according to this method of inference from true and absolutely certain premisses have a degree of certainty not higher than $\dfrac{S}{Z+S}$.

The statement that the scheme $P(x) \sim\to C(x)$ has a degree of infallibility k/l means that the ratio of the number of values of the variable x, for which both the premisses and the conclusions are true, to the number of all the values for which the premisses are true, is k/l.

On the other hand, the statement that the degree of certainty of the conclusions derived according to this method from true premisses does not exceed the value $\dfrac{S}{Z+S}$ means that, on the basis of accepting these conclusions, we are ready to undertake only such activities that will, if the conclusions are true, give at least a profit Z and, if they are false, at most a loss S.

These characteristics of our methods of inference will enable us to compute the lowest limit of the balance of profits and losses resulting from the activities based on the acceptance of conclusions derived according to this method from true premisses. Since these activities will, in the case of false conclusions, bring each time at most the loss S, and in addition, our conclusions will be k times true and $l - k$ times false, then

$$\text{total profit} \geqslant k \cdot Z,$$
$$\text{total loss} \leqslant (l - k) \cdot S$$

and hence

$$\text{the balance of profits and losses} \geqslant k \cdot Z - (l - k) \cdot S.$$

The sufficient condition for this balance to be non-negative is that

$$k \cdot Z - (l - k) \cdot S \geqslant 0$$

i.e. that $k \cdot Z \geqslant (l - k) \cdot S$.

Simple transformations of this inequality give

$$k \cdot Z \geqslant l \cdot S - k \cdot S$$
$$k(Z + S) \geqslant l \cdot S$$
$$\frac{k}{l} \geqslant \frac{S}{Z + S}$$

This is a sufficient condition for the balance of profits and losses resulting from activities based on conditions derived according to the above characterized method of inference from true premisses, after it has been applied for a long time, not to be negative; this is therefore a sufficient condition to accept this method of inference as rational from the practical point of view.

It is easy to see that the left side of the inequality (1) represents the degree of infallibility of our method of inference and the right side represents the upper limit of the degrees of certainty for the conclusion derived from true premisses according to this method.

We can formulate the result of our considerations in the following way: A sufficient condition for some method of inference to be rational from the practical point of view is that the degree of certainty of conclusions derived according to this method from true premisses does not exceed its degree of infallibility.

This is our answer to the question as to when some method of inference may be accepted as rational from the practical point of view. The answer given does not make the rationality of a particular method dependent exclusively on the degree of its infallibility, but on whether the degree of certainty with which the conclusions are accepted is defined with respect to the degree of infallibility of the method. And since we understand the degree of certainty as a readiness to undertake more or less risky activities, our answer makes the rationality of a method of inference dependent on whether it leads to readiness to undertake activities whose degree of risk is related to the degree of infallibility of the method of inference.

6. We have been dealing so far with the problem of the rationality of methods of inference from the practical point of view. Naturally, rationality of methods of inference may be considered with respect to goals other than practical ones. We may, for example, have in mind the purely theoretical goal of the recognition of truth and avoidance of falsity and so accept as rational those, and only those kinds of inference which from true premisses always lead to true conclusions. From this point of view we might accept as rational only deductive types of inference. Or we might weaken this theoretical goal and demand of methods of inference that they lead more often from truth to truth than from truth to falsity. We would then consider rational only those types of inference whose degree of infallibility is more than half. The question as to what conditions methods of inference should fulfil will be — as we have shown — different, depending on the goal we have in mind when considering their rationality, i.e. applicability.

7. I should also like to add that we have spoken only of the rationality of methods of inference and not of the rationality of concrete inferences. This concept may be defined in two ways. A concrete inference may be

considered rational from the point of view of a given goal, if it realizes that goal. Then all and only those inferences which lead to true conclusions would be rational from the practical point of view. We would then have to accept as rational, for example, the inference by which from the fact that 2 times 2 is 4 we reached, by chance, the correct conclusion regarding the number of the ticket that won the main prize in a lottery. This would surely be an inadequate concept. One might, however, consider rational, from the practical point of view, those concrete inferences which are made in a rational way from this point of view, i.e. in a way that guarantees a non-negative balance of profits and losses over a long period of time. Since by inferring in a way that is rational from the practical point of view one might sometimes reach conclusions that might lead one to carry out unfavourable actions, if we accept this concept of the rationality of concrete inferences, we shall have to regard as rational such an inference which makes the achievement of the practical goal harder rather than easier. I must confess that this consequence does not seem unreasonable to me. I do not consider the statement that somebody, although he acted rationally, did not reach his goal, to be in disagreement with the ordinary sense of the adjective 'rational'.

8. Finally several remarks directed towards an evaluation of our considerations. Our investigations might well seem extremely primitive and elementary to anyone well acquainted with the theory of probability and literature devoted to the problem of the probabilistic justification of induction. Our point consists in treating methods of inference as particular systems of gambling, where one may win or lose. And the development of this idea is simply a repetition of what has long been known about the conditions of reliability of game systems. Namely, that a game system is fair, if the mathematical expectation of winning equals the mathematical expectation of losing. The condition for the rationality of methods of inference we have given:

$$k \cdot Z \geqslant (l - k) \cdot S$$

is only a different formulation of this condition. For if we divide both sides of the inequality by l, we obtain

$$\frac{k}{l} \cdot Z \geqslant \frac{l-k}{l} \cdot S,$$

but k/l is the ratio of the number of correct conclusions to the number of all conclusions, and is therefore the probability of the conclusion being correct, i.e. the probability of winning. Hence k/l. Z is the same as the mathematical expectation of winning. Similarly $l - k/l$. S is the mathematical expectation of losing. Thus our condition for the rationality of a method of inference is coextensive with the well known condition of the fairness of a game system.

So there are no revelations in what we have said here; methods of inference are treated in the same way as gambling systems, so the familiar properties of the latter can be employed.

The arguments presented here may also receive criticism because the criterion of rationality we have laid down cannot be practically applied to types of inference which, like enumerative induction, are a matter of central interest to methodologists. Our criterion of rationality cannot be applied, because the degree of infallibility of these types of inference cannot be established in practice. This criticism may be softened, though, by the remark that in many cases where the degree of infallibility cannot be computed one can compare the degrees of infallibility of different types of inference. Consequently, one could decide which of two ways of inference is more rational. Nevertheless this remark also indicates the weak side of our achievements.

In spite of this, however, I feel I may venture to say that at least three results worthy of attention have been obtained here.

The first is in making precise the sense of the problem of the justification of induction and other fallible methods of inference. This problem has worried logicians and methodologists at least since Hume's time; and I must admit that I was never quite sure what the problem actually was. Max Black spoke about the problem of this vagueness at a recent international philosophical congress, but he did not clarify it either.

It seems that the problem of the legitimacy, i.e. rationality of non-deductive types of inference has been expressed clearly in my considerations. This has been achieved by classifying types of inference according to the general praxeological concept of types of action, as well as by taking advantage of the idea that a good course of action from some point of view, is one which is adequate in the long run for the goal which determines our evaluation of this activity. This general praxeological concept of sound reasoning should — it seems to me — be the compass of all considerations on the logical correctness of any act of reasoning. This concerns not only methods of inference, but also such things as constructing concepts, defining, classifying, etc.

According to this approach both the concept of the rationality of a type of inference, and, generally, any concept of the correctness of this or that reasoning requires relativization to the goal that is taken into consideration. If no such relativization is carried out, then this goal is tacitly assumed. It is one of the most important tasks of methodology to find those aims which, in fact, determine an evaluation of the various mental operations and their products in the sciences, if it is to understand the sciences as cultural phenomena in the humanistic sense.

The second point is the resistance to the influence of the term 'probability' found in the literature devoted to the question of induction. Formerly a 'probable sentence' was understood as a sentence which it was rational to believe, though the meaning of the adjective 'rational' was only vaguely understood. This original content of the concept of probability has entirely altered in the course of the development of what is known as the mathematical theory of probability. Neither in the classical, nor in the frequency, nor, finally, in the theory of probability that operates with the concept of the measure of a set, can we find any indication suggesting clearly that what is highly probable deserves rational belief. In spite of this many logicians believed that the problem of the rationality of induction or other non-deductive types of inference would be solved if we could demonstrate that inductive inferences have a high degree of probability in the mathematical sense. This attitude is quite wrong until the question has been answered why what is probable in the mathematical sense deserves rational belief. In order to answer this question one must make precise the concept of a statement deserving rational belief. This, however, is not done in most cases; under the influence of the term 'probability' it is believed that it suffices to demonstrate that some statement is probable in the mathematical sense in order to demonstrate that it is probable in the original sense of this word, i.e. that it deserves rational belief.

Drawing attention to the fact that the mathematical concept of probability is, as far as its content is concerned, different from the logical concept of probability is not our own discovery. Many authors have already pointed out the fact that it is not obvious at all that a sentence highly probable in the mathematical sense, is at the same time, a sentence that has a high degree of rational certainty. The point has been emphasized very strongly by Carnap who distinguishes the concept of logical probability (probability$_1$) from the concept of mathematical probability (probability$_2$). In his work mentioned above, *The Logical Foundations of Probability*, Carnap has constructed a definition of the concept of confirmation, treating the concept of confirmation as an explication of the intuitive concept of logical probability. He has developed a theory of confirmation on the basis of this definition, which he calls the logic of induction. But Carnap's definition of the degree of confirmation does not include anything that would allow the transition from a sentence belonging to a metalanguage and attributing to a hypothesis h under an assumption e a high degree of confirmation, to the adoption of any assertive attitude toward the sentence h belonging to the object language, when we accept the sentence e. Consequently, the same question arises with respect to the concept of confirmation, that arose with respect to the concept of probability: why are we allowed to and should we accept with a high degree of rational certainty sentences which have a high degree of confirmation? Until we are given an answer to this question, the whole theory of confirmation will not deserve the name of 'logic of induction'. Carnap draws a parallel between the theory of logical consequence constructed in a metalanguage and his theory of confirmation, which he treats as the logic of induction. But the theory of logical consequence deserves the name of logic of deduction, since metalinguistic theorems stating that a sentence b is a logical consequence of a sentence a enable us to evaluate as a rational procedure an inference in which, on the basis of the accepted sentence a we reach the acceptance of the sentence b. In other words, the metalinguistic theory of logical consequence deserves the name of logic of deduction, since, on the basis of its theorems, one may justify the rationality of the rules of deductive inference. But in order to do this we must bridge the gap between the sentences of a metalanguage assigning to the sentence h under assumption e some degree of confirmation, and the rationality of some rule of induction that on the basis of accepting the sentence e, allows acceptance with some degree of certainty of the sentence h in the object-language.

I should also like to suggest that an achievement of this article is in drawing attention to the fact that neither the mathematical theory of probability, nor the theory of confirmation are logic of induction until the gap has been spanned allowing, on the basis of the theorems of one or other of these theories, an indication of the rationality of the rules of inductive inference. But in order to span this gap, an analysis of the concept of the rationality of a rule of induction must be carried out. Such an analysis has been performed here and it was only this analysis that made it possible to form a link between the frequency theory of probability and the rational rules of, or methods of, inductive inference; though it was an unsophisticated analysis, and applicable only to the simplest situations. The link is the theorem that a method of inference that allows, on the basis of premises P, the acceptance of a conclusion C with a degree of certainty not greater than the degree of infallibility of this method, is a rational method. Since the degree of infallibility of a method is the relative frequency of true conclusions, derived according to this method from true premises, among all the conclusions derived according to this method from true premises, this theorem links the theorems concerning partial probability with the rationality of certain inductive methods. If the way by which the gap between the mathematical theory of probability and the rationality of the rules of inductive inference has been bridged is, in principle, correct, then the frequency theory of probability should be considered the logic of induction. The construction of some theory of confirmation would not then be necessary.

The third idea worth the reader's attention is − I believe − as follows. It is generally believed that a method of non-deductive inference may be considered correct only, if it very often leads to true conclusions, or at least if it leads more often to truth than to falsity. According to our approach to the problem, in which we have distinguished different degrees of certainty, a type of inference which very rarely leads to truth may also be considered rational, provided that the degree of certainty with which the conclusion is accepted is sufficiently low. I believe this particular detail to be important and in conformity with the normal use of non-deductive types of inference.

Contemporary statisticians refuse to acknowledge the existence of any fallible methods of inference. They state that in cases in which the logicians speak of fallible methods of inference we do not deal with the acceptance of certain conclusions on the basis of certain premises, but with a decision to act. Now, the way in which we have defined here the degree of certainty of accepting sentences seems to erase to some extent the difference between accepting a sentence and a decision to act, which will bring profit or loss depending on the truth of this sentence.

These are the three ideas contained in the article to which I wanted to draw the reader's attention.

NOTES

[1] A. Shimony in his article entitled 'Coherence and the Axioms of Confirmation' (*The Journal of Symbolic Logic* **20** (1955), 7) gives a definition of partial relative belief, which does not differ in principle from our definition of the degree of certainty with which a person X accepts a sentence h. Namely, Shimony states that X believes h on the basis of e in the degree r (symbolically: $B(h/e) = r$) "if and only if X would accept a bet on h on the following terms, or on terms more favourable to himself than these:

(a) To pay rS and collect nothing for a net gain of $−rS$ in case e is true and h is false;

(b) To pay rS and collect S, for a net gain of $(1 − r)$, in case e and h are both true;

(c) To annul the bet, i.e. to have a net gain of 0, in case e is false".

It is easy to notice that

$$r = \frac{r \cdot S}{r \cdot S + (1 - r)S} = \frac{\text{loss}}{\text{loss} + \text{profit}}$$

since negative profit is the same as loss.

The difference between the method of measuring the degree of certainty we have adopted here and Shimony's method consists only in that Shimony gives the measure of the degree of certainty of the sentence h given an assumption e, and we give as measure the absolute degree of certainty.

[2] It seems natural that the highest degree of certainty with which we may, acting rationally, accept a sentence h as the conclusion derived from premises e according to the scheme of inference S should be called the logical probability of the sentence h with respect to the sentence e and the scheme S (symbolically $P_S(h/e)$).

Using this terminology one might derive the following consequence from our theorem formulating the condition of the rationality of some method of inference: the logical probability of the sentence h with respect to the sentence e and the scheme S equals the degree of infallibility of the scheme S:

$$P_S(h/e) = T(S)$$

The theorem puts the sign of equality between logical probability and frequency probability, since the degree of infallibility of the scheme of inference is — as we have said above — frequency probability.

Carnap uses this or a very similar concept of logical probability in one of the unofficial explications of this concept, which he gives in a paragraph of the work mentioned above. The reasoning of this paragraph is very similar to our considerations aimed at establishing the condition of the rationality of non-deductive types of inference.

16. THE PROBLEM OF THE FOUNDATION OF
ANALYTIC SENTENCES*

(1958)

1. The purpose of this article is to find an answer to the question whether terminological conventions are sufficient to validate analytic sentences. Explications of the meanings of terms used in the formulation of the problem will be given at the outset.

2. We shall begin by explicating the meaning of the term 'analytic sentence'. In their researches published within the last few years logicians have been expressing the view that there are serious difficulties in defining this term. For in order to define it one would have to use concepts such as the meaning of terms or synonymity, concepts which in turn elude any precise explication. It is our belief that the difficulties mentioned were associated with the tendency to regard the concept of an analytic sentence as an absolute concept whereas it should be understood − like most concepts of semiotics − as a relative concept. No sentence is simply analytic or non-analytic just as no man is simply a friend, father or son, though he may be such in relation to another person.

There are many ways of relativizing the concept of an analytic sentence. One may say that a sentence is analytic for a person or in a given language, provided we have an appropriate conception of language. However, at the bottom of all these relativizations there is always one and the same relativization, viz. to some terminological conventions.

By a terminological convention we understand here a declaration of intent concerning the use of certain terms. Terminological conventions may be formulated either semantically or syntactically. So, for example, the declaration: "I decide to use the word 'centimeter' as a name for the length of one hundredth of a meter" is a semantical convention, since it concerns the semantic relation between the term 'centimeter' and the object to be designated by it. On the other hand, the convention: "I decide to use the term 'centimeter' in the same sense as 'one hundredth of a meter'" is a syntactical convention, since it concerns a relation holding between two expressions.

* Translated by Jerzy Giedymin. First published in *Studia Logica* **VIII** (1958), 259−72. Translation based on *Język i Poznanie*, II, 308−21. Reprinted here by kind permission of PWN.

Let us now agree on the following usage of the term 'language': if two persons make use of the same vocabulary of simple terms, obey the same rules for the construction of compound expressions out of simple ones and, moreover, accept the same terminological conventions, then we shall say that the two persons speak the same language.

3. The concept of an analytic sentence may be defined in either of two ways depending on whether the adopted convention is of semantic or syntactic character.

To construct the first of the two definitions we shall need the concept of a postulate which we shall presently explicate. We shall say, namely, that a sentence S is a postulate of the language L if in L there is a terminological convention which determines that a term λ occurring in S is to denote an object which satisfies S in place of λ.

If, for instance, there is consensus that in English 'centimeter' is the name of the length which satisfies the condition "A centimeter is one hundredth of a meter", then the quoted sentence is a postulate of English.

The definition of postulate may be generalized so that it concerns not one term (i.e. the one that denotes an object satisfying the condition) but several terms simultaneously. If, for example, there is a consensus that 'point', 'line', 'passes through' have in the language of geometry denotations which in suitable places satisfy the condition "Through two points passes one unique line", then the latter sentence will also be a postulate.

4. In our definition of 'postulate' we have used the term 'denotation', which also requires clarification. Now by the denotation of a proper name (i.e. of a particular name which is not a predicate) we shall mean an object whose name is the proper name. For example, the denotation of the proper name 'Socrates' is the philosopher Socrates. By the denotation of a predicate (either in the noun form, e.g. 'a living person' or as a verb, e.g. 'lives') we shall mean a class of objects of which this predicate may be truthfully predicated (in the distributive sense) i.e. the extension of the predicate. As a consequence, the denotation of the predicate 'lives' is the class of objects to everyone of which one can truthfully apply the predicate, i.e. it is the class of living organisms. The denotation of a binary predicate such as, for example, 'loves' is the class of ordered pairs of objects to which the predicate is applicable, i.e. the class of pairs $\langle x, y \rangle$ such that x loves y. Each proper name and each predicate has one and only one denotation. The denotation of a proper name is always an individual object, the denotation of a predicate is always a class. Instead of saying that the object A is the denotation of the expres-

sion B, we shall also say that the expression B denotes, names or designates the object A.

5. Now we are ready to formulate the first of the two definitions of an analytic sentence. We shall say that a sentence S is analytic in the language L in the semantic sense if it is a postulate of L or a logical consequence of the postulates of L.

The concept of a postulate used in this definition is semantical, i.e. its definition would be in terms of terminological conventions which have a semantic character. The concept of an analytic sentence so defined we shall call the semantic concept of an analytic sentence.

6. We shall now formulate the second definition of an analytic sentence. This one will not involve the concept of terminological conventions of semantic nature but terminological conventions of a syntactic nature. Hence the concept defined in this way will be referred to as the syntactical concept of an analytic sentence. We shall first introduce the auxiliary concept of logical truth. A sentence S is a logical truth of a language L if S is either a logical tautology or results from a logical tautology by substitution of a descriptive constant of L for a variable. So among the logical truths of English will be sentences: "Every A which is not B, is not B", as well as "Every unmarried man is unmarried". Using this concept of logical truth we shall define the syntactical concept of an analytic sentence as follows:

A sentence S is analytic in L in the syntactical sense if it is a logical truth in L or reduces to a logical truth in virtue of syntactical terminological conventions of L.

In conformity with this definition among analytic sentences of English will be not only the above quoted examples of logical truths but also, e.g. the sentence 'Every bachelor is unmarried'. For there is in English a syntactic terminological convention which permits one to use variously the terms 'bachelor' and 'unmarried man'. Consequently the sentence 'Every bachelor is unmarried' reduces to the logical truth 'Every unmarried man is unmarried'.

7. The terminology clarified, let us consider our main problem: are the analytic sentences of a language sufficiently validated by the terminological conventions of the language. In other words, the question is whether a sentence of a language is bound to be true provided there are in the language in question terminological conventions which give it analytic status.

The problem has to be considered separately for analytic sentences in the semantic and in the syntactic sense.

8. We shall begin with analytic sentences in the semantical sense. Let us restate the definition. A sentence $F(\lambda)$ is analytic in L if it is either a postulate of L or a logical consequence of the postulates of L. A sentence $F(\lambda)$ is a postulate of L if there is a convention in L according to which the term λ is to denote an object satisfying the condition $F(\lambda)$. It appears easy to prove on the basis of this definition that all postulates of a language must be true in that language. For the following argument appears at first sight convincing:

I. If the sentence $F(\lambda)$ is in L a postulate, then there exists in L a convention according to which the term λ is to denote an object satisfying $F(\lambda)$.

II. If there exists in L a convention according to which the term λ is to denote an object satisfying the condition $F(\lambda)$, then λ denotes in L an object satisfying the condition $F(\lambda)$.

III. If λ in L denotes an object satisfying the condition $F(\lambda)$, then the sentence $F(\lambda)$ is true in L.

Ergo: If the sentence $F(\lambda)$ is a postulate of L, then the sentence $F(\lambda)$ is true in L.

How shall we evaluate this argument which results in a positive answer to our main question? From the formal point of view it is undoubtedly valid, since it is a substitution instance of a valid hypothetical syllogism. The first premiss is a consequence of the definition of 'postulate' and is unobjectionable. Likewise unobjectionable is the third premiss: for to say that the term λ denotes an object satisfying the condition $F(\lambda)$ amounts to saying that $F(\lambda)$ is true. But what about the second premiss? At first sight it also appears convincing. Indeed, when constructing a language we are inclined to believe that we are completely free in choosing the objects which are to constitute the denotations of various terms of the language. Hence, if I decide that in my language — which is at least partially constructed by myself — the term λ is to denote this or another object, then the term in question will denote that object.

But is indeed my freedom so unlimited? Let us consider two different situations in which relations are established between the expressions of a language and their extralinguistic counterparts. In one situation we have an object and want to assign to it a term which is to designate it. In this case I am completely free to give it any existing term I please and if I do not like any existing one I am at liberty to invent a new one. The case is different, if I am given a term and want to assign to it an object as its denotation. Then I cannot choose an arbitrary object but only an existing one. If an object satisfying my conditions does not exist, then my decision to assign to the given term such an object as its denotation will not be sufficient for its creation. Therefore the decision that the term λ should denote an object satisfying the condition $F(\lambda)$ is insufficient for this to be the case if no object satisfies the condition $F(\lambda)$.

We see, therefore, that the second premiss of the argument which yielded the positive answer to our question, is false. It is not true that whenever there is a convention in the language L to the effect that the term λ should denote an object satisfying the condition $F(\lambda)$, that term *ipso facto* denotes such an object. The second premiss should be replaced by the following one:

If in the language L there is a convention to the effect that the term λ is to denote an object satisfying the condition $F(\lambda)$ and if, moreover, there exists an object satisfying that condition, then the term λ denotes in L an object satisfying the condition $F(\lambda)$.

From this it follows that a terminological convention alone is not sufficient to ensure the truth of a postulate based on it. It is able to give such a warrant only if it is conjoined with an existential statement which ascertains the existence of an object satisfying the postulate.

9. In support of our conclusion one may show some paradoxical consequences of the view according to which a terminological convention alone is a sufficient warrant of the truth of a postulate based on this convention. Now, if this view were true, one would be able to prove the existence of objects satisfying an arbitrary condition $F(x)$.

For in order to be able to assert with certainty that $F(\lambda)$ it would be enough to decide that the term λ should denote an object satisfying that condition. Then, in virtue of the well-known law of logic

$$F(\lambda) \rightarrow (\exists x) F(x)$$

we would be able to prove that

$$(\exists x) F(x)$$

In this way one would be able to prove, for example, the existence of a man 100 meters tall. To do so, it would be sufficient to decide, for instance, that the term 'Polyphemus' is to denote an object satisfying the condition: 'Polyphemus is a man 100 m tall' and to assert, in virtue of that convention, that

Polyphemus is a man 100 m tall.

Then in virtue of the mentioned law of logic we are entitled to infer that

there exists a man 100 m tall.

Up till now the result of our analysis reduces to the statement that the terminological convention to the effect that a term λ is to denote an object satisfying the condition $F(\lambda)$, on its own does not guarantee the truth of the sentence $F(\lambda)$ in the language in which the convention has been adopted. Such a guarantee is given only by the convention in conjunction with the existential premiss $(\exists x)F(x)$. This result is by no means a revelation. It is merely a generalization of a well-known theorem of the theory of definitions in mathematics. Definitions in mathematics are, as we know, nominal definitions which are accepted on the basis of terminological conventions or are themselves terminological conventions. They may be formulated either in the object or in the meta-language. A definition is in the object-language if the term defined and not its name occurs in it. So, for example, the sentence 'A square is an equilateral rectangle' is a definition of the term 'square' formulated in the object-language. A definition is in the meta-language if instead of the term to be defined its name occurs in it. Such a definition is, for instance, the sentence: 'the term 'square' means the same as the expression 'an equilateral rectangle' '.

Definitions formulated in the object-language are accepted on the basis of semantical conventions. Thus the definition 'a square is an equilateral rectangle' is accepted on the basis of the convention to the effect that the term 'square' is to designate a figure satisfying the mentioned condition. Generally speaking, a definition $D(\lambda)$ of a term λ is accepted on the basis of a convention to the effect that the term λ is to designate an object satisfying the condition $D(\lambda)$. As can be seen, mathematical definitions formulated in the object-language are postulates of a kind. Now, according to the theory of definitions, a convention to the effect that a term λ is to denote an object satisfying the condition $D(\lambda)$, of itself does not yet entitle us to accept the sentence $D(\lambda)$ as the definition of the term λ. We have the right to introduce such a definition only after it has been proved that it satisfies certain definite conclusions, one of which is known as the existence condition

$$(\exists x)D(x)$$

and the other is known as the uniqueness condition:

$$(\forall x)(\forall y)[D(x) \wedge D(y) \to x = y]$$

The uniqueness condition is required since the sentence $D(\lambda)$ is to be a definition of the term λ i.e. is to characterize uniquely its denotation. The demand for an existence proof as a condition for the acceptance of definitions in the object-language (which, are, as we already pointed out, kinds of postulates) is a special case of the condition which we have imposed here on all postulates.

The result of our inquiry is therefore a generalization to all postulates of what has been well known about the postulates which are unique (unambiguous) characterizations of the denotations of terms, i.e. about the postulates which are definitions formulated in the object-language. Nevertheless our inquiry and its result are not without a certain merit. They make it possible to understand better why one is not allowed to accept a definition, or in general a postulate, on the basis of conventions alone without an existence proof. Furthermore, the generalization of the existence condition to all postulates has certain important epistemological consequences which I will discuss in another article.

10. We have shown that terminological conventions alone are insufficient to ensure the truth of postulates. Hence, they are not sufficient to ensure the truth of the consequences of postulates either. But analytic sentences in the semantical sense have been defined as either postulates or their logical consequences. Our arguments, therefore, yielded the conclusion that semantic conventions alone are insufficient to ensure the truth of analytic sentences in the semantic sense; reference to suitable existential sentences is necessary for that purpose. In this way we have solved the main problem of this paper so far as analytic sentences in the semantical sense are concerned. We shall now discuss this problem with reference to the analytic sentences in the syntactic sense.

11. We have defined analytic sentences in the syntactical sense as either logical truths or as sentences derivable from logical truths in virtue of terminological conventions of syntactical nature. By a 'terminological convention of syntactical nature' we mean here any statement to the effect that expressions A and B are to be used interchangeably, i.e. in such a way that if one accepts a sentence involving one of those expressions one ought to accept also the sentence if that expression is replaced in it by the other expression. Syntactical conventions so characterized are simply rules of transformation of sentences into others. Now it is evident that such rules alone will never be sufficient to ensure the truth of any sentence whatever; apart from those rules one needs premises from which a given sentence is derivable in virtue of the rules. Hence terminological conventions of syntactical nature are insufficient to validate any sentence, henceforth also analytic sentences. To validate analytic

sentences laws of logic and their substitutions, i.e. logical truths are necessary apart from those conventions.

The negative answer to our question with regard to analytic sentences in the semantical sense we have thus supplemented by the negative answer to that question as regards analytic sentences in the syntactical sense: terminological conventions alone are insufficient to establish the truth of analytic sentences. The validation of analytic sentences requires, apart from conventions, also additional premisses. Along with this parallel there is, however, an essential difference between analytic sentences of the two kinds, which I should like to emphasize here. We have shown that to validate an analytic sentence in the semantical sense an existential premiss is necessary along with the laws of logic and terminological conventions. On the other hand, to validate an analytic sentence in the syntactical sense only laws of logic are necessary apart from terminological conventions; no existential premiss seems required.

12. The mentioned difference has certain consequences which appear paradoxical and which throw light on the problem of definitions formulated in the object-language. We have said that in mathematics definitions formulated in the object-language, i.e. definitions in which the term defined itself occurs rather than its name, are kinds of postulates, based on semantical terminological conventions. As a result, for their introduction an existential premiss is required. As an example of such a definition we have quoted the sentence:

'a square is an equilateral rectangle'

Now, it is easy to show that definitions in the object-language may be obtained with the help of syntactical conventions and so validated with the help of laws of logic alone; hence definitions in the object-language may also be regarded as analytic sentences in the syntactical sense. We shall show this on the basis of an example.

We adopt the syntactical terminological convention to the effect that the expression 'an equilateral rectangle' may be replaced in any asserted sentence by the expression 'a square' and vice versa. In virtue of this convention we derive from the laws of logic alone the definition in the object-language:

a square is an equilateral rectangle

Now we assert the law of identity:

(1) $(\forall x)(x = x)$

Hence by substitution:

(2)   an equilateral rectangle = an equilateral rectangle

In virtue of the convention which permits the substitution of the term 'equilateral rectangle' by the term 'square' we get from (2):

(3)   square = equilateral rectangle

In this way we have obtained a sentence which — being a postulate — seems to require an existential premiss for its validation. And yet we have derived this sentence in a way for which an existential premiss seems unnecessary.

This paradoxical conclusion makes us suspect that either we have made a mistake in our proof of the statement according to which an existential premiss is required for the validation of any postulate, or else that we have used an existential premiss in our last proof without having noticed it.

13. The latter conjecture turns out to be correct. Our derivation of the definition of the term 'square' in the object-language from the terminological convention and the laws of logic, presupposes an existential premiss. Such a premiss is necessary to obtain in a valid way from the law of identity $(\forall x)(x = x)$ its substitution instance: 'an equilateral rectangle = an equilateral rectangle'. The derivation of '$f(a)$' from the universal sentence '$(\forall x)f(x)$' is invalid, unless the existence of a has been proved.

This is due to the meaning of the quantifier '$(\forall x)$'. A universal sentence '$(\forall x)f(x)$' means the same as 'for every object x, $f(x)$'. Hence it is impossible to derive from such a universal sentence a particular conclusion '$f(a)$', unless we know that a is an object, i.e. that a exists and is unique:

$$(\exists x)(x = a)$$
$$(\forall x)(x = a \,.\, y = a \to x = y)$$

The first of these premisses is an existential premiss.

If no existential premiss were required for our method of deriving a definition in the object-language formulation from the laws of logic in virtue of a syntactical terminological convention, then one could prove in this way the existence of arbitrary objects.

For let us assume the following syntactical convention:

Instead of writing 'the tallest man over 100 m in height', one is permitted to write 'Polyphemus' and vice versa.

Starting with the law of identity $(\forall x)(x = x)$ we get by substitution:

The tallest man over 100 m in height = the tallest man

over 100 m in height

In virtue of the adopted terminological convention, we obtain from this:

Polyphemus = the tallest man over 100 m in height.

This sentence, in turn, in virtue of the law of logic

$$F(a) \rightarrow (\exists x) F(x)$$

yields the existential sentence:

$(\exists x)$ (x = the tallest man over 100 m in height).

This evidently false conclusion shows that there is an error in its derivation. The error is to be found in the transition from the law of identity $(\forall x)(x = x)$ to one of its instantiations: we have substituted for the individual variable 'x' the term 'the tallest man over 100 m in height' which has no denotation. We have made the substitution without having ascertained whether there exists an object denoted by that term, i.e. without finding out whether the existential premiss is true. In the case of Polyphemus it is not and this is why we have obtained an obviously false conclusion.

Our analysis shows that an existential premiss is just as necessary for the derivation of a definition formulated in the object language from a syntactical terminological convention as it is for the derivation of such a definition from a semantical convention.

14. What has just been said about the derivation of definitions formulated in the object-language from syntactical terminological conventions applies as well to the majority of analytic sentences in the syntactical sense. The latter are either so-called logical truths, i.e. laws of logic and their instantiations or sentences derivable from logical truths in virtue of syntactical terminological conventions. Now we have to use an existential premiss in order to justify the instantiation of a law of logic; without such a premiss this step in our derivation will be invalid. Thus the existential premiss is needed in the validation of any sentence which we intend to derive from the instantiation, hence also in the case when in further derivation syntactical terminological conventions are used.

We see now that the difference which at first sight seemed to distinguish the validation of analytic sentences in the semantical and in the syntactical sense, turned out to be only apparent. The claim that although an existential premiss is needed for the validation of analytic sentences in the semantical sense, no such premiss is needed for the validation of analytic sentences in the syntactical sense, has been shown to be false. On the contrary, an existential premiss is necessary for the validation of any analytic sentence in the syntactical sense, unless it is a law of logic; for it is necessary to validate any instantiation of a law of logic and any sentence which reduces to such instantiation in virtue of a syntactical convention; existential premisses are required to apply validly the laws of logic to particular instances.

15. The fact that the derivation of a particular conclusion from a universal sentence by substituting a constant for a variable requires an existential premiss, is not usually mentioned. The rule of substitution is usually formulated exclusively in syntactical terms, without recourse to semantical concepts, hence without the requirement that the substituted term should have a denotation. However, the purely syntactical rule is usually so formulated that it ensures the satisfaction of the semantical condition.

Which constant expressions may be substituted for variables in accordance with the rule of substitution?

For sentential variables one is allowed to substitute only sentences, i.e. constants whose denotations are truth or falsity. For individual variables one may, firstly, substitute constants which are proper names. Proper names are names which are assigned to individuals directly, i.e. they are assigned to individuals given in observation and not merely by indirect, verbal characterization. Experience in which individuals bearing proper names are given to us ensures the existence of the denotations of those names. The substitution rule for definite descriptions may be formulated in different ways but always so that only the substitution of non-empty descriptions is sanctioned.

For predicate variables one may substitute indefinite descriptions of the type '$(\hat{x})(...x...)$' or '$(...x...)$', i.e. so-called propositional functions. However, simultaneously the so-called definition axiom is accepted which states that for every propositional function there exists a class to which belong all and only the objects satisfying this function. The axiom ensures that every indefinite description, formed with the help of a propositional function, has a denotation.

Under certain circumstances one may also substitute for predicate variables definite descriptions which involve predicate variables; certain conditions are also imposed on the substitution of descriptions involving variables of higher order; those conditions are formulated variously but always so that they do not permit the substitution of terms which do not denote anything.

The substitution rules, therefore, in spite of being formulated in a purely syntactical way, always guarantee that constant symbols which may be substituted for variables do have denotations.

16. We have concluded that terminological conventions and laws of logic are insufficient to validate analytic sentences either in the semantical or in the syntactical sense; the only exceptions here are the laws of logic themselves. In order to validate any analytic sentence which is not a law of logic an existential premiss is required. Such a premiss sometimes asserts the existence of an individual object which satisfies a condition and then has the form:

$$(\exists x) f(x)$$

where 'x' is an individual variable.

In other cases the existential premiss asserts the existence of a class or relation determined by a propositional function which imposes a condition on its elements or members. Then the premiss has the form:

$$(\exists f)[f(x) \equiv_x (\ldots x \ldots)]$$

or

$$(\exists f)[f(x_1, \ldots, x_n, \ldots) \equiv_{x_1 \ldots x_n} (\ldots x_1 \ldots x_n \ldots)]$$

where 'f' is a predicate variable.

It may occur that the existential premiss asserts the existence of classes or relations which themselves satisfy a condition. In that case the existential premiss has the form

$$(\exists f) F(f)$$

where 'f' is a predicate variable.

In the first case, i.e. when the existential premiss has the form

$$(\exists x) f(x)$$

and when 'x' is an individual variable taking values from the domain of real objects, the existential premiss must invariably be justified, so it seems, by experience, whether directly or indirectly. For what is involved are premisses such as

$$(\exists x)(x \text{ is red})$$
$$(\exists x)(x \text{ is a man at least 2 m tall})$$

etc.

In the other case, i.e. when the existential premiss has the form

$$(\exists f)[f(x) \equiv_x (\ldots x \ldots)]$$

it is enough to appeal to the laws of logic, in particular to the definitional axiom which states that for every propositional function there exists a class determined by that function. Our previous conclusion to the effect that for the validation of an analytic sentence in the syntactical sense an existential premiss is required apart from the laws of logic and terminological conventions, must — therefore — be corrected. Since the laws of logic themselves provide the existential premiss, those laws together with conventions provide a sufficient justification.

In the third case, i.e. when the existential premiss has the form

$$(\exists f) F(f)$$

where 'f' is a predicate variable, the premiss can be justified in various ways. We believe that sometimes the premiss has to be validated by experience. It must be admitted that this belief may appear strange. For what is claimed is that in some cases an appeal to experience is necessary in order to establish the existence of a class with a certain property; the existence of the class itself, not of the fact that the class is not empty.

Let us try to justify this claim by analyzing the existence proof required for the acceptance of the stipulative definition of the term 'gram'. We shall use the symbol (D) for that definition:

1 gram is the mass of 1 cm^3 of water at 4 °C.

17. Let us assume that to introduce the definition of the term 'gram' the following convention (C) has been accepted:

It has been decided that the denotation of the term 'gram' is to satisfy the following postulate: 1 gram is the mass of 1 cm^3 of water at 4 °C.

In conformity with this convention the denotation of the term 'one gram' must satisfy the following conditions:

(1a) α is a mass
(2a)   if x is 1 cm^3 of water at 4 °C, then x has the property α

Using 'M' for 'mass' and '$ccw4$' for '1 cm^3 of water at 4 °C', we shall re-write conditions (1a) and (2a) as follows:

(1b) $\alpha \in M$
(2b) $(\forall x)(x \in ccw4 \rightarrow x \in \alpha)$

Mass is an equivalence class with respect to the relation of mass-equality. That relation may be defined as follows: bodies A and B have equal mass if A is identical with B or if A and B acting on each other induce in each other equal accelerations in opposite directions. An equivalence class with respect to the relation of mass equality (RwM, for short) is any class to which belong all and only those bodies which have equal masses. So our terminological convention decides to assign to the term 'one gram' as its denotation the class which satisfies the following conditions:

(1c) $\alpha \in RwM$

(2c) $(\forall x)(x \in ccw4 \rightarrow x \in \alpha)$

It should be emphasized that (1c) and (2c) characterize the class α in terms of conditions imposed on that class itself and not on its elements. The statement asserting the existence of this class will not have the form:

$$(\exists \alpha)[\alpha(x) \equiv_x (... x ...)]$$

but rather:

$$(\exists \alpha) F(\alpha)$$

The existence of a class which satisfies these two conditions simultaneously may be proved by constructing an example of a class whose existence may be proved and which does satisfy these conditions. In order to construct such a class let us choose a particular 1 cm^3 of water at 4 °C and let us designate it with w. We formulate now the propositional function

x is equal to w with respect to mass

This function determines a class

$$M_w = (\hat{x})(x \text{ is equal to } w \text{ with respect to mass})$$

whose existence is guaranteed by the definitional axiom. We see at once that M_w satisfies (1c), i.e.

(a) $M_w \in RwM$

In order, however, to ascertain that M_w satisfies the condition (2c), i.e.

(b) $(\forall x)(x \in ccw4 \rightarrow x \in M_w)$

it is necessary to appeal to experience, since only experience can decide whether or not all cubic centimeters of water at 4 °C belong to the class $M_w = (x)(x$ is equal to w with respect to mass), in other words, to decide whether all cubic centimeters of water at 4 °C are with respect to mass equal to a particular cubic centimeter of water, i.e. to w.

Experience shows that cubic centimeters of water at various temperatures are not all equal with respect to mass to a given one. If, on the other hand, we consider only cubic centimeters of water at the same temperature, e.g. at

4 °C, then they all turn out to be equal among themselves with respect to mass, in other words they all turn out to be equal to one of them with respect to mass, e.g. equal to w.

Therefore it is only with the help of experience that we can ascertain that M_w satisfies also the condition (2c) i.e. that

(b) $(\forall x)(x \in ccw4 \rightarrow x \in M_w)$

On the basis of premisses (a) and (b) stating that the class M_w satisfies conditions (1c) and (2c) we can prove, in virtue of the laws of logic, that an object satisfying these conditions exists:

(1) $(\exists x)\{\alpha \in RwM \wedge (\forall x)(x \in ccw4 \rightarrow x \in \alpha)\}$

in other words, there exists a mass of an arbitrary cubic centimeter of water at 4 °C. This is the existential premiss which has to be proved before one accepts on the basis of convention (C) the definition (D): '1 gram is the mass of a cubic centimeter of water at 4 °C'.

We see that the premiss in question concerns the existence of a class characterized by a condition imposed on the class itself and not on its elements. Hence its truth is not ensured by the definitional axiom and has to be proved. The example discussed here shows that the existence proofs of this type (i.e. of statements of the form $(\exists f) F(f)$, in some cases at least, have to appeal to experience.

18. The definition of one gram is an example of a postulate, i.e. of an analytic sentence in the semantical sense. Since we have shown that the validation of this definition requires an appeal to experience, we must conclude that in some cases the validation of analytic sentences in the semantical sense has to be based on experience. The statement of this result, which does not seem to be uninteresting, concludes the present paper.

17. SYNTACTICAL CONNECTIONS BETWEEN CONSTITUENTS OF DECLARATIVE SENTENCES*

(1960)

1. Problems of language analysis are of interest to both linguists and logicians. One of the most important differences between the linguistic and the logical analysis of language is the fact that linguistic investigations are concerned with natural languages whereas logicians study artificial ones. Those artificial languages constructed by logicians are simple in comparison with very involved and complicated natural languages. The relatively greater simplicity of the languages studied by logicians enables them to give a clearer account of the structure of those languages than is possible in the case of the analysis of complex natural languages.

However, since the languages studied by logicians are in many respects modelled on natural languages, it seems that logicians may be able to make some contribution to general linguistics. It is most probable that the results of the logical analysis of languages cannot be applied without qualification to the empirically given natural languages; that their analyses which ignore certain moments characteristic for natural languages require far-reaching modifications to be applicable to natural languages. Possibly this situation is similar to the one in physics. Physicists also formulate some of their laws for ideally simplified cases which do not occur in nature. They formulate laws for ideal gases, ideal liquids, for frictionless motion, etc. For those idealized cases it was possible to find simple laws which have contributed essentially to our understanding of reality; had physicists acted otherwise, trying to describe reality in all its complexity, they would probably not have been successful.

Now it seems that the languages analyzed by logicians may also be regarded as an idealization of natural languages and maybe this idealization makes it possible for logicians to reach deeper into the nature of linguistic entities than linguists have been able so far to do.

In this article I should like to discuss from the logician's point of view the problem of the connections between the constituents of a declarative sentence.[1]

* Translated by Jerzy Giedymin. First published in *Studia Filozoficzne* (1960), No. 6, 73–86. Translation based on *Język i Poznanie*, II, 344–55. Reprinted here by kind permission of PWN.

2. In the rest of the article I shall be concerned exclusively with the connections between the constituents of a declarative sentence which are determined by the relations between the extralinguistic entities corresponding to those constituents, i.e. I shall be concerned with those connections which are content-dependent (of substantive nature). I distinguish only two kinds of those connections between the constituents of a declarative sentence, viz. (1) syntactical connections, which are associated with the syntactical function performed by those constituents within the sentence, (2) reflective connections which assign to a constituent its objective correlate only with respect to another constituent of the same sentence. As an example of a syntactical connection may serve the connection between the subject and predicate or the connection between a noun and a qualifying adjective, or, finally, between a connective and the sentences which it combines into a compound sentence. As an example of a reflective connection may serve the connection between a noun and a pronoun which alone assigns a denotation to the pronoun.

In the present paper I shall be concerned exclusively with those connections which I have just called syntactical. What I intend to do is to make – with the help of the logic of language – a contribution to the analysis of the syntactical connections which are usually discussed by grammarians. I shall first show how in the logic of language one deals with the syntax of a declarative sentence (and in general with the syntax of a meaningful compound linguistic expression). Then I shall present the classification of linguistic expressions into so-called semantical categories. Finally, with the help of a few examples I shall exhibit a method which enables one to reduce the syntactical connections discussed in grammar to the concepts of the logic of language.

3. I begin with an account of the way the syntactical structure of a declarative sentence is dealt with in the logic of language.

Every meaningful and unambiguous expression, consisting of more than one word, hence every declarative sentence, can be decomposed without any residue into its components in exactly one way, so that one of those components relates to others and connects them into a meaningful whole. Such an analysis of the sentence

$$2 + 8 = 2.5$$

distinguishes the components '=', '2 + 8', '2.5', the first of which (the sign of equality) combines the two remaining ones into a meaningful whole. The analysis of the sentence

'Wise Socrates loves young Alcibiades'

into 'loves', 'wise Socrates', 'young Alcibiades' distinguishes the verb 'loves' as that component which connects the remaining ones into a meaningful whole.

Now if an expression A can be exhaustively decomposed into B and C_1, C_2, ..., C_n, where B relates successively to the expressions C_1, C_2, ..., C_n and connects them into a unit, then we say that the expression B is the main operator of the expression A, while C_1 is the first, C_2 the second ... C_n the nth argument of the operator.

In our first example the equality sign is the main operator[2] whereas the expressions '2 + 8' and '2 . 5' its first and second arguments. In the second example the verb 'loves' is the main operator while 'wise Socrates' and 'young Alcibiades' its first and second arguments.

The main operator of an expression A and its arguments are its first order or main constituents. They may be, in turn, compound expressions themselves and then in each of them its main operator and its arguments may be distinguished. They are then first order components of the first order components of the expression A and will be termed second order components of A.

So, for example, in the equation

$$2 + 8 = 2 . 5$$

the plus sign as the main operator of the first order component of the whole equation and the numerals '2' and '8' as its arguments are second order constituents of the equation. In general: First order constituents of the nth order constituents of an expression A are $(n + 1)$-order constituents of A. The expression A itself is its own zero-order constituent.

It follows from the above that every kth order constituent of a meaningful expression (with the exception of the constituent of order zero) is either the main operator of a constituent of order $(k - 1)$, or ith argument of the main operator of a constituent of order $(k - 1)$. That constituent of order $(k - 1)$ is, in turn, if $k - 1 \neq 0$, again either the main operator of a constituent of order $(k - 2)$ or else its jth argument.

The relations which hold between the first order constituents of an expression and that expression itself will be signified as the relations of direct (immediate) syntactical subordination. So the relation of direct syntactical subordination holds between the main operator of an expression and that expression itself, as well as between the arguments of the main operator of an expression and the expression itself. Since every constituent of kth order of a meaningful compound expression (with the sole exception of a constituent of order zero) is either the main operator of a constituent of order $(k - 1)$ or the ith argument of the main operator of a constituent of order $(k - 1)$, we can say that every constituent of kth order of an expression A (for $k \neq 0$) is correlated with some constituent of order $(k - 1)$ of that expression by the relation of direct (immediate) syntactical subordination. Every kth order constituent of an expression A is either identical with A (if $k = 0$), or else may be coordinated with A with the help of a chain of relations of direct syntactical subordination. Now that chain of relations of direct syntactical subordination which connects a constituent G of an expression A with that expression itself, or — in the extremal case when G is identical with A — the identity relation, is the *syntactical position* of the constituent G in the expression A. The syntactical position of G in A is determined by the enumeration of the relations of direct syntactical subordination with the help of which A is reached from G. As an example, let us consider the sentence:

(A)   'Wise Socrates talks with pious Euthyphro or discusses with Phaedo'.

This sentence has the following syntactical structure: the word 'or' is its main operator, while the two sentences joined by the connective are the operator's arguments. In the first of these two simple sentences the phrase 'talks with' is the main operator whose arguments are 'wise Socrates' and 'pious Euthyphro'. In the expression 'wise Socrates' the word 'wise' is the main operator while 'Socrates' is the argument. If, therefore, we want to indicate the syntactical position of 'Socrates' in this compound expression, we have to say: 'Socrates' is the only argument of the main operator of the first argument of the main operator of the disjunctive sentence (A). Our example shows that to indicate the syntactical position of the constituent of an expression within that expression is sometimes a complicated affair. Later on we shall introduce symbolism which will make it possible to indicate syntactical positions in a transparent way.

It is obvious that a compound expression cannot be uniquely characterized by an enumeration of words of which it consists, since various compound expressions may be built up from the same words by assigning to them different syntactical positions. So, for example, from the words 'John', 'loves', 'Ann' one may construe both the sentence 'John loves Ann' and 'Ann loves John'. For a unique characterization one must have methods of indicating the syntactical positions occupied by the particular constituents of a sentence. Different languages make use of different devices to achieve that purpose. In mathematical symbolism the syntactical positions of the constituents of sentences are indicated above all by their linear order, moreover by the use of brackets and parentheses as well as by conventions deciding which of two operation symbols binds arguments more strongly than the other. In natural languages the syntactical positions of the constituents of a sentence are indicated – apart from their linear order – also by inflection and by punctuation marks. Some languages make greater use of the order rather than of inflection forms, others rely more on inflection leaving to the speaker greater freedom with respect to the order of words. For example in the English sentence:

'John loves Peter'

the word order is essential to indicate which of the words is the first and which the second argument of the main operator 'loves'. In Latin, on the other hand, the difference between the first and second argument is indicated with the help of inflection. Both in the sentence

'Johannes amat Petrum'

and in the sentence

'Petrum amat Johannes'

'Johannes' is the first while 'Petrus' is the second argument of the main operator.

Languages which mark syntactical positions of the constituents of sentences with the word order exclusively are known as positional languages, while languages which use for this purpose inflection forms exclusively are known as purely inflectional. All natural languages approach either one or the other type more closely but none of them is purely positional or purely inflectional. Mathematical symbolism admittedly does not make use of inflections but cannot be regarded as purely positional since syntactical positions are indicated in it not only by the word order but also by brackets and parentheses.

In my article 'Syntactic Connexion' (*Studia Philosophica*, 1935)[3] I have constructed a purely positional language which does not make use of either inflections, parentheses or of any conventions concerning the 'binding strength' of operational symbols; the syntactical positions of all constituents are indicated in it by the word order exclusively.

Recently I have succeeded in constructing a purely inflectional language in which the word order is irrelevant[4] (it does not even have to be a linear order) and the syntactical positions are indicated with the help of inflections exclusively. This language cannot be constructed with the help of previously introduced symbols for syntactical positions. The new symbols are based on the following principles:

1. To the syntactical positions which an expression takes in itself, i.e. to the position of the constituent of zero order, we assign the symbol '(1)'.

2. If to the syntactical position of the constituent G of arbitrary order of an expression A in A the symbol '(K)' is assigned, then the syntactical position of the main operator of that constituent in A will be designated with the symbol '$(K, 0)$', while the syntactical positions of the first, second, ... nth argument of that operator are designated with symbols '$(K, 1)$', '$(K, 2)$', ... '(K, n)'.

Following these principles we are able to assign a symbol to the syntactical position of every constituent of a compound expression. To show this, let us consider the following Latin sentence:

(B)   '*Socrates est philosophus et Plato est philosophus*'

In accordance with our two principles we assign to the syntactical positions of the constituents of that sentence their indices in the following manner:

Socrates	*est*	*philosophus*	*et*	*Plato*	*est*	*philosophus*
(1,1,1)	(1,1,0)	(1,1,2)		(1,2,1)	(1,2,0)	(1,2,2)
	(1,1)		(1,0)		(1,2)	
			(1)			

It should be obvious that the whole syntactical structure of the expression (i.e. the syntactical positions of all its constituents) is uniquely determined by the specification of the syntactical positions of particular words. Hence, in order to specify the whole syntactical structure of an expression it is sufficient to designate with the help of our indices the syntactical positions of particular words. We write therefore:

Socrates	*est*	*philosophus*	*et*	*Plato*	*est*	*philosophus*
(1,1,1)	(1,1,0)	(1,1,2)	(1,0)	(1,2,1)	(1,2,0)	(1,2,2)

We can write now these words in any order whatever; we can even – disregarding their linear order – disperse them on a plane or in space; thanks to indices of syntactical positions, the words will remain to be interconnected and continue to occupy their respective syntactical positions. Positional indices, therefore, play a role analogous to inflections used to indicate syntactical positions, and when assigned to particular words may be treated as inflections. A language which would use only positional symbols to indicate syntactical positions of particular words, might – therefore – be regarded as purely inflectional.

This is what we wanted to say about the usual treatment of the syntactical structure of a compound expression in the logic of language. We should add, however, that what has been presentend here is only sufficient for the specification of the syntactical structure of those expressions in which no so-called bound variables or binding operators occur. If bound variables occur in a sentence, then the task of specifying its syntactical structure becomes considerably more complicated. We shall not consider this problem here since bound variables or binding operators do not occur explicitly in natural languages their role being rather performed by other kinds of expressions.

4. Let us take up now the second item of my paper, viz. the classification of linguistic expressions into so-called semantical categories. The concept of semantical categories must be clearly distinguished from the concept of syntactical categories. The term 'semantical category' was introduced for the first time by Husserl; however, the concept he associated with it would correspond better to the term 'syntactical category'. For Husserl pointed out that the expressions of a language may be classified according to the role they can play within a sentence. He defined, therefore, his categories from the syntactical viewpoint. Our classification of linguistic expressions will be based not on their syntactical function within a sentence but on the ontological categories of the entities to which linguistic expressions refer or – as we shall also say – which they denote. In the logic of language the term 'semantical' is used in a narrower sense to designate all those concepts which are concerned with the relations between linguistic expressions and the entities referred to. This is why a classification of linguistic expressions which reflects ontological categories denoted by them is more appropriately called a classification of semantical categories than one based on syntactical criteria. The concepts of syntactical and semantical categories differ at least with respect to their intension, this does not necessarily imply that they also differ with respect to their extensions.

In a classification of linguistic expressions into semantical categories one should mention first of all those which denote particular objects and which therefore are known as singular names (terms). Secondly, we shall mention sentences which differ from all other linguistic expressions in that they alone may be either true or false. Following Frege one assumes in logic that true sentences denote truth while false sentences denote falsity. Truth and falsity are known as 'logical values' (truth-values). The class of sentences may, therefore, be defined from the semantical point of view as that class of linguistic expressions each of which denotes a truth-value.

Singular terms and sentences are thus the first two semantical categories.

Singular terms, i.e. the names of individuals will here be assigned the symbol 'i'. Sentences, i.e. the expressions which denote a truth-value will be indexed with 'w'. Further semantical categories will be found among linguistic expressions which denote functions and which are therefore known as functional symbols or functors. The concept of function originates from mathematics but is often used outside mathematics. By a function we mean a relation which to every object of a certain kind or to two, three, etc. objects of a certain kind assigns another object as their correlate in a unique way. So, for example, the relation of fatherhood is a function which to every man (human) assigns another man as their father. The *sine* relation is a function which to every real number assigns another real number as its *sine*. Depending on whether functions assign uniquely objects to single objects, to pairs, triples, ... or n objects of a given kind, they are known as unary, binary, ... n-ary functions (One usually speaks of functions of one, two, ... n-variables).

An essential property of linguistic systems in the proper sense, by contradistinction to other systems of signs (e.g. the system of railway signs or of traffic signs), is the following one: in certain conditions from two expressions A and B which denote respectively objects α and β a compound expression may be formed which denotes neither α nor β but a different object γ. For if A is a functor which denotes a function α defined for objects of some kind and which is combined with an expression B denoting an object β of that kind, then the compound expression consisting of A and B denotes the object which the function α assigns to the object β. So, for example, the expression 'the father of Socrates' is a name of Sophroniskos and not of the fatherhood relation and of the particular object Socrates. It seems that all compound expressions which have denotations are constructed according to this principle.

After these general comments we shall enumerate various semantical functors. First of all we distinguish functors whose denotations are functions (unary or n-ary) which correlate particular objects with particular objects. These are functors which — when applied to one or more singular terms — form a new singular term. They are, therefore, functors forming singular terms out of singular terms. We shall assign to them indices $\dfrac{i}{i}, \dfrac{i}{ii}, \ldots$

Secondly, there are functors which denote functions (of one or more variables) correlating truth-values to truth-values. These are functors which used with one or more sentences form sentences (i.e. expressions denoting truth-values). Such a one-place functor is, for example, the negation-symbol which together with a sentence forms another sentence (the negation of the first sentence). A two-place functor of this kind is, for example, the disjunction functor 'or', since it forms a disjunctive sentence out of two sentences. These are functors forming sentences out of sentences and in our symbolism they will be assigned indices $\frac{w}{w}, \frac{w}{ww}, \ldots$

Next come functors whose denotations are functions (of one or more variables) correlating a truth-value to a singular object. These are functors which together with one or more singular terms form a sentence (i.e. an expression denoting a truth-value). The phrase 'is alive' is such a functor forming a sentence together with one singular term (e.g. 'Socrates is alive'). The verb 'loves' forms a sentence when combined with two singular terms. These are functors forming sentences out of terms; they will be assigned indices $\frac{w}{i}, \frac{w}{ii}, \ldots$

There are, finally, functions which correlate other functions with objects. These functions are denoted by functors which form meaningful expressions when combined with other functors. Each adverb is such a functor. To see that this is so let us consider the sentence 'The sun shines brightly'. 'Sun' is a singular term, 'shines' is a functor which forms a sentence together with a singular term, its index is therefore $\frac{w}{i}$. But the compound expression 'shines brightly' is of the same category $\frac{w}{i}$. Hence the adverb 'brightly' is an expression which combined with a functor of the type $\frac{w}{i}$ forms a functor of the type $\frac{w}{i}$. Such an expression will be assigned a symbol in the form of a fraction with fractions as its nominator and denominator:

$$\frac{\frac{w}{i}}{\frac{w}{i}}$$

5. We have given a sketchy survey of so-called semantical categories. Our survey is neither exhaustive nor has it been fully explained. We shall take up now the third task of our paper, i.e. we shall exhibit in a few examples a method of analyzing syntactical connections in terms of the logical concepts introduced in the two previous chapters.

We shall begin with an analysis of the relationship between the subject and predicate of a sentence.

First of all we have to clarify to ourselves the nature of this relationship: is it a relationship between linguistic expressions *in specie* or *in concreto*?

Linguistic expressions *in concreto* are utterances made *hic et nunc* or signs written *hic et nunc*. Linguistic expressions *in specie* are classes of such utterances or written signs. The difference between these two conceptions of linguistic expressions comes to light when we ask whether the sentence '2 = 2' consists of three words or of only two, one of which occurs in it twice. Those who give the first answer to this question have in mind words *in concreto*; those who give the second answer mean by 'word' an expression *in specie*. In the rest of this article whenever syntactical relationships are discussed 'expression' means 'expression *in specie*'; this is, I think, the established usage among linguists. If, therefore, the relationship between the subject and predicate is seen as a relationship between expressions *in specie*, then one must not say that two linguistic expressions in general stand to one another in the relationship of predicate to subject; they can only be so related within a particular sentence. For it is clear that one and the same expression *in specie* which in one sentence occurs as its predicate may in another sentence perform quite a different role. One must never say, therefore, that 'expressions A and B are related one to the other as predicate to subject' but only that 'Expressions A and B stand to one another in the relation of predicate to subject in a sentence C'. From the logical point of view this is expressed by saying that the subject-predicate relationship is a three-place relation holding between expressions A, B and a sentence C.

How should one analyze the predicate-subject relationship with the help of the concepts which have been introduced here: If the predicate-subject relation holds between A and B in a sentence C, then -- first of all -- A must take the syntactical position of the main operator in the sentence C while B must take *the position of its only argument*. In other words, the expression A must have in C the position $(1,0)$ and the expression B must have the position $(1,1)$. This is, however, not yet sufficient for a unique characterization of the relationship in question. In addition, the predicate must always be a sentence-forming functor. But even more is necessary for such an unambiguous characterization, for in a negative sentence consisting of the negation and the sentence negated (e.g. 'not-every man is happy'), the negation symbol is the main operator and at the same time it is a sentence-forming operator; we cannot say, however, that the negation sign is the predicate of that sentence. The predicate of a sentence must be the main operator which is a functor capable of forming a sentence when conjoined with the expressions of some but not arbitrary categories. In other words, in order to characterize the predicate-subject relation in terms of the operator-argument relationship it is necessary to restrict both the operator and its arguments to specific semantical categories.

If the main operator of the sentence belongs to the category $\frac{w}{i}$ and its argument is a singular term (i), then the syntactical relation holding between them will undoubtedly be regarded as the predicate-subject relation. From the logical point of view this is the predicate-subject relation of first order and the functors of the $\frac{w}{i}$ category which may occur in it are known as predicates of first order. However, logicians also speak of predicates of second and higher orders. A functor of type $\frac{w}{\frac{w}{i}}$, i.e. one which as main operator conjoined with a predicate of first order forms a sentence, is a predicate of second order. Hence, in the languages considered by logicians there are sentences in which one can predicate something of the predicates of first order using predicates, which may then be called predicates of second order. In natural languages predicates of first order are always *verba finita*, as e.g. 'lives', 'sings' or expressions such as 'is a man', etc. Now it seems that the syntax of natural languages would not tolerate *verba finita* as subjects of sentences. Expressions such as 'lives is *A*' appear to be syntactical nonsense.

One should realize, however, that languages analyzed by logicians consist of words which in every respect, both syntactically and semantically, may be regarded as atoms; they are not constructed from constituents which would determine their syntactical or semantical role. Such a language is, for example, the language of mathematics. Natural languages are different. In the expressions which constitute their single words one may distinguish: roots, prefixes, suffixes, inflectional endings, etc. These constituents determine both the syntactical and the semantical role of the words. It seems, in particular, that suffixes serve to determine the syntactical position of a word in a composite expression. *Verbum finitum* has a suffix or ending which assigns to it the syntactical position of an operator. This is why it is inadmissible or impossible to put a *verbum finitum* in the position of a subject, i.e. of an argument in a sentence. If, on the other hand, we treat the concept of a word *in specie* so broadly that all words *in concreto* with the same root and reference (denotation) are seen as examplars of one and the same word *in specie*, then we can say that a *verbum finitum* and a noun with the same root are one and the same word *in specie*; the only difference being that the former as a word *in concreto* takes the position of an operator, while the latter takes the position of an argument. If we take 'word' *in specie* in this broad sense, then we may consider so-called general terms, e.g. 'man', 'living', etc. to be the same words as *verba finita* 'is being a man', 'lives', etc.

If we do this, then we shall be able to speak also with respect to natural languages of sentences in which the functor $\frac{w}{i}$ performs the role of the subject while the functor $\frac{w}{\frac{w}{i}}$ performs the role of the predicate. The principles of the word-formation of natural languages require, however, that the functor $\frac{w}{i}$, functioning as the subject, i.e. as the argument in a sentence, should be a noun (i.e. a term).

Previously we have introduced the concept of a predicate of first order as a functor which, when conjoined with a singular term, forms a sentence. We have defined a second order predicate as a functor which, when conjoined with a predicate of first order as its argument, forms a sentence. We are now in a position to define by induction the general concept of an nth order predicate as a functor which, when conjoined with an $(n - 1)$ functor as its argument, forms a sentence. With the help of these concepts we can define in general the predicate-subject relation as the relation which holds between two expressions A and B in a sentence C if and only if A is the main operator in C, and B is its only argument, given that A is a functor with index $\frac{w}{i}$ and B is a singular term, or A is a predicate of nth order (for $n - 1$) and B a predicate of $(n - 1)$ order.

The above analysis has shown that to define the predicate-subject relationship it is necessary, firstly, to specify the syntactical positions in the sentence of both constituents so related and, secondly, to specify the semantical categories to which both constituents belong. This shows the way to a complete enumeration of all possible syntactical relationships between two components of a sentence. There exist in principle, as we have seen, an unlimited number of syntactical positions in a sentence and a similar variety of semantical categories. By reasonably combining both variants one may distinguish an unlimited number of syntactical relationships which should be characterized both in terms of the syntactical positions of their elements and in terms of those elements' semantical categories. However, only some of those relationships deserve attention.

6. In conclusion I should like to emphasize that for the concept of syntactical relations the concept of the relationship between the main operator of a composite expression and its argument is of fundamental importance. In our analysis we have not defined it precisely. What we have said was that if an expression A can be exhaustively decomposed into expressions $B, C_1, C_2, ...,$ C_n where B relates successively $C_1, C_2, ..., C_n$ and connects them into a

whole, then we say that the expression B is the main operator of the expression A with C_1 as its first argument, C_2 as its second argument, ... C_n as its nth argument. This explication of the main operator makes use of the metaphorical expression 'relates' which, so it seems, has a psychological meaning. Since whatever is psychological presupposes a thinking subject, the relation under discussion seems to require relativization to a speaker. I shall try now to define the relation of being the main operator in such a way that it reflects an objective relation holding between the entities denoted by linguistic expressions and no longer contains any subjective element. This may be done in the following way: If an expression A, which denotes α can be completely decomposed into expressions $B, C_1, ..., C_n$ which denote respecively $\beta, \gamma_1, \gamma_2, ..., \gamma_n$ and β is a function which to objects $\gamma_1, \gamma_2, ..., \gamma_n$ in this order assigns uniquely α, then B is in A the main operator with C_1 as its first argument, C_2 as its second argument, ... C_n as its nth argument. I propose this definition for discussion. Should it turn out to be correct, then the syntactical structure, i.e. the whole net of operator-arguments relations in an expression which − as a whole − denotes something (hence must be syntactically well constructed) would be determined uniquely as soon as the semantical categories of its first-order constituents have been determined. For my definition assumes that from the constituents whose semantical categories have been determined, it is possible to construct in one way only an expression which denotes something at all.

NOTES

[1] This was one of the problems discussed at the International Linguistic Symposium held in Erfurt from September 27 to October 2, 1958. The present article was the author's contribution to that Symposium.

[2] I have used the term 'operator' in place of the term 'functor' commonly used in Polish since the latter is ambiguous. The term 'functor' has two different meanings in the contexts:

' 'The expression f is a functor (simpliciter)' 'the expression f is a functor (performs the role of a functor)' in the expression W'. In the contexts of the first type 'functor' is the name of an (absolute) property of some expression; while in the contexts of the second type it is the name of a relation between the particular expression and another one. The use of the term 'functor' in both senses results in 'the expression f is a functor which is not a functor in the expression W'. To avoid this ambiguity and such paradoxical statements, I have introduced here the term 'operator' for those cases where we deal with a relation between the given and another expression, viz where we deal with the syntactical function performed by an expression within another one. The term 'functor' may then be used as the name of an absolute property of some expressions. The term 'operator' is clearly syntactical, while the term 'functor' is − at least as used in the present article − a semantical one.

[3] [Present volume pp. 118–139].

[4] ['Intensional Expressions', present volume pp. 320–347].

18. AXIOMATIC SYSTEMS FROM THE METHODOLOGICAL POINT OF VIEW*

(1960)

1. METHODOLOGY AND METASCIENCE

There are two disciplines which make axiomatic systems the object of their research. One of them is the branch of mathematical logic named meta-mathematics, or metalogic, or more generally metascience. The other is the traditional methodology of sciences, which is treated in separate chapters in the textbooks of logic and deals with problems bordering upon the philosophical theory of knowledge. The achievements of metascience are so numerous, its notions so precise, and its proofs so exact, that they have dissuaded many from examining deductive systems from any other point of view except that of metascience; they have produced an impression as if metascience could be identified with the theory of deductive systems, and as if no other problems concerning those systems could be stated but those treated by metascience.

In the present paper I wish, firstly, to give an account of the differences between the point of view of metascience and that of traditional methodology; secondly, to try to find what is essential to methodological problems; finally, to examine one of the problems of methodology, which concerns axiomatic systems but essentially belongs to the domain of the theory of knowledge.

The difference between the point of view of metascience and methodology consists chiefly in the fact that metascience does not take into account the part played by man in the construction of science; it considers science as a system of sentences, a system of inscriptions of definite forms whose correspondents are so-called models which fulfil the system. Methodology, by contrast, investigates also the part played by the human being that makes use of these sentences to acquire knowledge of reality. From this difference it follows that of all the notions of semiotics or the logic of language (which includes semantics, syntax, and pragmatics) in metascience there appear only the notions of syntax and semantics, while methodology has also recourse to the notions of pragmatics.

In metascience, of which metamathematics and meta-logic are so far the

* Revised translation by Jerzy Giedymin. First published in *Studia Logica* IX (1960), 205–18. Present translation based on *Studia Logica* and on *Język i Poznanie*, II, 332–43. Reprinted here by kind permission of PWN.

only representatives, there appears the term 'sentence' but it is defined there in a purely morphological way, without any reference to what a sentence expresses, namely as an inscription of a specific form, determined by the so-called rules of the formation of expressions. In addition, metascience has recourse to the notion of 'derivability under the rules of transformation', a notion which is also defined in a strictly morphological way, viz. as a relation holding between two sentences and with respect to their external form alone. Upon these purely morphological notions, that of a sentence and that of derivability in virtue of certain rules of transformation, several others are based. Such is the syntactic notion of a deductive system constructed according to certain rules of transformation, defined in metascience as the totality of sentences which are consequences, by virtue of these rules, of an empty class of sentences; the notion of axiom, which is defined as being a direct consequence of an empty class of sentences; the notion of proof, defined as a sequence of sentences which are consequences of axioms, etc. Besides these syntactic notions, which can be reduced to morphological ones, certain semantic notions are used in metascience, as e.g., the notion of an axiomatic system being satisfied by a model. On the basis of these notions a branch of science is constructed whose importance, theoretical at least, is considerable.

As we have said, metascience uses no pragmatic notions, i.e. no notions concerning the attitude of a thinking and acting human being towards linguistic expressions or towards what these expressions symbolize. Now, these notions play an essential part in the traditional methodology of science. Thus, for example, the notion of a sentence asserted by someone, completely alien to metatheory, is enormously important to methodology. It is true that sometimes the term 'asserted sentence' is used in metatheory too. So, for example, the *modus ponens* rule is sometimes formulated as follows: If one asserts a conditional sentence and its antecedent, one is also allowed to assert its consequent. But here the term 'asserted sentence' has quite a different meaning from that in methodology. There it denotes a sentence towards which someone takes an assertive attitude, or − to explain in what this attitude consists − a sentence that someone is willing to make a basis of his practical activity. In metascience, by contrast, the term 'asserted sentence' means the same as 'theorem', or, more precisely, the same as 'sentence which is a direct or indirect consequence of an empty class of sentences'. It can be seen that this metascientific notion of an asserted sentence has no reference to any human attitude. Consequently, the expression 'one is allowed to assert', which appears in the above formulation of the *modus ponens* and which, if taken literally, has a normative character, lacks this character in metascience.

In metascience the statement 'If the sentence x is asserted, one is allowed to assert the sentence y' only declares that if the sentence x is a consequence of an empty class of sentences, so is the sentence y. Methodology, by contrast, deals with man's various attitudes towards sentences; consequently, it deals with a certain behaviour of man. It evaluates this behaviour and formulates norms concerning it. In particular, it evaluates this behaviour as to its efficiency in attaining given aims. In methodology the rule permitting the assertion of a consequent on the basis of the assertion of a conditional sentence and its antecedent is taken in its literal sense. By stating this rule, the methodologist evaluates the behaviour described in it as being efficient in attaining the cognitive aim and expresses his own approval of such behaviour.

The central notion of methodology, and one that does not appear at all in metascience, is the notion of the validation of asserted sentences or of the justification of their acceptance. This is a notion of an obviously normative and evaluative character. For to validate a sentence means to justify its acceptance by a method that guarantees the attainment of the aim pursued, e.g. the true knowledge of reality. So by calling a sentence validated, one states that one has justified its acceptance by a procedure which is efficient from the point of view of the aim pursued, that, therefore, this procedure deserves to be evaluated positively and that, consequently, from the point of view of the given aim, it is a good behaviour. Upon this evaluation a norm may be based which will allow this procedure to be applied whenever the same aim is pursued.

We see that methodology, unlike metascience, is a humanistic science. This is so for the following reasons: firstly, because it deals with human behaviour, which consists in taking certain attitudes towards certain linguistic expressions; secondly, because it evaluates this behaviour and establishes the norms of good, that is to say, efficient behaviour. It evaluates not only the ways of validating sentences, but also those of forming notions, i.e. definitions and classifications. It does so not only to know whether they satisfy so-called formal criteria, but also non-formal ones. If, for instance, methodology evaluates the logical 'division of a concept', it does so not only to know whether this division fulfils the condition of exhaustiveness (which requires that the extension of the divided concept be identical with the sum of the extensions of the members of the division) and that of exclusiveness (which demands that the members have no element in common). For these two conditions form a part of the definition of a logical division itself, and to examine whether a mental procedure fulfils them or not would be tantamount to examining whether this procedure is a division or not. Methodology also evaluates a logical division from another point of view: it asks whether the members of a division are useful notions, conducive to achieving the aim of the given research.

The aim, involved in methodological evaluations is not being understood here anthropomorphically, i.e. as an objective consciously pursued. Scientists whose behaviour it guides are often unable to define it. The teleologic terminology in this case is only metaphorical and serves to describe the actions of the scientists in question. When studying, for instance, the history of zoology or of botany, one sees that at various periods various classifications of animals or plants were suggested, but did not stand up to criticisms and were replaced by others. The old ones were evaluated as bad, the new ones as good, or at least as better. So the question arises, which was the quality that the old classification lacked and the new one possessed? If one succeeds in finding an answer to such a question, one may formulate it metaphorically in a sentence of the following form: zoologists 'seek' to build up a classification of animals that would have such-and-such a property. Taken literally, this answer need not be true, for zoologists themselves may not even be aware of the property they seek. To avoid the metaphor, one can say either that zoologists proceed *as if* they sought to build up a classification possessing the quality in question, or else that such is the not necessarily conscious aim, or the *quasi*-aim, of their behaviour.

Now, the study of these *quasi*-aims of scientific behaviour constitutes a kind of synthesis of the procedure of science, an attempt at presenting it as a system organized in the same way as are actions consciously directed by an aim to be attained. In this way the reconstruction of the actual course of scientific procedure belongs to those results which Spranger had in mind when he spoke of the 'humanistic understanding' (*das geisteswissenschaftliche Verstehen*) of cultural phenomena. Humanistic understanding is a form of synthesis peculiar to humanistic sciences, just as the construction of an explanatory theory (which allows all the laws of the given domain to be deduced from certain basic principles) is peculiar to natural science. The humanistic understanding of the development of various sciences and their branches is one of the chief tasks of the methodology of science; for it is a necessary condition of any categorical evaluation. This is so because an evaluation consists in stating that something is useful in achieving a certain aim. As long as the aim has not been fixed, nothing but conditional value-statements can be made, which affirm that such a thing is useful for such an aim. But as soon as one has revealed either a real or a *quasi*-aim, one can make categorical value-statements, evaluating as good whatever is conducive to the aim which directs the process under consideration. If methodology is to evaluate certain ways of reasoning and certain mental constructions, including definitions and classifications, as good and others as bad, it must attain the knowledge of the aims or *quasi*-aims, pursued by the sciences, the knowledge which is synonymous with the humanistic understanding of the sciences.

This is the third and most important reason why methodology ought to be regarded as a humanistic science. Unlike methodology, metascience is not at all a humanistic science. It deals with certain constructs which are called sentences, expressions, proofs, deductive systems, definitions, and theorems; the axioms of the metascience attribute to those constructs certain properties from which then further properties are derived. Consequently, metascience is a science of the mathematical type, very remote in its nature from humanistic disciplines.

Having pointed out the difference between metascience and methodology, let us proceed to our proper subject, namely to the consideration of the axiomatic systems from the methodological point of view.

2. THE SYNTACTIC AND THE PRAGMATIC NOTIONS OF AN AXIOMATIC SYSTEM

The term 'axiomatic system' is used both in metascience and in methodology but in a different sense in each of them. In metascience it is defined in terms of syntactic notions alone, while in methodology pragmatic notions are also employed. In metascience a purely syntactic notion of an axiomatic system is used along with one defined in semantic terms. We shall from now on confine ourselves to considering the purely syntactic notion.

The syntactic notion of an axiomatic system in metascience is relativized to the rules of transformation of sentences, rules which in turn serve to define the relation of consequence. This relation, however, is understood in metascience in a peculiar way, quite different from those of ordinary language and traditional logic. In the latter, if one says that the sentence B is a consequence of the sentence A, one asserts that the truth of A implies the truth of B. In metascience, firstly, one does not say that a sentence is a consequence of another one, but that a sentence is a consequence of a class of sentences; such a class may either consist of several elements, or be a unit class or else an empty class, i.e. have no elements at all. Secondly, one does not speak of a consequence in an absolute sense, but only with respect to certain rules of transformation. By saying that a sentence A is a consequence of a class of sentences α in virtue of the rules of transformation I, one means that by applying these rules of transformation to the class α a finite number of times one arrives at the sentence A. It is not required that these transformations should always lead from a class of true sentences to a true sentence, but that the relation of consequence defined by these rules should fulfil certain formal conditions, e.g. be reflexive, transitive, etc.

With the help of the notion of consequence in virtue of the rules of transformation I, the notion of an axiomatic system relativized to those rules is defined in metascience, namely as the totality of sentences which are consequences, in virtue of the rules I, of an empty class of sentences. We shall call this notion of an axiomatic system the syntactic notion. An axiom of a system based on the rules I is defined as a sentence at which one arrives from an empty class of sentences by once applying one of the rules I, i.e. as an immediate consequence of the empty class. Sentences which are consequences of axioms, but are not themselves axioms, are called theorems.

By contrast, the notion of an axiomatic system in methodology is understood in such a way that it requires relativization not only to the rules of inference, but also to a person that constructs and develops the system. We shall refer to this notion of an axiomatic system as pragmatic. In methodology this notion can be defined as follows:

A set of sentences Z is an axiomatic system in the pragmatic sense for the person X if, firstly, Z is an axiomatic system in the syntactic sense relative to the rules of transformation I; secondly, the rules I are truth-preserving, i.e. always lead from true sentences to true sentences; thirdly, the rules I are entirely convincing to the person X, i.e. whenever X is to a certain extent convinced of the truth of a given sentence he is to the same extent convinced of the truth of the sentence resulting from it by transformation under the rules; and, finally, the person X constructs and develops the system in question by formulating the axioms and deductively deriving their consequences, i.e. theorems.

The notion of the deductive derivation of one sentence from another used in the above definition requires some comments. It is a wider notion than that of deductive inference. Deductive inference consists in asserting the conclusion on the ground of asserting the premisses, the conclusion being accepted with the same degree of certainty as the premisses. The verbal expression of an inference takes the form of a so-called inferential statement: p, therefore q. This statement expresses, firstly, the acceptance of the motivating sentence p, i.e. of the premiss; secondly, the acceptance of the motivated sentence q, i.e. of the conclusion; finally, the fact that the acceptance of p is, for the person making the inference a motive to accept q. Deductive inference is but a special kind of deduction in general; another kind of deduction is the mental process expressed by statements of the type 'Assume p – then q would also be the case'. Such a statement, unlike the inferential one 'p, therefore q', expresses neither the acceptance of the premiss p, nor of the conclusion q, but merely one's willingness to assert q if one asserts p. Mental processes expressed by such statements, and consisting in one's willingness to assert a certain sentence if one asserts another one can be called potential deductions to distinguish them from the ordinary deductive inference, which can be called actual deduction. We use potential deduction for example in indirect proof, when we derive the consequences of the negation of the thesis to be proved, without thereby asserting — by contrast to what is done in actual inference — either the negation of that thesis or its consequences. Potential deduction occurs also in the procedure of verifying hypotheses: in this case from a not yet accepted hypothesis, we derive consequences which are not accepted either.

The general notion of deduction, which we have used to define the pragmatic notion of a deductive system, is accordingly divided into two kinds: actual deduction, or ordinary deductive inference, and potential deduction.

3. CLASSIFICATION OF AXIOMATIC SYSTEMS IN THE PRAGMATIC SENSE

With respect to the attitude of a person X who constructs or develops an axiomatic system in the pragmatic sense, such a system may be either assertive or neutral. It is assertive for the person X if X accepts both its axioms and the theorems deduced from them; it is neutral for the person that constructs it if that person has no assertive attitude either towards the sentences of the system or towards their negations.

Assertive axiomatic systems can, in turn, be subdivided into deductive and reductive ones.

The definitions of these variants of assertive systems must be preceded by an explanation of the difference between deductive and reductive inference.

Deductive inference consists in accepting the consequent of a logically valid implication on the ground of having accepted the antecedent. Reductive inference, by contrast, consists in asserting the antecedent on the ground of having accepted the consequent of a logically valid implication. The latter type of inference is used e.g., in the natural sciences when, in verifying a hypothesis, one is induced to accept it on the basis of having ascertained that the consequences of that hypothesis are true.

Accordingly, an axiomatic system is assertive-deductive for the person X if X accepts both its axioms and its theorems, but first accepts the axioms and then derives the theorems from them and accepts the latter also.

On the other hand, an axiomatic system is assertive-reductive for the person X if X first accepts at least some of its theorems and is only afterwards induced to accept its axioms by reduction on the ground of those theorems. This does not preclude, moreover, that from the axioms grounded by reduction on certain theorems, X may later on derive some other theorems of the system.

According to the most common view the axiomatic systems of mathematics are assertive-deductive. The methodological structure of these systems is claimed to be the following: first of all, and independently of the acceptance of the theorems, the axioms are accepted; then, by way of deduction, one is brought to accept the theorems on the ground of having accepted the axioms. It must be stressed that it is the methodological, and not the meta-scientific, structure of the axiomatic systems that is being discussed here. If one examines their methodological structure, the problem is to discover the *proteron pros hêmas*, i.e. to discover which sentences are accepted first thus providing the motive for accepting others. On the other hand, if the meta-scientific structure of the systems is examined, the question is to find the *proteron tê physei*, i.e. to ascertain the basis from which the theorems are derivable in virtue of the rules of transformation or, in other words, the assumptions from which, by these rules, the consequence follows.

Apart from the view according to which the axiomatic systems of mathematics are assertive-deductive, there is another view, which considers them to be neutral-deductive. According to this latter view, a mathematician constructing his axiomatic systems accepts neither the axioms nor the theorems, but takes a neutral attitude towards both; he only considers them; what they express are not his convictions, but simply such states of mind which the Austrian philosopher Meinong used to call '*Annahmen*'. In deducing theorems from axioms, the mathematician – according to this view – effects not an actual, but only a potential deduction. His reasoning may be expressed as follows: if it were true that A, it would be true that B.

The assertive-reductive methodological structure is characteristic of those axiomatic systems which are used to formulate theories of natural science, such as mechanics, thermodynamics, electrodynamics, etc. The methodological structure of the system of electrodynamics, for example, is the following. Concrete experiments provide the premises; starting from these, we arrive, by induction, at universal empirical laws; from these laws we obtain theoretical principles, which are by no means the consequences of the former; on the contrary, empirical laws are consequences of the principles. Proceeding in this way we accept, by reduction, some fundamental principles from which all the subordinate theoretical principles and all the empirical laws are derivable, so that these fundamental principles constitute the axioms of the system, while the subordinate principles and the empirical laws are the theorems.

In philosophical literature one can meet with protests against attempts to give the form of axiomatic systems to theories of natural sciences. Those protests are based on the following argument: In axiomatic systems one begins by accepting the axioms from which then the theorems are deduced. By giving a theory of nature the form of such a system, one takes the basic principles of that theory as axioms and deduces its subordinate principles and empirical laws from these. Now this procedure reverses the order of accepting theses of any scientific theory of nature, which always begins by asserting the most subordinate empirical laws, from which later on, by induction or by reduction, all principles, including basic ones, are obtained. It can be seen that this argumentation mistakes the notion of a deductive system for that of a reductive one. All it shows is that a theory of nature must not appear under the form of a deductive system; but it does not at all show that it must not take the form of any axiomatic system whatever. In reality, a scientific theory of nature can have, and sometimes has, the form of an axiomatic system in the syntactic sense of the word, which means that some of its sentences have consequences that, taken as a whole, are identical with the entire theory. It can also have, and sometimes has, the form of an axiomatic system in the pragmatic sense of the word, namely that of an assertive-reductive system.

The problem of validation or justification arises in methodology not only with respect to the theorems but also with respect to the axioms of assertive-deductive systems. For in those systems one is brought to assert the theorems by deriving them, in virtue of certain rules, from the axioms. If this procedure is to secure the truth of the theorems to which it leads, it is first of all necessary that the rules of inference applied should be truth-preserving, i.e. such that they never lead from true premises to false conclusions; secondly, it is necessary that the axioms or premises from which the theorems are derived should be accepted not in an arbitrary fashion but by applying a method that also ensures their truth; this, in turn, means that they must be adequately founded or justified.

As we have already said, the fact that the theorems are derived from the axioms in virtue of truth-preserving rules confers validation on the theorems only if the axioms are not merely true but had also been validated. However, is it indeed necessary to validate axioms? Does it not follow from their very definition – as the sentences which are not derived from anything in the given system, but from which, on the contrary, all other sentences of the system are derived – that they need no validation? To dissipate this doubt, two kinds of validation must be distinguished: direct and indirect. Indirect validation consists in accepting a sentence on the basis of another one. In case of direct validation the ground for asserting a sentence is not the assertion of another sentence. If, for instance, I am stating at this moment that the sheet of paper in front of me is white, what convinces me of this fact is my perception of that sheet, and not the assertion of another sentence. Now the axioms of an assertive-deductive system are not validated indirectly by any other sentences of the same system. They can be validated indirectly only as theorems of another system, from whose axioms they are derivable. But even if they are derived from the axioms of another system, they are validated only provided the latter axioms are. As we see, the basis of any assertive-deductive system must, in ultimate analysis, be provided by the axioms which are not longer validated indirectly, i.e. are no longer inferred from other sentences, but whose validation is a direct one. Otherwise, we would either be involved in *regressus ad infinitum*, or base all our affirmations, ultimately, upon unfounded premisses, thus committing the fallacy of *petitio principii*. Consequently, the possibility of constructing an assertive-deductive system, whose theorems would be justified, unavoidably depends on the existence of a direct method of foundation.

In philosophical literature several methods of justification are presented as direct. One of these is associated with statements immediately based on perception and called observational sentences. The perception accompanying them is believed not only to motivate their assertion subjectively, but also to secure their truth. Recently the question has been raised whether there exist any observational sentences reporting 'pure facts' alone or whether every observational sentence is not already an interpretation of these facts, based not only upon the data of perception, but also upon previous knowledge, consequently upon certain asserted sentences. During the interwar period, the problem of observational sentences, or 'protocol sentences' as they were then called, was the object of a particularly animated discussion, in which their existence was generally doubted. It can be seen, therefore, that the problem of founding statements directly on the testimony of experience is highly controversial.

Philosophers who favour apriorism regard intuition as a method capable of directly justifying statements. This is questioned, in turn, by the adherents of empiricism. According to apriorists, besides sense experience in which particular objects and events alone are given to us, there is also experience through which we have knowledge of objects of higher order, such as universals, the so-called essences of things, etc. This other kind of experience was termed *'reine Anschauung'* by Kant, *'Wesensschau'* by Husserl. Others, who did not go so deeply into its analysis, called it intuition or simply self-evidence. As a method of direct foundation, it is called in question even more than sense experience.

Of all the methods of direct justification of statements, the least doubtful seems to be the third method, which consists in founding them upon terminological conventions. It can be described as follows: we decide that in the language we intend to use, a given term should denote an object satisfying a condition, formulated in a sentence which involves the same term. For instance, we decide that in the language of geometry, the terms 'point', 'straight line', 'contains' should denote elements satisfying the following condition: "If p and q are distinct points then there exists one and only one line containing p and q." On the basis of this decision, called terminological convention, the sentence in question is asserted. This method can be more generally represented in the form of the following schema: we decide that in the language which is being constructed, the term 'λ' should denote an object that satisfies the condition '$F(\lambda)$'. On the basis of this decision, called terminological convention, one arrives at asserting the sentence '$F(\lambda)$' in the language that one is constructing. A sentence asserted on the ground of such a convention is called a postulate.

Now, it is commonly believed that this method of asserting sentences on the basis of terminological conventions secures their truth in the language in which the conventions hold. For, since I have decided that the term 'λ', in the language that I am myself constructing, should denote a certain object (viz. one that satisfies the condition '$F(\lambda)$'), it is generally believed that this will be so, i.e. that the term will really denote such an object and that the sentence '$F(\lambda)$' will be true in the given language.

Thus the method of asserting sentences on the ground of terminological conventions seems to ensure the truth of these sentences. On the other hand, it seems to be a method of direct justification: To assert a sentence, no recourse is made to any other sentence as a premiss but only to a terminological convention; the latter is a decision, an act of will, the verbal statement of which is not an indicative sentence, affirming or denying something, but rather the following imperative sentence: "Let the term 'λ' denote an object that satisfies the condition '$F(\lambda)$'."

Consequently, since the method of arriving at a theorem on the ground of a terminological convention secures the truth of that theorem and, moreover, founds it upon no sentence as a premiss, one would be willing to consider it a method of direct validation.

It seems that many authors who reject the method of intuition believe that an assertive-deductive system can be constructed using nothing more than the method of terminological conventions (for directly founding the basic premisses which are not further proved) and that of deduction (for founding the theorems derived from these premisses).

We intend now to subject this view to criticism. We wish to demonstrate namely that the method of terminological conventions and of deduction do not suffice, by themselves, to validate any theorem; this means that by confining ourselves to these methods, we shall not be able to construct any assertive-deductive system consisting of validated sentences.

This follows from the fact that a terminological convention, stating that a given term 'λ' shall, in our language, denote an object that fulfils the condition formulated in the sentence '$F(\lambda)$', never suffices by itself as a validation for the truth of this sentence in our language; in other words, such a terminological convention may be valid in our language and nevertheless the relevant sentence may be false. This is so because our decision to make a term denote an object characterized in a specified way is not enough to make that term denote such an object. For if there exists no object to fulfil the condition '$F(\lambda)$' − in case, for instance, this condition is self-contradictory − then our decision does not suffice to make such an object the denotation of the term 'λ'. In fact, although we can decide to make every term denote any object we please, we cannot, for all that, create such objects by those same decisions. Hence it follows that to validate the postulate '$F(\lambda)$', one must use not only the convention by which λ shall satisfy '$F(\lambda))$', but also an existential premiss, stating that there is an object which satisfies this condition.

Consequently, the method of founding theorems on a terminological convention does not secure the truth of those theorems, unless they are also founded on a suitable existential premiss. Accordingly, if one were to confine oneself to the method of conventions and to that of deduction, one would possess no method of direct validation and would be committed either to the *regressus ad infinitum*, or to the use of unfounded premisses (i.e. the fallacy of *petitio principii*).

These considerations lead to the following conclusion: In order to be able to make justified assertions, consequently also to be able to construct assertive-deductive systems of validated sentences, one must possess a richer arsenal of methods than those of terminological conventions and of deduction alone. One must enrich that arsenal by adding a method of direct foundation to it, either that of experience or that of intuition, provided that these really are methods of direct foundation. Now, the method of experience is not well suited to validate the kind of axioms that usually appear in axiomatic systems. For, in general, such axioms affirm nothing that could be seen or heard. By the method of experience, one can at most validate the most remote consequences of the axioms. If, starting from these consequences one were to arrive by reduction at asserting the axioms, one would construct a reductive but not a deductive system. Consequently, the method of direct experience offers no prospect of constructing assertive-deductive systems of validated sentences.

There remains the method of intuition. It seems that to save the assertive-deductive system, which means saving the whole of our alleged knowledge a priori, we are constrained to rely upon this method. However, in many minds it provokes very far-going reservations, especially because of its lack of precision, because of the difficulty of controlling it, of the impossibility of settling the disputes between those who appeal to its testimony. If, under the influence of these reservations, one gives up this method, one ought also to renounce the possibility of constructing assertive-deductive systems, as well as all the knowledge called a priori.

Would such a renouncement amount to a catastrophe? It seems that the axiomatic systems of mathematics would lose nothing if they were constructed as neutral-deductive by the mathematicians and treated as assertive-reductive by the scientists who use them.

A certain doubt arises here, however. To construct neutral-deductive systems, sentences must be derived one from another by rules of deduction which, in turn, are based on the laws of logic. Consequently, is it not necessary to presuppose a system of logic, i.e. an assertive system (since it consists of asserted sentences) in order to construct any neutral-deductive system? We wish but to sketch this doubt and our intended answer. It is true that the theorems of logic are necessary to demonstrate that rules of deduction are truth-preserving. But to deduce sentences from one another, one need not prove that one is proceeding in accordance with truth-preserving rules. It is enough simply to proceed in conformity with such rules. Therefore, to construct neutral-deductive systems it is unnecessary to presuppose the theorems of logic. These are needed only for reflecting upon such systems from the methodological point of view, for instance for evaluating the correctness of their structure.

19. THE PROBLEM OF FOUNDATION *

(1963)

The concept of foundation or substantiation of a statement[1] seems to be essential for the methodology of sciences, which in its investigation of scientific statements is mainly concerned with the methods of their foundation and for which these methods form the *fundamentum divisionis* in the classification of the branches of science into deductive and inductive or into aprioristic and empirical, according to the methods of validation used.

It must be admitted, however, that in spite of its importance, the concept of foundation is by no means clear and precise. If we were asked what it means to substantiate a statement, at first we should perhaps be inclined to say that we substantiate a statement if we arrive at its assertion in the course of a procedure which assures the truth of the statement, in other words — using a method which always results in truth. This definition, however, is not only vague, but unsatisfactory in other respects. For it would classify most statements of science as unfounded, as none or hardly any are obtained in this manner. Therefore, we should, perhaps, modify our definition and say that a statement is substantiated if it is accepted as a result of a procedure which ensures either the truth of the statement or its high probability. Thus corrected our definition would still have undesirable consequences. We are not able to show that scientific methods, which result in the acceptance of statements — at least as we know them — ensure a high probability of these statements. What we can show is only that these methods increase the initial probability of statements, i.e., that these statements are more probable after the application of the methods than before. Since however, the initial probability of the statements remains unknown, we do not know if scientific methods, by increasing the unknown initial probability of the statements, make the latter thereby very probable, or more probable then their negations.

Both tentative definitions given above are unsatisfactory. Let us, however, say explicitly why. We did not criticize them from the formal point of view, though they may be unsatisfactory in this respect, too. We did not raise any

* Translated by Jerzy Giedymin. First published in *Studia Filozoficzne* (1963), No. 2, 4–13. Originally translated from the Author's manuscript. Reprinted here by kind permission of D. Reidel and PWN.

objection which would disqualify them as arbitrary conventions. What we did show was that by adopting the first definition we would commit ourselves to considering most scientific statements as unfounded, while by adopting the second, we would have to plead inability to recognize, which statements are founded and which are not, in an overwhelming majority of cases.

We want to understand the task of defining the concept of foundation in such a way that 'foundation' stands for those operations which result in the assertion of scientific statements by scientists, and we want our definition to indicate what is essential in those operations, i.e., what is responsible for the fact that the statements so obtained have the social status of scientific statements.

Our task is therefore the following:

We are confronted with science as an empirical fact, historical and social in character. In the history of mankind, it grew out of the practices of tribal magicians and sorcerers, from the speculations of philosophers and from the experience of practical life; its beginnings are difficult to delineate. Today, however, it appears distinct enough, though its limits are still blurred and will probably always remain so. For it comprises disciplines which vary in their scientific status, with mathematics and the exact sciences of nature forming its core and some of the humanities its outskirts.

Men of science are interested in the subject of their research and as long as they are concerned with it they speak an object-language. Science consists, however, in the collaboration of many, and it is inevitable that scientists should reflect upon the activity of their fellow-scientists. This they do using a meta-language, in which, among others, the term 'well-founded' or 'substantiated' occurs. A scientist will refer with this term to a statement which formulates the results of the research of one of his fellow-scientists, i.e., he will say that the statement was well-founded by the other, if applying the same procedure which led his fellow-scientist to its assertion, he himself will also be persuaded to assert the statement in question. In other words, a scientist will declare that the procedure which led the other scientist to the assertion of a statement substantiates this statement if the procedure applied by the other satisfies the criteria he himself respects in deciding whether or not to assert a statement. If the procedure of his fellow-scientist satisfies his own criteria, he will grant that the statement is well-founded and will himself assert it. If the procedure does not satisfy his criteria he will consider the statement as unfounded and will refuse to assert it, which, however, does not amount to his rejecting the statement and asserting its negation. Now a scientist may use the term 'founded' according to some criteria, but he is not concerned with defining those criteria. Therefore – it may be said – the term 'founded' has in the language of scientists an operational meaning, but it does not possess a definitional meaning.

Now, we understand the task of defining 'foundation' in such a way that we choose the operational concept of foundation, used by scientists, as our *explicandum* and want our definition to replace it by an *explicatum*. To put it in another way, we want to make explicit the criteria which govern the scientist's decision to assert statements which, moreover, have the property that, if satisfied by a procedure resulting in the assertion of a statement, this assertion will be acknowledged by the consensus of scientists as well-founded, and this procedure as its foundation.

The task formulated in this manner is a factual problem; it is not an attempt at making precise some vague, intuitive concept of foundation; even less is it a task undertaken to propose a convention how to use the term. This factual problem may only be solved by empirical observation and analysis of the procedure used by scientists. To give a precise description of the criteria or methods used in their scientific activity by scientists (who, as a rule, do not formulate them explicitly) is the central objective of empirical methodology. It seems to have given rise to logic and it dominated logical enquiry as late as the days of Mill and Jevons. Nowadays, the term logic is used rather to denote a mathematical discipline which originated from those enquiries, while the study of how science is actually being constructed is labelled the methodology or the philosophy of science.

However, is the above formulation of the objective of methodology unambiguous? Is there, in fact, a consensus among scientists as to which methods are appropriate for substantiating a statement? Is it not rather that one and the same method is considered by some scientists sufficient to render a statement well-founded (i.e., justifying its assertion) while others disagree? This surely happens, as is witnessed by controversies among scientists, some of whom may be ready to accept a given statement as well-founded while others are not. Disagreement of this sort is, however, temporary, and may be a symptom of temperamental differences; (some scientists exhibit a greater propensity to risk, while others are more cautious) or it may be indicative of the personal interest of one of the scientists, or of any other psychological or sociological motivation. In due time, the controversy will be resolved by the consensus of the community of those competent in the given branch of science. Anyway, there are many cases where no disagreement occurs and which may be studied in order to construct an empirical methodology.

Another objection that may be raised against the above programme of methodological inquiry is based on the claim that in different branches of science different methods are believed to justify the assertion of statements.

This is precisely why deductive and inductive sciences are distinguished, the former represented by mathematics and the latter by the natural sciences. This objection does not make our programme impracticable; rather it makes it imperative to study the differences in methods used in various branches of science and to distinguish various concepts of foundation.

Let us briefly summarize what has been said so far.

We understand the task of defining the concept of foundation as one that will be accomplished by a precise formulation of the criteria or methods which ought to be observed in any procedure terminating in the assertion of a statement, if the assertion so reached is to be acknowledged by scientists as justified and the procedure itself as its sufficient foundation (substantiation).

Has this task (someone may ask) not been accomplished already? Do we not know that in mathematics a statement is well-founded if and only if it has been derived by means of a deductive proof; in inductive science, on the other hand, those hypotheses are believed to be well-founded whose logical consequences have been sufficiently confirmed by the results of observation? Indeed, such claims have become trite by now; nevertheless we could hardly say that their meaning is clearly comprehensible. Do we in fact know what a deductive proof is that renders a statement well-founded? There exists, to be sure, a precise definition of the proof of a statement relative to assumptions and to rules of inference. However, we would not consider well-founded any statement which has been derived in the course of a proof from arbitrary assumptions and by virtue of arbitrary rules. Any statement may easily be derived by a proof from some assumptions by virtue of some rules. Nevertheless, a proof relative to some arbitrary assumptions and rules is not sufficient to render a statement well-founded, or justified in the sense in which mathematicians use these terms. The proof of a statement, from an assumption by virtue of some rules, is believed to constitute a deductive proof of the statement and to render it well-founded, only if the assumption and the rules have certain properties. Now we are faced with the problem: what properties are the assumptions and rules of derivation to possess in order that the proof based on them may become the *foundation* of a statement and justify its assertion by the representative of a deductive science? This is the problem of the proper choice of such axioms which, in the view of scientists, may be accepted without proof, and the problem of the choice of appropriate rules of inference. Different solutions of these problems have been proposed. The solution of the problem of the appropriate choice of axioms offered by the adherents of Platonism among methodologists differs from that offered by conventionalists. The third solution, proposed by radical empiricists, who believe the axioms of deductive science to be hypotheses founded on the conformity of their consequences with the results of observation, reduces deductive to inductive sciences; consequently, it cannot be classified as an attempt to describe the methods of substantiation of statements peculiar to deductive sciences. There is no problem of the foundation of statements in the deductive sciences for those who see these sciences as so-called hypothetico-deductive systems. In such systems nothing is being asserted, therefore there is no need to justify any assertions, nor is there room for the foundation of statements. Sentences are derived from other sentences or rather from sentential functions and thus a deductive apparatus is prepared for those who will find reason to assert certain values of those functions.

But even for those who hold that the deductive sciences are hypothetico-deductive systems, just as for all others, there is another problem: the problem of distinguishing appropriate rules of inference, i.e., such rules of derivation which the derivation of a statement must follow if it is to be accepted by mathematicians as a proof justifying the assertion of the statement in question, that is to say, as a foundation of the statement. Better solutions of this question are known than of any other associated with the problem of foundation. The solution was rendered by formal logic in its codification of the methods of inference given in mathematics. But even here the agreement reached is not perfect. There are, namely, many logics: there are multivalued logics alongside the bivalued one; there is the logic of material implication and the logic of strict implication; alongside the classical non-constructivist logic there is the constructivist logic of intuitionists. Which of them is respected by mathematicians when they prove their statements?

This *quaestio facti* is posed by empirical methodology for solution. Perhaps the answer will never state simply that all mathematicians always adhere to this and not to another logic in the course of proving statements, i.e., in the derivation of statements which justify their assertion. Perhaps they disagree in their choice of logic appropriate for the foundation of statements. If so, and this seems to be the case indeed, then empirical methodology ought to register this fact of disagreement among mathematicians as to when a statement is well-founded, and at a further stage of inquiry to subject those different methods of foundation to the so-called 'understanding analysis' in the Sprangerian sense of this term, which will be mentioned at the end of this lecture.

We see, therefore, that we are far from being able to say that the task of empirical methodology with respect to deductive science has been accomplished. To say that in deductive science a statement is well-founded if it has been derived in the course of a deductive proof, is not to say much, since we do not know exactly what is a deductive proof that in the mathematicians' opinion would justify the assertion of a statement, i.e. would constitute its foundation.

The state of our problem with respect to the inductive sciences is even less satisfactory. There we find at least two other concepts of foundation. It should be noted first of all that in deductive science 'substantiated' is a classificatory concept. A statement is believed to be substantiated if it has been deductively proved, otherwise it has no foundation at all. In the deductive sciences, to say that one statement is better substantiated than another or that a statement is now better founded than it formerly was, has no sense. The situation is different in the inductive sciences. Here, more and more positive results of the verification of a hypothesis entitle one to an ever-stronger assertion of the same hypothesis, which deserves the name of a better and better substantiated hypothesis. This shows that in inductive science we have a comparative concept of foundation, unknown in the deductive sciences. As a consequence, in inductive science there emerge such problems as e.g., the question: which testing procedure justifies in the opinion of scientists an increase in the strength of the assertion of a statement? or the question: when would scientists approve of a decision to assert one of several alternative hypotheses stronger than the others? The former question is concerned with the degrees of foundation of one and the same hypothesis, while the latter, with comparing the degrees of substantiation of alternative hypotheses. Many other questions involving the comparative concept of substantiation may be cited. Apart from this comparative concept of substantiation, inductive scientists appear to know also a classificatory concept of substantiation, though its existence may seem somewhat problematic. However that may be, this classificatory concept in the inductive sciences is different from that in the deductive sciences. In the latter a statement is founded if its absolutely positive assertion, precluding any thought of its being revocable, was the result of a procedure which in the opinion of mathematicians entirely justifies such an assertion. Statements so substantiated may be referred to as entirely substantiated or completely founded.

The theorems of the deductive sciences are their completely substantiated statements. Besides being completely founded, they have the property that competent opinion approves of their being publicly propagated in schools, from university chairs, in textbooks, and thereby, recommended as a guide to practical human activity.

Inductive science also yields statements which by the consensus of those competent are propagated as truths in schools, in universities and as guides to practical activities. These statements might also be referred to as theorems. But these 'theorems' of inductive science in contradistinction to deductive theorems are not completely founded. An entirely categorical assertion of these statements, such that its revocation would be inconceivable is not approved by competent opinion. The so-called theorems of the inductive sciences remain hypotheses forever; they are hypotheses which have successfully passed a long process of verification but the latter never terminates; it can always be extended, and we can never be sure that the outcome of verification will always be positive for the hypotheses.

Now the existence of the 'theorems' of inductive science in the sense of statements whose public dissemination in spite of their being hypotheses is approved of by competent opinion, seems to be an empirical fact. This fact generates a problem for empirical methodology, namely, what makes scientists distinguish these accepted statements from other hypotheses, incompletely asserted. What property must they possess for their public propagation to meet the scientist's approval? Here we encounter the classificatory concept of foundation, peculiar to inductive science and different from that of deductive science. Hypotheses, possessing the property that their public dissemination is approved of by scientists, may be said to be substantiated in this new sense of this term. It would be the task of empirical methodology to make explicit those criteria which distinguish the 'theorems' of inductive sciences in the sense explained above from other hypotheses. Is this criterion definable in terms of the comparative concept of substantiation, e.g., does it distinguish as asserted statements those hypotheses which are better founded than their negations? Or, perhaps, in order to make it explicit must we have recourse to a metrical concept of substantiation, and distinguish as asserted statements those hypotheses which are substantiated in a higher degree than a given limit? Or, perhaps, is any attempt at making explicit the criterion which guides scientists when they promote hypotheses to the status of asserted statements doomed to failure? Perhaps it is merely a question of the intuition of scientists who begin to believe strongly in a hypothesis as soon as its verification reaches a certain, unknown limit, if it conforms to the totality of their views, if it provides simple and elegant explanations of the so-called results of observation, etc. Were this the case, we should, perhaps, say that there does not exist a method capable of a verbal description and approved in the inductive sciences, of promoting hypotheses to the status of asserted statements; or to put it briefly, that a scientific method of induction does not exist. The last formulation would have to be made more precise.

Or can we exclude the possibility of doubting the very existence of 'theorems' of inductive science, i.e., of hypotheses which have successfully passed verification, however inconclusive but sufficient, in competent opinion,

to make their public dissemination advisable? Perhaps the scientific community only consents that a hypothesis, together with the report on the results of its
testing, be presented to the public, but does not commit itself to the assertion
of a hypothesis. This view would be an even more radical rejection of induction as a scientific method.

These are all *quid facti* questions. They are all concerned with ascertaining
the criteria which in fact govern the scientist's decisions to acknowledge
the assertion of certain statements as justified and the statements themselves as founded; or to be explicit, the criteria scientists adopt when they
consider the strengthening of the assertion of a statement as justified or when
they consider it justified to assert one statement more strongly than another.
It is only when these and similar questions are answered that we shall know
what the so-called scientific method is, or rather, which methods terminating
in the assertion of statements or in the strengthening of their assertion, etc.,
are approved of in science, in other words, which methods are scientific.

Again, it might be supposed that the codification of methods approved
of in the inductive sciences had been completed long ago. Does not every
textbook of methodology published over the last decades contain a list of
methods, such as the method of enumerative induction, the method of
inference by analogy, the method of the verification of hypotheses, the
methods of eliminative induction codified by Mill and many more? We may
seriously doubt, however, whether these are the methods we are interested
in. We are not concerned with making a list of methods which are in fact
applied in science, but with such methods, terminating in the assertion of
statements, which in the opinion of scientists actually do justify the assertion,
i.e., which substantiate the statements in the sense in which scientists
understand this term. Most methods described in the textbooks of methodology
do not belong here. As an example, let us consider enumerative induction. It
is certainly not unknown in science, and inductive inference may sometimes
be considered as furnishing foundation to a statement. Nevertheless, the
method of enumerative induction, as such, is not believed to be capable of
furnishing foundation. In other words, if by enumerative induction a conclusion is arrived at from legitimately asserted premisses, then this does not
constitute the foundation of the conclusion. Only certain particular cases of
enumerative induction are considered by scientists as substantiating statements.
Enumerative induction is considered capable of substantiation only if it results
in a universal conclusion that goes as little as possible beyond the given
evidence; otherwise, i.e., when the conclusions are more general, induction is
accused of yielding over-hasty generalizations. Or perhaps some other restric-

tion is necessary to make enumerative induction a method which furnishes substantiation.

Similar comments would probably apply to other methods listed in the textbooks of methodology as methods of inductive science. These methods are indeed used in science; it is, however, only with certain qualifications that they are considered by scientists as substantiating methods.

It is evident, then, that the descriptive task of empirical methodology has not yet been accomplished and awaits those ready to undertake it. The more so that, besides studying the restrictions which would turn the methods listed in the textbooks into those respected in science as substantiating, it is necessary also to study other procedures of science to make the list complete. In this respect empirical methodology may be assisted by the theory of mathematical statistics which in its inferential schemes reconstructs, consciously or unconsciously, some methods applied in science. As an example, I should like to quote the so-called principle of maximum likelihood, which is a variant of a method of choice of hypotheses used in science.

So far, I have discussed the descriptive task of empirical methodology. This is, however, not its only task. Having answered the *quid facti* question, i.e., which methods are considered in science as substantiating or as justifying the assertion of statements, empirical methodology asks the following question: what end may be attained by following in our assertion of statements the criteria whose satisfaction is necessary to obtain the scientist's approval, i.e., what end may be attained by following in our assertion of statements the rules of scientific method? We may also ask a more specific question; namely, having specified an end, we may ask whether, by following scientific methods in our assertion of statements, it is possible to attain this end. This is exactly what philosophers do when they ask, if by following scientific methods we may always or in most cases be sure of accepting a true statement. We know that the answer to this question is "no", and that it is mainly due to the fallibility of induction. This negative answer seems, however, premature as long as no rules of the scientific method of induction have been formulated. So far no one has succeeded in formulating such rules for the promotion of hypotheses to the status of accepted statements — and this is exactly what we mean by an inductive method — which would be approved of by scientists: we do not even know whether rules of this kind exist.

Were it the case, however, that by following scientific methods in the assertion of statements (in our decisions whether or not to assert statements) we should have no guarantee of the truth of statements, the question what end might be served by following scientific methods would be even more

interesting. An answer to this question would constitute a sympathetic understanding of science as a social phenomenon.

The above question has usually been considered in a purely academic
manner, i.e., by disregarding the fact that scientific procedure is interrelated
with other human activities. This one-sidedness was due to the lack of an
adequate analysis of the concept of assertion. The latter was regarded as a
peculiar attitude, known to everybody from introspection, but no analysis
in terms of behaviour was attempted. So far as I know, Peirce was the first
to comprehend the behaviouristic sense of assertion, though neither he himself nor his followers have succeeded in giving a precise definition of this
attitude in behavioural terms. Their main idea is as follows: the assertion
of a statement consists in our readiness to undertake an action which will
result in our loss, if the statement is false, but will result in our gain, if the
statement is true. The greater the loss resulting from our decision to act upon
the statement in case the statement is false, and the smaller the gain, in case
the statement is true, the stronger must be our assertion of the statement, if
we are ready to take the decision to act. Assertion in terms of behaviour
is reduced, therefore, to our readiness to choose a course of action. Thus:
the methods we follow in order to arrive at the assertion of statements,
are methods of deciding which course of action to choose. These methods
may be evaluated according to their effectiveness as means to some end.
From the same viewpoint we may evaluate methods of arriving at the assertion of statements, i.e., scientific methods.

The above remarks emphasize the pragmatical point of view in the evaluation of scientific methods. This is precisely the viewpoint of mathematical
statistics in evaluating the methods of statistical inference, which some prefer
to refer to as methods of decision-making. It has proved to be fruitful
there. One may suggest, therefore, that one should follow the same approach
in general methodology. Having this in view we have formulated the subject
of our conference as "The problem of the foundation of statements and of
decisions".

I should now like to conclude my talk. But before I end, I wish to add a
few words to explain the intention I had in presenting this paper. I did not
intend to solve any problem, nor did I want to explain concepts. My intention was to give an outline of the problems of foundation as I understand
them. I do not pretend to have formulated the problems with sufficient
clarity; they are barely outlined. I hope, however, that by the very sketchiness
of its character and by the diversity of the problems mentioned, my talk has
succeeded in alerting the participants of the Conference intellectually on

many points, and so may serve as an introduction to the discussion of specific problems with which other speakers will deal in detail.

NOTE

[1] [The problem of the foundation of statements and of decisions was the subject of the International Methodological Colloquium, Warsaw, September 18–23, 1961. This is the text of the inaugural speech delivered at the Colloquium.]

20. THE PROBLEM OF EMPIRICISM AND THE
CONCEPT OF MEANING*

(1964)

The Problem of Empiricism and the Concept of Meaning[1]

The expression 'the problem of empiricism' may be understood in various ways. In the present context I shall mean by 'the problem of empiricism' the question 'Are there a priori judgments?' The negative answer to this question is the thesis of radical empiricism. The positive answer to the question is shared by moderate empiricism, according to which only analytic judgments may be a priori, and by apriorism, according to which there exist also synthetic judgments a priori. The answer to the question 'Are there a priori judgments?' depends, of course, on how one understands the terms involved, in particular on how one understands the term 'judgment' and the predicate 'a priori'. We shall begin our inquiry with the clarification of the meanings of these terms.

By judgment we shall mean the meaning which a declarative sentence has in the given language. The term 'declarative sentence of the language *L*' may be defined in various ways: semantically, as an expression which has a truth-value in *L*; syntactically, as an expression which has a certain structure; pragmatically, as an expression which expresses in the given language the mental phenomenon of asserting a state of things; misunderstandings are not likely to arise from this, however. The case of the term 'meaning' is different since one may understand it differently depending on one's conception of language.

The various conceptions of language and the various concepts of 'meaning' associated with them, will be outlined presently. In doing this we shall aim at showing that the answer given to the question 'Are there a priori judgments?' will depend on one's conception of language. This will be the main thesis of the present article.

---

* Translated by Jerzy Giedymin. First published in *Studia Filozoficzne* (1964), No. 1, 3–14. Translation based on *Język i Poznanie*, II, 388–400. Reprinted here by kind permission of PWN.

THE PROBLEM OF EMPIRICISM AND THE CONCEPT OF MEANING

There are two versions of the problem of empiricism. I shall refer to one as epistemological and to the other as methodological. The epistemological problem is concerned with the question whether knowledge is attained by asserting judgments on the basis of experience. If a positive answer is given to this question then the next question is whether knowledge is attained only by asserting judgments on the basis of experience. If this question is answered in the negative, then we ask under what conditions judgments asserted without reference to experience constitute knowledge. These questions are usually formulated ambiguously, e.g. as follows: Is there knowledge based on experience? Is there only knowledge based on experience? What kinds of knowledge based on experience exist? These formulations are ambiguous since, for instance, the question 'Is there knowledge not based on experience?' may be understood as either *questio facti*, i.e. 'Is it the case that we assert judgments without consulting experience?', or as *questio iuris*, i.e. 'Do we have the right to assert judgments which are not based on experience?', or – in other words – 'Is the assertion of judgments which are not based on experience legitimate?' or 'Is the assertion of judgments without appeal to experience justifiable?'.

Only on the second, i.e. *quid iuris* interpretation of the question of the existence of non-empirical knowledge the question itself is an epistemological problem. If the problem is understood as a *quid facti* question, then we are within the domain of empirical psychology. The mentioned ambiguity is avoided if instead of asking whether there is knowledge not based on experience we ask whether the assertion of judgments without appeal to experience may contribute to knowledge. One should realize, however, that the term 'knowledge' which occurs in this question has for an epistemologist not only a descriptive but also an evaluative meaning. For 'knowledge' does not simply consist in the assertion of judgments; it is justified or legitimate assertion of judgments.

This being so, it is the epistemologist's duty to clarify the concept of knowledge he uses, i.e. the concept of justified or legitimate knowledge. How difficult this task is, we know from our recent experience. For we have spent a great deal of effort at two conferences, one national and another international, on the clarification of this concept, without – unfortunately – making much progress.

This question is, however, not essential for the methodological version of the problem of empiricism. For a methodologist observes and analyses the procedure whereby scientists assert judgments and elevate them to the status of accepted theses; he notices that there are two varieties of that procedure, one of which he calls a priori and the other empirical. The methodologist tries to characterize both varieties as precisely as possible without, however, attempting to do what was essential for the epistemologist, i.e. without attempting to evaluate each of the two varieties of the procedure. In other words the methodologist does not consider the question whether the a priori or the a posteriori assertion of judgments deserves the honorific title of knowledge, i.e. whether only one or both these methods are able to justify judgments. The question which he attempts at first is this: Are, as a matter of fact, both the a priori and the a posteriori methods used by scientists? So formulated this is a *questio facti*, similar to the one which we have already classified as belonging to empirical psychology. However the task of giving an account of the actual procedure used by scientists to assert judgments is hopelessly difficult. The difficulty lies not only in the fact that to achieve this task one would have probably to read a vast amount of scientific publications and conduct an equally wide-ranging questionnaire survey of scientists; it lies moreover in the fact that in many cases the interviewed scientist is unable to answer the question whether he accepts a given theory on the basis of experience or does so a priori. This can be seen from frequent disputes among scientists over the question whether certain laws of nature, e.g. the law of inertia, the law of conservation of energy, are generalizations of observed facts or are merely based on terminological conventions which establish the meanings of terms.

These difficulties should be sufficient, I believe, to deter methodologists from attempting the question whether in science conceived as a historical fact all theories are based on experience or whether some of them are accepted a priori. This descriptive question, which concerns the actual state of things, may — however — be replaced by another question of a speculative nature, viz. the question whether it is possible to construct science in such a way that no theories are accepted a priori but all are based on experience. It is this problem whether all a priori elements may be eliminated from science that constitutes the methodological version of the problem of empiricism.

Before this question is considered, however, it will be necessary to clarify the concepts which are essential for its understanding, among other things, to clarify what is meant by an a priori and what by an empirical thesis. By a thesis I mean here an asserted judgment and by a judgment the meaning of a sentence, or — more precisely — such a meaning that an expression endowed with it is a sentence. No explication of the term 'meaning' is given here since it would depend on the conception of language not to be prejudged yet. Nor do I explicate here the term 'assertion' which may be understood either psychologically, as a certain mental attitude, or else in a neutral way, as the property of a judgment which consists in the fact that the judgment in question is incorporated into the system of science, in other words, becomes a thesis of science. In the rest of this paper I shall have the former, psychological interpretation of assertion in mind, though I would like my analysis to remain both meaningful and useful on the other, neutral interpretation of assertion. Whether this proves possible, I do not know.

I shall begin by clarifying what it means to say that a thesis, i.e. the assertion of a judgment has an a priori character. An a priori assertion may be either directly a priori or indirectly a priori. The assertion of a judgment is directly a priori if it is the assertion of a judgment which may be accepted but which cannot be rejected under any circumstances. This definition of the directly a priori nature of the assertion of a judgment resembles definitions of immediately a priori statements (also known as self-evident statements) familiar from the history of philosophy. According to the latter a statement is self-evident if one cannot conceive that things could be otherwise than stated in it. 'Das Nichtandersdenkenkönnen', 'the inconceivability of the opposite', these are expressions with the help of which philosophers used to explicate the meaning of 'self-evident' or 'immediately a priori' whenever they attempted to go beyond a purely negative definition according to which a statement is a priori if it is legitimately accepted but without an appeal to experience. However, most philosophers understood the impossibility of the rejection of a self-evident judgment as a factual impossibility. Man cannot reject a judgment meant: man's mind is such that he cannot believe that things could be otherwise. Moreover, this was not meant to be the impossibility which affects one individual's thinking but may not affect another's. The impossibility was claimed to affect all humanity since its origin was sought in so-called human nature, common to all people. Hence self-evident judgments were regarded as universally valid (allgemeingültig, in German). This is perhaps why apriorism was usually associated with epistemological idealism according to which the objects of knowledge were restricted to the products of the human mind, i.e. to so-called intentional objects.

The impossibility of rejecting the directly a priori judgments may also be understood, however, in a different way, i.e. not as factual (man's inability to conceive that things could be otherwise) but as logical impossibility. To say that the rejection of a judgment J is logically impossible is to say that the supposition that someone rejects J involves a contradiction. Now, there is a conception of language according to which with respect to certain judgments one can show that the supposition that any of them is being rejected involves a contradiction. We have defined judgment as the meaning of a sentence in a language. To reject a judgment J means to reject the sentence S whose meaning is J in the language which we use while rejecting S. In other words, to reject a judgment J means to reject the sentence S while regarding at the same time J as the meaning of S.

According to the conception of language mentioned before, there is a strict relationship between the meaning in which one uses the sentences of the language and the rules which govern one's acceptance or rejection of those sentences.

For example, if we were to meet someone who gives a negative answer to the question 'Does every square have four sides?', i.e. who seriously rejects the sentence 'Every square has four sides', we would regard this behaviour as an infallible indication that the person in question does not attach to the given sentence its usual meaning in English. For one associates with the sentence 'Every square has four sides' the meaning appropriate to it in English only on condition that one does not reject that sentence under any circumstances. Sentences which can never be rejected if they are understood in the sense they have in the given language, may be called the axioms of the language.

Now, given these assumptions it is easy to show that the supposition that somebody rejects a judgment which in the language L constitutes the meaning of an axiom of L, involves a logical contradiction. For to reject a judgment J_A which constitutes the meaning of the sentence A in the language L, is to reject also the sentence A understood in the sense which it has in L. If the sentence A is an axiom of L, then to reject A means not to understand it in the sense which it has in L. Hence to reject the judgment J_A which constitutes the meaning of A in L when A is an axiom of L, would mean to reject the sentence A taken in its appropriate sense in L (since otherwise the rejection of the sentence A would not amount to the rejection of the judgment J_A) and not taken in its appropriate sense (for otherwise the sentence A would not be an axiom of L). This shows that to suppose that someone rejects the judgment which is the meaning of an axiom of a language is to make a contradiction. For the supposition implies (1) that whoever rejects such a judgment rejects also a sentence whose meaning is that judgment in the given language, (2) that the sentence is then being used in the sense which it has in the given language and that it is not so used.

So, given the conception of language under discussion, the judgments which constitute the meaning of the axioms of the language have the property that while they can be accepted it is impossible to reject them; the impossibility, moreover, is not a factual one, resulting from the peculiar nature of the human mind: it is a logical impossibility which results from the structure of the language.

This is what we wished to say regarding the clarification of the concept of a directly a priori assertion of a judgment.

Let us turn now to the clarification of the concept of an indirectly a priori assertion of a judgment. The assertion of a judgment is indirectly a priori if this assertion occurs in the conclusion inferred from directly a priori premisses in an argument-chain, each argument of which is conclusive (compelling). I call an argument conclusive (or compelling) if it is impossible for anyone to accept the judgments asserted in its premises and not to accept the judgment asserted in its conclusion. Again this terminology resembles the terminology of traditional philosophers. The assertion of judgments indirectly a priori corresponds to their assertion of judgments mediately evident, 'mittelbar evident'; they regarded as mediately evident assertions obtained from immediately evident premises with the help of — what they called — compelling inference (in German 'ein zwingendes Schlussverfahren').

The impossibility of rejecting the conclusion while the premises are accepted may again be understood here as factual impossibility which originates from the nature of the human mind. On the other hand, given the conception of language discussed before, the impossibility in question may be understood as logical impossibility: the supposition that anyone might accept the judgments asserted in the premises of a compelling argument while rejecting its conclusion, results in a logical contradiction.

For according to that conception of language it is believed that to use the sentences of a language in the sense they have in the language it is necessary not only to refrain from the rejection of the axioms of the language under any circumstances; it is claimed, moreover, that if anyone were to accept sentences of a certain form and were at the same time to reject sentences of a form related in a certain way to the form of accepted sentences, his behaviour would show that he did not attach to the sentences the meaning which belongs to them in the language in question. For example, if anyone accepts the sentence of the form 'If today is Sunday, then tomorrow is Monday' as well as the sentence 'Today is Sunday' and at the same time rejects the sentence 'Tomorrow is Monday', his behaviour is an indication of the fact that presumably he understands those sentences not in the sense which they have in English. Again, if anyone accepts the sentence of the form 'Some birds are birds of prey' and at the same time rejects the sentence 'Some birds of prey are birds', he indicates thereby that he does not understand those sentences as they should be in English. If the acceptance of the sentence A and simultaneous rejection of the sentence B indicate that the sentences are not being used in the sense appropriate to them in the language L, then we shall say that B directly (or immediately) follows from A in L (or that B is a direct consequence of A in L).

Now let us assume that B follows directly from A in the sense just mentioned. It can be shown on this assumption that the supposition that someone accepts the judgments J_A which is the meaning of the sentence A in L while rejecting the judgment J_B which is the meaning of the sentence B in L, results in a contradiction. For to accept the judgment J_A and to reject the judgment J_B means to accept the sentence A and reject B, both understood in the sense which they have in L. Since, however, B follows directly from A in L, it means that whoever accepts A and rejects B, does not attach to those sentences the meaning they have in L. If B follows directly from A in L, then whoever accepts judgment J_A and rejects judgment J_B, would have – in accepting A and rejecting B – to take both in the sense they both have in L (for otherwise when accepting A and rejecting B he could not accept judgment J_A and reject judgment J_B); on the other hand, whoever accepts A and rejects B cannot possibly take them in their appropriate meaning, for B follows directly from A in L.

So we see that according to the conception of language under discussion the supposition that someone accepts judgment J_A assigned to the sentence A as its meaning, while rejecting judgment J_B, assigned to B as its meaning, implies a contradiction, if B follows directly from A in L. On this conception it is logically impossible for anyone who accepts judgment J_A to reject judgment J_B, provided B follows directly from A in L and J_A and J_B are assigned in L as meanings to sentences A and B respectively. If B follows directly from A in L, then the argument (inference) leading from the acceptance of J_A to the acceptance of J_B is a conclusive (compelling) one. Hence, if from the assertion of judgment J_A the assertion of judgment J_B were derived in a finite number of argument-steps, each of which links judgments corresponding in L to sentences linked in L by the relation of direct consequence (i.e. if each step in the argument chain is compelling), then the assertion of judgment J_B would be indirectly a priori.

According to the above outlined conception of language there exist in every language sentences which cannot be rejected without thereby violating meanings which they have in the language. Such sentences we call the axioms of the language. So-called axiomatic rules of language determine those sentences which cannot be rejected without thereby violating their meaning. Furthermore, according to the same conception of language, in every language some of its sentences follow directly from others (the former are direct consequences of the latter), i.e. one cannot reject certain sentences (without violating their meaning) if one accepts others. So-called deductive rules of language determine those sentences which follow directly from others in the sense just clarified. It should be clear that the conception of language we are now concerned with ensures in every domain of thought in which such a language is used (hence also in every science) room for the assertion of both the direct a priori and for the indirect a priori judgments. Directly a priori will be the assertion of judgments which constitute the meaning of the axioms of the language; indirectly a priori — the assertion of judgments inferred from the direct a priori ones with the help of an argument chain each argument of which links the assertion of such premises to the assertion of such a conclusion that the relation of direct consequence holds between the sentences corresponding to them in the language.

Let us now turn our attention to the definition of empirical knowledge. Its analysis is much more difficult than the analysis of a priori knowledge. One of the fundamental difficulties concerns the question whether in order to define empirical knowledge one should first define an isolated empirical assertion or rather an empirical system of assertions. This is related to the question whether in an empirical system there exist any irrevocable basic elements which support the whole theoretical superstructure and uniquely determine it, or whether one can erect this superstructure in one way or another, rejecting previously accepted basic elements and replacing them, for the purpose of supporting a new superstructure, by others, different but equally acceptable ones. This controversial issue is associated with the names of Duhem and Poincaré and with their dispute over the relation between facts and hypotheses and over the difference between facts and their interpretations. This exciting methodological problem, discussed in Poland in the nineteen-thirties by Wundheiler and Poznanski, has unfortunately not been analysed by any of our logicians or methodologists since. It is in my view well worth investigating.

In the present sketchy analysis I shall take the traditional viewpoint, according to which there exist irrevocable, basic assertions of empirical knowledge, viz. so-called perceptual assertions. These constitute our direct (immediate) empirical knowledge. The indirect empirical knowledge consists of the assertions of hypotheses which have been adquately verified by their direct empirical consequences.

We shall have to analyse more closely the procedure of testing hypotheses through their consequences. The procedure consists, as we know, in deriving from the hypotheses (usually in conjuction with additional assumptions) consequences which are then confronted with experience. We are here interested in the question in what way are the consequences to be derived from the hypotheses. Is it the same way which has to be used to infer a judgment from immediately a priori premisses in order to make its assertion mediately a priori? In other words, is it to be a process of deriving judgments from other judgments of which every step is a compelling argument? It is generally believed that it must be so.

Given the conception of language according to which in every language there are so-called axiomatic rules distinguishing the axioms of the language (those sentences which cannot be rejected without violating the meaning of the sentences) as well as so-called deductive rules (prohibiting the rejection of certain sentences as long as one accepts certain other sentences) the question of deriving consequences from hypotheses is simple. The consequences must be derived from hypotheses (and possibly other assumptions already accepted) in conformity with the deductive rules of the language. The deductive rules of the language are determined by the choice of the language made by us and cannot be changed except by the transition to another language. Moreover it would have to be a transition to a language not translatable into the given one, since a translatable language is based on rules which the dictionary transforming one language into the other maps isomorphically on to rules of the original language.

On the conception of language under consideration not only the a priori knowledge but also at least a part of empirical knowledge (viz. the indirect empirical knowledge) is at least partially determined by the choice of the language of science, which choice is however independent of experience. .

Until now we have discussed the concepts of the a priori and empirical knowledge from the viewpoint of a conception of language according to which in every language there are axiomatic rules, distinguishing those sentences which cannot be rejected without the violation of their meaning, and deductive rules determining the relation of direct consequence between sentences in such a way that it is impossible (without the violation of meaning) to accept a sentence and reject its consequence. Apart from presenting that conception of language, however, we have also indicated its consequence relevant to the problem of methodological empiricism. The consequence states that every science which uses a language is bound to contain a priori knowledge and that even in empirical knowledge there are elements determined by language and independent of experience.

To the majority of my audience today it is no secret that the conception of language which I have so often mentioned here was developed by myself in the nineteen-thirties, mainly in my treatises 'On the Meaning of Expressions'[2] and 'Sprache und Sinn' (Language and Meaning)[3].

Since then many changes have occurred in my views. At that time I claimed that between the meaning of expressions and the rules of meaning (this is the common name of the axiomatic and deductive rules apart from which I also distinguished at the time so-called empirical rules) two relations hold. I believed that the meaning-rules are invariant under the exchange of synonymous expressions, i.e. the meaning-rules remain unchanged if the name of one or two synonymous expressions is replaced in them by the name of the other expression. I also claimed that the inverse relation holds, for I was inclined to believe that if the meaning-rules are invariant under inter-change of certain expressions, then those expressions are synonymous.

These two assumptions made it possible for me to give the definition of the equality of meaning of two expressions, according to which two expres-sions are synonymous in the language L if and only if the meaning-rules of L are invariant under the interchange of those expressions, in other words, if the meaning-rules of the language say the same things about both expressions.

That definition of meaning may be easily criticized if the meaning-rules are restricted to the axiomatic and deductive rules. Let us consider a language whose axiomatic rules dictate the unconditional acceptance of the axioms of the functional calculus with identity and of the following two axioms:

$$A \neq B$$
$$B \neq A$$

where A and B are new primitive constants. Let the deductive rules of the language be the inference rules of the functional calculus with identity.

It is easy to see that the meaning-rules of the language under consideration are invariant under interchange of A and B. Hence my definition of equality of meaning would imply that A and B are synonymous. However, according to the axioms $A \neq B$ and $B \neq A$ the two terms have different denotations. This shows that in the language in question one could have two synonymous terms with non-identical denotations, a consequence which seems unac-ceptable.

This objection which soon after the publication of 'Language and Meaning' was communicated to me by Tarski in a conversation, seems to me unanswerable at least with respect to languages whose only rules are axiomatic and deductive ones. It also seems to show that the concept of meaning is not definable in purely syntactical terms without the use of semantical terms in the narrower sense.

However, the objection in question undermines only the thesis according to which the invariance of meaning-rules is sufficient for the synonymity of two expressions; it does not affect the converse of the thesis, viz. the claim that the invariance of meaning-rules is necessary for synonymity.

I continued, therefore, to hold the thesis according to which the meaning of expressions of language determines its meaning-rules (hence it is impossible to change meaning-rules without thereby altering the meaning) though I have given up its converse (i.e. the meanings of expressions are determined by the meaning-rules). On this basis I was inclined to defend the view according to which since every science uses a language there are inevitably a priori elements in every science.

In particular I rejected as untenable Łukasiewicz's claim according to which experience will decide the choice between the two-valued logic and the many-valued logics constructed by him. I believed that the axioms of logic are determined by the language which we use and that the choice of a language or of the conceptual apparatus associated with it must precede any experience. I believed, for example, that one cannot expect experience to decide whether the law of contradiction, or the law of the excluded middle are true. In order to refute the law of contradiction, experience would have to induce us to accept both a sentence and its negation. However, were we to accept two sentences of the form 'p' and '$-p$', we would admittedly accept two sentences of the form which two contradictory sentences have in English but these two sentences would not be synonymous with any two contradictory sentences in English; for in English there is an axiomatic rule to the effect that in order to use the symbol of negation in the sense it has in English it is necessary not to accept two sentences one of which results by prefixing the other with the negation sign.

I think I held this view on the a priori nature of logic until 1947 when I noticed that as a factual account of how this or that person uses the negation sign and other logical constants, my view is perhaps true but that logical terms need by no means be assigned a meaning such that they are governed by the axiomatic sense rules prohibiting the rejection of the axioms of logic on pain of violating their meaning. In other words, without prejudging the question of the methodological status of the axioms of logic in actual science, I came to the conclusion that there is nothing to prevent one from constructing science in a language in which the axioms of logic are not dictated by the rules of the language, provided there are in it deductive rules distinguishing certain forms of inference to be observed on pain of violating the meaning of expressions. If science were formulated in such a language then the axioms of logic could be regarded as hypotheses indirectly based on experience through the empirical testing of their consequences derived in virtue of the deductive rules of the language. It has been known for some time that in verifying a scientific hypothesis consequences are derived not from the hypothesis alone but from several laws belonging to the theory within which the testing is conducted. Strictly speaking, however, in the procedure of verifying hypotheses we make use not only of those scientific laws but also of the laws of mathematics and logic to greater or lesser extent, depending on how rich is the apparatus of the deductive rules of our language. What is regarded as the confirmation of the tested hypothesis, in fact is the confirmation of the conjunction of all those assumptions, among them the laws of logic used as premises in deriving consequences. Whatever confirms the hypothesis to the same extent confirms other assumptions, among them the laws of logic.

As we see, a minor change in the conception of language which results in the admission of languages with only deductive and no axiomatic rules, made possible an essential change in my view of the methodological problem of empiricism. By allowing the elimination of axiomatic rules, my answer to that question turned out to be as follows: it is possible for science to have such a methodological structure that there will be no a priori scientific judgments.

However, this transition from the position of methodological apriorism to that of empiricism appeared to me half-hearted. There remained deductive rules which − though not themselves accepted statements of science − are nevertheless independent of experience and completely determined by the language used to construct science. And surely our system of indirect empirical knowledge depends to a large extent on what deductive rules there are. In order to free scientific knowledge completely from the choice of language, it was necessary to abandon deductive rules as well. This would mean complete abandonment of that conception of language which I have recalled here. In the absence of deductive rules as meaning-rules, the procedure of testing hypotheses would contain (apart from statements tested) as an additional element, to be accepted or rejected, the rule of inference used in deriving consequences. If conflict arises between the statement of the theory and direct experience, consistency might be restored not only by modifying the statements of the theory but also by changing the rules of inference and yet without transition to a different language, i.e. without the change of meanings of expressions.

A new conception of language was, however, required to adopt this radical empiricist position. The previous conception, with the meaning-rules whose violation amounts to the violation of the meaning of expressions, was intended to clarify the difference between what an expression denotes and what it means. For, as we know, two expressions may have identical denotations and yet different meanings. For example, the term 'a polygon with 9 diagonals' and the term 'a polygon whose angles add up to 720°', denote the same, viz a hexagon, but they have different meanings. I saw the difference in their meaning in that different meaning-rules apply to each of them. If one denied the sentence 'a polygon with 9 diagonals has 9 diagonals' one would violate the rules of the language; on the other hand, no violation of the rules of language would result from denying the sentence 'a polygon whose angles add up to 720° has 9 diagonals'. Language rules are not invariant under the interchange of these two different terms which have identical denotations, and this constitutes the difference in their meanings, the identity of denotation notwithstanding.

By giving up meaning-rules as an essential feature of a language I could no longer characterize in that way the difference between the meanings of two expressions which have the same denotation.

Three years ago a new conception of meaning occurred to me which one may use to attempt the solution of that problem in a different way. I presented in outline the new theory of meaning in 1958 at a meeting of the Warsaw Section of the Philosophical Society but have not published it yet. My new conception is similar to Mill's. One may even regard it as a development and explication of the latter. Having distinguished the meaning of an expression from its denotation Mill reduces meaning to its connotation. I have introduced the concept of co-denotation of an expression and propose to identify co-denotation with the meaning of the expression.

I have defined the concept of co-denotation in terms of the concept of denotation and the concept of the syntactical position which in a composite expression is occupied by its constituent expressions. Syntactical positions are, for example, the positions of the main functor, the position of its first argument, etc. I find in this way a definition of the meaning of expressions, as distinguished from the denotation of an expression, without using the idea of meaning-rules and without committing myself to those consequences which my previous conception of meaning had for the methodological problem of empiricism.

However, the new conception of meaning when applied to simple expressions faces certain difficulties which will be only briefly mentioned here. One may try to avoid those difficulties in one of two ways. One of them is the position of intensionalism which claims, among other things that two properties may be different though every object and only the object that has one of them has also the other. The other way would mean the return to the conception of meaning-rules. It would again imply certain consequences with regard to empiricism. I do not find either of the two ways attractive. I am searching for a third solution which would involve the restitution of meaning-rules but not as rules whose violation alters the intersubjective meaning expressions have in a language shared by different people; rather it would be the restitution of the meaning-rules whose violation alters the subjective meaning which expressions have for particular individuals. I believe that the restitution of meaning-rules in this role will have no implications for the methodological problem of empiricism.

I am aware of the fact that these words do not communicate much to my audience. However there is not enough time to explain what I have in mind. I have taken the liberty to say a few words about the last stage in the development of my views in order to complete, however sketchily, the account of the evolution of my conception of meaning and of my position, associated with it, concerning the methodological problem of empiricism.

NOTE

[1] [The text of the paper 'The Problem of Empiricism and the Concept of Meaning' read by K. Ajdukiewicz on Feburary 18th, 1962 at the conference organized to celebrate his 70th birthday, is preceded here by a fragment of an article, under the same title, on which Ajdukiewicz was working just before his death, and which has remained unfinished – Editor.]

[2] [This volume, p. 1.]

[3] [This volume, p. 35.]

21. INTENSIONAL EXPRESSIONS*

(1967)

1. Intensional expressions can be either expressions containing free variables or expressions which do not contain such variables. An expression E, which contains no free variables, is an intensional expression if it can be transformed into a non-equivalent expression E' by replacing one of its constituents by an expression which is equivalent with that constituent.

An expression E, which contains one or more free variables, is an intensional expression if two non-equivalent expressions can be obtained from it by substituting for each of the variables two different but equivalent constant expressions. As is known, expressions which are not intensional are called extensional.

The sentence 'Newton knew that $8 > 5$' (Z_1) may be given as an example of an intensional expression (for a certain interpretation of its syntactic structure). For if in that sentence we substitute for '8' the equivalent expression 'the atomic number of oxygen', we obtain the sentence 'Newton knew that the atomic number of oxygen > 5' (Z_2). The first of these two sentences (Z_1) is true, and the second (Z_2) is false, which means that they are not equivalent, although the second is obtained from the first by substituting for '8' the equivalent expression 'the atomic number of oxygen'.

An example of an intensional expression containing a free variable is the formula 'Newton knew that $x > 5$', because we obtain from it non-equivalent sentences (Z_1) and (Z_2) by substituting for the variable respectively the expressions '8' and 'the atomic number of oxygen', which are equivalent.

The notion of an intensional expression has been defined here in a general way, so that it can be applied to expressions belonging to different semantic categories. We may thus speak of intensional sentences, intensional predicates, intensional operators, etc. The most disturbing problem, however, is that of intensional sentences and intensional sentential formulae, and only these will be the subject discussed in the main part of this paper.

Intensional sentences are primarily sentences which resort to so-called indirect speech, e.g. 'John believed that ...', 'John said that ...', etc. Further,

* Revised translation by David Pearce. First published in *Studia Logica* **XX** (1967), 63–86. Reprinted here by kind permission of PWN.

sentences which include so-called modal terms, such as 'it is necessary that ...', 'it is possible that ...', etc., are also considered intensional sentences. For various reasons, chiefly those of time limits, only sentences which make use of indirect speech will be discussed in this paper.

2. Two terms used in the definitions given above require additional explanations, viz. the terms 'equivalent expressions' and 'a constituent of an expression'.

An expression A is equivalent with an expression B either if A and B are proper names of the same object, or A and B are sentences having the same logical value, or A and B are (non-binding) operators with the same number of arguments, and such that these operators form equivalent expressions when combined with equivalent arguments.

We assume that all expressions between which the relation of equivalence may hold have some objective reference which will be called their denotation, and further, that two equivalent expressions denote the same thing.

In particular, we assume that the denotation of a proper name is the object named by it, and the denotation of a sentence is its logical value, i.e., truth or falsity. As far as non-binding operators are concerned, we assume that the denotation of an operator of n arguments is the relation of $n+1$ arguments, holding between the denotations of its arguments and the denotation of the expression which that operator forms jointly with its arguments.

As for the term 'a constituent of an expression', we say that an expression A is a constituent of zero order of the expression B if A is the same as B. In other words, every expression is its own constituent of zero order.

An expression A is called the first order constituent of an expression B if A is the main operator in the expression B or if A is an argument of that operator.

In general: the expression A is a constituent of the $n+1$th order of the expression B if A is a first order constituent of an nth order constituent of the expression B.

An expression A will be called simply a constituent of an expression B if it is a constituent of any order of the expression B.

The following notation will be used to indicate the syntactic position occupied by a constituent in a given expression:

The syntactic position occupied by a given expression in itself will be marked with the figure 1. To indicate the syntactic position of other constituents the following principle will be adopted: if the position occupied by the expression A in the expression E is symbolized by m, the syntactic position occupied in the expression E by the main operator of the expression

A will be symbolized $(m,0)$, and the position occupied by the nth argument of that operator will be symbolized (m,n). For instance, in the following expression the syntactic positions of its constituents of different orders will be indicated thus:

$$
\begin{array}{ccccccc}
2 & + & 3 & = & 6 & - & 1 \\
(1,1,1) & (1,1,0) & (1,1,2) & & (1,2,1) & (1,2,0) & (1,2,2) \\
 & (1,1) & & (1,0) & & (1,2) & \\
 & & & 1 & & &
\end{array}
$$

3. It must be emphasized that for an expression to be intensional it is not enough that it can be transformed into a non-equivalent expression by replacing any of its parts by an equivalent expression, but it is necessary that the part to be replaced should be a constituent of the expression so, for example, the true sentence

$$5 + 3 . 4 = 17$$

changes into a false one if its part

$$5 + 3$$

is replaced by the equivalent expression

$$2 + 6$$

because the sentence

$$2 + 6 . 4 = 17$$

is false. Yet the sentence under discussion is not intensional: the transformation performed did not consist in the replacement of any of its constituents.

The point just mentioned is essential for further analysis. An expression will qualify as an example of an intensional expression only if its part whose replacement transforms it into a non-equivalent expression is one of its constituents. Now the syntactic structure of colloquial expressions, from among which examples are usually drawn, is not sufficiently unequivocal to allow only one way of dividing an expression into its constituents. If an expression can be dismembered in two different ways, such that in one case the expression must be considered intensional but not in the other case, then by making more precise the language which determines its syntactic structure we may choose a syntactic structure which avoids intensionality. In this way we may free our language from intensional expressions.

4. There are several reasons for which it may be desirable to free our

language from intensional expressions, in particular from intensional sentences and sentential formulae.

Some of these reasons will be recalled here, and attention will be drawn to some others, which — as far as I know — have been disregarded up till now.

First of all, the presence of intensional formulae in a language prevents us from adopting Leibniz's definition of identity. The definition in question is as follows:

$$a = b \leftrightarrow \prod_{.F} \{F(a) \leftrightarrow F(b)\}.$$

If there exists an intensional formula $\ulcorner F_1(x) \urcorner$, then there exist two expressions a and b such that $a = b$ and yet $\sim \{F_1(a) \leftrightarrow F_1(b)\}$, which is in contradiction with the above definition.

Furthermore, every extensional sentential formula with one variable establishes a correspondence between the value of that variable and the logical values, viz. truth for those values of the variable which satisfy the formula, and falsity for those which do not. In other words, every extensional sentential formula $\ulcorner (... x ...) \urcorner$ determines a functional relationship

$$(... x ...) = t$$

in which the variable $\ulcorner x \urcorner$ is the independent variable ranging over the entire universe of a suitable order, and the variable t is the dependent variable which may take the values truth or falsity. This means that every extensional sentential formula determines a class of those values of the variable x for which the formula becomes true. This fact is reflected in the rule, adopted in the logical systems based on type theory, which permits us to state for any sentential formula $(... x ...)$ that

$$\sum_f \{f(x) \equiv (... x ...)\}.$$

Now in contrast to extensional formulae, which always determine functional relationships between the values of the variable and truth or falsity, intensional formulae determine no such functional relationship.

Let us consider, for instance, the intensional formula

$\ulcorner$Newton knew that $x > 5\urcorner$.

This formula does not establish any correspondence between a definite value of the variable $\ulcorner x \urcorner$ and a definite logical value. For instance, in the case of the number '8' the formula turns either into truth or into falsity depending on which name of this number we choose. Thus, an intensional formula does not determine any class of values of the variable which satisfy that formula. Consequently, if the formula

$$\ulcorner(\dots x \dots)\urcorner$$

is an intensional one, then it is not true that

$$\sum_f \{f(x) \equiv (\dots x \dots)\},$$

or in another formulation:

$$\sum_f \{(x \in f) \equiv (\dots x \dots)\}$$

i.e. it is not true that there exists a class f to which belong all those, and only those, objects which satisfy the formula

$$\ulcorner(\dots x \dots)\urcorner.$$

It follows from the above that any logical system in which for any sentential formula $(\dots x \dots)$ the equivalence

$$\sum_f \{f(x) \equiv (\dots x \dots)\},$$

holds, confines the range of sentential formulae to extensional formulae and justifies this restriction by the rule of extensionality.

It seems that what we have just said requires a revision of the prevalent view that the presence of intensional formulae in a language prevents us from adopting Leibniz's definition of identity. Leibniz's definition

$$a = b \leftrightarrow \prod_F \{F(a) \leftrightarrow F(b)\},$$

is formulated exclusively in the object language and does not refer to any expressions, in particular to any sentential formulae.   The quantifier $\prod_F$ should not be read 'for any predicate F', but rather at object-language level, 'for any class F' or 'for any property F'. Now, in the light of what has been said before, the introduction into a language of intensional formulae does not lead to the introduction of new classes or properties, since – as we have just seen – no classes correspond to intensional formulae. This means that if

$$\ulcorner(\dots x \dots)\urcorner$$

is an intensional formula, then it is not true that

$$\sum_f \{(x \in f) \equiv (\dots x \dots)\}.$$

Hence, in conformity with Leibniz's definition, a may be identical with b, i.e. the name $\ulcorner a \urcorner$ may denote the same object as the name $\ulcorner b \urcorner$, in spite of the fact that there exists an intensional sentential formula $\ulcorner(... x ...)\urcorner$ which becomes true when the name $\ulcorner a\urcorner$ is substituted for the variable $\ulcorner x\urcorner$, and becomes false when the name $\ulcorner b\urcorner$ is substituted for the variable $\ulcorner x\urcorner$.

The third peculiarity of intensional expressions, on account of which they are suspect, is the following.

It seems obvious that the denotation of a compound expression which, apart from first order constituents, has constituents of the second and possibly of still higher orders, cannot change as a result of a change in the denotation of a constituent of a higher order if the change does not involve a change in the denotation of lower order constituents. In other words, the denotation of an expression of the form

$$F\{a, \varphi[\chi(b), c]\}$$

cannot change as a result of a change in the denotation of the constituent b (here a constituent of the third order) if such a change does not involve a change in the denotations of the second order constituents $\chi(b)$ and of the first order constituents $\varphi[\chi(b), c]$. For within expressions there is no *action at a distance* which could make a constituent influence some other constituent, separated from it by constituents of intermediate orders, without causing any changes in those intermediate constituents.

Extensional expressions comply with this obvious principle which, however, is violated by certain expressions if they are syntactically interpreted as intensional expressions.

If we take, for instance, the sentence 'Caesar knew that the capital of the Republic lies on the Tiber' and interpret it syntactically as shown by the brackets below: {Caesar} knew that {[the capital (of the Republic)] lies on [the Tiber]} we see that it will be an intensional sentence because from a true one it changes into a false one when its constituent

'[the capital (of the Republic)]'

is replaced by an equivalent constituent

'[the capital (of the Popes)]'.

In other words, the sentence quoted above changes its logical value when its third order constituent '(of the Republic)' is replaced by the expression '(of the Popes)'. The change in the denotation of the third order constituent resulting from such a replacement brings about a change in the denotation of the entire expression, that is, also of the zero-order constituent, although it does not influence the denotation of the intermediate, second order constituent 'the capital of the Republic', or of the intermediate, first order constituent 'the capital of the Republic lies on the Tiber'.

The fact that the obvious principle, mentioned above, which excludes *action at a distance* between constituents of expressions is violated by certain expressions if their syntactic structure is interpreted so that these expressions become intensional, raises misgivings about such a syntactic interpretation of their structure and induces one to search for some other interpretation of their syntactic structure, for which the principle in question will neither be violated, nor will it be possible to consider such expressions as intensional ones.

5. Such are the motives which may induce us to try to eliminate from our language intensional expressions, and in particular intensional sentences and sentential formulae. We shall now consider the problem of how to eliminate them. It has been stated above that intensional sentences appear in the form of sentences which make use either of such indirect speech phrases as 'said' or such psychological terms as 'thought', 'knew', etc., connected with indirect speech. Moreover, it seems that those sentences which include modal terms are also intensional sentences.

Now we can avoid intensional sentences and sentential formulae by eliminating from our language those indirect speech phrases, psychological and modal terms which give rise to intensionality. This is the way mathematics avoids intensional sentences and sentential formulae: it does not introduce those phrases or terms into its language.

It would be implausible to suggest such a radical measure for ordinary language for the elimination of all those terms would deprive it of the means of expression which its practical function requires.

There is, however, another method of eliminating intensional expressions from the language, a method which does not demand giving up all statements to the effect that someone thought, or believed that something is so and so, or statements saying that something is necessary or possible. This other method, already hinted at above, consists in interpreting the syntactic structure of sentences in a way different from the one which makes them intensional.

This is precisely our task in this paper. We want, firstly, to show the possibility of such a syntactic construal of sentences regarded as intensional, for which they are no longer intensional. Furthermore, we want to analyse the meaning of those allegedly intensional sentences in order to show that a syntactic interpretation which deprives them of their intensional character is in conformity with the meaning of those sentences. As mentioned before, the analysis given in this paper will be confined to sentences with psychological terms.

6. As an example of a sentence, which for a certain interpretation of its syntactic structure is intensional, we take the sentence (Z_1):

> '{Caesar} believed that {[Rome] lies on [the Tiber]}'.

This sentence is intensional because if the word 'Rome', which is one of its constituents, is replaced by an equivalent expression, viz. 'the capital of the Popes', then the sentence changes its value from truth to falsity. It has been suggested that the sentence in question will no longer be intensional if it is interpreted as expressing a certain attitude of Caesar towards the sentence 'Rome lies on the Tiber', rather than towards what is stated by the sentence. This interpretation implies that Caesar believed in the sentence 'Rome lies on the Tiber'. As a result, intensionality disappears. Nevertheless, one would be reluctant to adopt this interpretation because the interpreted sentence (Z_1) 'Caesar believed that Rome lies on the Tiber' is true, whereas the sentence 'Caesar believed in the sentence "Rome lies on the Tiber"' is false (since Caesar did not know English and hence did not believe in any English sentence).

The following interpretation will be free from this objection:

(Z_1^t) Caesar believed in a sentence which is a translation of the English sentence 'Rome lies on the Tiber' into some other language.

This present interpretation does not substitute any false sentence for the true sentence (Z_1), but is not satisfactory, because for the sentence (Z_1), which is an object-language sentence, it substitutes the sentence (Z_1^t), which is a metalinguistic sentence. In the sentence (Z_1), 'Caesar believed that Rome lies on the Tiber' we are clearly dealing with Caesar's mental attitude with regard to Rome, the relation of lying on, and the Tiber, but not with Caesar's attitude towards some verbal entity. Our aim is to give such an interpretation of the object-language sentence (Z_1) and of other sentences of this type which would itself be an object-language sentence but no longer intensional. We shall attempt such an interpretation through the analysis of the interpretation (Z_1^t), which refers to the notion of translation.

To begin with, what does it mean to say that an expression A is a translation of an expression B from the language L_1 into the language L_2? First of all, let us note that the language L_1 need not be different from the language L_2, so that it is not only about two expressions belonging to different languages that we may say that one is a translation of the other; we may also say this about two expressions belonging to the same language. To simplify our formulations we shall hereafter disregard relativization to a particular language. This can easily be added if required.

To define the notion of translation we shall not refer to the notion of meaning, in particular, we shall not say that an expression A is a translation of an expression B if both these expressions have the same meaning; such a definition would burden the notion of translation with all those obscurities which are connected with the term 'meaning'. Our definition of translation will be based on the notions of denotation and of syntactic position.

Before we define the notion of translation we must realize that one may speak of translations of varying degrees of precision, more or less literal.

We say that an expression A is a literal translation of an expression B if, and only if, after the resolution of all the abbreviations which they contain, they are transformed into two abbreviation-free expressions A' and B', such that there is a one-to-one correspondence between all the constituents of one expression and the constituents of the other expression; moreover, the constituents between which such a correspondence is established, (1) occupy in A' and B', respectively, the same syntactic positions, and (2) are reciprocally equivalent, i.e., they denote the same object.

We say that an expression A is a translation of nth degree of an expression B if A and B are reciprocal literal translations provided their constituents of orders higher than nth are disregarded, i.e. if their constituents of nth order are treated as simple constituents.

More precisely: an expression A is a nth degree translation of an expression B if, and only if, after the resolution of all the abbreviations which they contain they are transformed into two abbreviation-free expressions A' and B', such that there is a one-to-one correspondence between all the constituents of nth and lower orders of each expression; moreover, if the constituents between which such a correspondence is established (1), occupy in A' and B', respectively, the same syntactic positions and (2) are reciprocally equivalent, i.e. they denote the same object.

It can be seen from these definitions that a literal translation of an expression A is the same as its translation of the highest degree of precision possible for a given expression, i.e. its translation of the degree equal to the highest order shared by the constituents of the expression A.

We shall illustrate this by the following expressions:

(A)	$2 + (3 \cdot 5)\ \ = 3 + (2 \cdot 7)$
(B)	$2 + (5 + 10) = 3 + (10 + 4).$

We assume here that the single symbols which appear in A and B are not conventional abbreviations of any compound expressions. It can easily be verified that these expressions are reciprocal translations of zero-degree, for each expression is its own constituent of zero-order. Thus by establishing a one-to-one correspondence between the expression A and the expression B we establish a one-to-one correspondence between the constituents of zero-order of these two expressions; moreover, these constituents (1), occupy respectively the same syntactic positions, viz. the positions occupied by each of these expressions themselves, and (2), are reciprocally equivalent since both are true sentences.

If we establish a one-to-one correspondence between the first order constituents of the expressions concerned:

$$
\begin{array}{ll}
A & B \\
= & = \\
2 + (3 . 5) & 2 + (5 + 10) \\
3 + (2 . 7) & 3 + (10 + 4)
\end{array}
$$

we also establish a one-to-one correspondence betwen zero and first order constituents such that (1) the constituents between which this correspondence is established occupy in A and B, respectively, the same syntactic positions, and (2), are reciprocally equivalent, since they denote the same objects.

It can be easily seen that the expressions A and B are reciprocal translations of second degree; if the above correspondence between constituents of zero and first order is supplemented, as below,.by a one-to-one correspondence between second order constituents:

$$
\begin{array}{ll}
A & B \\
2 & 2 \\
+ & + \\
(3 . 5) & (5 + 10) \\
3 & 3 \\
+ & + \\
(2 . 7) & (10 + 4)
\end{array}
$$

we obtain a one-to-one correspondence of constituents of zero, first and second order, such that the constituents between which this correspondence is established, (1), occupy in A and B, respectively, the same syntactic positions, and (2) denote the same objects.

However, the expressions A and B are not reciprocal translations of third degree; for if we establish a one-to-one correspondence between the third order constituents (of these expressions), which occupy the same syntactic positions:

A	B
3	5
.	+
5	10
2	10
.	+
7	4

we find that they are not reciprocally equivalent.

Since the expression A is not a third degree translation of the expression B, whereas the highest order which the constituents of these expressions can have is the third order, the expression A is not a literal translation of the expression B.

Similarity between the definition of literal translation, given above, and Carnap's definition of intensional isomorphism (*Meaning and Necessity*, first ed., p. 56) can easily be noticed. The difference between these two definitions consists above all in the fact that Carnap requires that if two expressions are to be intensionally isomorphic then their constituents occupying respectively the same positions must be L-equivalent, whereas our definition is in terms of ordinary extensional equivalence.

To prepare the way for an answer to the question, whether sentences of the type (Z_1), 'Caesar believed that Rome lies on the Tiber', remain intensional if they are interpreted as (Z_1^t), 'Caesar believed in some translation of the sentence "Rome lies on the Tiber"', the following analysis will be given.

Every sentence is characterized by a correspondence between its syntactic positions and the expressions which occupy those positions. Since each such expression has a definite denotation, every sentence is characterized by a correspondence between the syntactic positions of its constituents and certain definite objects. As an example, let us consider the sentence 'Rome lies on the Tiber'. Its constituents are assigned syntactic positions as follows: (1), its main operator (1,0), the first argument of that operator (1,1), the second argument of that operator (1,2); the whole sentence is therefore characterized by the following correspondence:

(1) – Verum, (1,0) – the relation of lying on, (1,1) – Rome, (1,2) – the Tiber.

Let the correspondence, characteristic for a given sentence, between the syntactic positions of all its constituents and those objects which those constituents denote, be called the full content of the sentence.

It can easily be seen that all the sentences which are literal translations of the same sentence have the same full content. For, in conformity with the definition of literal translation, the sentences which are literal translations of the sentence A have in their individual syntactic positions expressions with the same denotations as the expressions occupying the corresponding syntactic positions in A. We may say, therefore, that a literal translation of a sentence A is identical with a sentence which has the same full content as the sentence A.

Let the correspondence between the syntactic positions occupied in the sentence A by simple expressions and the objects denoted by those simple expressions be called the basic content of the sentence A. Now, to determine unequivocally the full content of a given sentence it suffices, except for some cases which will be discussed later on, to give the basic content of that sentence. In other words, if the denotations of the simple expressions contained in a sentence are given, then the denotations of the compound expressions contained in that sentence as its constituents are thereby unambiguously determined. For instance, the denotations of the simple expressions which appear in the sentence

$$2 + 3 = 5$$

– i.e., the expressions '2', '+', '3', '=' and '5' – determine the denotations of the compound expressions which are its constituents, i.e., its first order constituent '2 + 3', and the denotation of its zero-order constituent, hence of the entire sentence itself.

However, this is not always the case. It is not the case when the sentence Z is itself an intensional expression or contains an intensional expression as its constituent. For intensional expressions are characterized by the fact that the denotations of their constituents do not unequivocally determine the denotation of the expression formed from those constituents. Thus the claim that the basic content of a sentence unequivocally determines its full content is applicable only to those sentences which are neither intensional expressions nor include such expressions among their constituents.

It has been stated above that a literal translation of a sentence Z is identical with a sentence which has the same full content as the sentence Z. It has also been stated that as far as sentences free from intensional constituents are concerned, they have the same full content if and only if they have the same basic content. Consequently, with respect to sentences free from intensional constituents, we may say that a literal translation of a sentence Z is identical with a sentence which has the same basic content as the sentence Z.

The sentence 'Rome lies on the Tiber' (which hereafter will be written in the abbreviated form 'R l T') does not include intensional constituents. Therefore a literal translation of the sentence 'R l T' is a sentence which has the same basic content as the sentence 'R l T'. But the basic content of the sentence 'R l T' is the correspondence between the syntactic positions occupied in that sentence by certain words and the objects denoted by those words. Consequently, the basic content of the sentence 'R l T' = the set of ordered pairs: $(1,1)$ – Rome, $(1,0)$ – the relation of lying on, $(1,2)$ – the Tiber; or in an abbreviated form:

$$[(1,1) - R,(1,0) - l,(1,2) - T].$$

It follows from the above that instead of

(t) 'a literal translation of the sentence 'R l T' '

we may say

(c) a sentence with the basic content $[(1,1) - R,(1,0) - l,(1,2) - T]$.

Let it be recalled, for the sake of avoiding any misunderstandings, that the basic content of a sentence is the correspondence between the syntactic positions in that sentence and the objects denoted by the simple expressions occupying such syntactic positions in that sentence. It is not the correspondence between the syntactic positions and the words which occupy them. The correspondence between the syntactic positions in a sentence and the words which occupy them is sufficient for an unequivocal description of that sentence. This is why such a correspondence between the syntactic positions in a given sentence and the words which occupy them will be called the basic description of that sentence. The basic description, for example, of the sentence 'Rome lies on the Tiber' is the following correspondence: $[(1,1) -$ 'Rome', $(1,0)$ – 'lies on', $(1,2)$ – 'the Tiber']. Consequently the basic description of a sentence should not be confused with the basic content of that sentence. In the former, a correspondence is established between the syntactic positions and the words which occupy them, in the latter, between the syntactic positions and the objects denoted by the words occupying their respective positions.

Let us now draw attention to the following fact which is of essential importance for further analysis. The expression (c) is extensional. In particular, it does not change its extension if its constituents 'R', 'l', 'T' are replaced by other equivalent expressions. Thus, for instance, the class of sentences with the basic content $[(1,1) - R,(1,0) - l,(1,2) - T]$ is identical with the class of sentences with the basic content $[(1,1) -$ the capital of the Popes, $(1,0) - l,(1,2) - T]$. The former includes sentences which in the syntactic position $(1,1)$ have some simple expression denoting Rome, and the latter, sentences which in $(1,1)$ have some simple expression denoting the capital of the Popes. But since Rome is the same as the capital of the Popes, this means that each and only those expressions which denote Rome denote *eo ipso* the capital of the Popes.

7. What has been said above will now be used to expand the previous interpretation of the sentence

(Z_1) 'Caesar believed that R l T'

as

(Z_1^t) 'Caesar believed in a translation of the sentence 'R l T'.

Attention has been drawn to the fact that when we speak about translations we may mean translations of different degrees of precision. It seems that the interpretation (Z_1^t) can appear correct only if by 'translation' we mean 'literal translation'. So we reformulate our interpretation as

$(Z_1^t lit)$ 'Caesar believed in a literal translation of the sentence 'R l T'.'

But a literal translation of the sentence 'R l T' is the same as a sentence with the basic content

$$[(1,1) - R, (1,0) - l, (1,2) - T],$$

and this leads to the following version of our interpretation:

(Z_1^c) 'Caesar believed in a sentence with the basic content $[(1,1) - R, (1,0) - l, (1,2) - T]$.'

There is an essential difference between $(Z_1^t lit)$ and (Z_1^c). To understand this let us state first that the expression " 'Rome lies on the Tiber' ", built of single quotes " ' ' " and the sentence contained therein, was used as an abbreviation of the following expression:

"the English language sentence in which the position $(1,1)$ is occupied by the word 'Rome', the position $(1,0)$, by the word 'lies on' and the position $(1,2)$, by the word 'the Tiber'."

Making use of the term 'the basic description of a sentence', introduced above, we may say that the expression

'Rome lies on the Tiber'

was treated as an abbreviation of the expression

'the English language sentence with the basic description $(1,1)$ − 'Rome', $(1,0)$ − 'lies on', $(1,2)$ − 'the Tiber'.'

Consequently, after resolving the abbreviation contained in the quotation marks, the interpretation $(Z_1^t lit)$ may be written as follows:

$(Z_1^t lit)$ Caesar believed in a translation of the English language sentence with the basic description: $(1,1) -$ 'Rome', $(1,0) -$ 'lies on', $(1,2) -$ 'the Tiber',

(where the quotation marks enclosing the inscriptions 'Rome', etc., are to be understood as ostensive names of those inscriptions).

The interpretation (Z_1^c) has the form:

(Z_1^c) 'Caesar believed in a sentence with the basic content: $(1,1) -$ Rome, $(1,0) -$ lies on, $(1,2) -$ the Tiber.'

In order to understand clearly the difference between the formulations $(Z_1^t lit)$ and (Z_1^c) we must briefly explain the quoting expressions which appear in $(Z_1^t lit)$ and which are built of the quotation marks and the words contained therein.

Quotation marks may play various roles. One of them was explained above. The quotation marks which appear in the formulation $(Z_1^t lit)$ play a quite different role: here they cannot be treated as an operator which together with the word which it contains as its argument forms the name of the name of the object denoted by that word. In other words, we may not assume that for instance

'Rome' = the name of Rome.

For the extension of the term on the right-hand side of the equation includes such expressions as 'urbs aeterna', 'the capital of Italy', etc., since both the first and the second expression quoted above is a particular name of Rome. Yet these expressions do not belong to the extension of the left-hand side of the equation since neither of them is the word 'Rome'. The quoting expressions must here be treated like ostensive names which consist of an indicating gesture and the object which that gesture indicates. Here the quotation marks play the role of the indicating gesture, and the inscription which they contain is the object which it indicates. And as the ostensive name, which consists of the indicating gesture and the object indicated by it, is one simple word, and not an expression composed of an operator and an argument, so the quoting expression is not an expression with a compound syntax, but one simple word of which the word contained in the quotation marks is a physical part, but not a syntactic constituent. The inscription inside the quotation marks, which on other occasions may be used as a separate word, is part of the entire quoting expression in the same way as 'lack', which also may be used as a separate word, is part of the word 'lackey'. But as in the word 'lackey' the inscription 'lack' does not appear as a separate word, so that inscription which appears in a quoting expression does not function as a separate word but only as a physical part of one simple word.

If the quoting expressions which appear in the formulation $(Z_1^t lit)$ are understood in this way, then we must conclude that $(Z_1^t lit)$ does not include the word 'Rome' as its constituent. Suppose we decide to transform $(Z_1^t lit)$, by replacing some of its constituents by other expressions, into:

$(Z_1^t lit)$ Caesar believed in a translation of the English language sentence with the basic description: (1,1) – 'the capital of the Popes', (1,0) – 'lies on', (1,2) – 'the Tiber'.

We might do this only by replacing the quoting expression " 'Rome' " by the quoting expression " 'the capital of the Popes' ". But one sees immediately that these quoting expressions are by no means equivalent since one of them is a name of an inscription quite different from the other. By drawing attention to this fact we ward off the invasion of intensionality, since the word 'Rome' does not appear as a constituent of a supposedly intensional sentence in the case of the interpretation $(Z_1^t lit)$.

However we cannot get rid of intensionality in the same way if we adopt the interpretation (Z_1^c), since in that interpretation the word 'Rome' appears as a constituent of the sentence and not as part of a quoting expression. And this is just the difference between the interpretation $(Z_1^t lit)$ and the interpretation (Z_1^c). In the latter, the words 'Rome', 'lies on', and 'the Tiber' appear as constituents of the sentence; a certain relation between Caesar and the objects denoted by those words is stated. Thereby, the interpretation (Z_1^c) better suits our purpose, i.e. finding an object language interpretation, rather than a meta-linguistic interpretation, of the sentence (Z_1) 'Caesar believed that Rome lies on the Tiber'. The interpretation (Z_1^c) is still not quite satisfactory since it retains a certain meta-linguistic aspect: reference is made to the fact that Caesar recognized a certain sentence. Yet it comes nearer to our objective since it refers to Rome, to the relation of lying on, and to the Tiber, and not to any names of those objects. In the concluding part of our analysis we shall see that the meta-linguistic component can easily be eliminated. Before proceeding to that point, however, we shall demonstrate that the interpretation (Z_1^c) is not an intensional sentence.

8. Let us bear in mind that the intensional character of (Z_1) 'Caesar believed that Rome lies on the Tiber' was proved by stating that: (Z_1) is a true sentence, but if we replace its constituent 'Rome' by its equivalent expression

'the capital of the Popes' (hereafter abbreviated as '$c(p)$'), we obtain the sentence:

(Z_2)   'Caesar believed that the capital of the Popes lies on the Tiber',

which is false. This shows that the sentence (Z_1) is intensional.

Let us see whether a similar proof may still be used when the sentence (Z_1) is replaced by its interpretation (Z_1^c), and the sentence (Z_2), by its interpretation (Z_2^c). Now if in the sentence

(Z_1^c)   'Caesar believed in a sentence with the basic content: $[(1,1) - R,(1,0) - l,(1,2) - T]$'

the constituent 'R' is replaced by its equivalent expression '$c(p)$', we obtain

$\overline{(Z_1^c)}$ 'Caesar believed in a sentence with the basic content: $[(1,1) - c(p),(1,0) - l,(1,2) - T].$'

Now, as stated above, the class of sentences with the basic content: $[(1,1) - R,(1,0) - l,(1,2) - T]$, is identical with the class of sentences with the basic content: $[(1,1) - c(p), (1,0) - l,(1,2) - T]$. Consequently, both the sentence (Z_1^c) and the sentence $\overline{(Z_1^c)}$ state about the same class of sentences that Caesar believed in a sentence belonging to that class. Therefore, if (Z_1^c) is true, than $\overline{(Z_1^c)}$ is also true. The sentence (Z_1^c) does not change its logical value, i.e., its denotation, if one of its constituents is replaced by another, equivalent expression. Consequently, there are no reasons to consider that sentence to be intensional.

Let us further take note of the fact that the sentence $\overline{(Z_1^c)}$, obtained from (Z_1^c) which – in conformity with the recognized principles of interpretation – is an explication of the sentence (Z_1), may not, in conformity with those principles, be interpreted as an explication of the sentence (Z_2). For in the sentence

(a)   'the capital of the Popes lies on the Tiber'

the syntactic positions occupied by the simple words are: $(1,1,0)$, $(1,1,1)$, $(1,0)$, $(1,2)$. To obtain the basic content of that sentence we require that a correspondence be established between all those syntactic positions and the objects denoted by the words occupying those syntactic positions in that sentence. Consequently, the basic content of the sentence (A) is as follows: $(1,1,0)$ – the capital, $(1,1,1)$ – the Popes, $(1,0)$ – lies on, $(1,2)$ – the Tiber. Therefore, in conformity with the principles we have adopted, the sentence (Z_2) is interpreted as

(Z_2^c) 'Caesar believed in a sentence with the basic content $(1,1,0) - c,(1,1,1) - p,(1,0) - l,(1,2) - $ T'.

Firstly, (Z_2^c) is false since Caesar never believed in any sentence containing a word denoting the Popes, because he was not aware of that notion at all. On the other hand, $\overline{(Z_1^c)}$ is true. Secondly, $\overline{(Z_2^c)}$ includes as one of its constituents the expression '$c(p)$' ('the capital of the Popes'), whereas (Z_2^c) does not contain any such constituent. This reveals the basic idea of our method of eliminating the intensionality of sentences of the type 'x believes that ...'. It will be more evident still when we proceed to analyse another course of reasoning intended to demonstrate the intensional character of certain sentences.

Let us start from the sentence not analysed so far:

(Z_2) 'Caesar believed that the capital of the Popes lies on the Tiber',

and let us replace in it the expression 'the capital of the Popes' by the equivalent expression 'the capital of the Republic'. We thus obtain the sentence

(Z_3) 'Caesar believed that the capital of the Republic lies on the Tiber'.

Now (Z_2) is false, and the sentence (Z_3), obtained from it by means of substituting one equivalent expression for another, is true. Thus, in this way (Z_2) changes its logical value, i.e., its denotation. Consequently, (Z_2) is an intensional sentence.

How is this argument affected if we apply to the sentences (Z_2) and (Z_3) our principles of interpretation? (Z_2) will then take on the form:

(Z_2^c) 'Caesar believed in a sentence with the basic content: $(1,1,0) - $ the capital, $(1,1,1) - $ the Popes, $(1,0) - $ lies on, $(1,2) - $ the Tiber',

and (Z_3^c) will appear as:

(Z_3^c) 'Caesar believed in a sentence with the basic content: $(1,1,0) - $ the capital, $(1,1,1) - $ the Republic, $(1,0) - $ lies on, $(1,2) - $ the Tiber'.

Now (Z_2^c) does not include as one of its constituents the expression 'the capital of the Popes'; it has among its constituents only the simple words 'the capital' and 'the Popes'. Consequently, if we replace in (Z_2^c) the expression 'the capital of the Popes' by the expression 'the capital of the Republic', we do not replace any constituent of (Z_2^c) by its equivalent; we merely replace a loose string of words of the sentence (Z_2^c), which is not a constituent of that sentence, by its equivalent. In this way we proceed as if we replaced in the sentence

(C) $5 + 3 . 2 = 11$

the expression '5 + 3' by its equivalent, e.g., '1 + 7' and thus obtained the sentence

(D) $1 + 7 . 2 = 11$

Therefore, on replacement of one equivalent by another, we passed from a true sentence to a false one, but this fact does not in the least prove the intensional character of the sentence in question. For a sentence is intensional only if it can change its logical value on replacement of any of its constituents, and not just of any string of words, by its equivalent.

Thus the basic idea of our method of eliminating intensionality is as follows. The intensional operator, e.g., 'believes that ...', is an analyser which breaks the syntactic structure of the subordinate clause into separate simple words, by considering the original syntactic role they played in that subordinate clause. It breaks that structure in the sense that all those expressions which were constituents of the subordinate clause are not constituents of the entire compound sentence; it is only the simple words of the subordinate clause, characterized by their syntactic positions (occupied in the clause) that are constituents of the compound sentence. This can be explained more clearly with the help of our notation of syntactic positions.

The usual interpretation of the syntactic structure of the sentence (Z_3) for which the intensional character of that sentence can be proved, is as follows:

Caesar believed that the capital of the Republic lies on the Tiber
(1,1)   (1,0)   (1,2,1,0)   (1,2,1,1) (1,2,0)   (1,2,2)
                                (1,2,1)
                                  (1,2)

In our interpretation, as in the usual one, the words 'believes that' form the main operator of the entire sentence (Z_3); similarly, the word 'Caesar' is its first argument according to both interpretations. But whereas in the usual syntactic interpretation of the sentence (Z_3) the second argument of the main operator, 'believes that', is the entire subordinate clause 'the capital of the Republic lies on the Tiber', in our interpretation that clause is not the second argument of the operator 'believes that'. The second, third, etc., arguments of that operator are, in our interpretation, the various words constituting the subordinate clause, together with the syntactic positions they had when the subordinate clause was still an independent sentence. What are the syntactic positions of the various words in the sentence 'the capital of the Republic lies on the Tiber'? They can be indicated by means of our indices for syntactic positions in the following way:

the capital of the Republic lies on the Tiber
(1,1,0)   (1,1,1)   (1,0)   (1,2)

Consequently, in our interpretation, the syntactic structure of the compound sentence (Z_3) is as follows:

Caesar believed that the capital of the Republic lies on the Tiber
                    (1,1,0)   (1,1,1)   (1,0)   (1,2)
(1,1)   (1,0)   (1,2)   (1,3)   (1,4)   (1,5)

In such interpretation of the syntactic structure of sentences of the type 'x believes that ...' their intensionality, which can be proved in the case of the usual interpretation of their syntactic structure, disappears – as we have shown above. Thus, to remove intensional expressions of the type in question it is enough to pay the low price of choosing a different syntactic interpretation of the expressions concerned.

We face an alternative: either to treat the syntactic structure of expressions of the type 'x believes that ...' in the usual way, with all the paradoxical consequence of intensionality, or to choose a different interpretation of their syntactic structure and so remove intensional expressions from the language.

I do not presume to claim that the interpretation of the syntactic structure of the expressions concerned in which intensionality disappears is the correct one. We are dealing with expressions of a natural language in which no syntactic interpretation is the only and 'correct' one. After all, there may be disagreement as to whether the sentence

'John likes Peter'

consists of two constituents: the simple subject 'John' and the compound predicate 'likes Peter', or of three constituents: the main operator 'likes' and its two arguments of the same order, 'John' and 'Peter'; there is no way of settling this dispute which would not admit of any arguments to the contrary. All this refers a fortiori to the syntactic structure of the complex sentences which are usually adduced as examples of intensional sentences. A natural language leaves room for different syntactic interpretations. That is why I refrain from claiming that my interpretation is the correct one, and confine myself to demonstrating its possibility and the advantages that can be obtained from it.

The objection might be raised that the problem has not been presented

in a sufficiently general manner. For I have shown in *only* two examples
that if we abandon the usual syntactic interpretation of sentences of the
type 'x believes that ...', etc., their intensionality is thereby eliminated. So
I shall try now to give a general formulation.

Let us consider the general schema:

(A_1)　　　x believed that (...).

We interpret it syntactically so that the arguments of its main operator
'believed that' are not 'x' and the clause (...) which follows that operator, but
'x' and the simple words of which that clause consists. Thus the sentence
(A_1) includes as its constituents, apart from the expression 'x', only simple
words which form the subordinate clause (...). The transformation of the
sentence A_1 into some other sentence A_2 by replacing a constituent of A_1 by
one of its equivalents may consist only in replacing a simple word, never in
replacing an expression which was a constituent in the subordinate clause but
is no longer a constituent of the entire compound sentence. Consequently,
excluded are such operations as replacing the expression 'the capital of the
Republic' by its equivalent 'the capital of the Popes'. The equivalent replacing
a simple word which is a constituent of the entire sentence 'x believed that
(...)' may be either a simple word or a complex expression. When we analysed
the transition from (Z_1), 'Ceasar believed that Rome lies on the Tiber', to
(Z_2), 'Caesar believed that the capital of the Popes lies on the Tiber', we
discussed the latter case. We have shown that in a different interpretation of
the syntactic structure of the sentence (Z_1), expressed by the sentence (Z_1^c),
the replacement of 'Rome' by the expression 'the capital of the Popes', does
not result in the sentence (Z_2) in its interpretation (Z_1), but results in the
sentence $(\overline{Z_1^c})$, which always has the same logical value as the sentence (Z_1^c).

We have not, however, examined the former case when a simple word
which is a constituent of a sentence of the type 'x believed that (...)' is
replaced by another simple word equivalent to it. This case will be considered
now. We take as our example the sentence:

(A_1)　　　John believed that Dr Jekyll was a gentleman,

and replace in it the simple word 'Dr Jekyll' by another simple word, 'Mr
Hyde', which is its equivalent since it denotes the same person. We thus
obtain the sentence:

(A_2)　　　John believed that Mr Hyde was a gentleman.

In the usual interpretation of the syntactic structure of these sentences (if
John did not know that Dr Jekyll was identical with Mr Hyde) the first is

true and the second is false. Let us now see whether intensionality is eliminated if we interpret these sentences as suggested above, i.e. if we interpret (A_1) as:

(A_1^c) 'John believed in a sentence with the basic content: $(1,1)$ – Dr Jekyll, $(1,0)$ – was, $(1,2)$ – a gentleman',

and (A_2) as

(A_2^c) 'John believed in a sentence with the basic content: $(1,1)$ – Mr Hyde, $(1,0)$ – was, $(1,2)$ – a gentleman'.

Here, too, it can easily be seen that the class of sentences described as sentences with the basic content: $(1,1)$ – Dr Jekyll, $(1,0)$ – was, $(1,2)$ – a gentleman, is identical with the class of sentences with the basic content: $(1,1)$ – Mr Hyde, $(1,0)$ – was, $(1,2)$ – a gentleman. Therefore (A_1^c) and (A_2^c) state about the same class of sentences that John believed in a sentence belonging to that class, and consequently, if one of them is true, then the second is true also.

If the sentence (A_1) seems to us to be true, and the sentence (A_2) to be false, this is probably because we understand them not as sentences stating a certain relation between John and the man whose name was both 'Dr Jekyll' and 'Mr Hyde' and the kind of people called gentleman, but as sentences stating a certain relation between John and the corresponding words. More precisely, if we think that (A_1) is true and (A_2) is false, it is because we do not understand them as the object language sentences (A_1^c) and (A_2^c), but as metasentences.

9. We have shown, it seems, in a general way that sentences of the type

(Z_1) 'x believes that (...)',

interpreted as

(Z^c) 'x believes in a sentence with the basic content (...)'

ceases to be intensional. Yet the interpretation (Z^c) still contains a certain metalinguistic residue since it refers to believing in a sentence, whereas the sentence (Z) under consideration seems to be free from any admixture of metalinguistic elements. Consequently, we must attempt to transform the interpretation (Z^c) so that no reference is made to the assertive attitude of a given person towards a certain sentence, i.e., a certain linguistic entity; in such a transformation reference would be made to the assertive attitude of the person towards something taking place in the objective sphere.

Now, we may say both 'I believe in the fact that the sun shines' and 'I believe in the sentence 'the sun shines''. In these two cases the word 'I believe' has different meanings. Let us distinguish them by writing: 'I believe$_1$ in the fact that the sun shines' and 'I believe$_2$ in the sentence 'the sun shines''. What is the connection between the object of the belief$_2$, i.e. the sentence 'the sun shines', and the object of the belief$_1$, i.e., the fact that the sun shines? Everyday speech has a certain term for naming that connection: in conformity with the colloquial interpretation of words one may say that the sentence 'the sun shines' states that the sun shines. In everyday speech the term 'states that' has a meaning in conformity with which we may say that a sentence A states the same as a sentence B if and only if A is a literal translation of B. But we have seen above that a sentence A is a literal translation of a sentence B if and only if the two sentences have the same full content, and — in the case where these sentences include no intensional constituents — if and only if, the two sentences have the same basic content. Hence it follows that two sentences state the same thing if and only if, they have the same full or basic content. We have obtained this result on the basis of statements governed by the colloquial meaning of the phrase 'states that', and we shall continue to conform to that result if we assume that what is stated by a given sentence is its full or basic content.

Confining ourselves to an analysis of sentences which do not contain any intensional constituents, we adopt the following definition:

What is stated by a sentence A = the basic content of A.

Further, I think we may agree that between the term 'believe$_1$' and 'believe$_2$' the following connection occurs which seems to be in conformity with their colloquial interpretation:

X believes$_1$ in what is stated by a sentence $A \equiv X$ believes $_2$ in a literal translation of A.   (1)

However, in conformity with the definition just adopted, what is stated by a sentence A is the same as its basic content; and a literal translation of A is the same as a sentence whose basic content is identical with the basic content of A. For example, let the basic content of a sentence A have the form

$$[m_1 - x_1, m_2 - x_2, ..., m_n - x_n].$$

In that case what is stated by the sentence

$$A = [m_1 - x_1, m_2 - x_2, ..., m_n - x_n]$$ (2)

A literal translation of A = a sentence with the basic content

$$[m_1 - x_1, m_2 - x_2, ..., m_n - x_n] \tag{3}$$

By substituting (2) and (3) respectively, for the two sides of the equivalence (1) we obtain:

X believes$_1$ in $[m_1 - x_1, m_2 - x_2, ..., m_n - x_n] \equiv X$ believes$_2$ in a sentence with the basic content $[m_1 - x_1, m_2 - x_2, ..., m_n - x_n]$. (4)

The last equivalence will be applied for the formulation

(Z^c) 'X believes$_2$ in a sentence with the basic content $[m_1 - x_1, m_2 - x_2, ..., m_n - x_n]$'

which seemed unsatisfactory as an interpretation of the sentence

(Z) 'X believes$_1$ $x_1, x_2, ..., x_n$,
                             $m_1, m_2, ..., m_n$

because the sentence (Z) is formulated exclusively in the object language, and (Z^c), which refers to believing in a sentence, contains a certain metalinguistic element. Now, in conformity with the equivalence (4), (Z^c) will be transformed into

(Z^h) 'X believes$_1$ that $[m_1 - x_1, m_2 - x_2, ..., m_n - x_n]$'.

This is the interpretation of a sentence of the type (Z) which we shall finally adopt as being completely adequate. The interpretation (Z^h), like the interpretation (Z^c), is not an intensional sentence. This may be proved by repeating, *mutatis mutandis*, what has been said above in demonstrating that the interpretation (Z^c) is not an intensional sentence.

In this interpretation one disturbing detail remains, namely the introduction of ordered pairs, each consisting of a syntactic position and a word, as constituents of sentences of the type

X believes that Rome lies on the Tiber.

In the ordinary interpretation of such a sentence its constituents are words and expressions, not ordered pairs of syntactic positions and words. With the help of the notation we have adopted for syntactic positions, the ordered pairs of positions and of words which occupy them can easily be represented. What corresponds however to such pairs in ordinary languages, which have no special symbolism for syntactic positions?

To answer this question let us note the ambiguity of 'word'. Consider the sentence

$$2 = 2$$

Of how many words does it consist? Our answers will differ according to how we understand 'word'. If we reply that the sentence, understood as an inscription localized *hic et nunc*, consists of three words, viz. two two's and one symbol of equality, we thereby reveal that by 'word' we understand a name the *designata* of which are definite inscriptions, localized in time and space and separated from other inscriptions by spacing. This interpretation of 'word' we shall call 'word *in concreto*'. But someone may say that the sentence in question consists of two words only, viz. the numeral two which appears twice, and the symbol of equality which appears once. Such an answer proves that the speaker understands the term 'word' so that its *designata* are not concrete inscriptions but certain classes of inscriptions, i.e., certain species, which may become concrete entities in the form of the various inscriptions occurring *hic et nunc*. When interpreting the term 'word' in this way we shall say 'word *in specie*'.

This ambiguity of the term 'word' is well-known. But there is still another ambiguity in the case of the term 'word *in specie*'. To illustrate this let us consider the following Latin sentence

'Petrus amat Petrum'

and ask whether the word *in concreto 'Petrus'* and the word *in concreto 'Petrum'*, as they appear in that sentence, are concrete occurrences of the same word *in specie* or of two different words *in specie*. The word *in concreto 'Petrus'* differs from the word *in concreto 'Petrum'* by its inflectional ending which in Latin serves to indicate the syntactic position in a sentence. Consequently, if we answer that the words *in concreto 'Petrus'* and *'Petrum'* are concrete occurrences of the same word *in specie*, we indicate that we understand the term 'word *in specie*' so that its *designata* (individual word species) may concretely occur in various syntactic places. However, if we answer that the word *in concreto 'Petrus'* is an occurrence of a different word *in specie* than the word *in concreto 'Petrum'*, we show that our understanding of the term 'word *in specie*' is such that its *designata* are word species which may occur only in certain definite syntactic positions. In the first instance we shall say 'word *in specie*, not determined as to its syntactic position', in the latter 'word *in specie*, determined as to its syntactic position'. The individual word species which are *designata* of the term 'word *in specie*, determined as to its syntactic position' require for their unambiguous characterization two co-ordinates: a definite word *in specie*, not determined as to its syntactic position, and a definite syntactic position. In other words, a given word *in specie*, determined as to its syntactic position, is an ordered pair, consisting of a syntactic position and a word *in specie*, not determined as to its syntactic position.

For example, if we say that in the sentence '2 = 2' the word '2' occupies the positions of the first and of the second argument, we understand the term 'word' as 'word *in specie*, not determined as to its syntactic position', because only in the case of such an interpretation of the term 'word' may we say that the word '2' occupies two different syntactic positions in a particular sentence. In general, when we say that a word occupies a certain syntactic position in a given sentence, we understand the term 'word' as 'word *in specie*, not determined as to its syntactic position'. For a word *in specie*, determined as to its syntactic position in a given sentence A, is itself an ordered pair consisting of a particular syntactic position in that sentence and a word *in specie*, not determined as to its syntactic position in that sentence, and such a pair is not a constituent of that sentence and so does not occupy any syntactic position in A.

If, however, sentence A becomes a syntactic part of some other sentence B it may happen that the constituents of B, which occupy in it certain syntactic positions, are words *in specie*, determined as to their syntactic positions in A. In our opinion, this occurs, for instance, when a given sentence, e.g., the sentence 'Rome lies on the Tiber', becomes part of another sentence, e.g., 'X believed that Rome lies on the Tiber'. The syntactic structure of the simple sentence (if the position which that sentence itself occupies is marked '2') is

(Z_1) Rome lies on the Tiber
          (2,1)   (2,0)   (2,2)

and the syntactic structure of the compound sentence is

(Z_f^h) X believed that (2,1) – Rome (2,0) – lies on (2,2) – the Tiber.
      (1,1) (1,0)   (1,2)   (1,3)   (1,4)

The above analysis now permits us to answer the question of what corresponds to the ordered pairs, each consisting of a syntactic position and a word which occupies it in ordinary languages which have no special symbolism to mark syntactic positions. What corresponds to such a pair is the word *in specie*, not determined as to its syntactic position. For such a word *in specie* is something which for its unequivocal indication requires both the specification of a syntactic position and a word *in specie*, not determined as to its syntactic position. The latter word is assigned a syntactic position of its own.

Different languages have different means to indicate the syntactic positions of words. Inflectional languages perform this function by means of word-endings. E.g., in the Latin sentence

'*Roma sita est ad Tiberim*'

the fact that the word '*Tiberis*' (word *in specie*, not determined as to its syntactic position) plays the role of the second argument of the main operator '*sita est*', i.e., the role of object, is indicated by using that word in the accusative case. The word '*Tiberis*', not determined as to its syntactic position, by adopting the accusative ending is located in the place of the second argument of the main operator. The word '*Tiberis*', whose syntactic position is not determined, is a constituent of that sentence. However in the sentence

'*Caesar credidit Roman ad Tiberim sitam esse*'

it is not the word '*Tiberis*', undetermined as to its syntactic position, which is a constituent of that sentence, but the word '*Tiberim*', determined as to its syntactic position and assigned a certain place in that compound sentence.

This completes our explanation of how our interpretation (Z^h), which uses symbols for syntactic positions, is expressed in those languages which have no such symbolism.

10. Our analysis has been confined to sentences with such psychological terms as 'believes that', etc., but I think that the results obtained here are applicable to sentences containing modal terms as well. The intensional character of the sentence

(M_1) 'It is necessary that $\sqrt{81} = 9$'

is usually proved by pointing out that if in the true sentence (M_1), we replace the expression '$\sqrt{81}$' by an equivalent expression 'the number of planets', we obtain a false sentence

(M_2) 'It is necessary that the number of planets $= 9$'.

It follows that (M_1) is an intensional sentence, but only under the assumption that the expression '$\sqrt{81}$', for which we have substituted its equivalent 'the number of planets', is a constituent of the sentence (M_1).

Now, this assumption is not satisfied if, as before, we interpret the operator 'it is necessary' as an analyser which breaks up the sentence '$\sqrt{81} = 9$'

into separate words in the sense that not all the constituents of the sentence which follow the operator 'it is necessary' are arguments of that operator, but that the arguments are only simple words together with their syntactic positions. In this case the expression '$\sqrt{81}$', which is a constituent of the simple sentence '$\sqrt{81} = 9$', is no longer a constituent of the compound sentence 'It is necessary that $\sqrt{81} = 9$'.

However to adopt this approach and interpret the modal operator as an analyser we would have to begin with an interpretation of modal sentences which agrees with our intuition, and then demonstrate, as has been done with sentences containing psychological terms, that on this interpretation the modal operator in fact becomes an analyser. I intend to do this in another article.

22. PROPOSITION AS THE CONNOTATION OF
A SENTENCE*

(1967)

1. Every meaningful sentence, whether true or false, states something. What is stated by a sentence is called in German *'Sachverhalt'*. A literal translation of that term, e.g., 'state of things' or 'state of affairs', is seldom used in English. In the latter language, what is stated by a sentence is usually called a 'proposition'. In this sense, a proposition is neither a linguistic expression, nor a psychological act of thinking, nor any 'ideal meaning', but something which belongs to the sphere of objects to which a given sentence refers. The relation of stating, which holds between the sentence and the proposition, is therefore a semantic one, but should be distinguished from the semantic relation of denotation as it was understood by Frege. According to Frege, every true sentence denotes one and the same object, namely a mysterious object called 'truth', and every false sentence denotes one and the same object, still more mysterious, called 'falsity'. But different true sentences may state different propositions, and different false sentences need not state the same state of affairs. Hence it follows that the semantic relation of stating differs from another semantic relation, namely that of denoting (in Frege's sense), and the proposition stated by a given sentence is neither truth nor falsity.

2. The concept of proposition seems to be important for any study which has science as its object. In such a study the notion of a scientific law or theory is fundamental. Scientific laws and theories are usually identified with the sentences in which they are formulated, and metascience adopts the notion of a sentence as a fundamental concept. Yet such an identification of scientific theories with sentences leads to undesirable consequences. For instance, it implies that there is not *one* Newtonian theory of gravitation, but as many theories as there are languages in which the Newtonian idea can be formulated. A scientific theory is, therefore, not a sentence, but something which is common to all those sentences which state the same thing, or, in other words, which are connected with the same proposition. The simplest

* Revised translation by David Pearce. First published in *Studia Logica* **XX** (1967), 87–98. Reprinted here by kind permission of PWN.

answer to the question of what scientific theories are, seems therefore to be this: scientific theories are propositions.

The need for a definition of proposition can also be seen in connection with the puzzling question of what is stated by a false sentence. A true sentence states some fact, but what is stated by a false sentence is not a fact, although it seems to be something. The difference between a meaningless sentence and a false one consists just in that the former states nothing whereas the latter states something – which, however, is not a fact. The definition of proposition should provide an answer to the question of what is stated by a sentence, whether true or false. Such a definition would have to point to kinds of entities which in the case of true sentences may be called 'facts'.

The distinction between propositions which are facts and those which are not is the same as the distinction between true and false propositions. Since propositions are conceived as objective entities, their truth or falsity are properties of objective entities and as such belong to the objective word. They may, therefore, be understood to be those mysterious objects which Frege called 'truth' and 'falsity' and related to sentences as their denotations. A definition of true and false propositions would therefore help elucidate the fundamental semantic ideas of Frege.

It is to be hoped that the definition of proposition will also be helpful in solving another perplexing meta-logical problem, namely that of intensional sentences, but this question will be the subject matter of another paper.

3. All this seems to justify an attempt to define proposition as an objective entity. Carnap in his *Meaning and Necessity* has given his own definition of the term 'proposition', but his definition characterizes proposition by means of syntactic terms alone, without resorting to any semantic concepts. Consequently, what Carnap calls a proposition belongs to the linguistic sphere and not to the sphere of objects, and does not promise a solution to the problems stated above.[1]

In this paper it is intended to give such a definition of proposition which conceives it as an objective, and not a linguistic or psychological, entity, connected with the sentence by a semantic, and not a syntactic or pragmatic, relation, viz., the relation of stating. This is why, with reference to sentences, beside the semantic relation of denoting, another semantic relation, namely that of stating, must be established.

4. To begin with, the traditional semantics of names distinguishes two semantic relations for them. In conformity with this traditional semantics,

every name (i.e., such a name as may be used as a predicate in a sentence and consequently may be called a predicable name, as distinguished from a proper name) denotes its extension or denotation, and connotes its intension or connotation. The extension or denotation of a predicable name is the class of all individual objects with reference to which that name be truly used as a predicate. Those objects are called the *designata* of that name. The intension or connotation of a name is a set of properties whose conjunction holds with reference to all, and only those, objects which are elements of the extension of that name. In other words, the connotation of a name is a set of properties which unambiguously determines the extension of that name. The properties of the objects designated by a name belong to the objective, and not to the linguistic sphere, and that is why the relation between a name and its connotation is a semantic and not a syntactic one.

Now, in connection with distinguishing two semantic relations for names, one is tempted to look for such a generalization of those relations which would enable us to speak not only of the denotation and connotation of names, but also of the denotation and connotation of other expressions. Further, one might try to generalize them so that the denotation of sentences would be, in conformity with Frege, their truth value, and the connotation of sentences would be an entity which we might call a proposition, in conformity with our unanalysed, intuitive interpretation of that term. Such a solution will be sought in this paper.

5. First of all, the concept of denotation will be broadened so that one can speak of the denotation of proper names, sentences, and operators which bind no variables. Thus, we define the denotation of a proper name to be the object named by it; the denotation of a sentence to be its truth value, the denotation of an operator which binds no variables to be the relation between the denotations of its arguments, and the denotation of the expression formed by that operator together with its arguments. For instance, the denotation of a truth operator (e.g., of the implication symbol) is its matrix. The denotation of the sentence-forming operator 'shines' is the relation between any individual object and the truth value of the sentence obtained from the sentential formula 'x shines' when the proper name of that object is substituted for the variable 'x'. The concept of denotation is applied neither to variables, nor to formulae containing variables, nor to operators binding variables. Other semantic notions, analogous to the notions of designating and denoting, are applicable to those expressions; for instance variables represent their values but do not designate them, and they range over the set of their values but do not denote it. An analysis of the semantic notions referring to

variables and to expressions connected with them would go beyond the limits of this paper. The fact that these notions are disregarded means that what is said in this paper refers only to those languages which include neither variables nor operators binding variables. This undoubtedly reduces the value of the results presented here and imposes upon the author the duty to endeavour to formulate such a concept of proposition which would be applicable to languages that make use of variables.

6. It is much more difficult to generalize the concept of connotation, because the notion of the connotation of names itself, which is to be generalized, has no unique definition in traditional logic. The formulation that the connotation of a name is the set of properties which unambiguously determines its extension, cannot be considered as a definition of the connotation of a name, since a given class of objects, forming the extension of a name, can be unambiguously determined by different sets of properties. And the connotation of a name is not just any set of properties which uniquely determines its extension, but a set distinguished among those which satisfy that condition.

The connotation of a name is understood in such a way that between the denotation, the connotation and the meaning of a name the following relations take place: the meaning or the sense of a name uniquely determines its connotation; the connotation of a name uniquely determines its denotation; but the denotation of a name does not uniquely determine its connotation, i.e., two names with the same denotation may have different connotations; and the connotation of a name does not uniquely determine its meaning, i.e., two names with the same connotation may differ in their meanings because, for example, they may differ in their emotional tinge which also belongs to the meaning of a name. Hence a name that has a definite meaning has a definite connotation. Therefore it does not suffice to say that the connotation of a name taken in some meaning is the set of properties which uniquely determines the extension of that name, because such a formulation does not single out any definite object, which is uniquely determined.

In order to define properly the connotation of a name, let us see how the connotation of a name is formulated in practice. In traditional logic, this practice was confined to names which are either conjunctions of two or more other names, e.g., 'circular and red', or are conventional abbreviations of such conjunctions e.g., 'square', which may be considered as a conventional abbreviation of the conjunction: 'tegragon, equilateral, rectangular'.

Now, in considering such names which are either explicitly or implicitly conjunctions of other names, the practice was to give as their connotations the sets of properties corresponding to the component names forming a given conjunction. For instance, the connotation of the name 'circular and red' was said to be the set of the property of circularity and the property of redness; the connotation of the name 'square' — if considered as a conventional abbreviation of the name 'tegragon, equilateral, rectangular' — was said to be the set of properties of tetragonality, equilaterality and rectangularity.

This practice permits us to formulate a rule for constructing the connotation of those names which are either explicit or implicit conjunctions of other names, but does not allow the formulation of a general rule that would be applicable to all names. For there exist names which are composed of other names, but not on the conjunction principle. For example, the name 'circular or red' is based not on conjunction but on alternation. The connotation of the name 'circular or red' may not be considered to be the set of properties of circularity and redness. Should one think so, one would ascribe to the name 'circular or red' the same connotation as to the name 'circular and red'. Since the two names differ in their extensions, that is, in their denotations, this would be in contradiction with the principle that the connotation of a name uniquely determines its extension.

If as the connotation of a name composed of simple names one wants to give something which would uniquely determine its extension, then it is not enough to pay attention only to the objective references of the component names by themselves, but it is necessary to take into consideration the objective reference of that component of the compound name which binds these component names together. The connotation of such names as 'circular and red' or 'circular or red' is determined not only by the component names, in which these two compound names agree, but also by the words which bind the component names together to form the compound name, in which they differ.

Further, there are names which are composed of other names in a non-symmetrical way, i.e., in such a way that if the order of the component names is changed, the extension of the compound name changes too. For example, the extension of the name 'the brother of John's mother' differs from the extension of the name 'the mother of John's brother'; the extension of the name 'red but not circular' differs from that of the name 'circular but not red'. Hence, if the connotation of a name is to be interpreted as something which uniquely determines the extension of that name, it does not suffice to define connotation as a set of certain properties or other objective referents of the constituents of the given name, but it is also necessary to take into consideration the syntactic role, or syntactic position, of those constituents within the compound name in question.

It follows from the above that in looking for the definition of the connotation of expressions it is necessary: (1) To determine the connotation of the expression E in such a way that its component parts should be the objective referents of all component expressions of the expression E, and not only of its component names. To take into consideration not only those component expressions of the expression E which are contained in it explicitly, but also those which are contained in it implicitly and which can be seen clearly when all conventional abbreviations present in the expression E are developed. (2) To determine the connotation of the expression E in such a way that it should reflect not only the words contained in that expression, but also the syntactic positions which those words occupy in the expression E.

Thus the way is paved for a definition of connotation sufficiently general to cover not only names, but any expressions as well. This, however, must be preceded by an explanation of the concept of the syntactic position of a given constituent expression in a compound expression. This concept seems very important, not only from the point of view of the analysis contained in this paper.

7. In explaining the concept of a syntactic position it must be stated first that every compound expression consists of constituents which form a certain hierarchy. If only those expressions which contain no binding operators are taken into consideration, it may be said that in each such expression one can distinguish the main (principal) operator and its successive arguments. The main operator contained in the expression E is that operator which together with its arguments exhausts the entire expression E. The main operator of the expression E and its arguments are called *first-order constituents* of the expression E. First-order constituents of first-order constituents of the expression E are called *second-order constituents* of the expression E. In a general way, first-order constituents of nth-order constituents of the expression E are called $(n + 1)th$ *order constituents* of the expression E. Further, the expression E itself will be called its own *constituent of 0-order*.

As can be seen from the above, every nth-order member of the expression E, for $n > 0$, is either the main operator of an $(n-1)$th-order constituent, or one of the successive arguments of that operator. That $(n-1)$th-order constituent, if it is not the expression E itself, is in turn either the main operator of an $(n - 2)$th-order constituent, or one of the successive arguments of that operator, and so on, until the expression E is reached.

Now, the description of the syntactic position occupied by the expression

A in the expression E (if A is an nth-order constituent of E) consists in the information stating both for the expression A and for every constituent of the expression E which includes the expression A, whether it is the main operator of a constituent one order lower than the order of the expression of which it is a component part, or the first, second or kth argument of that operator. For instance, let the expression

$$3 \, . \, 4 = 5 + (8 - 1)$$

be analysed. The syntactic position of the expression '$5 + (8 - 1)$' in the expression E is described by the statement saying that it is the second argument of the main operator of the expression E. The syntactic position of the expression '$8 - 1$' in the expression E is described by the statement saying that it is the second argument of the main operator in the second argument of the main operator of the expression E. Still more complicated is the description of the syntactic position occupied by the numeral '8' in the expression E. The numeral '8' is the first argument of the main operator in the second argument of the main operator in the second argument of the main operator of the expression E.

As can be seen from the above, the indication of the syntactic position by means of a verbal description is very complicated. To simplify it a special symbolism will be introduced. The syntactic position of an expression E will be marked with the symbol of a natural number, e.g., the symbol of the number 1. Further, if the syntactic position occupied by the expression A in the expression E is marked $\ulcorner m \urcorner$, then the position of the main operator of the expression A in the expression E will be marked $\ulcorner (m,0) \urcorner$ and the position occupied in the expression E by the nth argument of that operator will be marked $\ulcorner (m,n) \urcorner$.

Thus, if the syntactic position of the sentence E:

'*Plato est philosophus et Aristoteles est philosophus*'

is marked with the numeral '1', then the positions occupied in that sentence by the constituents of that sentence will be marked as follows:

| 111 | 110 | 112 | | 121 | 120 | 122 |

Plato est philosophus , et Aristoteles est philosophus

11   (1,0)   12

This symbolism makes it possible to indicate in a simple way even the most remote syntactic positions.

For the unambiguous description of a compound expression it is not enough to enumerate (write out) the simple constituents of which it consists, but also necessary to describe in some way the syntactic positions they occupy in that expression. For instance, from '5', '>', '3' one can build the sentence '5 > 3' and the sentence '3 > 5'. In arithmetical symbolism the order of the elements and sometimes the use of brackets serve to indicate the position occupied by simpler expressions within more complex ones. Such languages in which the syntactic positions of constituents of compound expressions are indicated by their order and by the semantic categories of simple elements are called positional languages. There are, however, languages which indicate syntactic positions of words not only by means of their order, but also by their inflectional forms. For instance, in the Latin sentence

'Petrus amat Paulum'

the fact that the word 'Petrus' is the first argument of the operator 'amat', i.e., the subject, the word 'Paulus' its second argument, i.e., the object, is indicated by the fact that 'Petrus' is in the nominative case, and 'Paulus' in the accusative. Even if the order is changed into

'Paulum amat Petrus'

the syntactic role of the elements of that sentence does not undergo any change.

Such languages which resort to inflection to indicate the syntactic position of words are called inflectional. Yet no natural language indicates the syntactic positions of words exclusively by means of inflectional forms, but resorts to word order, punctuation, etc., so that no natural language is purely inflectional.

Now, a purely inflectional language can be built by means of the symbolism indicating the syntactic position of words, as described above. Those symbols, when attached to words, can be treated as their inflectional endings which themselves, regardless of the order of the words in question, indicate their syntactic positions. Words with such endings can be scattered in an arbitrary way, and yet on the strength of these endings they will continue to form definite wholes.

Such a purely inflectional language will be used later in an attempt to define true proposition.

8. After this digression on syntactic positions the previously announced definition of the connotation of expressions will be given.

For that purpose a given expression E must first be transformed so that all the conventional abbreviations contained in it are expanded and consequently none of its simple constituents are abbreviations of compound expressions. The syntactic positions occupied by simple constituents in such an expanded expression E will be called the ultimate syntactic positions of the expression E. Thus, in the expression E there is a one-to-one correspondence between those ultimate syntactic positions and separate words. Such a one-to-one correspondence between words and syntactic positions in the expression E, i.e., the function, determined for those positions, which establishes a one-to-one correspondence between those positions and words, is the characteristic function of the expression E. But there is a one-to-one correspondence between the words occupying the ultimate places in the expression E and their denotations. If there is agreement on this, it follows that for every expression E there exists a function establishing a one-to-one correspondence between every ultimate syntactic position in the expression E and a certain object, namely the object which is the denotation of the word occupying that position.

It is suggested that that very function should be considered as the connotation of the expression E. Consequently, the following definition is adopted:

> The connotation of the expression E is the function determined for the ultimate syntactic positions of the expression (obtained from the expression E by the expansion of all the abbreviations it contains) which establishes a one-to-one correspondence between those positions and the denotations of the words occupying such positions in the expanded expression E.

For instance, the connotation of the expression

'circular and red'

is the relation establishing a one-to-one correspondence:
  (1) between the syntactic position of the main operator $(1,0)$ and the denotation of the word 'and',
  (2) between the syntactic position of the first argument $(1,1)$ and the denotation of the word 'circular',
  (3) between the syntactic position of the second argument $(1,2)$ and the denotation of the word 'red'.

Every binary relation, and consequently every function of one argument, can be identified with the class of ordered pairs of objects between which that relation holds. If that class is finite, it can be symbolized by the enumeration of those pairs. Thus the function which is the connotation of the expression

'circular and red'

may be written

$\langle (1,1) - \text{circular}; (1,0) - \text{and}; (1,2) - \text{red} \rangle.$

If bound variables and abstraction symbol were used, the above expression might be replaced by the equivalent one:

$$(\hat{x}, \hat{y}) \{x = (1,1) \wedge y = \text{circular}] \vee$$
$$[x = (1,0) \wedge y = \text{and}] \vee [x = (1,2) \wedge y = \text{red}]\}$$

Such a way of symbolizing the relation, which resorts to an operator binding the variables is, however, not necessary if the domain of the relation is finite and may be replaced by an enumeration.

It can easily be seen that the definition of the connotation of an expression, as suggested above, satisfies the conditions previously formulated with regard to such a definition.

Firstly, in the case of the above definition of connotation, the connotation of an expression uniquely determines its denotation. If the name of the connotation of the expression E is given by enumeration, the name of its denotation is obtained by the juxtaposition of the second element of every pair contained in that name and by writing below every such element the first member of its pair. For instance, from the symbol for the connotation of the expression 'circular and red', which has the form

$\langle (1,1) - \text{circular}; (1,0) - \text{and}; (1,2) - \text{red} \rangle$

the symbol of its denotation is obtained by writing

circular and red
  1,1   1,0 1,2

It can also be noticed that although the connotation of an expression, defined in this way, determines its denotation, it is not conversely determined by its denotation.

Secondly, the definition of connotation, as given above, makes the connotation of an expression depend on the objective references of all its component expressions, and not only its component names; moreover, not only those components of a given expression which appear in it explicitly are to be taken into consideration, but also those which will appear in it after the abbreviations have been expanded.

Thirdly, the above definition of connotation takes into account not only the objective references of the words of which a given expression consists, but also their syntactic roles, i.e., their syntactic positions.

9. The above definition of connotation is so general that it may be applied not only to names, but to any expression whatever. Consequently, it may also be used with respect to sentences. Now, *the connotation of a sentence will be called the proposition stated in that sentence*. This is the definition of proposition, which this paper suggests.

Now, in the light of this definition, what is the proposition stated, for example, in the sentence

'Socrates likes Alcibiades'?

Transcribed with the help of symbols indicating the syntactic positions, this sentence can be written thus:

Socrates   likes   Alcibiades
$(1,1)$ $(1,0)$ $(1,2)$

The connotation of this sentence, i.e. the proposition stated by the sentence, is the function establishing a one-to-one correspondence between the syntactic positions of its words and their denotations, that is

$\langle (1,1) -$ Socrates; $(1,0) -$ likes; $(1,2) -$ Alcibiades$\rangle$.

Is such an interpretation of the concept of proposition in conformity with our intuitive interpretation of proposition as that which is stated in a given sentence? It seems so. Objects exist in the world regardless of whether and what people think about them. Socrates exists, Alcibiades exists, and − in a sense − the relation of liking exists. These objects are either related to one another, or not. For instance, the relation of liking either occurs between Socrates and Alcibiades, or it does not, regardless of what people think about them. The thought that Socrates likes Alcibiades, does not by itself create the objective fact which consists in the occurrence of the relation of liking between Socrates and Alcibiades. But by thinking that Socrates likes Alcibiades we think about those objects as being related to one another in that way. And it seems that the best description of what the thought about those objects, so related to one another, consists in is that of a one-to-one correspondence between the relation of liking and the syntactic position of the main operator, between Socrates and the syntactic position of its first argument, i.e., the subject, and between Alcibiades and the syntactic position of its second argument, i.e., the object. Thus, when one states with understanding the sentence 'Socrates likes Alcibiades', one establishes a one-to-one correspondence between the syntactic positions in that sentence and the objects denoted by the constituents of that sentence occupying such positions.

Such a correspondence between the syntactic positions and the objects in question is what is stated by that sentence, and is, consequently, a proposition.

So much for attempting to achieve an intuitive approval for the definition suggested in this paper.

As a result of this definition of a proposition, to every sentence, whether true or false, there corresponds the proposition stated by that sentence. The puzzling question of what is stated in a false sentence, seems to have been solved in this way.

The correspondence between syntactic positions and objects may, or may not, agree with the relative positions of those objects in reality. If the sentence stating a given proposition is true then the relative positions occupied with respect to one another by the objects referred to in the sentence, correspond to the syntactic positions which are allotted to them in the proposition stated in that sentence. In that case it seems natural to call the proposition stated in a true sentence a fact.

10. The propositions stated in true sentences may be called true propositions. But here the question arises, whether a true proposition might not be defined directly, without reference to the concept of a true sentence. It is known that in defining the truth of a sentence one must resort both to the object language and the meta-language, whereby considerable difficulties are involved. Perhaps a definition of the truth of a proposition, i.e. of an entity which can be referred to in an object language, might itself be built in an object language, too.

For the time being I cannot build a satisfactory definition of the truth of a proposition, or even a general schema of such a definition, and I do not know whether this is possible at all. This is why only partial definitions of the truth of propositions will be given here, to serve as a possible starting point for the formulation of a general definition.

It has been shown above how to pass from a symbol of the connotation of an expression to a symbol of its denotation. If, e.g. the connotation of the expression

'circular and red'

is written in the form

$$\langle(1,1) - \text{circular}; (1,0) - \text{and}; (1,2) - \text{red}\rangle,$$

in a language which makes use of symbols of syntactic positions, the name of its denotation is obtained in the form

circular   and   red
 (1,1)   (1,0) (1,2)

This will help to understand the following partial definition:

(1) $\langle(1,1) - \text{Socrates}; ((1,0) - \text{likes}; (1,2) - \text{Alcibiades}\rangle$ is true $\equiv$
         $\equiv$ Socrates likes Alcibiades
              (1,1)   (1,0)   (1,2)

The expression in pointed brackets on the left side of the above equivalence is the name of a proposition the truth of which is stated; the right part is occupied by the sentence stating that proposition.

The above equivalence resembles a partial definition of the truth of a sentence, e.g.,

(2)   'Socrates likes Alcibiades' is true $\equiv$ Socrates likes Alcibiades.

The difference between (1) and (2) consists in that in (2) reference is made both to words and to the objects named by those words, whereas in (1) reference is made to objects only, but not to words. That is why the partial definition (1) may *cum grano salis*, be considered as formulated exclusively in an object language. The reservation is due to the fact that although the symbols of syntactic positions appear on the right hand side not as words but as inflectional endings of words, yet on the left side they are taken as words, namely as names of syntactic positions. Consequently, the definition (1) may not be considered as formulated exclusively in an object language. This problem, very important for the present analysis, will be discussed later.

Starting from the partial definitions of the truth of propositions, here represented by the formulation (1), one might consider the following formulation as the first approximation of a general definition of the truth of propositions:

(3) $S \in \text{true} \equiv$

$$\sum_{\substack{n \in Nat}} \sum_{\substack{x_1, x_2, ..., x_n \in \text{object} \\ m_1, m_2, ..., m_n \in \text{synt. position}}} \left\{ (S = \langle m_1 x_1, m_2 x_2, ..., m_n x_n \rangle) \wedge \begin{pmatrix} x_1, x_2, ..., x_n \\ m_1, m_2, ..., m_n \end{pmatrix} \right\}$$

Many objections may be raised against this formulation. First of all, it does not hold for all S's, because for those S's which are not propositions the right side of the definition is a syntactic nonsense. For, if S is not a proposition, i.e. a connotation of a sentence, and S is a connotation of the expression $\ulcorner x_1, x_2, ..., x_n \urcorner$ $m_1, m_2, ..., m_n$, then that expression is not a sentence and consequently may not meaningfully appear as an argument of the symbol of conjunction on the right hand side of the definition. The only way of avoiding this difficulty seems to be to change the definition into a rule permitting, if it is already known that S is a proposition, the adoption of the equivalence (3).

The second objection refers to the fact that this equivalence is written in a mixed language: everything in it is written in a language which does not use special symbols for marking syntactic positions, except for the last constituent, which is formulated in just such a language. One might think of re-formulating the definition in the sort of language in which its last member is written. But to do so one would have to expand the system of syntactic positions so as to make it possible to mark the syntactic positions of quantifiers, and the above analysis refers to languages which do not include quantifiers.

The third objection refers to the claim of defining the truth of propositions exclusively in an object language. The above definition is not built in this way, because it contains names of syntactic positions.

The second and third objections point to the direction in which research should be continued. The concepts of connotation and of proposition must be generalized so as to make them applicable to languages which include binding operators. Further, the concepts of connotation and proposition must be freed from the meta-linguistic concept of syntactic position. I see a possibility of solving both these problems, but my ideas are still too vague to be presented here. Yet there seem to be prospects for a solution.

NOTE

[1] [See, however, Carnap's own remarks on this point which apparently stand in contradiction to Ajdukiewicz's claim. *Meaning and Necessity,* 1958, University of Chicago Press, p. 27. – *Translator*]

BIBLIOGRAPHY OF AJDUKIEWICZ'S WORKS

Monographs, textbooks, articles, reviews, abstracts of papers
Compiled by Professor Tadeusz Czeżowski
(*Ruch Filozoficzny* **XXII** (1964), 119–124)

[Translation by Jerzy Giedymin, based on *Język i Poznanie*,
II (1965, 409–13]

Abbreviations: PF Przegląd Filozoficzny, RF Ruch Filozoficzny

1913

W sprawie odwracalności stosunku wynikania [On the Relation of Deducibility and Its Converse], *PF* **XVI**, 287–297.
W sprawie interpretacji kantowskiego wyrażenia 'forma zjawiska' [On the Interpretation of the Kantian Term 'the Form of a Phenomenon'] *RF* **III**, 71a, b.
B. Bornstein, Prolegomena filozoficzne do geometrii [B. Bornstein's Philosophical Prolegomena to Geometry, A Review], *RF* **III**, 193a–195b.

1914

Nowa aksjomatyka arytmetyki Hilberta [Hilbert's New Axiom System for Arithmetic], *RF* **IV**, 136a, b.
L. Chwistek, Zasada sprzeczności w świetle nowszych badań Bartranda Russella [Review of L. Chwistek's 'The Principle of Contradiction in the Light of Bertrand Russell's Recent Research'], *RF* **IV**, 173b–176b.

1919

Definicja dowodu w znaczeniu logicznym [A Definition of Proof in the Logical Sense], *RF* **V**, 59b.

1920

Pojęcie istnienia w naukach dedukcyjnych [On the Notion of Existence in Deductive Sciences], *RF* **V**, 112a, b.

1921

Czas względny i bezwzględny [Absolute and Relative Time], *RF* **VI**, 70b.
Czas względny i bezwzględny [Absolute and Relative Time], *PF* **XXIII**, 1–18.
Z metodologii nauk dedukcyjnych [*From the Methodology of Deductive Science*], Wydawnictwo Polskiego Towarzystwa Filozoficznego we Lwowie, vol X, 66.

1922

Redukcja czy indukcja [Reduction or Induction?], *RF* **VII**, 39a, b.

1923

Główne kierunki filozofii w wyjątkach z dzieł ich klasycznych przedstawicieli. Teoria poznania, logika, metafizyka [Principal Philosophical Theories in the Excerpts from Classics: Theory of Knowledge, Logic, Metaphysics], Lwów 1923, K. S. Jakubowski, VIII + 284 pp.
O intencji pytania 'Co to jest P?' [On the meaning of the Question 'What is P?'], *RF* VII, 152b–153a.

1924

K. Sosnicki, Zarys logiki-recenzja [Review of K. Sosnicki's 'An Outline of Logic'], *RF* VIII, 62a–64b.
O wartości logiki formalnej [On the Value of Formal Logic], *RF* VIII, 87b.

1925

Nazwy i zdania [Terms and Sentences], *RF* IX, 23b–24b.
J. Nuckowski, An Introduction to Logic for Schools. Review of J. Nuckowski's 'An Introduction to Logic for Schools', *RF* IX, 128a–131.
Składniki zdań [Constituents of Sentences], *RF* IX, 164a, b.

1926

Założenia logiki tradycyjnej [The Assumptions of Traditional Logic], *RF* X, 67a.
Analiza semantyczna zdania pytajnego [A Semantical Analysis of Interrogative Sentences], *RF* X, 194b–195b.
Założenia logiki tradycyjnej [The Assumptions of Traditional Logic], *PF* XXIX, 200–229.

1927

O stosowaniu kryterium prawdy [On the Application of the Criterion of Truth], *PF* XXX, 280–283.

1928

O zasadzie podziału rozumowań [On a Classification of Arguments], *RF* XI, 166b–167a.
W sprawie klasyfikacji rozumowań [Concerning a Classification of Arguments], *PF* XXXI, 148–152.
Główne zasady metodologii nauk i logiki formalnej. Skrypt autoryzowany z wykładów wygłoszonych w Uniwersytecie Warszawskim wr. ak. 1927/28, zredagował M. Pressburger [Fundamental Principles of the Methodology of Sciences and of Formal Logic – An Authorized Transcript of Lectures Delivered in Warsaw University in 1927/28, edited by M. Pressburger], 304 pp.

1930

Studium krytyczne: Elementy teorii poznania, logiki formalnej i metodologii nauk, Tadeusza Kotarbińskiego [Review-article: T. Kotarbiński's Elements of the Theory of Knowledge, Formal Logic and the Methodology of Science], *PF* XXXIII, 140–160. Reprinted in the 2nd ed. of T. Kotarbiński's Elements of ... 1961, 607–631.
O pojęciu substancji [On the Notion of Substance], *RF* XII, 208b–209b.

1931

O znaczeniu wyrażeń [On the Meaning of Expressions], *Księga Pamiątkowa Polskiego Towarzystwa Filozoficznego we Lwowie*, Lwów, 31–77.
On the Notion of Substance, *Sprawozdania Poznańskiego Towarzystwa Przyjaciół Nauk*, 11–13.
O obiektywności poznania zmysłowego [On the Objectivity of Experiential Knowledge], *RF* **XII**, 212b–214a. *Sprawozdania Poznańskiego Towarzystwa Przyjaciół Nauk*, 13–16.
Konwencjonalizm w zastosowaniu do geometrii [Conventionalism in Geometry], *RF* **XII**, 214a–215a.
O zagadnieniach filozoficznych [On Philosophical Problems], *Filomata* **26**, Lwów, 435–444.
Paradoksy starożytnych [The Paradoxes Dicussed by Ancient Philosophers], *Filomata* **35, 36**, Lwów, 6–14, 51–58.

1932

W obronie uniwersaliów [In Defence of Universals], *RF* **XIII**, 40b–41b.

1933

Analiza i synteza [Analysis and Synthesis], *Zarys encyklopedyczny współczesnej wiedzy i kultury*, I, Książnica-Atlas, Lwów-Warszawa, pp. 204–213.

1934

Doświadczenie [Experience], *Świat i Życie* I, 1226–1233.
O stosowalności czystej logiki do zagadnień filozoficznych [On the Applicability of Pure Logic to Philosophical Problems], *PF* **XXXVII**, 323–327.
Ontologiczne założenia uniwersalizmu socjologicznego [The Ontological Assumptions of Sociological Universalism], *RF* **XIII**, 134a, b.
Logiczne podstawy nauczania [The Logical Foundations of Teaching. Offprint from *Encyklopedia Wychowania*], Nasza Księgarnia, ZNP, Warszawa, 79.
Sprache und Sinn [Language and Meaning], *Erkenntnis* **IV**, 100–138.
Das Weltbild und die Begriffsapparatur, *Erkenntnis* **IV**, 259–287.
Dusza, Duch [Soul and Spirit], *Świat i Życie* II, 24–33.
Krytycyzm [Criticism], *Świat i Życie* III, 148–153.
Logika [Logic], *Świat i Życie*, 358–367.

1935

Die wissenschaftliche Weltperspektive, *Erkenntnis* **V**, 22–30.
Der logistische Antiirrationalismus in Polen, *Erkenntnis* **V**, 151–164.
Sinnregeln, Weltperspektive, Welt, *Erkenntnis* **V**, 165–168.
W sprawie uniwersaliów [On the Problem of Universals], *PF* **XXXVII**, 219–234.
Pola filosofia penso enlasta jarcentkvartuo, *Pola Esperantisto*, **XXXIX** Jaro.

1936

Die syntaktische Konnexität, *Studia Philosophica* I, 1–27.
Okres warunkowy w mowie potocznej i w logistyce [Conditional Statements in Ordinary Language and in Logic], *RF* **XIV**, 134a, b.

Über die Anwendbarkeit der reinen Logik auf philosophische Probleme, *Actes du VIII Congrès International de Philosophie, Prague,* 170–174.
Die Definition, *Actes du I. Congrès International de Philosophie scientifique, Paris,* 1–6.
Empiryczny fundament poznania [The Empirical Foundation of Knowledge], *Sprawozdania Poznańskiego Towarzystwa Przyjaciół Nauk,* 27–31.
Rozumowanie [Reasoning], *Świat i Życie* IV, 653–666.

1937

Problemat transcendentalnego idealizmu w sformułowaniu semantycznym [A Semantical Version of the Problem of Transcendental Idealism], *PF* XL, 271–287.
Kierunki i prądy filozofii współczesnej [Theories and Schools in Contemporary Philosophy], *Kalendarz IKC,* Kraków, 78–84.

1938

Propedeutyka filozofii dla liceów ogólnokształcących, Książnica-Atlas, Lwów-Warszawa, 2nd ed. 1947, 3rd ed. 1948, 4th ed. 1948, 5th ed. 1950, p. 216.
Mscisław Wartenberg – Obituary, *RF* XIV, 177–184.

1939

O sprawiedliwości [On Justice], *RF* XV, 7–8.
O sprawiedliwości [On Justice], *Kultura i Wychowanie,* 109–121.

1946

Co to jest wolność nauki? [What is Freedom of Science], *Życie Nauki* I, 6, 417–426.
O tzw. neopozytywizmie [On So-called Neo-Positivism], *Myśl Współczesna* II, 155–176.
Logika a doświadczenie [Logic and Experience], *PF* XLIII, 3–22.
Analiza paradoksów Zenona z Elei [An Analysis of Zeno's Paradoxes] *Sprawozdania Poznańskiego Towarzystwa Przyjaciół Nauk* 1/36, 26–27.
Czas prawdziwy [The True Time], *Problemy* III, 1, 43–46.
Konwencjonalne pierwiastki w nauce [The Conventional Elements in Science], *Wiedza i Życie* XVI, 304–313.

1948

Zmiana i sprzeczność [Change and Contradiction], *Myśl Współczesna* (1948), Nos. 8/9, 35-52. Also in *Zycie Nauki* VI, 31/32, 4-15. French abstract in *Synthese* VII, 244.
Epistemologia i semiotyka [Epistemology and Semiotics], *PF* XLIV, 4, 336–347.
Epistemology and Semiotics, *Proceedings of the Xth Congress of Philosophy, Amsterdam,* 607–609.
Kazimierz Twardowski jako nauczyciel filozofii [Kazimierz Twardowski as a Teacher of Philosophy], *Z zagadnień dydaktycznych wyższego szkolnictwa* red. J. Rutkowski, *Poznańskie Towarzystwo Przyjaciół Nauk,* 55–60.
Frenkel Karol 1891–1920. Entry on Frenkel Karol in *Polski Słownik Biograficzny* PAU, VII, Kraków, 129.
Z dziejów pojęcia materii [From the History of the Concept of Matter], *Wiedza i Życie* XVII, 307–312.
Promieniotwórcza rewolucja [Radioactivity – A Revolution in Science], *Wiedza i Życie* XVII, 706–712.

1949

The Scientific World-Perspective, *Readings in Philosophical Analysis*, eds. H. Feigl and
W. Sellars, Appleton-Century-Crofts, New York, 182–190.
Definicja prawdy a zagadnienie idealizmu [The Definition of Truth and the Problem of
Idealism], *Spawozdania Poznańskiego Towarzystwa Przyjaciół Nauk*, 54.
O pojęcia istnienia [On the Notion of Existence], *Sprawozdania Poznańskiego Towar-
zystwa Przyjaciół Nauk*, 55–56.
Zagadnienia i kierunki filozofii: Teoria poznania. Metafizyka. [*Theories and Problems
of Philosophy: Theory of Knowledge, Metaphysics*], Czytelnik, Warszawa, 234 pp.

1950

Logic and Experience, *Synthese* **VIII**, 6/7, 289–299.

1951

Logika, jej zadania i potrzeby w Polsce Ludowej [Logic – Its Uses and Needs in People's
Poland], *Myśl Filozoficzna* 1/2, 50–67.
On the Notion of Existence. Some Remarks Connected with the Problem of Idealism,
Studia Philosophica **IV**, 7–22.

1953

W sprawie artykułu prof. A. Schaffa o moich poglądach filozoficznych [A Reply to
Professor A. Schaff's Article Concerning my Philosophical Views], *Myśl Filozoficzna*
2, 292–334.
Zarys logiki [*An Outline of Logic*], Państwowe Zakłady Wydawnictw Szkolnych, Warszawa,
188 pp. 7 editions between 1953 and 1960.

1955

Klasyfikacja rozumowań [A Classification of Arguments], *Studia Logica* **II**, 278–299.
Sprawa planu prac badawczych w zakresie logiki [The Problem of Planning Research in
Logic], *Studia Logica* **II**, 267–276.
Franciszek Bacon-Novum Organum, edited by K. Ajdukiewicz with an introduction
and annotations, Biblioteka Klasyków Filozofii PWN, VII–XCVIII, 373–435.

1956

Okres warunkowy a implikacja materialna [Conditional Statement and Material Implica-
tion], *Studia Logica* **IV**, 117–134.
W sprawie programów logiki usługowej [On the Teaching of Logic to Non-Philosophers],
Myśl Filozoficzna 2, 126–136.
O definicji [On Definitions], *Normalizacja* Nos. 2, 3, 131–136, 201–207.
Über Fragen der Logik – A Contribution to the Discussion, in *Deutsche Zeitschrift für
Philosophie*, vol. 4, No. 3, 318–338.

1957

O wolności nauki [On the Freedom of Science], *Nauka Polska, PAN,* Warszawa, 1–20.
On the Freedom of Science, *Review of the Polish Academy of Science* **II**, 1/2, 1–19.
Descartes, Medytacje o pierwszej filozofii Meditations on First Philosophy, translated

by Maria Ajdukiewicz and Kazimierz Ajdukiewicz, Biblioteka Klasyków Filozofii, PWN, Warszawa.

1958

Abriss der Logik, translated by M. Dobrosielski. Aufbau Verl., Berlin, 204 pp.
Zagadnienie racjonalności zawodnych sposobów wnioskowania [The Problem of the Rationality of Non-Deductive Types of Inference], *Studia Filozoficzne* 4, 14–29.
Trzy pojęcia definicji [Three Concepts of Definition], *Studia Filozoficzne* 5, 3–16.
Three Concepts of Definition, *Logique et Analyse* I, 3/4, 115–126.
Le problème du fondement des propositions analytiques. *Studia Logica* VIII, 259–272.

1959

Pozanaukowa działalność Kazimierza Twardowskiego-Działalność dydaktyczna i organizacyjna [Kazimierz Twardowski as Teacher], *RF* XIX, 1/2, 29–35.
La notion de rationalité des méthodes d'inference fallibles, *Logique et Analyse*, 5, 3–18.
Co może zerobić szkoła dla podniesienia kultury logicznej uczniów [What the School Can Do to Improve the Standard of Logical Thinking of Students], *Nowa Szkoła* 2, Warszawa, 2–8.

1960

Axiomatic Systems from the Methodological Point of View, *Studia Logica* IX, 205–218.
Związki składniowe między członami zdań oznajmujących [Syntactical Connections between Constituents of Declarative Sentences], *Studia Filozoficzne* 6, 73–86.
Język i Poznanie, Language and Knowledge – Selected Papers 1920–1939, PWN, Warszawa, VIII + 376 pp.

1961

A Method of Eliminating Intensional Sentences and Sentential Formulae, *Atti del XII Congresso Internat. di Filosofia, V, Firenze*, 17–24.
Pomiar [Measurement] *Studia Logica* XI, 223–232.

1962

Subiektywność i niepowtarzalność metody bezpośredniego doświadczenia [The Subjective and Non-Repetitive Nature of the Method of Direct Experience], *Studia Logica* XIII, 209–211.

1963

Zagadnienie uzasadnienia [The Problem of Foundation], *Studia Filozoficzne* 2, 4–13.
Czas [Time], *Wielka Encyklopedia Powszechna* PWN, vol. 2, 703–4.
Definicja [Definition], *Wielka Encyklopedia Powszechna* PWN, vol. 2, 846–7.

1964

Zagadnienie empiryzmu a koncepcja znaczenia [The Problem of Empiricism and the Concept of Meaning], *Studia Filozoficzne* 1, 3–14.
Dowód i wyjaśnienie [Proof and Explanation], in *Szkice filozoficzne Romanowi Ingardenowi w darze*, PWN, Warszawa-Kraków, 211–220.

1965

Logika pragmatyczna, PWN, pp. 408.
Foundations of Statements and Decisions (ed. by K. Ajdukiewicz), PWN and D. Reidel, 1965, 'The Problem of Foundation', pp. 1–11.
Język i Poznanie, Language and Knowledge – Selected Papers 1945–1963, Vol. II, PWN, Warszawa, 425 pp.

1966

From the Methodology of Deduction Sentences, translated by J. Giedymin, *Studia Logica* **XIX**, 9–46.

1967

Intensional Expressions, *Studia Logica* **XX**, 63–86.
Proposition as the Connotation of a Sentence, *Studia Logica* **XX**, 87–98.
Syntactic Connexion, in *Polish Logic 1920–1934*, (ed. by Storrs McCall), Oxford U.P., pp. 207–231.

1973

Problems and Theories of Philosophy, translated by H. Skolimowski and A. Quinton, Cambridge U.P.

1974

Pragmatic Logic, translated by O. Wojtasiewicz, D. Reidel and PWN, Synthese Library, vol. 62. XV + 460 pp.

INDEX OF NAMES

Ajdukiewicz, K. vii, ix–xii, xiii–xviii, xix–xxii, xxvi–viii, xxxv–liii, 64, 66, 89, 154, 181, 191, 281, 319, 361
Aristotle xx, 97–102, 107, 109, 140, 195

Baden School 148
Bellarmino, R. xliii
Bergson, H. xxviii, xxxii, xxxv, lii, 87, 197
Berkeley, G. xx, 148, 184–6
Bernard, C1. xxix
Black, M. 249
Bolzano, B. ix, xx, 141
Bonola, R. li
Bosanquet, B. lii
Boutroux, E. xxviii
Bradley, F. H. lii
Brentano, F. xiii, 38

Cantor, G. xxii
Carnap, R. xxvi, xliii, 64–5, 89, 129, 139, 141, 181, 243, 250–1, 299, 330, 349
Cohen, H. 148
Comte, A. xxix, xxxii
Couturat, L. ix
Czerwinski, Z. xiv

Dedekind, J. 1
Dilthey, W. ix, xx
Duhem, P. xxviii, xxxii–v, li–ii, 313

Eubulidus 81

Frege, G. 140, 348–9, 350

Gauss, C. F. xxiii
Geach, P. x, lii
Grünbaum, A. li

Harrah, D. xi
Hempel, C. 141
Hilbert, D. xiii
Hume, D. xx, xlv, 249
Husserl, E. ix, x, xiii, xx, 2, 14, 34, 37, 64, 95, 118, 119, 139

Jevons, S. 297
Johnson, V. E. 96, 109
Jordan, Z. xiv

Kant, I. ix, xiii, xxii, xxiv, xxxvi, xliv–v, 86–7, 148, 188
Klein, F. li
Kotarbiński, T. xiv, xx, 97–106, 109, 119

Leibniz, G. W. 91, 323–4
LeRoy, E. vii, xi, xx, xxii, xxvii–ix, xxxii, xxxiv–xxxvi, xlv, lii, 68, 87, 89
Leśniewski, S. x, xiv, 34, 95, 97, 101–2, 107, 118–21, 138, 139, 140
Lie, S. xxiv
Lobatchevsky, N. xxiii
Łukasiewicz, J. xiii, xiv, 65, 128, 139, 181, 316

Mach, E. xx
Malewski, A. xiv
Marburg School 148
Marty, A. 2, 34
Mehlberg, H. xiv, 141
Meinong, A. 37
Milhaud, G. xxviii, xxxi, lii
Mill, J. S. 18, 21, 34, 53, 297, 302, 318
Morris, Ch. xlvi

Newton, I. xliv, 70, 245
Nicod, J. 141

Ossowski, S. 34
Ossowska-Niedźwiecki, M. 8

Peano, G. 1
Peirce, Ch. 304
Pelc, J. xiv
Plekhanov, M. 199
Poincaré, H. vii, ix, xix–xx, xxii–xxviii, xxxii, xxxiv–vi, xxxviii–xxxix, xliii, xlix, li, lii, 67, 86, 88, 89, 313
Popper, K. xxvi
Poznański, E. 313
Przełęcki, M. xii, xiv

Quine, W. V. O. xxvi, xlix, 228
Quinton, A. xliv, liii

Raoult, F. M. 171–2
Reinach, A. 198–9
Rickert, H. 148–9, 50
Riemann, B. xxiii
Russell, B. xxiii, lii, 53, 89, 107, 118,
127, 135–6, 142

Schaff, A. 181
Scholz, H. 131
Shimony, A. 252
Sierpiński, W. xiii
Simmel, G. 243
Skolimowski, H. xliv, liii
Spranger, E. ix, xx, lii, 285, 299
Şuszko, R. xiv

Świeżawski, S xv
Szaniawski, K. xii, xiv, xv

Tarski, A. x, xiv, xxxviii, xliv, xlvi, xlvii,
xlix–l, 141, 147, 153, 315
Tuomela, R. lii
Twardowski, K. xiii
Twardowska-Ajdukiewicz, Maria xiii

Wang, H. l
White, M. G. xxvi
Whitehead, A. N. 53, 89, 90, 135, 140–1
Wilbois, J. xxviii, lii
Wittgenstein, L. 65
Wójcicki, R. xli
Wundheiler, A. 313

Zeno 193–202

INDEX OF SUBJECTS

Acceptance
  of a sentence 22–9, 38
  motivated by belief 22–9
  and language (meaning)rules 27–9,
    40–7
  v. rejection 38, 74, 88–9, 113, 309–12,
    314
  see also Assertion
Aim (goal)
  of science 81, 85, 117
  quasi-aims of science 285
Analytic sentence xlix, 174–6, 254–6,
    260
  and axiomatic meaning rules 173–4,
    177
  and apriorism, empiricism, convention-
    alism 174–5, 307–18
  principles 72
  semantic concept of 256–7, 260–1,
    268
  syntactic concept of 256–7, 260–1
  validation of 256, 260–1, 263–8
Answer (to a question),
  complete 159, 161
    direct complete 160–1
    indirect 160–1
  exhaustive 160
  improper 159, 161
  partial 159, 161
  proper 159, 161
  refuting the positive assumption 160
Apparatus, Conceptual *see* Conceptual
A priori, Apriorism 165, 174, 194,
    306–18
  methodological 317
Articulated
  judgment 36–8
  non-articulated judgment 36
  well-articulated expression 122
Assertion
  see Acceptance
  assertion-moment 37–8
    negative 37
    positive 37
  assertive and non-assertive axiomatic
    system, *see* axiomatic system
Associationism

linguistic 7–8
  criticism of linguistic 8–18
Assumptions (of a question) 158–9
Axiom
  axiomatic system xl, 282–294
  assertive v. non-assertive (neutral) a.s.
    288–94
  in the semantical sense
    syntactical sense 286
    pragmatic sense xli, 286, 288–94
  axiomatic meaning rule 45–7, 58–9,
    309–13
  of a language xli, 71, 174, 178

Belief (in the truth of a sentence) 22–9
  see Acceptance, Assertion

Category 95–109
  ontological 105
  semantical 95–109
  syntactical 95–109
  categorical grammar, Ajdukiewicz's x
Change
  and contradiction 192–208
  of language 50–7, 60–1, 67–80,
    83–9
  in the total scope of meaning-rules
    45–50
  scientific, replacing one conceptual
    apparatus by another 79–88
Co-denotation xlvii, 318–19
Conceptual apparatus (Framework) xi,
    xix, xxxix–xl, 57, 62, 67–89,
    104–105, 113–17
  choice of 104
  evolutionary tendencies of 84–6
  epistemological changes in 117
  of classical and relativistic physics 76
  and the structure of the language-
    matrix 62
  and the world-perspective 113–17
Classical concept of truth *see* Truth
Conditional statement 222–5, 235–8
Connotation 18–23, 348, 350–3, 356–9
Connected language *see* Language, Syn-
    tax
Connection (connexion), syntactical *see*

Syntax
Consequence relation 28–30, 45, 141, 144–6
  direct (immediate) 144–7, 149–50
  indirect (mediate) 144–7
Constituent of an Expression 122–3, 127, 269–81
  see also Expression
Continuity, Principle of 203
Contradiction
  and change 192–208
  contradictory sentences in terms of rejection rules 88–9
  law of contradiction 192
  and tendencies in scientific development 85
Convention 67, 77–8, 85
  problems unsolvable without a convention 67, 85
  terminological 254, 257–60, 263
Conventionalism xix–liii
  ordinary 67, 77–9, 298
  radical, of Ajdukiewicz vii, xi–xii, xix–liii, 72–6, 79, 81, 86
  radical, of LeRoy (nominalism) xxviii–xxxv, 68, 87–9
  and vague expressions 77–9
  and the law of excluded middle 152–3
Critique, la nouvelle des sciences xx, xxviii–xxxii

Datum questionis 156–7, 161
Decidable sentence, in virtue of meaning-rules 65
Decision question, see Question
Deduction 168–9
  actual and potential 287–8
  principle of a deduction 158–9
Deductive
  meaning-rule 45–7, 58–9
  system, see Axiomatic system, Consequence
  complete and incomplete 147
  inference 24–30, 41–7, 49–50
  see also Consequence, Axiomatic system, Deduction Hypothesis testing, Inference
Definition
  as a rule of inference 54
  in the meta-language 54–259
  in the object language 259–63
  classical definition of 'truth' see Truth
  of 'meaning' see Meaning

Degree of Certainty 239–41, 245–6, 251–2
  subjective 239
  measure of 239–42, 252–3
Degree of confirmation 250–1
Denotation xlvii, 18–23, 182–3, 255, 257–60, 264, 266–7, 315, 328, 349–50, 356–8, 360
  adequate definition of 182–3
  co-denotation xlvii, 318
  of operators 321
  of predicates 255
  of proper names 255, 264, 321
  of propositional functions 264
Derivation, derivable see Consequence
Derivative of the index sequence of an expression, see Expression

Empirical
  hypothesis elevated to a principle xxxviii, 70–1
  knowledge 313–14
  meaning-rules xxxvii, xli, xlviii–ix, 27–9, 39–44, 45–9, 58–9, 68–9, 112–13
  methodology 297–303
  sentence 65, 166, 174, 180
Empiricism xxi, xxii, xlvii, xlix, 165–7, 172–181, 306–19
  genetic xxii
  geometric xxiii, xxvii
  methodological v. epistemological 307, 317
  moderate v. radical xix–xxii, 165–7, 172–5, 176–7, 298
Epistemology (theory of knowledge) xi, xix, 81–4, 117, 140–1, 174, 182–91, 282
  semantical theory of knowledge 142
  epistemological v. methodological problems of empiricism 307
  pluralist epistemology xix
Existence xxvii–xxviii, 209–21
  in mathematics xxvii
  real v. intentional 209, 211, 214–20
  relativity of xxviii
  and the thesis of idealism 209–21
Experience 46–7, 59, 68, 72–6, 87, 165–81, 307–8, 314, 317
  and empirical meaning rules 46–7, 68
  experiential data and the language matrix 59
  experiential data do not uniquely

impose any world-picture 67, 72–6
and factual reports v. interpretations
77–9
and radical conventionalism of LeRoy
87
and logic 165–81
Expression 1–34, 50–62, 66, 95, 104,
118, 121–2, 133–8, 229, 320–47,
353–4, 356, 358
composite 121–2, 127–8, 131
compound 353, 355–6
constituent of 320–2, 325, 328–9,
331–2, 335, 337–40, 345–7, 353–5
nth order constituent of 122–4,
127–8, 329, 353
equivalence of 320–2, 325, 329–30,
335–9, 346
exponent of 123, 125, 127, 131–2,
134
extensional 320
first derivative of 124
final derivative of 125, 131–4
intensional 320, 322–3, 325–6, 331,
339
partial index sequence of 132
proper index sequence of 124–6,
131–3
proper word sequence of 124
well-articulated 122
well-articulated throughout 122–3,
125
Extension 350–2
of a predicate 255
extensionalism, thesis of extensionality
90–2
extensionalism v. intensionalism 318
Evolution(ary)
view of science xl, 84–5
e. tendencies of conceptual apparatuses
84–5

Fact xxix–xxxv, 77–9, 87, 114–15
facts v. interpretations xxxix–xl, 77–9
reciprocal accommodation of facts
to theories 114–15
scientists create facts xxix, 87
Falsity xlv, 348–9
see also Truth
Foundation (justification, validation)
295–305
Functor 119–20, 122–3, 125, 127–31
135–8
main 122–5, 127, 136

n.-adic 127
sentence-forming 120–137
truth- 129–30

Game system 248–9
Geisteswissenschaft ix, 117
understanding methodology ix
hermeneutic understanding xx

Hypothesis
empirical hypotheses transformed into
principles 70–2
hypothetical syllogism 196–7
logical theorems as hypotheses 179
testing (verification) of 169–72

Idealism xxi, xliii, xlvi, 140–53, 182,
184–8, 209–21
metaphysical 182
objective (logical) 186–9, 219–21
subjective 148, 184–8, 211, 218–19
transcendental xlvi, 140–53, 186
and existence 209–21
ideal (intersubjective) meaning xi, xlv,
xlii, 35
idealised assumption xlviii, 63–4, 88
Identity
Leibniz's definition of 323–4
Index of an expression, see Expression
Induction 239
justification of 239
see non-deductive inference
Inference 24–30, 41–7, 49–50
deductive 24–30, 41–7, 49–50, 166–
9
non-deductive 239–253
see also Hypothesis testing, meaning-
rules, Axiomatic systems
Inflection(al) see Language
Interrogative sentence 155–64
see also Question, Answer

Judgment 36, 67–8, 72, 116–17
in the logical sense 36, 148–9
in the psychological sense 36

Knowledge xix, xliv, 35, 87, 113,
141–3, 146, 149, 165–82, 306–13
A priori 165–81, 306–12
empirical 307–313
in the logical sense 141, 143
psychological sense 141, 143
indubitable component of 113

and epistemology 141
semantic theory of knowledge 142–3, 146

Language
  Ajdukiewicz-language xl–xliv
  axioms of a language, axiomatic meaning rules 45–50, 58–9, 145–6, 151, 309–13
  change of 49–57, 61, 70–2, 76, 79–81, 84–8, 114–17
  closed 50–6, 58, 69, 79–80
  conception of l. and epistemology (apriorism, empiricism) xlix, 4, 36, 178, 307–19
  connected 51–2, 58, 69, 79–80
  as a deductive (axiomatic) system 144–6, xl–xliv
  discursive l. structure 63
  empirical structure of a l. 63
  idealized xl, 88, 63–4
  inflectional 273–4, 346, 355
  isolated part of 51, 69
  learning to speak 26, 28
  matrix of xi, xxxvii, 58–61
  meta-language 140, 147, 150, 183–6, 188–91, 335, 341, 343, 359
  object-language 184, 186–90, 324, 327, 335
  open 50–3, 58, 69
  ordinary language 63–4, 104–9
  positional 273, 355
  rules of language (axiomatic, deductive, empirical) 27–9, 39–44, 45–7, 58–9, 68, 112–13, 147, 149, 309–13
  structure 62–3
  transition to a non-translatable l. 76
  translatable languages xxxvi, 56–62, 69, 72, 76
  non-translatable xxxvi, 76–80
  universal 80–1
Law
  of contradiction 165, 176, 192–4, 199, 203, 207
  of excluded middle 147, 150–3, 166–7, 176–8, 199, 207
Logic 44, 89, 90–4, 95, 121, 140–1, 165–81, 199–203, 209, 222, 282–8
  change of 81, 179
  tautology 167–8, 175
  see also law, semantics, syntax
  truths of 256, 258–61
Matrix of a language xi, xxxvii, 58–62

Meaning
  and acceptance 22, 38, 43
  associationist theory of 7–8, 33
  -change xxxviii, 31–3, 50–1, 70–1, 93
  and conceptual apparatus 57, 69, 71–2
  connotation 18–23
  and dispositions to motivational relations xxxvi, 20, 23–9
  definition of 23, 31–2, 35, 57–63
  denotation 22–3
  as equivalence class of positions in the language-matrix 62
  ideal (linguistic) xi, 35, 141, 148, 161, 176
  identity of (synonymity) 53, 60
  intention of the act of 33
  knowledge as 35
  and language rules 27–9, 39–47
  and language-matrix 62
  meaningless sentence 65
  procedure to discover (misunderstandings) difference in 40–1
  psychological 141, 161
  meaning-related expressions xxxviii, 48, 54–6, 69
  rules of xxxviii, xlviii–ix, 27–9, 39–44, 45–9, 68, 78, 82–3
  specification (assignment) 39, 45–9, 50, 63–4, 68–70
  synonymity 30–2, 53–4, 60
  translation 53–4
  universe of 79–80, 83
  universal invariant xxxiv
  and vagueness 104–5
  verbal and intuitive 32–3
  violation of 40–4, 68, 112
Meta-language, *see* Language
Modal
  operators 346–7
  terms 320, 326, 346

Names 18, 30, 119, 350–52, 358
  in suppositione personali 120
  in suppositione simplici 120
  general 119
  proper 119, 350
Name category 119–20, 130
Non-deductive, *see* Inference

Objective mind 141
Ontology 101, 105–9, 209

see existence
see also Leśniewski
o. category 10, 109
o. thesis of extensionality 91
Operator 128–31, 135, 138, 321, 334, 350–1, 353, 355, 357
circumflex 135–8
main 321, 334, 340, 346, 353–4, 356–358
sentence-forming 350

Phenomenology
intention of the act of meaning 33
phenomenological method 93
see also Husserl
Postulate 255–62
existential xxvii
Pragmatism 85, 304
pragmatic xi
see Axiomatic systems in the pragmatic sense
pragmatics xlvi
Precision 77–8, 151–3, 156–7
and acceptance (meaning) rules 156
expressions made precise by conventions 156–7
and vagueness 151–3, 156
Principle xxxviii–ix, xliv, xlix, 72, 133, 203–6
of continuity 203–6
and change of language 72
of transition 203–6
hypotheses elevated to the status of principles 70–2, xliv
and the tendency to rationalisation 133
Probability 248–250
classical 250
frequency concept of 244, 250–53
logical 250–3
mathematical concept of 250–2
Proposition 251–3, 348–61
false 349
true 349, 355, 359
Psycho-physical identity thesis 90–1

Question, *see* also interrogative sentence 157
Assumption of a 158
complementation q. 158
decision q. (whether -q) 158
didactic q. 162
heuristic q. 163

Quotation
expression in q. marks 4–5
-marks 334–5

Rationalism v. empiricism, *see* Apriorism
Rationality 239–53
of actions 245, 249
of beliefs 250
of concrete inferences 247–8
of methods of inference 245–53
Realism xliii, xlvi, 184
see also Idealism
Reism 105–8
see also Kotarbiński
Rules, *see* Language 45–7, 58–9, 68, 147, 149–50, 17, 177
axiomatic
deductive
empirical

Science xix, xxi, xxxviii
changes in xix, xxi, 70–2, 79–89, 114–17
s. facts xxix, xxxii
tendencies in the development of 84–6
rejection of universality 79–81
goals and quasi-goals of 81, 85, 117
see also Conceptual apparatus
Semantic(s) 2, 95–7, 99, 103, 107–9, 140–154
category 95–7, 99, 103, 107–9, 270, 275–7
of ordinary language 95–7
index of a s. category 99–100
s. theory of knowledge 142
see also Syntax, Semiotic, Semasiology, Pragmatics
Semasiology
semasiological 35, 63
Semiotics 182–91
Sentence 22–9, 38, 119, 348–50, 358–9
acceptance of 22–9, 38, 225–6, 228–31, 234, 237–8, 239–42
basic content of 331, 336–7, 341–3
basic description of 332–5
full content of 330–1, 342
equivalent, equiexpressive 235–6
what is asserted by 229–33, 237–8
what is expressed by 229–33, 236–38
what is stated by 327, 342
category 120, 130, 136

Signs, Signals 1–2
Synonymity 30–2, 53–63, 254, 315
  as inferential substitutivity 30, 32
  isotopic expressions 60
  necessary condition for s. of two
    expressions of *L* 53, 315
  and invariance of meaning rules 315
  s. of two expressions of two languages
    54–60
Syntax, Syntactical
  category 10–19, 95, 118
  connected 118, 123, 125, 127–8,
    135–8
  connexion 118–39, 269–81
  position of a constituent 272, 321–2,
    328–32, 338–9, 343–7, 353–9
  index of position 274
  structure of a sentence 272
  subordination 271–2
  see also Semantics, Pragmatics, Semi-
    otics

Terms
  general and singular 146–7, 159
  in suppositione materiali 142–3
  maximally universal 155, 158
  universal 143, 159
  vague 151
Terminological convention 254–61,
    257–60, 265–6
  semantical 254–6, 259, 263
  syntactical 254–6, 260–3
Theorem
  finitistic v. infinitistic concept of 150
Transcendental, Idealism 140–53
  semantical paraphrase of 149
  norms 149, 187
  subject 190
Translation 53–63, 79–89
  and conceptual apparatus 57
  literal and incomplete 65–6, 328,
    330–3, 342–3
  of *n*th degree 328–30
  translatable v. non-translatable lan-
    guages 56–7, 60–2, 69, 72, 75,

80, 84, 88, 108
  see also Synonymity, Conceptual ap-
    paratus
Truth, True
  adequate definition of 182–3
  classical concept of 186–8
  coherence concept of 187
  criteria of 187
  falsity xlv, 165, 348–9
  of world-perspectives 81–4, 116–17
  non-classical concepts of 187–8
  relativised to a conceptual apparatus
    84
  syntactical definition of 188–9

Understanding ix, 117
  hermeneutic xx
  methodology ix
Universal(s) 95–110
  universale 101
  language 80–1
  see also Term, Name, Reism
Utility 243

Vague(ness) 104–5, 107–8, 151
Variable 129–131
  apparent 129, 131
  bound 129, 131, 135

World 340, 343–4
  in concreto 344
  in specie 344–5
  see also Expression
World-perspective, Scientific 111–17
  see also Conceptual apparatus
World-picture 67–89
  connected 81
  different world-pictures 81
  linguistic 83, 89
  and truth 81–84
  see also Conceptual apparatus

SYNTHESE LIBRARY

Monographs on Epistemology, Logic, Methodology,
Philosophy of Science, Sociology of Science and of Knowledge, and on the
Mathematical Methods of Social and Behavioral Sciences

Managing Editor:
JAAKKO HINTIKKA (Academy of Finland and Stanford University)

Editors:

ROBERT S. COHEN (Boston University)
DONALD DAVIDSON (University of Chicago)
GABRIËL NUCHELMANS (University of Leyden)
WESLEY C. SALMON (University of Arizona)

1. J. M. Bocheński, *A Precis of Mathematical Logic.* 1959, X + 100 pp.
2. P. L. Guiraud, *Problèmes et méthodes de la statistique linguistique.* 1960, VI + 146 pp.
3. Hans Freudenthal (ed.), *The Concept and the Role of the Model in Mathematics and Natural and Social Sciences, Proceedings of a Colloquium held at Utrecht, The Netherlands, January 1960.* 1961, VI + 194 pp.
4. Evert W. Beth, *Formal Methods. An Introduction to Symbolic Logic and the Study of Effective Operations in Arithmetic and Logic.* 1962, XIV + 170 pp.
5. B. H. Kazemier and D. Vuysje (eds.), *Logic and Language. Studies Dedicated to Professor Rudolf Carnap on the Occasion of His Seventieth Birthday.* 1962, VI + 256 pp.
6. Marx W. Wartofsky (ed.), *Proceedings of the Boston Colloquium for the Philosophy of Science, 1961-1962,* Boston Studies in the Philosophy of Science (ed. by Robert S. Cohen and Marx W. Wartofsky), Volume I. 1973, VIII + 212 pp.
7. A. A. Zinov'ev, *Philosophical Problems of Many-Valued Logic.* 1963, XIV + 155 pp.
8. Georges Gurvitch, *The Spectrum of Social Time.* 1964, XXVI + 152 pp.
9. Paul Lorenzen, *Formal Logic.* 1965, VIII + 123 pp.
10. Robert S. Cohen and Marx W. Wartofsky (eds.), *In Honor of Philipp Frank,* Boston Studies in the Philosophy of Science (ed. by Robert S. Cohen and Marx W. Wartofsky), Volume II. 1965, XXXIV + 475 pp.
11. Evert W. Beth, *Mathematical Thought. An Introduction to the Philosophy of Mathematics.* 1965, XII + 208 pp.
12. Evert W. Beth and Jean Piaget, *Mathematical Epistemology and Psychology.* 1966, XII + 326 pp.
13. Guido Küng, *Ontology and the Logistic Analysis of Language. An Enquiry into the Contemporary Views on Universals.* 1967, XI + 210 pp.
14. Robert S. Cohen and Marx W. Wartofsky (eds.), *Proceedings of the Boston Colloquium for the Philosophy of Science 1964-1966, in Memory of Norwood Russell Hanson,* Boston Studies in the Philosophy of Science (ed. by Robert S. Cohen and Marx W. Wartofsky), Volume III. 1967, XLIX + 489 pp.

15. C. D. Broad, *Induction, Probability, and Causation. Selected Papers.* 1968, XI + 296 pp.
16. Günther Patzig, *Aristotle's Theory of the Syllogism. A Logical-Philosophical Study of Book A of the Prior Analytics.* 1968, XVII + 215 pp.
17. Nicholas Rescher, *Topics in Philosophical Logic.* 1968, XIV + 347 pp.
18. Robert S. Cohen and Marx W. Wartofsky (eds.), *Proceedings of the Boston Colloquium for the Philosophy of Science 1966-1968,* Boston Studies in the Philosophy of Science (ed. by Robert S. Cohen and Marx W. Wartofsky), Volume IV. 1969, VIII + 537 pp.
19. Robert S. Cohen and Marx W. Wartofsky (eds.), *Proceedings of the Boston Colloquium for the Philosophy of Science 1966-1968,* Boston Studies in the Philosophy of Science (ed. by Robert S. Cohen and Marx W. Wartofsky), Volume V. 1969, VIII + 482 pp.
20. J.W. Davis, D. J. Hockney, and W. K. Wilson (eds.), *Philosophical Logic.* 1969, VIII + 277 pp.
21. D. Davidson and J. Hintikka (eds.), *Words and Objections: Essays on the Work of W.V. Quine.* 1969, VIII + 366 pp.
22. Patrick Suppes, *Studies in the Methodology and Foundations of Science. Selected Papers from 1911 to 1969.* 1969, XII + 473 pp.
23. Jaakko Hintikka, *Models for Modalities. Selected Essays.* 1969, IX + 220 pp.
24. Nicholas Rescher *et al.* (eds.), *Essays in Honor of Carl G. Hempel. A Tribute on the Occasion of His Sixty-Fifth Birthday.* 1969, VII + 272 pp.
25. P. V. Tavanec (ed.), *Problems of the Logic of Scientific Knowledge.* 1969, XII + 429 pp.
26. Marshall Swain (ed.), *Induction, Acceptance, and Rational Belief.* 1970, VII + 232 pp.
27. Robert S. Cohen and Raymond J. Seeger (eds.), *Ernst Mach: Physicist and Philosopher,* Boston Studies in the Philosophy of Science (ed. by Robert S. Cohen and Marx W. Wartofsky), Volume VI. 1970, VIII + 295 pp.
28. Jaakko Hintikka and Patrick Suppes, *Information and Inference.* 1970, X + 336 pp.
29. Karel Lambert, *Philosophical Problems in Logic. Some Recent Developments.* 1970, VII + 176 pp.
30. Rolf A. Eberle, *Nominalistic Systems.* 1970, IX + 217 pp.
31. Paul Weingartner and Gerhard Zecha (eds.), *Induction, Physics, and Ethics: Proceedings and Discussions of the 1968 Salzburg Colloquium in the Philosophy of Science.* 1970, X + 382 pp.
32. Evert W. Beth, *Aspects of Modern Logic.* 1970, XI + 176 pp.
33. Risto Hilpinen (ed.), *Deontic Logic: Introductory and Systematic Readings.* 1971, VII + 182 pp.
34. Jean-Louis Krivine, *Introduction to Axiomatic Set Theory.* 1971, VII + 98 pp.
35. Joseph D. Sneed, *The Logical Structure of Mathematical Physics.* 1971, XV + 311 pp.
36. Carl R. Kordig, *The Justification of Scientific Change.* 1971, XIV + 119 pp.
37. Milič Čapek, *Bergson and Modern Physics,* Boston Studies in the Philosophy of Science (ed. by Robert S. Cohen and Marx W. Wartofsky), Volume VII. 1971, XV + 414 pp.

38. Norwood Russell Hanson, *What I Do Not Believe, and Other Essays* (ed. by Stephen Toulmin and Harry Woolf), 1971, XII + 390 pp.
39. Roger C. Buck and Robert S. Cohen (eds.), *PSA 1970. In Memory of Rudolf Carnap*, Boston Studies in the Philosophy of Science (ed. by Robert S. Cohen and Marx W. Wartofsky), Volume VIII. 1971, LXVI + 615 pp. Also available as paperback.
40. Donald Davidson and Gilbert Harman (eds.), *Semantics of Natural Language.* 1972, X + 769 pp. Also available as paperback.
41. Yehoshua Bar-Hillel (ed.), *Pragmatics of Natural Languages.* 1971, VII + 231 pp.
42. Sören Stenlund, *Combinators, λ-Terms and Proof Theory.* 1972, 184 pp.
43. Martin Strauss, *Modern Physics and Its Philosophy. Selected Papers in the Logic, History, and Philosophy of Science.* 1972, X + 297 pp.
44. Mario Bunge, *Method, Model and Matter.* 1973, VII + 196 pp.
45. Mario Bunge, *Philosophy of Physics.* 1973, IX + 248 pp.
46. A. A. Zinov'ev, *Foundations of the Logical Theory of Scientific Knowledge (Complex Logic)*, Boston Studies in the Philosophy of Science (ed. by Robert S. Cohen and Marx W. Wartofsky), Volume IX. Revised and enlarged English edition with an appendix, by G. A. Smirnov, E. A. Sidorenka, A. M. Fedina, and L. A. Bobrova. 1973, XXII + 301 pp. Also available as paperback.
47. Ladislav Tondl, *Scientific Procedures*, Boston Studies in the Philosophy of Science (ed. by Robert S. Cohen and Marx W. Wartofsky), Volume X. 1973, XII + 268 pp. Also available as paperback.
48. Norwood Russell Hanson, *Constellations and Conjectures* (ed. by Willard C. Humphreys, Jr.). 1973, X + 282 pp.
49. K. J. J. Hintikka, J. M. E. Moravcsik, and P. Suppes (eds.), *Approaches to Natural Language. Proceedings of the 1970 Stanford Workshop on Grammar and Semantics.* 1973, VIII + 526 pp. Also available as paperback.
50. Mario Bunge (ed.), *Exact Philosophy – Problems, Tools, and Goals.* 1973, X + 214 pp.
51. Radu J. Bogdan and Ilkka Niiniluoto (eds.), *Logic, Language, and Probability. A Selection of Papers Contributed to Sections IV, VI, and XI of the Fourth International Congress for Logic, Methodology, and Philosophy of Science, Bucharest, September 1971.* 1973, X + 323 pp.
52. Glenn Pearce and Patrick Maynard (eds.), *Conceptual Chance.* 1973, XII + 282 pp.
53. Ilkka Niiniluoto and Raimo Tuomela, *Theoretical Concepts and Hypothetico-Inductive Inference.* 1973, VII + 264 pp.
54. Roland Fraïssé, *Course of Mathematical Logic* – Volume 1: *Relation and Logical Formula.* 1973, XVI + 186 pp. Also available as paperback.
55. Adolf Grünbaum, *Philosophical Problems of Space and Time.* Second, enlarged edition, Boston Studies in the Philosophy of Science (ed. by Robert S. Cohen and Marx W. Wartofsky), Volume XII. 1973, XXIII + 884 pp. Also available as paperback.
56. Patrick Suppes (ed.), *Space, Time, and Geometry.* 1973, XI + 424 pp.
57. Hans Kelsen, *Essays in Legal and Moral Philosophy*, selected and introduced by Ota Weinberger. 1973, XXVIII + 300 pp.
58. R. J. Seeger and Robert S. Cohen (eds.), *Philosophical Foundations of Science. Proceedings of an AAAS Program, 1969*, Boston Studies in the Philosophy of

Science (ed. by Robert S. Cohen and Marx W. Wartofsky), Volume XI. 1974, X + 545 pp. Also available as paperback.

59. Robert S. Cohen and Marx W. Wartofsky (eds.), *Logical and Epistemological Studies in Contemporary Physics*, Boston Studies in the Philosophy of Science (ed. by Robert S. Cohen and Marx W. Wartofsky), Volume XIII. 1973, VIII + 462 pp. Also available as paperback.

60. Robert S. Cohen and Marx W. Wartofsky (eds.), *Methodological and Historical Essays in the Natural and Social Sciences. Proceedings of the Boston Colloquium for the Philosophy of Science, 1969-1972,* Boston Studies in the Philosophy of Science (ed. by Robert S. Cohen and Marx W. Wartofsky), Volume XIV. 1974, VIII + 405 pp. Also available as paperback.

61. Robert S. Cohen, J. J. Stachel and Marx W. Wartofsky (eds.), *For Dirk Struik. Scientific, Historical and Political Essays in Honor of Dirk J. Struik*, Boston Studies in the Philosophy of Science (ed. by Robert S. Cohen and Marx W. Wartofsky), Volume XV. 1974, XXVII + 652 pp. Also available as paperback.

62. Kazimierz Ajdukiewicz, *Pragmatic Logic*, transl. from the Polish by Olgierd Wojtasiewicz. 1974, XV + 460 pp.

63. Sören Stenlund (ed.), *Logical Theory and Semantic Analysis. Essays Dedicated to Stig Kanger on His Fiftieth Birthday*. 1974, V + 217 pp.

64. Kenneth F. Schaffner and Robert S. Cohen (eds.), *Proceedings of the 1972 Biennial Meeting, Philosophy of Science Association*, Boston Studies in the Philosophy of Science (ed. by Robert S. Cohen and Marx W. Wartofsky), Volume XX. 1974, IX + 444 pp. Also available as paperback.

65. Henry E. Kyburg, Jr., *The Logical Foundations of Statistical Inference*. 1974, IX + 421 pp.

66. Marjorie Grene, *The Understanding of Nature: Essays in the Philosophy of Biology*, Boston Studies in the Philosophy of Science (ed. by Robert S. Cohen and Marx W. Wartofsky), Volume XXIII. 1974, XII + 360 pp. Also available as paperback.

67. Jan M. Broekman, *Structuralism: Moscow, Prague, Paris*. 1974, IX + 117 pp.

68. Norman Geschwind, *Selected Papers on Language and the Brain*, Boston Studies in the Philosophy of Science (ed. by Robert S. Cohen and Marx W. Wartofsky), Volume XVI. 1974, XII + 549 pp. Also available as paperback.

69. Roland Fraïssé, *Course of Mathematical Logic* – Volume 2: *Model Theory*. 1974, XIX + 192 pp.

70. Andrzej Grzegorczyk, *An Outline of Mathematical Logic. Fundamental Results and Notions Explained with All Details*. 1974, X + 596 pp.

71. Franz von Kutschera, *Philosophy of Language*. 1975, VII + 305 pp.

72. Juha Manninen and Raimo Tuomela (eds.), *Essays on Explanation and Understanding. Studies in the Foundations of Humanities and Social Sciences*. 1976, VII + 440 pp.

73. Jaakko Hintikka (ed.), *Rudolf Carnap, Logical Empiricist. Materials and Perspectives*. 1975, LXVIII + 400 pp.

74. Milič Čapek (ed.), *The Concepts of Space and Time. Their Structure and Their Development*, Boston Studies in the Philosophy of Science (ed. by Robert S. Cohen and Marx W. Wartofsky), Volume XXII. 1976, LVI + 570 pp. Also available as paperback.

75. Jaakko Hintikka and Unto Remes, *The Method of Analysis. Its Geometrical Origin and Its General Significance*, Boston Studies in the Philosophy of Science (ed. by Robert S. Cohen and Marx W. Wartofsky), Volume XXV. 1974, XVIII + 144 pp. Also available as paperback.

76. John Emery Murdoch and Edith Dudley Sylla, *The Cultural Context of Medieval Learning. Proceedings of the First International Colloquium on Philosophy, Science, and Theology in the Middle Ages – September 1973*, Boston Studies in the Philosophy of Science (ed. by Robert S. Cohen and Marx W. Wartofsky), Volume XXVI. 1975, X + 566 pp. Also available as paperback.

77. Stefan Amsterdamski, *Between Experience and Metaphysics. Philosophical Problems of the Evolution of Science*, Boston Studies in the Philosophy of Science (ed. by Robert S. Cohen and Marx W. Wartofsky), Volume XXXV. 1975, XVIII + 193 pp. Also available as paperback.

78. Patrick Suppes (ed.), *Logic and Probability in Quantum Mechanics*. 1976, XV + 541 pp.

79. Hermann von Helmholtz: *Epistemological Writings. The Paul Hertz/Moritz Schlick Centenary Edition of 1921 with Notes and Commentary by the Editors*. (Newly translated by Malcolm F. Lowe. Edited with an Introduction and Bibliography, by Robert S. Cohen and Yehuda Elkana), Boston Studies in the Philosophy of Science (ed. by Robert S. Cohen and Marx W. Wartofsky), Volume XXXVII. 1977, XXXVIII+204 pp. Also available as paperback.

80. Joseph Agassi, *Science in Flux*, Boston Studies in the Philosophy of Science (ed. by Robert S. Cohen and Marx W. Wartofsky), Volume XXVIII. 1975, XXVI + 553 pp. Also available as paperback.

81. Sandra G. Harding (ed.), *Can Theories Be Refuted? Essays on the Duhem-Quine Thesis*. 1976, XXI + 318 pp. Also available as paperback.

82. Stefan Nowak, *Methodology of Sociological Research: General Problems*. 1977, XVIII + 504 pp.

83. Jean Piaget, Jean-Blaise Grize, Alina Szeminska, and Vinh Bang, *Epistemology and Psychology of Functions*, Studies in Genetic Epistemology, Volume XXIII. 1977, XIV+205 pp.

84. Marjorie Grene and Everett Mendelsohn (eds.), *Topics in the Philosophy of Biology*, Boston Studies in the Philosophy of Science (ed. by Robert S. Cohen and Marx W. Wartofsky), Volume XXVII. 1976, XIII + 454 pp. Also available as paperback.

85. E. Fischbein, *The Intuitive Sources of Probabilistic Thinking in Children*. 1975, XIII + 204 pp.

86. Ernest W. Adams, *The Logic of Conditionals. An Application of Probability to Deductive Logic*. 1975, XIII + 156 pp.

87. Marian Przełęcki and Ryszard Wójcicki (eds.), *Twenty-Five Years of Logical Methodology in Poland*. 1977, VIII + 803 pp.

88. J. Topolski, *The Methodology of History*. 1976, X + 673 pp.

89. A. Kasher (ed.), *Language in Focus: Foundations, Methods and Systems. Essays Dedicated to Yehoshua Bar-Hillel*, Boston Studies in the Philosophy of Science (ed. by Robert S. Cohen and Marx W. Wartofsky), Volume XLIII. 1976, XXVIII + 679 pp. Also available as paperback.

90. Jaakko Hintikka, *The Intentions of Intentionality and Other New Models for Modalities*. 1975, XVIII + 262 pp. Also available as paperback.

91. Wolfgang Stegmüller, *Collected Papers on Epistemology, Philosophy of Science and History of Philosophy*, 2 Volumes, 1977, XXVII + 525 pp.
92. Dov M. Gabbay, *Investigations in Modal and Tense Logics with Applications to Problems in Philosophy and Linguistics*. 1976, XI + 306 pp.
93. Radu J. Bogdan, *Local Induction*. 1976, XIV + 340 pp.
94. Stefan Nowak, *Understanding and Prediction: Essays in the Methodology of Social and Behavioral Theories*. 1976, XIX + 482 pp.
95. Peter Mittelstaedt, *Philosophical Problems of Modern Physics*, Boston Studies in the Philosophy of Science (ed. by Robert S. Cohen and Marx W. Wartofsky), Volume XVIII. 1976, X + 211 pp. Also available as paperback.
96. Gerald Holton and William Blanpied (eds.), *Science and Its Public: The Changing Relationship*, Boston Studies in the Philosophy of Science (ed. by Robert S. Cohen and Marx W. Wartofsky), Volume XXXIII. 1976, XXV + 289 pp. Also available as paperback.
97. Myles Brand and Douglas Walton (eds.), *Action Theory. Proceedings of the Winnipeg Conference on Human Action, Held at Winnipeg, Manitoba, Canada, 9-11 May 1975*. 1976, VI + 345 pp.
98. Risto Hilpinen, *Knowledge and Rational Belief*. 1978 (forthcoming).
99. R. S. Cohen, P. K. Feyerabend, and M. W. Wartofsky (eds.), *Essays in Memory of Imre Lakatos*, Boston Studies in the Philosophy of Science (ed. by Robert S. Cohen and Marx W. Wartofsky), Volume XXXIX. 1976, XI + 762 pp. Also available as paperback.
100. R. S. Cohen and J. J. Stachel (eds.), *Selected Papers of Léon Rosenfeld*, Boston Studies in the Philosophy of Science (ed. by Robert S. Cohen and Marx W. Wartofsky), Volume XXI. 1977, XXX + 927 pp.
101. R. S. Cohen, C. A. Hooker, A. C. Michalos, and J. W. van Evra (eds.), *PSA 1974: Proceedings of the 1974 Biennial Meeting of the Philosophy of Science Association*, Boston Studies in the Philosophy of Science (ed. by Robert S. Cohen and Marx W. Wartofsky), Volume XXXII. 1976, XIII + 734 pp. Also available as paperback.
102. Yehuda Fried and Joseph Agassi, *Paranoia: A Study in Diagnosis*, Boston Studies in the Philosophy of Science (ed. by Robert S. Cohen and Marx W. Wartofsky), Volume L. 1976, XV + 212 pp. Also available as paperback.
103. Marian Przełęcki, Klemens Szaniawski, and Ryszard Wójcicki (eds.), *Formal Methods in the Methodology of Empirical Sciences*. 1976, 455 pp.
104. John M. Vickers, *Belief and Probability*. 1976, VIII + 202 pp.
105. Kurt H. Wolff, *Surrender and Catch: Experience and Inquiry Today*, Boston Studies in the Philosophy of Science (ed. by Robert S. Cohen and Marx W. Wartofsky), Volume LI. 1976, XII + 410 pp. Also available as paperback.
106. Karel Kosík, *Dialectics of the Concrete*, Boston Studies in the Philosophy of Science (ed. by Robert S. Cohen and Marx W. Wartofsky), Volume LII. 1976, VIII + 158 pp. Also available as paperback.
107. Nelson Goodman, *The Structure of Appearance*, Boston Studies in the Philosophy of Science (ed. by Robert S. Cohen and Marx W. Wartofsky), Volume LIII. 1977, L + 285 pp.
108. Jerzy Giedymin (ed.), *Kazimierz Ajdukiewicz: The Scientific World-Perspective and Other Essays, 1931 - 1963*. 1978, LIII + 378 pp.

109. Robert L. Causey, *Unity of Science.* 1977, VIII+185 pp.
110. Richard E. Grandy, *Advanced Logic for Applications.* 1977, XIV + 168 pp.
111. Robert P. McArthur, *Tense Logic.* 1976, VII + 84 pp.
112. Lars Lindahl, *Position and Change: A Study in Law and Logic.* 1977, IX + 299 pp.
113. Raimo Tuomela, *Dispositions.* 1978, X + 450 pp.
114. Herbert A. Simon, *Models of Discovery and Other Topics in the Methods of Science,* Boston Studies in the Philosophy of Science (ed. by Robert S. Cohen and Marx W. Wartofsky), Volume LIV. 1977, XX + 456 pp. Also available as paperback.
115. Roger D. Rosenkrantz, *Inference, Method and Decision.* 1977, XVI + 262 pp. Also available as paperback.
116. Raimo Tuomela, *Human Action and Its Explanation. A Study on the Philosophical Foundations of Psychology.* 1977, XII + 426 pp.
117. Morris Lazerowitz, *The Language of Philosophy, Freud and Wittgenstein,* Boston Studies in the Philosophy of Science (ed. by Robert S. Cohen and Marx W. Wartofsky), Volume LV. 1977, XVI + 209 pp.
118. Tran Duc Thao, *Origins of Language and Consciousness,* Boston Studies in the Philosophy of Science (ed. by Robert S. Cohen and Marx. W. Wartofsky), Volume LVI. 1977 (forthcoming).
119. Jerzy Pelc, *Semiotics in Poland, 1894 - 1969.* 1977, XXVI + 504 pp.
120. Ingmar Pörn, *Action Theory and Social Science. Some Formal Models.* 1977, X + 129 pp.
121. Joseph Margolis, *Persons and Minds, The Prospects of Nonreductive Materialism,* Boston Studies in the Philosophy of Science (ed. by Robert S. Cohen and Marx W. Wartofsky), Volume LVII. 1977, XIV + 282 pp. Also available as paperback.

SYNTHESE HISTORICAL LIBRARY

Texts and Studies
in the History of Logic and Philosophy

Editors:

N. KRETZMANN (Cornell University)
G. NUCHELMANS (University of Leyden)
L. M. DE RIJK (University of Leyden)

1. M. T. Beonio-Brocchieri Fumagalli, *The Logic of Abelard.* Translated from the Italian. 1969, IX + 101 pp.
2. Gottfried Wilhelm Leibniz, *Philosophical Papers and Letters.* A selection translated and edited, with an introduction, by Leroy E. Loemker. 1969, XII + 736 pp.
3. Ernst Mally, *Logische Schriften,* ed. by Karl Wolf and Paul Weingartner. 1971, X + 340 pp.
4. Lewis White Beck (ed.), *Proceedings of the Third International Kant Congress.* 1972, XI + 718 pp.
5. Bernard Bolzano, *Theory of Science,* ed. by Jan Berg. 1973, XV + 398 pp.
6. J. M. E. Moravcsik (ed.), *Patterns in Plato's Thought. Papers Arising Out of the 1971 West Coast Greek Philosophy Conference.* 1973, VIII + 212 pp.
7. Nabil Shehaby, *The Propositional Logic of Avicenna: A Translation from al-Shifā: al-Qiyās,* with Introduction, Commentary and Glossary. 1973, XIII + 296 pp.
8. Desmond Paul Henry, *Commentary on De Grammatico: The Historical-Logical Dimensions of a Dialogue of St. Anselm's.* 1974, IX + 345 pp.
9. John Corcoran, *Ancient Logic and Its Modern Interpretations.* 1974, X + 208 pp.
10. E. M. Barth, *The Logic of the Articles in Traditional Philosophy.* 1974, XXVII + 533 pp.
11. Jaakko Hintikka, *Knowledge and the Known. Historical Perspectives in Epistemology.* 1974, XII + 243 pp.
12. E. J. Ashworth, *Language and Logic in the Post-Medieval Period.* 1974, XIII + 304 pp.
13. Aristotle, *The Nicomachean Ethics.* Translated with Commentaries and Glossary by Hypocrates G. Apostle. 1975, XXI + 372 pp.
14. R. M. Dancy, *Sense and Contradiction: A Study in Aristotle.* 1975, XII + 184 pp.
15. Wilbur Richard Knorr, *The Evolution of the Euclidean Elements. A Study of the Theory of Incommensurable Magnitudes and Its Significance for Early Greek Geometry.* 1975, IX + 374 pp.
16. Augustine, *De Dialectica.* Translated with Introduction and Notes by B. Darrell Jackson. 1975, XI + 151 pp.